The Politics of Utopia

the
LIFE
OF
IDEAS

Series Editor
Darrin McMahon, *Dartmouth College*

After a period of some eclipse, the study of intellectual history has enjoyed a broad resurgence in recent years. The Life of Ideas contributes to this revitalization through the study of ideas as they are produced, disseminated, received, and practiced in different historical contexts. The series aims to embed ideas—those that endured and those once persuasive but now forgotten—in rich and readable cultural histories. Books in this series draw on the latest methods and theories of intellectual history while being written with elegance and élan for a broad audience of readers.

The Politics of Utopia

A New History of John Law's System, 1695–1795

ARNAUD ORAIN

Translated by Andrew Brown

The University of Chicago Press
Chicago and London

The University of Chicago Press, Chicago 60637
The University of Chicago Press, Ltd., London

Published 2024
Printed in the United States of America

33 32 31 30 29 28 27 26 25 24   1 2 3 4 5

ISBN-13: 978-0-226-82535-9 (cloth)
ISBN-13: 978-0-226-82536-6 (e-book)
DOI: https://doi.org/10.7208/chicago/9780226825366.001.0001

Originally published in French as *La politique du merveilleux* by Arnaud Orain

Library of Congress Cataloging-in-Publication Data

Names: Orain, Arnaud, author. | Brown, Andrew (Literary translator), translator.
Title: The politics of utopia : a new history of John Law's system, 1695–1795 / Arnaud Orain ; translated by Andrew Brown.
Other titles: Politique du merveilleux. English | Life of ideas.
Description: Chicago : The University of Chicago Press, 2024. | Series: The life of ideas | Includes bibliographical references and index.
Identifiers: LCCN 2023053679 | ISBN 9780226825359 (cloth) | ISBN 9780226825366 (ebook)
Subjects: LCSH: Law, John, 1671–1729—Influence. | Finance, Public—France—History—To 1789. | France—Economic policy—18th century. | France—Politics and government—18th century. | BISAC: HISTORY / Modern / 18th Century | BUSINESS & ECONOMICS / Economic History
Classification: LCC HC275 .O7313 2024 | DDC 330.944/034—dc23/eng/20231128
LC record available at https://lccn.loc.gov/2023053679

♾ This paper meets the requirements of ANSI/NISO Z39.48-1992 (Permanence of Paper).

Contents

INTRODUCTION

In the evening of March 16, 1720, the spectators at the Théâtre-Français in Paris, then located on the left bank of the Seine, were preparing to leave when the veteran actor Pierre Le Noir de la Thorillière addressed them. For once, he said, it was he who wanted to applaud them. La Thorillière began his brief speech by lamenting the fact that for months, even years, the public had deserted the theater. The company, worried and offended, had feared that "love for the theater had died." But lately things had changed, and La Thorillière wanted to thank the Parisians "very seriously": "Gentlemen, let us forget the past. You have more than made up for your desertion. The state's newfound abundance has revived the taste of the people for the arts. You have come back in droves to our performances. Never have the ancient beauties been so admired, never have new beauties been so undisputed. Indeed, it would seem that we and the public are henceforth inseparable." This speech was greeted with thundering applause in a scene of communion between actors and spectators.[1]

What was happening in France—and more especially in Paris—for La Thorillière to speak in this manner and for the public to react as it did? The accomplished thespian did not mention the success of new plays, nor did he congratulate himself on the mediocrity of other theatrical establishments. Rather, he referred to an external cause to explain what had apparently breathed new life back into the theater, namely, the return of generalized prosperity throughout the old kingdom of France. Had the country truly been in such bad shape that the people had abandoned the pleasures of the stage prior to 1719–20? La Thorillière was undoubtedly exaggerating the seriousness of the situation, but it is precisely this exaggeration that is so interesting. It reveals something about the time at which he spoke: a period of euphoria and lightheartedness that the French capital had not known for decades and that contrasted sharply with the previous era, that of the end of the reign of Louis XIV and the beginning of the Regency of his nephew Philippe I, Duke of Orléans. To understand this context fully, it is necessary to go back a few years.

After an incredibly long and turbulent reign, the Sun King died in September 1715 in Versailles, leaving the country in a very difficult situation. The previous quarter century had indeed been a litany of disasters. The Nine Years' War (1688–97) had exhausted Europe's most powerful monarchy. It had precipitated a major economic crisis provoked by taxes that were too heavy, agricultural prices that were too low, thus discouraging land cultivation, and trade that was greatly hampered by the war. All this was compounded, during this period of the Little Ice Age, by repeated natural disasters. After the great famine of 1693–94, a peace treaty was signed in 1697 in Ryswick near The Hague. Unfortunately for the kingdom of France, this peace would last less than five years. From 1701 until 1713, France was plunged back into conflict with the War of the Spanish Succession. After meager successes, the monarchy was confronted with a series of defeats and the defection of important allies such as the Duchy of Savoy. Nor was nature itself on the side of the French Empire. Severe epidemics decimated cohorts of children in the north of the country and in Brittany. Above all, an exceptionally cold winter (1709) resulted in the worst harvest of the century and the last great famine of the ancien régime. The average price of cereals soared, hundreds of thousands of people died, and the number of marriages and births dropped dramatically. In 1713, the harvest failed again, causing another severe famine, while a mysterious disease ravaged the country's herds of cattle.[2] And, on top of this series of disasters, the kingdom also experienced an unprecedented financial crisis. Indeed, the period between 1708 and 1713 saw exorbitant war-related expenditure at the same time as tax revenues fell sharply as a result of the economic difficulties. Each year, the state had to rely on loans to cover more than half its expenses. Once peace was restored, the burden of indebtedness was such that the government managed the shortfall from day to day: the salaries of officers and soldiers, the bills of suppliers to the armies, and the interest on the debt were paid irregularly, depending on more pressing emergencies. While the situation should be neither exaggerated nor played down, it is obvious that by 1715 the kingdom of France had not yet recovered from these years of poverty.[3]

At the time, Louis XV, born in 1710, was too young to rule. After some trouble with Louis XIV's legitimized sons and the annulment of the late king's will by the *parlement* of Paris, Philippe, Duke of Orléans, emerged victorious from the power struggle for the appointment as regent of France. A grandson of Louis XIII's, the Duke of Orléans was a former military officer who had served with great distinction. An avid lover of science and the arts, renowned for his loose morals, he ruled the kingdom with a free hand until his death in 1723. In a clever balancing act, he quickly managed to relax the tense atmosphere he had inherited. His stroke of genius to rally the protesters was to implement a form of aristocratic government known as a *polysynody*, a series of councils (of war, finance, the navy, conscience, etc.) bringing together the elite of the aristocracy, the magistracy, and the church. The regent also managed to convince several figures of the Jansenist Party to recognize his authority.[4] Moreover, he established a common ground with the *parlements*—which served as courts of law and had ambitions to control the executive power—by returning to them the prerogatives that Louis XIV had suspended. A fragile political understanding emerged,[5] even if progress was slow from the point of view of the economic and financial situation, which remained volatile.

If the writers of the time are to be believed, levels of poverty in the kingdom did not subside at the beginning of the Regency.[6] An internal devaluation of the currency led to a shortage of cash and the flight of capital,[7] which impeded commerce and trade. The exceptional legal proceedings that took place between 1716 and 1717 under the name of "chamber of justice" accentuated the phenomenon. These proceedings involved indicting a number of financiers and tax collectors who, through their practices during the previous reign, had made outrageous profits, to the detriment of the state. The case caused a good deal of commotion but brought little money (in the form of fines) into the state's coffers. Above all, it contributed to increasing distrust in public finances and, more generally, to widespread suspicion that blocked financial and commercial transactions. No solution was found between 1716 and 1718, but it was at this time that the decisive experiment of the Regency, known as *John Law's experiment*, began to be set up.[8]

Law was born in 1671 into the family of a banker and goldsmith in Edinburgh, Scotland. Very little is known about his youth except that he studied at Eaglesham, south of Glasgow. He moved to London in 1692, where he led a life of pleasure, gambling, and romantic intrigues, taking the latter to extremes. In 1694, he killed a man in a duel. He was imprisoned but escaped—perhaps with the complicity of the authorities—and fled to Europe. There he led a life of wandering during which he became a kind of professional gambler, occupying the place of the banker or the bookmaker at the gaming table. It was in the early years of the eighteenth century that he began to write about monetary and financial issues. In 1703–4, he wrote the *Essay on a Land Bank*, and, in 1705, he published *Money and Trade Consider'd: With a Proposal for Supplying the Nation with Money*.[9] The general idea was to establish a bank that would allow for increasing the supply of money in circulation. Law was, indeed, convinced that the increase in the quantity of money, along with a lowering of the interest rate, was the instrument that would allow the revival of economic activity through the rise in consumption and in trade in general. He envisaged the creation of an establishment that would issue paper money backed by capital made up of land estates. As his plan was not adopted in Scotland, Law decided to propose it to the government of France in 1706–7, where it was also rejected. Abandoning the idea of a land bank, in 1711 he proposed to the Duke of Savoy the establishment of a private bank along the lines of the Bank of England that, on the strength of capital in the form of cash, would issue banknotes and facilitate investments and the liquidity of the public debt. Law, who had been living in France since 1714, presented an almost identical project to the controller general of finances, Nicolas Desmaretz (1648–1721), in the summer of 1715. Desmaretz was interested, but the king was ill, and plans were put on hold. As an acquaintance of the Duke of Orléans, Law raised the issue again in the fall and was finally authorized to create his "General Bank" in May 1716.[10] This marked the beginnings of what would go on to become the famous "System," the canonical narrative of which follows.[11]

With a small share capital and its private status, the bank took deposits by individuals, among whom were many nobles who were friends of the regent. In exchange, it issued its paper money to its clients, undertook cash management and foreign currency exchange transactions, and granted credit, even though it did not have the right to do the latter. Its activities progressed regularly during the first few months, and, in April 1717, the Council of State authorized its banknotes to be used in the payment of royal taxes. This rapprochement with the central power was finalized in December 1718 when the General Bank became the Royal Bank, in other words, an official institution of the French state. Meanwhile, in August 1717, Law created the Compagnie d'Occident, which aimed to increase the colonization of and trade relations with Louisiana. At this time, the name *Louisiana* referred to a vast area of the North American continent, from the great lakes marking the border between Canada and the United States today, to the mouth of the Mississippi River in the current state of Louisiana. The French territory was bordered on the east by the English colonies along the Atlantic coast and extended on the other side to the lands west of the Mississippi. The Compagnie d'Occident obtained from the regent in September 1718 the *ferme des tabacs*, that is, the monopoly of the importing, processing, and sale of tobacco in France, a very lucrative activity. It then absorbed other commercial enterprises, in particular the Compagnie du Sénégal in December 1718, which specialized in the slave trade, and finally in the spring of 1719 the Compagnie de Guinée, which was also involved in the slave trade, as well as the Compagnie des Indes orientales and the Compagnie de la Chine. This immense trade conglomerate controlled by the state (the directors were appointed by the king) took the name of Compagnie des Indes in May 1719. Law immediately conferred certain sovereign prerogatives on the Compagnie. In July 1719, it obtained the monopoly of the manufacture of currency in the kingdom and, the following month, the recovery of all indirect taxes.

To enable all these acquisitions, Law issued shares. The subscribers paid into the capital of the Compagnie d'Occident, now the Compagnie des Indes, sums in cash but also in French public debt securities. In other words, the latter received money to finance its purchases, but the practice also served to absorb part of the loans contracted by the monarchy, which thus benefited from a certain respite because, unlike individuals, the Compagnie was less demanding: the payment by the state of the interest on its debt could wait, not to mention the repayment of capital. But, on August 27, 1719, Law changed scale. He requested and obtained the conversion of the whole of the French public debt (rentes)—the long-term debt held by individuals and institutions (convents, trade associations, hospitals, etc.)—into shares in the Compagnie des Indes. Tens of thousands of people were thus forced to become shareholders of the company. But, since the share price continued to rise (encouraged by the Compagnie, which bought back its own securities) and the income of what was then referred to as *actions rentières* (rentier shares) was fixed, guaranteed, and tax free, it was in the interest of the public debt holders to proceed with the conversion. The strategy was a huge success, with the share price rising from 500 to nearly 10,000 livres at the beginning of 1720.

In February, the Royal Bank and the Compagnie des Indes merged, the former becoming the coffers of the latter. Law was now at the height of his power: having converted to Roman Catholicism, he was appointed in January controller general of finance, the most senior minister of the kingdom of France. This period marked the end of the polysynody and the recentralization of power around the Duke of Orléans. This was the golden age of the famous rue Quincampoix in Paris, which acted as a generalized stock exchange: all sorts of banknotes, public papers, and shares were exchanged in cafés, cabarets, and inns and even in the street. The euphoria swept everyone along in its wake: the speculators became richer, consumption was high, agricultural prices rose, and even the entertainment venues in the capital profited from this newfound good fortune. But this was also when the situation started spiraling out of control. Many new *millionaires* (the term was coined at this time) wanted to convert their shares and notes into hard cash, jewelry, and land. This liquidating of the shares—turning paper money or shares into coins was, under the System, termed *to realize*—led to a dual problem.

First, the sale of the shares caused a drop in their price. Second, by converting the shares into gold and silver, the Royal Bank was soon emptied of its cash reserves. This caused the state to implement a whole series of measures between February and March 1720. On the one hand, it was a case of preventing individuals from paying in and even holding gold coin. The value of metal coins was reduced in relation to the money of account (the livre): the purchasing power of coins was reduced, while the notes retained a fixed value. The idea, ultimately, was to demonetize gold while retaining silver coins and banknotes. On the other hand, Law decided on March 11, 1720, arbitrarily to fix the price of the shares at 9,000 livres. This time, it was a case of preventing it from rising higher while at the same time monetizing the shares to make them a means of payment in the strict sense of the term. But there was nothing to be done. The paper money supply was too vast and the share price too high compared to the real activities of the Compagnie des Indes. The "realizations" multiplied: the Royal Bank was on the verge of filing for bankruptcy, inflation was high, there were fewer and fewer coins to be found in circulation, and agitation and distrust grew. In an attempt to put an end to this situation, a decree of the Council of State of May 21, 1720, ordered the gradual reduction of the share price to 5,000 livres by December 1 of that year. All the major shareholders opposed this ruling, which was nullified six days later by the regent. This led to an outbreak of panic. Between May 27 and 31, everyone wanted to sell, and the price of the shares fell by almost half. The panic increased, and incidents of violence occurred at the Royal Bank. Law's enemies went on the warpath, causing him gradually to lose control of operations: the share price did not rise again, banknotes were demonetized, gold and silver resumed their natural place and importance, and there was a return to the traditional instruments of public debt (rentes). To these difficulties was added the plague epidemic that began in Marseille in July. Law, whose life had been threatened several times and who was now politically isolated, hurriedly left the kingdom in December 1720 never to return, and the dismantling of the System continued inexorably. Of this undertaking, only the Compagnie des Indes would remain in the following years, even though it lost its sovereign activities and would soon be under private control. And thus ends what would have been a singular financial and monetary adventure, that of a solitary and misunderstood genius named John Law.

This canonical narrative has generated three major interpretive models since 1720. The first is that of economic history, in which the System is reconstituted from a technical and statistical point of view in order to establish retrospective assessments.[12] This work begins with Law's monetary conceptions, generally emphasizing their depth and current relevance. It then focuses on the operation of the bank, the variation in the price of the shares, the scope of this or that royal edict, and the claimed "contradictions" or "conspiracies"[13] considered to have precipitated the fall of the undertaking.[14] Finally, it discusses the effects of the System on the economic activity of France in the years 1720–60: the experiment was considered an absolute catastrophe by some and a profitable and salutary remedy by others.[15] The second interpretive model, sometimes interwoven with the first, is that of political history. Law had opened up three fronts: the first with the former financiers, who lost the collection of indirect taxes; the second with the rentiers and their advocates of *parlements*, who considered themselves to have been robbed and cheated; and the third with the whole of the French population, which was denouncing despotism as a result of arbitrary and persecutory measures. Studies of these conflicts long focused on anecdotes and quarrels between people[16] but today fall within the context of the power relations between the monarchy and "public opinion,"[17] that of political détente after the personal reign of Louis XIV,[18] or again the perspective of international relations in Europe.[19] The third interpretive model is that of literary and iconographic history. Leaving aside the way in which the System was conceived by its promoters, works in this area are interested only in the myth it generated, that of a so-called financial disaster. The cultural materials left by the experiment serve a story of representations of "speculation," "paper money," "bubbles," and "panic."[20]

This book was born of a deep dissatisfaction with these interpretations, all stemming from the canonical narrative: the System had been a monetary and financial experiment, the fruit of a demiurge called John Law, that began in 1717 and (tragically) ended in 1720. It completely rejects this view and instead posits a simple hypothesis: the System was an undertaking whose goal was the total transformation of society into a social utopia based on the dream of an omniscient, benevolent, and all-powerful authority. The experiment was designed to sweep away all the theoretical and practical constructs that the greatest legislators had developed since antiquity in order to institute a new regulation of human communities, one unknown until that point. Monetary and financial issues were, at best, only the tip of the iceberg. The System represented the crossroads of several intellectual movements born in the late seventeenth century and converging under the Regency. As for John Law, he was but one actor among others in this foolish hope and perhaps not even the most important. Seriously considering this hypothesis involved nothing less than a paradigm shift in the treatment of the subject. It was from reviewing and reexamining the sources that this change was able to take place.

The historian Paul Harsin (1902–83), the editor of Law's *Oeuvres complètes* (1934) in three volumes, was often accused of having published texts that were not written by the Scotsman or whose attribution was uncertain. Harsin also made choices by selecting some versions of manuscripts he thought were by Law while leaving out variants. Moreover, he dismissed certain letters, articles, and other supporting documents published in the semiofficial gazette of the time, the *Nouveau Mercure*, or elsewhere, while he considered that others deserved to appear in the *Oeuvres* under the name of John Law. It has been customary since—the serious nature of the studies in question being at stake—not to use what was not written by Law and to use only with infinite precautions—always taking the most rational and technical versions or passages—those texts whose attribution was uncertain.[21] This is a first major and fundamental problem: the assumption that only Law could explain Law (and thus his System). It was necessary to remove all impure sources in order to understand the essence of a financial experiment conceived and implemented by this redeemer from a foreign land.

To undertake the complete opposite of this approach, it was first necessary to assemble the known, rare, and unpublished texts written in favor of the System and those prior to the System that had been falsely attributed to Law. It was then necessary to identify their authors or to confirm the intuitions and rumors that had caused them to be attributed to others, especially the administrator Jean Pottier de la Hestroye (d. 1719), the philosopher, theologian, and mathematician Jean Terrasson (1670–1750), the man of letters and administrator Jacques Pannier, sieur d'Orgeville (1680–1739), the man of letters and writer of fables Antoine Houdar de la Motte (1672–1731), and the journalist Pierre-François Buchet (1679–1721), to name but a few. Finally, these works had to be studied as seriously as any other source because whether they were dismissed or, on the contrary, attributed to Law was purely and simply arbitrarily decided. It is quite true that numerous documents were not penned by him or, in any case, not by him alone. But the fact that they were attributed to him is significant; it is even precisely what renders them so important and interesting. Did other theorists have ideas similar to Law's? Could some even have prepared proto-Systems before or during the Regency, independently of Law? Could the System have possibly stemmed from other government programs that had nothing to do with the Scotsman? Was there a team around Law and the regent? Did the subordinate employees and all those who went on to publicize and build the adventure confer on it a color, a shade, or generally one or more directions that escaped the control of those at the head of the System? Did the directors and captains of the Compagnie des Indes as well as the settlers of Louisiana implement and even fulfill the sometimes daring expectations of the System that had nothing to do with finance? Did the experiment not present itself as something of a fairy tale? Were the opponents of the System not right, as late as the French Revolution, to see in it an enemy of property and liberty?

The book goes back much further than the experiment of 1719–20 to understand its origins. Since the end of the seventeenth century, utopians, theologians, travelers, economists, and what Daniel Defoe called *projectors*—individuals who promote projects or schemes that combine public benefit and private profit, meaning the English propagandists of a grand plan of the years 1710–11—had all pointed out the vice inherent in the existence of rentes (annuities) and rentiers (annuitants) and denounced competition, greed, and taxation as forms of civil war. The solutions they proposed constituted the basis of what the System—its architecture and its goals—would become. The latter was, thus, not an accident but rather the result of an intellectual dynamic that had been initiated twenty years before and that had little to do with John Law. By studying the archives dealing with North America, on the Académie des sciences and the metallurgical experiments of some of its scholars, and on the famous *Enquête du régent* (Survey of the regent), dedicated to mines and factories, it was obvious that the French monarchy had not waited for Law to launch scientific, colonial, and commercial programs that were then continued under the System. The same was true for Louisiana, which since the seventeenth century had represented much more than just a continent to be exploited. It had occupied the French and European imagination around repressed desires (of abundance, adventure, sexuality) for a very long time, and this fantasy both nourished the System and was nourished by it in a kind of self-perpetuating phenomenon.

Law was not alone in building and disseminating the System under the Regency, far from it. For a better understanding of the subject, I started from the very many printed or handwritten documents that justified or promoted the experiment, whatever their origin and form (treaties, letters, newspapers, stories, maps, engravings, poems, songs), and I sought to discover the links and relationships that united their authors. Art collectors, men of letters and philosophers of the clan of the "Moderns," cartographers and ecclesiastics, all constituted several networks busy in Paris, Versailles, and Louisiana. The largely unpublished and scattered archives on the colonial trade and the Compagnie des Indes also played an important role in understanding how the System had been deployed as a major project for controlling and directing all the productive forces of the kingdom. To this end, I examined the trade expeditions, the naval bases, the slave trade, the organization of the price system, the settlers, and the mineral exploration and its discoveries. I took the liberation of desires stated by various promoters of the experiment seriously. In the same way, I studied the (al)chemical, theological, and fabulous references, not in a metaphoric way, as they have been so far, but for their very concrete roles in the proper functioning of the System (its use of metals and the logic of expenditure).

Concerning the anti-System literature and imagery, I concentrated on unknown or unpublished sources from three main origins: the trading sphere, frightened by the birth of a protodirigiste capitalism; the Jansenists, who took a stand against an experiment they considered to be sacrilegious; and songwriters and poets, who denounced a world of illusion and the shame felt by the subjects of the kingdom of France at the end of the year 1720. As for the posterity of the System, I first studied it in the vast intertextual network of the rococo fables published between 1720 and 1750 that referred to it, then in the debate over the termination of the Compagnie des Indes at the end of the 1760s, and, finally, under the French Revolution in the debate between the moderate and the radical republicans concerning private property and the demonetization of coins. In each of these cases, this book traces the echo throughout the century of the true ambition of the System. Could the freedom of individuals, their desires, and their property be sacrificed in a great jubilee from which would be born a new society regulated by an all-powerful authority?

As in all revolutionary experiments, the ideas that emerged and the consequences that followed went well beyond the intentions of the first to implement the change. Who are we to reject these ideas and consequences in a nonscientific sphere, to dismiss or despise them on the pretext that they did not come from a hero named John Law or that they did not fall within the interpretive framework of a financial experiment? Following the debate initiated in the 1970s around the "death of the author,"[22] the question of intentionality is central to history as it is told today. Both events and the meaning of a work escape the control of those traditionally regarded as their authors, and this was precisely the case for Law and his System. Since Law's contemporaries had read and listened to the discourses and seen the images that shaped the experiment, they came to conclusions about its nature. It was these discourses and images that dictated and established the System. They were constitutive of it in the same way as the royal edicts and other decrees of the Council of State. Better yet, they produced other ideas and other acts often much more concrete than a host of decrees and laws that were never applied, all these serious texts that conferred its supposedly financial meaning on the experiment.

In summary, it was necessary to start earlier (at the end of the seventeenth century) and finish later (the French Revolution) to understand the real issues of the System. To take up this question again while integrating this paradigm shift, we had to stop believing that certain sources are legitimate while others are not, to stop thinking that publicity, propaganda, and imagination have no effect in the real world. The book seeks to transcend the heroic, personal, event-driven, and even political history in its restrictive sense.[23] This book looks at the conditions of possibility of a project such as the System and the plural way in which it was implemented. It shows how the experiment crystallized forces and influences prior to it and external to Law. Above all, it takes a step aside from the intellectual tradition that seeks to reconstruct a genealogy of "economic liberalism."

This book posits a major discontinuity with respect to the classic narrative of the steady and triumphant rise of self-regulating systems and to that of the harmonious convergence of private interests.[24] The System is, indeed, considered here as an enterprise that was both Hobbesian and commercial at the same time. It was a case of establishing a huge economic Leviathan: an authority that was finally all-powerful, that would have replaced royal sovereignty and the free will of individuals to bring about their material prosperity, without their consent. The experiment is understood as a complete refoundation of the French monarchy that was to allow, for the first time in the history of human societies, for reconciling private interests and the public good in a perfect way. A new social form was to emerge, a sort of totalizing utopia that was both Promethean and disturbing inasmuch as everything was soon to disappear: taxes, debts, competition, free prices, and a part of the private properties as well as the rentiers, the intermediary bodies, the former hierarchies, the poor, and repressed sexuality. The System called for an almost anthropological change in societies. It instituted new truths and, thereby, led to a policy of fantasy.

Emptied of its hidden content and unfathomable, esoteric marvels and wonders, the fantasy (*merveilleux*) of the beginning of the eighteenth century, artisanal and mechanical, was that which would allow for renewing the explanation of the machinery of the world. It was bold but plausible. The fantasy fiction of the time used an imaginary taken from nature and its secrets, the famous "marvelously true," but also the tale and the fable, both of which call on the imagination to understand the universe. This fantasy was philosophical, secularized, a heuristic process that developed new "systems of nature,"[25] new explanations of the world and its laws, and that is precisely what the System of 1720 was.[26] It aimed to be more beautiful, more coherent, more useful, and above all more true than all the systems of nature that had preceded it, precisely because it was an artifact, because it was built, like the celestial machines of Huygens or Bacon that were "true *because* built." And, like most systems of nature of the late seventeenth century and the early eighteenth, it needed fiction to be instituted. It was "the tool to demonstrate that which cannot be demonstrated," to "show the invisible, the inaccessible," that which had eluded understanding until that point.[27] Fantasy—that is to say, this use of the imagination and surprise first to disconcert, then to explain the phenomena, and, finally, to convince readers and listeners, this sense of wonder at work in literary fiction, iconography, social utopias, reform projects, and economic or theological texts—constitutes the point of entry and the common thread chosen to analyze the System.[28] It makes it possible to reveal previously neglected elements of the experiment, its links with global history and utopia. The fantasy calls for decentering our view to see how the System interacted with the Atlantic world, real or fantasized. Another aspect is that of the intervention of fiction in the public sphere, writing becoming a motor of history. At the time of the intensive use of print in general and of newspapers in particular,[29] this book invites us to see in the fantasy something other than a discourse on events. It not only produced meaning; it was a political will that transformed individual practices and behaviors. The discursive elements around the System were mobilized in different contexts, they were recycled to produce various behaviors, but they were always performative: they generated acts in the real world.

The Politics of Utopia begins with the famous "crisis of the European mind" of the turn of the seventeenth and eighteenth centuries.[30] The libertines and the deists invented natural religion, morality became secular, and epic poetry and classical tragedy were dying, while science, the novel, and the opera prevailed. In France, there was a questioning of the Louis XIV model in a rash of texts denouncing the unprecedented violence of his reign, its equalizing despotism, its fiscal tyranny, its shameful but fascinating finance, and its widespread poverty. Three major approaches emerged to try to break this impasse. The first was the liberation of trade and individual interests. This was, however, very quickly perceived as a war of all against all. The second vaunted a wild and natural elsewhere, which would free the subjects from their chains. The third turned to an ideal world governed by an omnipotent state that controlled the will of individuals and the entire economic sphere. The System thus resulted from this criticism of the freedom of trade, from this call to indulge one's wild side, and from this dream of a perfect society organized by a tutelary power. All these elements suggest that, even if Law had remained an obscure gambler at a few gaming tables, an experiment similar to the System would very probably have emerged under the Regency.

Chapter 2 focuses on unveiling the networks and rhetoric that prepared and accompanied the System. This involved, first, the pressure group that, since the reign of Louis XIV, considered it possible to turn Louisiana into a French El Dorado and, second, the scientists investigating the geology and exploitation of the colonies. The kingdom of France did indeed launch into a race against time with England, which had just (in 1711) created a company to exploit Spanish America and to eliminate a part of its floating debt. To promote this enterprise of credit and distant trade, the English theorized the use of fantasy and the imagination and, thus, prepared what would happen in France during the System with the network of the Moderns. This chapter introduces these Moderns, what brought them together, their modes of expression, and their pro-System productions. It concludes with an analysis of the relationships between power and literature, the different levels of propaganda, and their uses in the experiment.

The next three chapters are devoted to the System in and of itself but in different ways. Chapter 3 begins by revealing the ambition of its followers, who saw in it a way to institute a social pact of a new nature. Contrary to the doctrine of national interest and modern theories of natural law, not only was the System intended to promote civil peace; it would also ensure the material prosperity of individuals by forcing them to invest in, to work for, or to unite through the Compagnie des Indes. Using a metaphor employed by Thomas Hobbes, who inspired Terrasson, the Compagnie became the "heart" of the kingdom and gradually replaced the state (for war and alliances with foreign powers, price controls, supply chains, etc.). It materialized the mystical promise of the body of the king, which was to embrace all the bodies of his subjects. It embodied the general will and replaced the former glory of the warring and conquering sovereign with a new glory, that of commerce, which became an attribute of the monarchy. Social taxonomy, credit relations, and the political form of the kingdom had to disappear in favor of a society of individuals, not of subjects, all in the service of the System.

Chapter 4 revisits the notion of system of nature and looks at how the Moderns attempted to change beliefs and behaviors. Maps, travel stories, and engravings praised the abundance of precious metals, the kindness and naïveté of the natives, and the fertility of the land in Louisiana. It will be seen that this was not mere propaganda: the Compagnie des Indes did indeed discover significant mineral deposits, and many settlers were able to start new lives, acquire large amounts of land, or lead a life filled with danger and adventure. In the same way, the fabulous allegories and the assimilation of the System to a theodicy served to educate in the ways of unbridled consumption. These fictions explained and vaunted the passage from a mercantilist logic (the maintaining of workers in poverty) to a logic of expenditure (prosperity through debt relief and global demand). But where the authority probably went too far—in order to propagate the idea that the working classes were the major winners under the System—is when it accredited and disseminated all types of long-winded tall tales about poor people who had suddenly become rich. This was a mistake that would cost the System dearly.

Chapter 5 focuses on the immediate counterattacks by the opponents of the System. Some merchants believed that, by becoming a huge public conglomerate, the Compagnie des Indes killed off the principles (emulation, competition, innovation) that allowed the creation and distribution of wealth and that France was becoming a country of "idiots and idlers." Drawing on the scholastic tradition, the Jansenists wanted to prove that the shares in the Compagnie des Indes were both "unjust and ungodly" under the laws of the church. Other opponents of the System saw a boon in the publicity that the authority generated around the experiment. They cried out against the widespread inversion of values and hierarchies: the poor supplanting the legitimate privileged classes, Louisiana and its chimeras, liberated sexuality as no more than prostitution, and bad chemistry that resulted in poverty. But, more than an opposition to the System, it was guilt that dominated these textual and iconographic productions. If the System was the original sin of the century to come, it was because the heart and the soul were ready to give themselves up to it. It was monstrous and, therefore, called for an era of redemption.

The sixth and final chapter focuses on the refractions of the System throughout the eighteenth century. In the decade immediately following the experiment, the plays of the official theater and the new utopias called for a return to virtue and innocence and contempt for wealth and grandeur. At the end of the 1720s, and in the next two decades, a war of memory began and reused the grammar of the Moderns, that of fantasy. The fairy tale was used to mock those who believed in the fables of the System or, on the contrary, to remake the experiment a desiring and desirable moment. Later on (1730–70), the great debate concerned the despotic, authoritarian, and egalitarian nature the System that its enemies erected into a trauma of memory so that people would forget the disasters of the end of the reign of Louis XIV. This last chapter ends with the French Revolution and, more particularly, the National Convention, where fierce republicans wanted to introduce the total demonetization of metal coins. These *ultrarevolutionaries*, as Danton calls them, considered in a very favorable light the great jubilee of property and wealth that could have been the System of 1720, replayed seventy years later during a revolutionary episode that was, however, not sufficiently bold as to want to entrust to a public entity the control of all the productive forces of the nation.

1

The Crisis of Conscience of the Monarchy of Louis XIV

The modern state was said to have flourished thanks to the fact that it had overcome the civil wars within it, both religious and political. Its justification was internal pacification and the rationalization of public action in order to increase productive forces.[1] But in France, at the end of the seventeenth century, pamphleteers, theologians, and economists felt that the state had failed in both of the ways that were meant to legitimize it. More precisely, in their view, the Louis XIV model of government had not ensured civil peace; on the contrary, it had ignited a perpetual war between the monarch and his subjects. These opponents attributed this new kind of internal war to a destructive system of finance, taxation, and trade management that caused the destruction of the wealth of a now-impoverished kingdom and, ultimately, led the state itself to the verge of implosion. To put an end to this logical impasse—that of a state that destroyed its own bases by using various instruments to maintain itself—these men imagined fundamental changes in the organization of the French monarchy.

This chapter begins by describing the different attitudes toward public credit in France at the beginning of the eighteenth century. Many economic, literary, or pictorial works, often in the form of pamphlets, reveal a deeply ambivalent posture toward finance: it was seen as, on the one hand, odious and repulsive and, on the other, useful and desirable. However, the rentes repaid by the state for what it had borrowed from the so-called respectable classes were increasingly attacked as a vast enterprise of destruction of productive wealth. For many theologians and economists who claimed to be the spokesmen of the workers against the idle and the privileged, the rentiers became the new usurers and rentes the quartermaster behind the oppression of the working classes through taxation. According to them, the kingdom of France was regarded by the state as a foreign country, its wealth as tribute taken from the enemy. Hence their desire to set the productive classes at the heart of a new social project that would put an end to injustice and fiscal tyranny: taxes would be paid by all, their collection would be more rational and less brutal, etc. However, these plans led to new problems: the privileged protested at what they saw as extortion, social leveling, and the overthrow of the constitution. They did not hesitate to defend their tax exemptions and to blame farmers, who, they believed, were solely responsible for their misfortune thanks to their attempted tax fraud.

Since no one seemed satisfied with the situation, whether or not there were financial and fiscal reforms, men of letters, royal administrators, and economists imagined other, much more radical possibilities of organizing human societies. The first involved utopias. Faced with a precarious, uncertain, unjust world, the literati, often exiled or marginalized, held up in contrast the figure of the perfect legislator, the rule of law, and the all-powerful state. For them, collective happiness involved a total socialization of wealth, in worlds where individual freedom was constantly being violated. Others turned to an ideal and egalitarian nature, to utopias in which the blessed abundance of the so-called savages contrasted with the poverty of the European peoples. The omniscient and benevolent state, on the one hand, a wonderful America, on the other—these were two elements that would be found in the System. The second possibility was that of the complete exclusion of the state from the sphere of the production and exchange of wealth. For theologians and economists, the material prosperity of societies resulted from a natural balance of forces, that is, from the free exercise of individual greed spurred by competition. This revolutionary idea immediately aroused broad opposition. Many men—magistrates, clergymen, and administrators—saw this liberation from self-interests as a presocial chaos, another civil war on top of the tax war. The third possibility for the reorganization of society, then, was not reducing the state but expanding it. In an echo of narrative utopias, and in reaction to the liberation of individual interests, it was the economic Leviathan that was placed on the agenda in several projects from the very end of Louis XIV's reign and the beginnings of the Regency. These proto-Systems sought to go far beyond the Colbertist management of commerce so as to bring under public control large swathes of the economy and society and to put an end to the divisions of the social body. The System itself was just one of the avatars of this totalizing intellectual dynamic, which it extended and from which it had arisen.

The Criticism of Rentes

Leaving aside the expedients, French public debt took two main forms at the start of the eighteenth century. The first was that of the famous *rentes sur l'Hôtel de Ville de Paris*. Individuals or institutions invested part of their income with the state, which used the funds to pay for its expenses. In return, the investors received interest for life or, if the rentes were transferable, in perpetuity at a rate that was fixed but that could still be modified by the public authorities. These investments were considered safe because, while the interest might go down, payments would not normally stop. Subscription to these rentes was originally voluntary, but this was less and less the case during the last two decades of the reign of Louis XIV: holders of offices, corporations, and provincial states were forced to acquire them so that government spending could be financed. When the Sun King died, the number of rentiers was estimated at several tens of thousands of people and institutions (communities, hospitals, cities, etc.), mostly in Paris. During periods of "reduction of rentes"—in other words, when the beleaguered monarchy had to resolve to pay less than it had promised—the rentiers sent their go-betweens in the law courts into action. There was an outcry, bewailing the imminent ruin of the entire kingdom. Tears were shed on the subject of orphans, poor widows, and hospitals that had no other income on which to live. Recent studies, however, all come to the same conclusion: the overwhelming majority of rente holders were nobles, judicial officers, and wealthy merchants and belonged almost exclusively to the urban elites.[2]

The second form of public debt was that of loans made to the monarchy by wealthy individuals, generally referred to as *financiers*. A few hundred such people formed a motley collection of varied statuses, but most were linked with taxation. They could be officers in charge of collecting direct taxes, associates of the Fermes générales (the General Farm, the private company that collected indirect taxes), and hundreds of other people who gravitated around these two main categories by forming companies with them. The king very often appealed to them for subsidies, which in theory he was supposed to repay later, with interest. But things were not always that simple. During his wars, Louis XIV had to secure the support of financiers. He borrowed at extremely high interest rates, which allowed the financiers to get immensely rich. But the crown sometimes "invited" these same financiers to provide the state with money, either without interest (a form of advance) or as a supertax, without their being able to hope for any future reimbursement. In the period that concerns us, this is what the controller general Desmaretz tried (with some success) to do in 1709 and 1711. A last means for the state to obtain money from financiers was to establish a "chamber of justice." The scenario was always pretty much the same: after having coddled and pampered them during a conflict, once peace returned the crown denounced their intolerable profits. Called by such infamous names as *partisans*, *traitants*, and *maltôtiers*, they were suddenly accused of a great number of embezzlements that had not appeared as such a few years before. Brought before a special legal hearing, they found themselves condemned to heavy fines for the benefit of public finances. Figure 1.1 illustrates this idea. This print was published at the very beginning of the Regency on the occasion of the chamber of justice of 1716. The figure of extortion personified in the center of the scene, her right hand raised, had shamelessly enriched herself by inflicting on the people taxes or interest on loans paid by taxes during the War of the Spanish Succession. She is here being "purged" of her money on behalf of the state (which will, in fact, recover very little of it) by "Mr. throw it all up, Grand Physician of France."[3]

The two main types of loan appeared to offer a stark contrast. There were, on the one hand, honorable rentiers, families and institutions above all suspicion, and, on the other, shady, underhanded characters, a den of thieves. The former would be easy to locate in the taxonomy of the ancien régime, with recognizable, transparent, legible practices and jobs, living in honest ease. The latter would, on the contrary, be parasites living in luxury and pleasure, oppressors shamelessly taxing the poor. In the eyes of the church, rentes were also a lawful instrument, while the loan with interest of financiers was usury, a monster of illegality. But did contemporaries think of things only according to this dichotomy? With the abandonment of the notion of mentalities in history, and on closer inspection, this is far from obvious.

If the classic studies on the subject are to be believed, the last years of Louis XIV's reign were marked by the explosion of a new cultural genre: anti-financier literature and printmaking. Large numbers of prints, pamphlets, novels, and plays unanimously described financiers as miserable creatures of low extraction subject to all the destructive passions. These leeches with the low customs of commoners were said to be full of falsehood, dissimulation, and boundless greed.[4] Figure 1.2 is an etching also published on the occasion of the chamber of justice of 1716.[5] It shows lackeys (bottom left) who start by emptying "the chamber pots," but, after studying (bottom right), they become "big financiers" like the one at the top to whom Fortune is presenting a horn of abundance. This prosperity is explained by the central scene of desolation, which shows Greed attacking a woman and her child to take away their money.

The image of the lackey-financier, though very frequent, has no historical reality since financiers very largely came from the upper bourgeoisie and the nobility. The problem is that many historians tend to give this myth a probably exaggerated instrumental role. If we follow their argument, the lackey-financier was, if not a construction of power itself, at least a fiction useful to power, a sort of social lightning rod. Vilifying financiers served as an outlet for both ends of the social spectrum. The upper nobility, who found it difficult

FIGURE 1.1. Engraving entitled *La maltôte à l'agonie* (Paris: Chez Gaillard rue de Sèvres, ca. 1716). Courtesy Bibliothèque nationale de France, Département des estampes et photographies, FOL-QB-201(88).

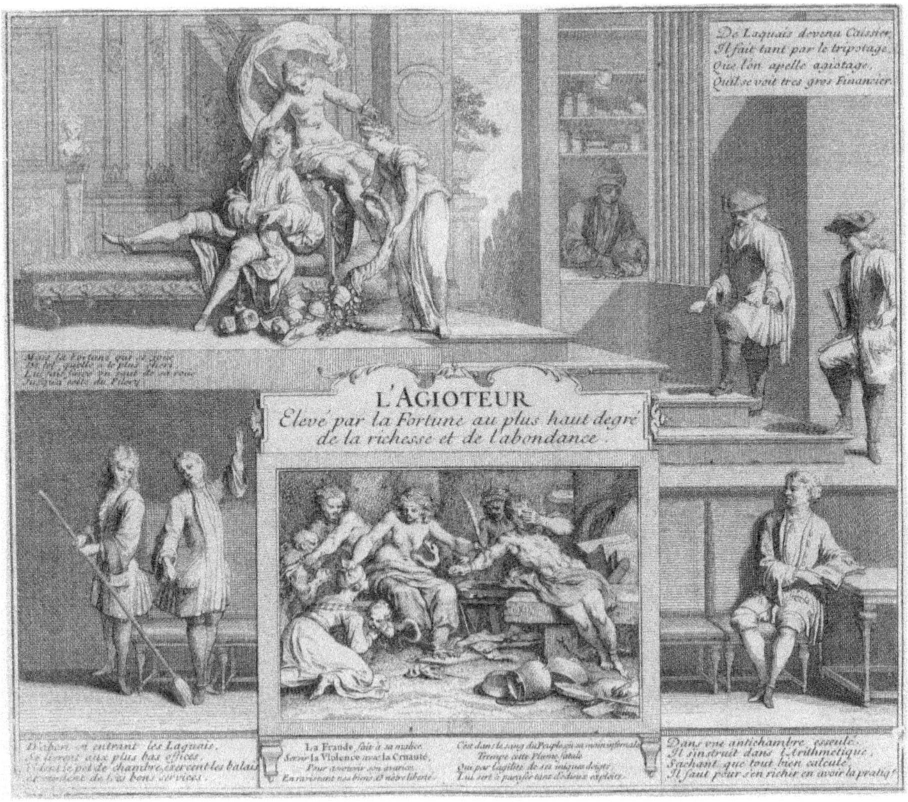

FIGURE 1.2. Engraving entitled *L'agioteur élevé par la fortune au plus haut degré de la richesse et de l'abondance* (ca. 1716). Courtesy Bibliothèque nationale de France, Département des estampes et photographies, FOL-QB-201(89).

to see financiers being integrated into the highest spheres of power, on the one hand, and the common people, who regarded them as oppressors, on the other, were overjoyed to see them mocked and punished on the stage and in images. The crown had thus found a cheap way to divert the resentments of both groups toward these scapegoats.[6] Such an interpretation is problematic because, to begin with, in most of the literary works of the period it is not the financial figures who are the most odious. Those who cheat them often appear more cunning, more dishonest, and much more wicked than the money handlers. Second, to interpret this literature as entirely opposed to financiers is to ignore the dialogism of most of the works in question, in other words, the different—and sometimes contradictory—discourses that they convey within them. Finally, it is to ignore the flood of underlying desires transmitted by short stories, plays, novels, and prints whose plots revolve around finance.

Two successful works by the actor and playwright Florent Carton (1661–1725), known as Dancourt, can serve as an introduction to the first problem. *La foire de Bezons* (1695) and *Les agioteurs* (1710) feature financiers caught up in amorous intrigues. In both plays, they are abused by more wicked, more terrible characters, and the negativity is certainly not all on their side. So, at the fair (*foire*), we find an abbé in clerical garb who is openly a ladies' man, a debauched and adulterous notary, and, above all, a female servant who is the embodiment of vice: "[She] herself enlisted her husband in the army to have the pleasure of being widowed sooner. . . . [T]o appropriate the small property of her family, she had her brother put in the Petites maisons [an asylum in Saint-Germain-des-Prés], & sent her uncle to the galleys." Compared with her, the financier is a colorless figure. No doubt he too has had affairs with the wives of those to whom he once lent, but today he is a well-behaved man who is willing to marry his niece and who is sincerely in love. He is one of the dupes of the play, but he does not hold a grudge against anyone: he finally gives everything to his goddaughter for a marriage to which he initially did not want to consent, gets married himself, and does not fall down the social ladder. It is finally thanks to him that a happy ending occurs. Likewise, *Les agioteurs*, a play with little or no plot and featuring several moneylenders, cannot be interpreted as a one-sided critique of finance. We discover a crooked prosecutor, the offspring of a fallen noble family who uses stratagems to move up the social ladder ("I ruin anyone who has ruined me"), a baroness addicted to gambling, a Gascon trickster, and in the midst of this gallery of characters two prudent financiers—Monsieur Zacharie and Madame Sara—who are going to teach their godson Trapolin a lesson. By the end of the play, not all stockjobbers are ruined, and finance ultimately appears only as a necessary evil to satisfy the vices of men and women.[7] But, in this regard, it is definitely *Turcaret* (1709), by Alain-René Lesage (1668–1747), that is the most telling.

The traditional interpretations that saw this famous play as a satire on the tax farmer (*traitant*) have been completely overturned, and, in the wake of recent studies, I here subscribe to the idea that it is a misunderstanding to see it as a critique of the financier and his morals. Turcaret, a great naive dupe, is certainly corrupt, and he has certainly lied by pretending to be widowed while he is only separated, but he does not do evil, unlike all the others. He is "less odious than pitiful." He calls for feelings of compassion, even liking, rather than disapproval. He is ultimately a character "endowed with a disquieting positivity."[8]

The baronesses in Dancourt and Lesage treat the Trapolins and the Turcarets as beneath their notice. Thus "aristocratic contempt" is exhibited with "extreme violence."[9] When he learns that the woman he covets, a spineless and dissimulating aristocrat, despises him and is using his money to support a chevalier who is one of her noble lovers, Turcaret sees red and smashes some pieces of china. But the baroness wraps him round her little finger and makes him kneel down to apologize for his outbursts, even though they are perfectly legitimate. Duped once again, he floods her with gifts so as to earn her forgiveness in a scene that is more embarrassing than comical. Turcaret, in fact, is also the only truly generous character. He gives without counting, while Lesage portrays nobles who are always penniless and who never pay anything: Turcaret practices selfless giving, something of which no representative of the noble class is now capable. He is constantly being reminded of his common origins, and he is openly mocked for his manners and his language, all in such an outrageous way that he inspires pity rather than disgust. Above all, it is the nobles who are full of vices, not the Turcarets. The baroness deceives the financier; the chevalier, who is an unrepentant gamer, does not give a damn about the baroness, who maintains him; the marquis is constantly drunk; the servants rob the masters. In comparison, Turcaret is not wicked, and his sister, a certain Madame Jacob, is a very positive character. When her brother falls down the social ladder, she is the only one to express feelings of humanity.[10] There is no monologic message here. Competing discourses unfold, and each has its own legitimacy. So it is with desires for social advancement: sometimes they are mocked and repressed, sometimes permitted and justified.

Les tours industrieux, subtils et gaillards de la Maltôte (1708)—Maltôte is extortion personified—is a merry prose tale that supposedly describes the lives of several financiers, real or fictitious. The title pretty much indicates the content of the book. It stages all kinds of ways in which money handlers aim to achieve their ends; of course, they have all emerged from the commonest and grimiest of backgrounds. But the first chapter is very instructive as dialogism is there at its height. On the one hand, in fact, the author seems to regret the way that "[we] love money today beyond all imagination," but, on the other, he describes with biting irony the good times of "Lacedaemon," where "the good was shared by all men." Anyone in need could enter an individual's house, "rummaging through the Chests & Cabinets, picking up the Furniture, Rags & Money he needed." The Greeks themselves these days would call "thieves those who came to their homes to pay such compliments." In addition, he denounces the "exactions" and the "looting" of the financier, whom he compares to the "city executioner," but at the same time he depicts as desirable a condition "where people of nothing who have come into the world without a penny" and, "having amassed & dissipated several millions, still leave an infinity of goods & riches to their family." *Pluton maltôtier* (Pluto the extortioner) (1709) is a little prose novel that of course castigates the financiers but also makes their way of life seem alluring, especially from a sexual point of view. We see "Deschiens" (a pun on *dogs*), alias the financier Pierre Deschien (1631–1704), become the prime minister of Pluto after the latter has taken him from the underworld. Deschiens and his friends the partisans are portrayed with dreadful features, but their adventures are highly enticing. They are lusty devils, always emerging from a private room or a princess's house. Here again, fascination is never far away, and the underlying desire is clearly identifiable. This is also the case in figure 1.2, in which wealth and pleasure are presented in a very ambiguous way. For, as the author of *Les tours industrieux* reveals, if everyone cries out against the name "partisan," in fact "everyone moves mountains to have the happiness of bearing it." "Everyone runs toward it; this position is viewed as eminently distinguished." This is not surprising since, in the tale itself, these men get all they want. They are rarely punished for their wrongdoing, as if, in the end, the social elevator was able to work. *Turcaret* offers another example of this dialogism. While the unfortunate hero of the play is chastised for having sought to rise too much, his clerk, Frontin, and his accomplice, Lisette, succeed in breaking out of their condition. They behave in a more controlled, more sensible way than Turcaret does and end up enriching themselves more modestly than their former master does but in a way that is, one can imagine, more stable and lasting. Likewise, the little extortioner from *La coquette de village* (first performed in 1715) by the playwright and songwriter Charles Dufresny (1657–1724) is the play's most likable character. There is no doubt of his future success and ascension as he has triumphed over the nobles and the rich to marry the tax farmer's daughter, and he says of his rivals: "They have made their fortune, & I have a fortune to make. . . . Nobility is acquired, as well as wealth."[11] The thirst is there, and under certain conditions it can be quenched. This deeply ambivalent literature allows us to glimpse the desires and fears aroused by finance within a society defined, conditioned, and tormented by social taxonomy. However, as we will see, the attitude toward rentes and rentiers—who are supposedly honorable—is also very ambiguous.

The critique of rentes has, curiously enough, hardly interested economic historians. However, this is an important element in the ideological construction of the System. To understand this, we must dwell for a moment on the question of the legality of interest on money. Drawing on Aristotelian philosophy, medieval scholasticism viewed money as a sterile entity, incapable of procreating. Money was a fungible good, a consumable, and, since time itself belonged only to God, it was impossible to sell it. From this point of view, you could lend your money and be legitimately reimbursed, but you could not demand anything beyond the capital. There were three major exceptions, however. These were called *extrinsic titles*, that is, causes external to the loan that could justify a compensatory indemnity. The first was the *poena conventionalis*, or the borrower's payment of a supplement in the event of late repayment. The second was the *damnum emergens*, or damages paid to the lender while his money was tied up in the hands of the borrower. If the former was able to prove that he had suffered major and unforeseen difficulties, he could demand from the latter a supplement to the amount initially granted. The third, more contentious exception was that of *lucrum cessans*. When a lender judged that he had missed out on the opportunity to turn a profit when his money was no longer in his hands, he could attempt to prove the fact and ask the borrower for compensation beyond the amount loaned.

Thanks to theological quibbling, rentes had been authorized in France at least since the sixteenth century without the need to resort to the doctrine of extrinsic titles. The argument was simple, at least at first glance at least: a rente was not a "loan" but a "sale" of money. In other words, a "buyer," for example, the state, accepted a sum from a "seller," an individual or an institution, which then received interest. The buyer (the borrower) was authorized, if he so wished, to repay the principal of the seller (the lender), but the latter could not force the buyer to return it to him. He had to consider his capital as lost. If this was not the case, as in rentes "redeemable on both sides," prohibited in France, this was usury. So ran the theory. In practice, it is known that in many cases it was possible for the lender to recover his money from the borrower, especially in court. In order to obtain liquid assets, one could also assign one's rente to a third party in return for hard cash.[12] Separating a rente from a loan with interest was, therefore, a fiction, denounced as early as 1682 in a work that was to have quite an impact, the *Traité de la pratique des billets entre les négociants* by the theologian and Jansenist sympathizer Jean Le Correur (d. 1693).

Seeking to justify the legality and usefulness of the loan with interest between merchants—and between merchants only—Le Correur was to lay the foundations for the debate on usury over the coming century among many Jansenist authors and economists, some even active in the heart of Diderot's *Encyclopédie*.[13] With Le Correur, the question being asked is no longer that of the scholastics. He is interested, not in what happens to the lender, but only in the use of the money loaned. When traders borrow from each other to increase their business and make a profit, then interest on money is fully justified. If, on the contrary, the loan is only for living and consuming, then there is usury. This is the case of the rich person who lends to a poor person to feed his family; any interest must in this case be prohibited. But it is also the case with rentes, which Le Correur views as an instrument that is both morally unjust and economically destructive.

Le Correur begins his argument by explaining that fairness involves always keeping a proportion between the thing "that one gives [lends] & that which one receives." When one merchant lends to another, then the first receives interest in proportion to the profits made by the second. In the case of rentes, the borrower does not "derive any profit from this money," which is perfectly "sterile." Most of the time, the king or the individual consumes the capital for his expenses, without creating new wealth. Now: "[I]f the debtor does not earn with the money given to him, at least the interest he is required to pay on it, to give him rentes is to ruin & overwhelm him. . . . This injustice, which is very common among rentiers, & even among many who profess piety & equity, is the cause of several disorders, & particularly of the ruin of a very large number of families." The notion of proportion is broken since the man who has borrowed does not earn anything and must pay interest. Rente is an oppression: "In it, one clearly notices the most cruel injustice, which is essential to usury, & it even seems that there is no difference between these ordinary rentes of which one speaks, & the usury that is so rightly condemned by God's law."

A rente is usurious, unlike a loan with interest, which is not. This is an apparent paradox that Le Correur maintains throughout his book. The problem is both moral, in that interest is expected only from people who can pay it, and economic, in that it is the fact that money produces profits through creative activity that justifies paying interest. What is even more serious is that, the more public borrowing increases, the more economic activity suffers because "the money used in *rentes constituées*" withdraws capital from trade and inflicts "a double harm on the state": it "stop[s] the trade that is so necessary" and induces "idleness."[14]

Le Correur's work went through no fewer than four editions until 1696, and its publication provoked debate. Several prelates approved of the author's doctrine, but rigorists of all stripes strongly condemned it. In 1702, a canon of Beauvais, Nicolas Le Maire, published the *Réfutation du traité de la pratique des billets entre les négocians* a rebuttal to Le Correur's treatise that was immediately given a positive review in the *Journal de Trévoux*, a Jesuit periodical. The author deployed arguments of authority: *rente* is legitimate, then, "since all the Doctors agree," and, even if a rich man "acquires a rente from a poorer one, he may well be acting against charity; but there can be no usury, because his bond is not a loan contract, but a genuine purchase & sale." Le Maire refuses to discuss the substance of Le Correur's argument on increasing wealth as a justification for interest. According to him, "[t]he usury is any addition, demanded or hoped for, to the thing loaned," which is the case with commercial loans. They are forbidden, and that is the end of the matter.[15]

However, in his *Traité du négoce et de l'usure*, published five years earlier, Father Louis Thomassin (1619–95), a theologian and famous teacher of the congregation of the Oratoire, had begun to yield some ground to Le Correur. Discussing the legality of rentes at length, he insisted that "it should not be said that these buyers of *rentes constituées* are Usurers, or similar to them." Besides the argument that a "sale" and not a "loan" was involved, he put forward the idea that the buyer of the rente could acquire "lands & funds, from which he will derive annual fruits & income." So why, in this case, will the seller "not take a share in the income from these lands, that is to say in the fruits of his money"? To justify rentes in this way was to get involved in a dangerous mechanism, one that brought the question of interest down to wealth creation and the nature of the activity underlying the loan. Thomassin would thus later return to arguments of authority. More interesting, in this debate, is the refutation of Le Correur proposed by the theologian Jacques-Joseph Duguet, the great figure of Jansenism. In a dissertation written at the end of the seventeenth century, Duguet recalls the traditional interpretations of the scriptures, the church fathers, and the church councils against usury and comes to the question of rentes. They are, he says, "more innocent than usury," but he concedes that "it is true that *rentes constituées*" are subject "to a thousand inconveniences, a thousand uncertainties, a thousand dangers."[16] In fact, Duguet seeks to put an end to any form of loan. What is interesting is that he wants to do so mainly for economic reasons.

In the *Institution d'un prince*, which was published for the first time in 1739 but also written at the very end of the seventeenth century and circulated in manuscript form,[17] Duguet explains that "although Religion must serve as our guide in all . . . my aim is to regard Usury less as forbidden by God's Law and more as pernicious to the state." According to him, trade would be much more secure if merchants exercised their profession in a company, sharing gains and losses, while by borrowing they exposed themselves to bankruptcy. Besides "idleness," usury leads to a bad allocation of capital: "When we have experienced how convenient Usury is, & how quickly it bears fruit, we regard the best lands as slow and unproductive holdings." Therefore, if the true prince wants to be independent and, therefore, fully sovereign, if he wishes to allow capital to flow into agriculture and commerce, he should never borrow, or at least only in exceptional circumstances, and if possible without interest. If it is free from all debt, this is, moreover, "[t]he most certain sign that a state is well governed."[18] Pierre de Boisguilbert (1646–1714), a civilian lieutenant general and later police lieutenant in Rouen, writer, projector, unofficial adviser to several ministers, former student of the *petites écoles* of Port-Royal, and Jansenist sympathizer, shares these views and concludes his argument by criticizing the harmful effects of rentes on taxation.

In 1707, when he republished the *Détail de la France* (1695), his great work, Boisguilbert added a fairly short but incisive text, the *Factum de la France*. His hatred of "tax farmers" and other "partisans" is obvious: the economist attributes to direct and above all to indirect taxation a large part of the kingdom's misfortunes, and he also worries about the frightening habit into which the French monarchy has fallen of borrowing from its subjects. The "constitutions of rentes on the prince" are for him one more heresy in this desolate landscape. It is "the same thing as if the peoples constituted themselves, since it also falls upon them to pay the capital and the interest, although people are so willfully blind these days that they believe the contrary . . . , so that they prefer the monarch to constitute on them a million in rentes at an appalling *denier* or rate of interest, rather than to ask for an écu from each individual." Instead of the fair, proportional, and rational tax levy that the economist calls for, the king goes into debt, and "the money taken in rentes will cost the people more than the maintenance of the war, so that it will be a perpetual war that they have to support." In other words, a rente is a tax, but a hundred times more.[19] It is a perpetual tax on the most industrious and the most useful people, who live in their own land as if they were in an enemy country.

Taxation as an Internal War

The Louis XIV tax system has recently been called by the historian Michael Kwass "a welfare state for the privileged." It can be characterized as an alliance between the crown and the elites, one "in which tax revenue was extracted from lower orders of society and redistributed (by means of pensions, interest payments, military outlays and outright gifts) up the social hierarchy."[20] These upward transfers of wealth were based on direct taxes, the main one being known as the taille. Collectors who were not professionals but residents of the parish or town in question were responsible for ensuring collection on behalf of the state. In the provinces imposing a "personal taille," it was based on the "faculties" of individuals, subjectively assessed by these men. It goes without saying that this principle of collection left room for all the pressures exerted by the powerful to ensure that their clients were not taxed highly. In these provinces, the tax did not apply to the privileged, nobles, clergymen, or holders of offices. So, as soon as their numbers increased in one place, everyone else's burden inevitably increased. It was different in the regions imposing a "real taille," where normally all goods were subject to tax regardless of who owned them. This mode of taxation was less frequent, however, and a major problem with the taille was the general feeling that it was a regressive tax, that is, one that tended to fall mainly on the less well-off of the kingdom's subjects.

Upward transfers of wealth also came from indirect taxes, which were based on the consumption or circulation of goods. While their share in the monarchy's revenue was initially small, it increased dramatically at the end of the seventeenth century, representing over 60 percent of tax revenue at the time we are dealing with. Their collection was not ensured by the state but delegated to a private company, the General Farm. The latter signed leases with the crown in which the *fermiers généraux*—the owners of the company—agreed to pay a fixed sum to the state for a certain number of years. During this time, the General Farm collected the taxes in question. The difference between what was collected from the taxpayers (after the deduction of collection costs) and what was paid to the king constituted the company's profits. Its great efficiency was matched only by the immense resentment it aroused among the population.

First, the very principle of tax leasing and the wealth accumulated by the owners of the company suggested a huge difference between what was collected and what was paid to the king. And the subjects, then, were far from being taxed on an equal footing. Quite apart from the differences between provinces, which led to extensive smuggling (especially of salt), many privileged people were exempt from paying some taxes when they owned vineyards. This alone gave nobles and religious institutions an immediate price advantage in agricultural markets over their competitors among the less well-off peasantry. Finally, the practices of the paramilitary contingent made up of the employees of the General Farm contributed to the institution getting a bad reputation. Authorized to enter the homes of individuals, the General Farm troops were still able to force certain purchases and could imprison anyone who sought to oppose their wishes. In short, the General Farm was constantly associated with a vast enterprise of violence and harassment.[21] In addition to these structural defects of the ancien régime, there was a sharp increase in the tax burden at the turn of the seventeenth and eighteenth centuries. And many observers of the time had no qualms about equating overtaxation with an internal war that was quietly leading the kingdom to the abyss.

The *Détail de la France* (1695) by Pierre de Boisguilbert is a work that had a significant impact on the last decades of the reign of the Sun King. The book, anonymous and secretly published, was widely distributed with no fewer than fifteen editions between 1695 and 1713, much more than most of the works of famous men of letters such as Jean Racine (1639–99), Charles Perrault (1628–1703), or Blaise Pascal (1623–62).[22] For Boisguilbert, things were simple: "[T]he first and main cause of the decrease in wealth in France comes from the fact that in the means, both ordinary and extraordinary, employed to find money for the King, France is considered with regard to the prince as an enemy country." Much longer, more painful, and more costly than foreign war is "this internal war" caused by the tax system under Louis XIV. The term *fermiers généraux* is not an apt name, says the author. The vocation of true farmers is to maintain the field that they cultivate and make it prosper, but this kind of *fermiers*, on the contrary "believed they could improve on the master's product solely by destroying everything, and causing more havoc than enemy armies that had undertaken to lay waste to everything." Writing his *Institution d'un prince* at around the same time, Duguet used the same vocabulary:

> In the beginning it was the pretext of War which served to justify everything, but in Peace itself everything is accepted. The state no longer has foreign enemies, but it does have domestic ones. . . . In this way the People are kept in a continual trembling. The designs of the tax collectors cause [the people] anxiety & an alarm that nothing can calm. . . . They do not know what they can consider to their property, & they think only with terror of that authority which is no longer a protection, & which almost always favors those who think only of oppressing their brothers. The state is thus divided into two parties, as in a civil war: some behave as enemies; & the others are in despair of falling prey to them. Some seek, & others hide. Some pursue, & others flee. . . . Citizens are no longer recognized. People no longer know why they are united under the same government. They feel they draw hardly any advantage from Society.[23]

Subjects are described by the theologian as beasts stalked by an oppressive entity. Why should they assemble in a society if they are always seen as enemies of the foreign body they have to feed? In a pamphlet entitled *L'Alcoran de Louis XIV* (1695), the anonymous author (authors?) imagines a dialogue between Mazarin and the Sun King, presented here as Mazarin's disciple. The latter makes his profession of faith by affirming his belief "in Niccolò Machiavelli" and his wish to imitate in all things the practices of "Cesare Borgia." "What is the conduct of a skillful Tyrant?" asks Mazarin, and Louis XIV answers: "A skillful tyrant, to support his tyranny, must maintain division among his subjects." Later he becomes more precise. Mazarin asks: "Are Civil Wars useful?" Yes, answers the pupil: "Dissensions & Civil Wars are useful, & are not to be criticized." What Boisguilbert, Duguet, and certain pamphlets are referring to are not the widespread ructions caused by taxation, which are at most the tip of the iceberg.[24] What these authors and these texts point to are the aggressions committed by the state or its representatives against the people, despite the principles that must govern and ensure the sustainability of that state.

As shown by philosophers and historians as dissimilar as Carl Schmitt and Michel Foucault, in the sixteenth and seventeenth centuries the theory of raison d'état, which placed politics outside moral considerations by allowing the state to have recourse to extraordinary measures and to violence to maintain or strengthen itself, in Niccolò Machiavelli, Jean Bodin, Francis Bacon, and Thomas Hobbes always requires the sovereign to guard against sedition. One can try to maintain divisions of interest so as to avoid coalitions that would lead to the overthrow of the prince, but, generally speaking, disunity in the kingdom becomes a failing and internal peace a goal. After the ravages of the wars of religion, European states must control internal violence by building peaceful spaces. Within their borders, it is law and order that must reign, while war, now external, allows nation-states to assert themselves.[25] However, if we are to believe the critics of Louis XIV's policies, this principle of raison d'état is constantly under strain since the taxation that must allow this internal pacification and this external display of force is the same taxation that leads to a new kind of civil war. Fiscal oppression becomes so great that it engages one army of collectors equipped to the teeth to fight another, an elite troop of smugglers and the rank and file of the people who are subject to taxation. In this sense, the king of France is a bad prince from his own point of view: the monarch should embody the building and the preservation of the state, but he is purposely maintaining war in his kingdom.

Neither Boisguilbert nor Duguet question taxation itself; they point to a contradiction in the formation of the modern state, which, in order to halt the internal war, needs another internal war. The establishment of a military and police monopoly by the nation-states was meant to allow the creation of peaceful geographic spaces within which the impulses of individuals were normally repressed or at least controlled by the public force. Indeed, the sociologist Max Weber teaches us that the state defines itself as the sole holder of legitimate violence. But it is necessary that the dominated should submit to the authority claimed each time by the dominators, which is not obvious. If we use Weber's typology, this domination can be exercised in the name of "traditional authority," "charismatic authority," or "legal-rational authority."[26] We could try to argue around these three modalities to justify the overtaxation under Louis XIV: the past provides examples of extraordinary tax increases in the event of extremity; the king of France, now known as the Sun King, can be presented, in particular to the Académie française, as an exceptional hero who should be followed without reservation; and the increase in taxation is legally justified by authentic royal acts. Conversely, opponents could try to demonstrate that never in the past had a king been seen to put so much pressure on his subjects, that Louis XIV was a tyrant rather than a model of a Christian prince, and, finally, that *parlements* stripped of the right of remonstrance had not been able to register this astronomical increase in the tax burden legally. This argument is present, but only behind the scenes, in Boisguilbert, Duguet, and the pamphleteers. The real problem for them, when they compare tax collection to a civil war, is that, in order to save the state, the state is being ravaged. Taxation destroys the sovereign's income. In short, power undermines its own foundations. The question is, therefore, not so much that of the legitimacy of violence as that of its disutility. Beyond brutality toward individuals, it is the brutality that is exerted on the creation of wealth that is at stake.

All of its opponents blame taxation for widespread misery. For Duguet: "They are taking away from people who have worked all year . . . what little they have left to live on. They seize cattle, & furniture, & beds, & generally anything that can be removed. . . . They make the industrious ones repent the very success of their work, because they are made surety for the insolvent. They are spreading consternation everywhere." In Boisguilbert's view, at the time he was writing "poverty is three times greater in the countryside than it has ever been." The taille is now the "ruin of goods, bodies and souls." Now, "a ruined person no longer consumes anything" so that "[t]his disorder . . . costs France more than five hundred millions lost per year, and life has as many unfortunate people who perish, both in sickness and in health, for lack of food and relief." The famous engineer, architect, and Marshal of France Sébastien le Prestre de Vauban (1633–1707) established the same causal link in his various royal tithe projects. Having sought "the cause" of the poverty of the people, "I have found," he said, "that it corresponded perfectly to what the author of *Le détail de la France* wrote about it, which discussed and laid bare quite naturally the abuses and defects that are common in the imposition and the collection of Tailles, Aids and provincial Customs [*Douane*]." So he describes the situation in the kingdom, in a version of the text dating from the year 1700:

> From all the research I have been able to do, . . . I have noticed very plainly that in recent times, nearly a tenth part of the people are reduced to beggary and do indeed beg; that of the other nine parts, there are five that are not in a condition to give alms to the former, because they themselves are reduced almost completely to this unfortunate condition; that of the four other parts which remain, three live in very straitened circumstances and are embarrassed by debts and lawsuits; and that in the tenth, where I include all the people of the sword [*gens d'épée*], the people of the robe [*gens de robe*], ecclesiastics and

> laity, all the upper nobility, the distinguished nobility and the people with military and civil responsibilities, the good merchants, the rentiers and better-off bourgeoisie, one cannot count on a hundred thousand families who can truly be called well-off.

In the last lines of his text, Vauban adds that taxes "have brought countless people to the hospital and out onto the streets, and in part depopulated the kingdom." In a letter dated 1694 and addressed to the king (who probably never saw it), the theologian, writer, and archbishop of Cambrai François Fénelon (1651–1715) laments:

> [Y]our peoples, whom you should love like your children, . . . are starving. The cultivation of the land is almost abandoned, the towns and the countryside are depopulated; all trades languish and no longer feed the workers. All commerce is destroyed. Therefore you have destroyed half of the real forces within your state, in order to make and defend vain conquests abroad. Instead of taking money from these poor people, we should give them alms and feed them. The whole of France is now nothing but a big desolate hospital with no provisions. . . . It is you, Sire, who have brought all these difficulties on yourself; for, now that the whole kingdom has been ruined, you have everything in your hands, and no one can live except on your gifts.[27]

If we translate the logic of this literature into modern terms, the process would be as follows: too heavy a tax system based mainly on the industrious elements of the kingdom would have led to a drop in generalized consumption. The latter would itself have resulted in a major economic depression, price reductions, and destruction of wealth—and, therefore, of the tax base—on a scale hitherto unknown, which would have led the kingdom to misery and depopulation. This last element is probably not the most important. With Boisguilbert and Vauban, we are indeed abandoning the idea that increasing the population is the goal of all good policy. The increase in the number of people now becomes more of an indicator of the situation than a goal to be achieved. What matters now is to create wealth and to spend in order to renew it. On this basis, Boisguilbert constantly denounces another illusion that goes hand in hand with the populationist question, that of chrysohedonism, or the belief that the wealth of a state is a function of its stock of precious metals. In *Le détail de la France*, he explains that "money is only the means and the channel, and the foodstuffs useful for life are the end and the goal; and so a country can be rich without a great deal of money." Boisguilbert clarifies his ideas in his *Dissertation sur la nature des richesses* (1707). He castigates this "unfortunate idolatry of money," which "prevents one from being able to traffic by credit and banknotes." He would like to replace all metallic currencies with a "simple piece of paper, which costs nothing and nevertheless performs all the functions of money." In his view, metals maintain a false conception of wealth, one that resides solely in the great consumption of commodities that are continually being remade. Using paper money should help dispel this illusion. This desire, shared at the same time by the John Law of *Considérations*, was on the verge of being realized. But let us not get ahead of ourselves. What matters for now is that the king, as Boisguilbert, Vauban, and Fénelon think, may well have all the money in the kingdom but that this does not make him any the richer since he can no longer buy anything there.[28] Whether this argument is true or false—in other words, whether fiscal pressure played an important role in the poverty that afflicted the end of the reign[29]—matters less for our purposes than the fact that a good number of contemporaries continued to say it and believe it and then tried to fix it.

At the end of 1694, Vauban presented the controller general of finances, Louis de Pontchartrain (1643–1727), and then, a few weeks later, the king himself with a first "poll tax" (*capitation*) project. Meant to last for the duration of the war, this involved a proportional tax levied "without distinction on all with the means to pay, and in particular on the clergy, the salaries, wages, and pensions of all the civil and military officers of the kingdom, the King's household, and the troops of land and sea, without excepting any of those who can pay it." In short, it was a tax on the income of all subjects of the kingdom, including the clergy and the nobility. To Vauban's mind, this would be a kind of experiment that "could very well serve as a model for the establishment of the King's income in the future." Over the years, his ideas became more precise, and, in his *Plan d'une dîme royale*, published in 1707, he proposed the establishment of a universal tax in kind on agricultural income and in money on "all other kinds of income." Vauban and Boisguilbert met in December 1694, and they exchanged letters and were in contact via an abbé from Rouen, Vincent Ragot de Beaumont (1624–1714). In his *Détail de la France*, Boisguilbert proposed not a new tax but an abolition of all existing taxes, which would be replaced by a revised taille and another tax on "chimneys" (a tax increasing with the number of chimneys, i.e., rooms). The taille would become a universal tax based on taxpayers' declarations of income. In 1707, he simplified the plan by defending the idea of a single poll tax in money based on all incomes, of both nobles and commoners. Vauban and Boisguilbert were convinced that, far from decreasing, the sovereign's income would increase if their projects were implemented. Their reasoning was simple: if all existing taxes and the heinous means used to collect them were removed, subjects were sure to become wealthier again. Therefore, a small levy on this immense wealth would provide the king with everything he needed.[30]

If, like Vauban, Boisguilbert presented his ideas to various ministers, the minister of finance implemented his own projects over the period 1695–1717. I cannot here go into the technical details of these tax innovations. But what is of interest is that the two new taxes—the poll tax (1695–98) and the "tenth" (*dixième*) (1710–17)—opened a breach in the upward transfer of wealth from the poor and the active to the privileged and the idle. These new taxes were, in fact, based on the wealth of individuals, whatever their condition, according to a complete classification of "states" (poll tax) or a declaration of income (the tenth). Even though their impact was much greater on the commoners than on the privileged, and even though the clergy were unaffected by them, they were "important inroads into the income of noble landowners [and] officers of justice."[31] But it was, of course, the ideological shock that was the hardest to take for these men who had only recently boasted of paying taxes not in money but in the blood they had shed in war.

Michel Le Vassor (1648–1718) was a former Oratorian who converted to Protestantism and took refuge first in Holland and then in England. In 1695 in Liège he published the *Lettres d'un gentilhomme françois sur l'établissement d'une capitation générale en France*. From the first lines of the text, the tone is set: "What! The Princes of the blood, the great of the Kingdom, the Officers of the Crown, all the gentlemen will have to pay the taille like the peasants?" This is indeed "something capable of rousing everyone to rebellion," something that will "end up changing the face of the state." For what provokes Le Vassor's disgust and anger is the advent of a new social organization in which "we are all rushing into slavery." He thus refers to "the most tyrannical" of reigns and recalls that, if the "peoples of the East [were] accustomed to suffer the despotic power of their Kings," "the inviolable maxims of the Gauls and of the nations of the North" had always preserved them from such tyranny. Even before the introduction of the poll tax and the tenth, a famous pamphlet to which Le Vassor undoubtedly contributed already drew on the same lexical field. *Les soupirs de la France esclave* (1689) aimed to show the "oppression & tyranny, under which all the orders of France groan, & the misery to which they are reduced under a Despotic Power."[32]

If the 1694 edition of the *Dictionnaire de l'Académie française* is to be believed, the name *tyrant* is given to princes "when they rule with cruelty, with injustice, and without any respect for divine & human laws": "*Tyrants* is also the name given to all those who abuse their authority to indulge in various harassments and extortions." This last idea is important. The vocabulary of tyranny is not only associated with violence; it also refers to the violation of property rights. The jurists of the sixteenth and seventeenth centuries drew the border between sovereignty and tyranny on the basis of respect for private property, yet it was precisely this boundary that Louis XIV crossed with his forced loans and his universal and inquisitorial taxes.[33]

Despotism and *despot* do not appear in the dictionaries of the time, but, "with *Les soupirs de la France esclave* (1689), a decisive step was taken": "Insisting on the adjective 'despotic,' the author of this pamphlet drew a close connection between what had been, according to him, the decline of the customary constitution, with the confusion between absolute monarchy and 'despotic empire,' and the notion of *social leveling*." This important idea was linked to the tax question. Let us listen again to *Les soupirs* on the subject of the relation between taxation and social classification: "[I]n the present government, all are People. We no longer know what quality, distinction, merit, birth is. . . . Oppression & misery have been spread to the noblest & most elevated parts of the state. This oppression of the people is effected first by the prodigious number of Taxes & by the excessive rates of interest that are levied throughout France." The gentlemen were also affected: "This nobility once had great privileges, today it is reduced to extremity. . . . Their farmers and their lands pay the King such excessive taxes that all the income from their holdings is consumed."[34]

In 1716, an anonymous author published the *Réflexions sur le traité de la dixme royale de M. le Maréchal de Vauban*. After having defended the taille against the attacks of the *Détail de la France* and the *Dîme royale*, he explains that removing the tax privileges of the nobility exposes them to "a general overthrow":

> All the exemptions, says the Author [Vauban] on page 32, are a disorder in the state, which it is necessary to correct. Given this, there should no longer be any difference between the Subjects of a State; merit, fidelity, virtue & fine deeds, must be without reward; & the Clergy, the Nobility & the People without distinction; . . . would that not mean annihilating the monarchical state in France, to introduce the Republican state into it.[35]

The question posed by the author is clear. Should this social leveling not gradually lead France to modify its constitution? If everyone becomes equal before tax, does that mean that the old orderly society will have to disappear? The author of the *Réflexions* is a zealous defender of the privileged, and what is very interesting in his argument is that he tries at the same time to make agricultural farmers feel guilty, those "vagabonds who change their homes all the time, often to avoid paying their taille." It would be much less expensive to collect, and there would be more to collect if "good faith reigned among the peoples who must pay for it." But this is far from being the case: "They do not forget anything that will keep them from paying; this is where the harm is; this is what causes the burden which they have thus indirectly imposed on themselves, & which creates the need for *Fermiers* [i.e., the *fermiers généraux* this time, who collected taxes], Clerks & Guards."[36]

What did the *Réflexions* attempt to ward off in 1716? Two elements: the clamor that attributed the poverty of the kingdom to the tax system and the discourses that were starting to place the farmers and more generally all the productive classes at the center of a project for the renewal of society on the other. Boisguilbert expressed things with disarming simplicity in 1707: "Today men are entirely divided into two classes, namely one that does nothing and enjoys all the pleasures, and the other, which has been working since morning until the evening, and barely has the necessities of life." Now, he himself "is merely the advocate of all the laborers and traders in the kingdom, that is to say all those who are the source and principle of all the wealth of the state." He keeps explaining that we should think only of defending and enriching the working classes rather than fleecing them. Vauban says the same. "[T]he common people" are, according to him, "the most ruined and miserable part of the kingdom; it is, however, *the part that is the most significant in its numbers and in the real and effective services it renders*."[37] This people, which is "so useful," which produces and consumes, is what the two men now want to put at the heart of the concerns of the kingdom. This is a promotion of the working classes against the idleness of the unproductive privileged often immune from taxation. It is, therefore, a matter not only of making the latter pay taxes but much more profoundly of questioning the social organization based on upward transfer of wealth.

Thus, behind a widely shared discontent, very distinct aspirations lay hidden. For advocates of the productive classes, the end of Louis XIV's reign bordered on civil war, in the sense that the state apparatus had become an enterprise for the extortion and destruction of wealth. For defenders of the privileged, a despotic slavery regime was being established, something that was not, or not only, tyranny. In this sense, taxation became a pretext for the equalization of conditions and the end of any social taxonomy based on birth, the church, or military glory. From the point of view of the social organization of the kingdom, the fears and hopes that flowed from these two analyses were contradictory. In one case, the idleness and uselessness of the rentier and privileged classes were denounced and a new ideology promoted. The warrior value and the self-representation of the ruling classes were to be replaced by the promotion of work and production (agriculture and trade), which would allow increased wealth and consumption. In the other case, people struggled to win lost prerogatives and distinctions. The nobility sought to relive a mythical past, and, in this dream, the industrious classes were not at the center of their concerns. All these tensions found an initial expression in the utopias of the end of the reign, which for the most part attempted to combine collective happiness and the maintenance of social hierarchies.

Resorting to Utopia

It was during the "crisis of the European mind" at the end of the seventeenth century that a new literary genre emerged in France, that of the narrative utopia. It arose from a threefold interrogation: a questioning, first, of the foundations of the political order, second, of institutional Catholicism, and, finally, of traditional novels. This new genre was not always that of a prospective fiction, in the sense that utopias do not necessarily offer models of society to be applied or transposed to European nations. Rather, they are formulations of another historical possibility. They point out what poses a problem for contemporaries—their concerns and their hopes—and imagine, through the use of critical reason, what the conditions for collective happiness could be.[38] In the first place, narrative utopia generally represents "a human community subjected to the tablets of the law as a social cement." The ideal city is very often the result of perfect legislation that establishes obligatory happiness. It is fixed, and its order is intangible since it is irreproachable. It is always anti-individualistic since utopia is a philosophy of totality: citizens do not have an autonomous existence; their happiness derives from that of the collective. Second, "every utopian impulse is guided by the demand for justice or redress for injustice."[39] However, many contemporaries of the reign of Louis XIV shared the idea that ancestral laws and practices had given way to an uncertain and precarious world, one in which, of course, injustice was to be found everywhere. This last concept, however, covered different meanings. For a large part of the nobility, it was the equalization of conditions that was unfair, while, for the defenders of the productive classes, it was the inequalities of wealth that were unjust.

Against the chaos of Louis XIV's reign, with its internal and external wars, its famines, its pillage, and its power, which was both tyrannical and disorderly, a utopia imagined a completely different world of order and peace, a rational organization in which the state regulated the smallest details of the citizens' lives. One of the most famous and influential utopias of the period, the one that both defined the canonical paradigm of utopia for the following decades and truly launched the genre in the French language, followed this path.[40] This was the *Histoire des Sévarambes* (1677–79) by Denis Vairasse, a Protestant exiled in England. Opportunely reissued in 1715–16, the book tells how Sévarias, the very model of the omniscient and benevolent administrator, founded a society in the southern lands, one that was simultaneously prosperous, peaceful, and perfectly ordered. The country no longer suffered from "war, poverty, & idleness" because it was rigorously controlled. The state organized subjects' lives from birth to death: towns and houses were built according to an identical geometric plan, meals were taken together, and children were raised and allocated to different types of work by the public authorities, which more generally organized the production and the distribution of wealth (food, clothing, etc.). Everything was governed by immutable laws and an immovable hierarchy, any deviation being met with ruthless punishments. The *Histoire des Ajaoiens* (1682) by the famous scientist and man of letters Bernard Le Bovier de Fontenelle (1657–1757) was built on the same model. On the island of Ajao, space was rationally organized, there was collective child-rearing, and everything belonged to the state. The state ensured the land was cultivated, and it owned the fishermen, hunters, butchers, and public bakers. Thanks to "granaries & stores," necessary goods were centralized and then redistributed by the magistrates, without a price system. In *Histoire de Caléjava* (1700) by the lawyer Claude Gilbert (1652–1720), there are no longer any idle people, and it is again the state that allocates children to various trades after training them. Very strict social and economic control is also exercised in the kingdom of Salento in *Télémaque* (1699) by Fénelon and the kingdom of Butrol in the *Voyages et aventures de Jacques Massé* (1710) by the writer Simon Tyssot de Patot (1655–1738). Thanks to the wise advice of Mentor, Télémaque's guide, Salento is reformed in three stages: first, luxury is rooted out by the suppression of the arts and "useless" trades; then frugality is inculcated through an education that teaches contempt of wealth; and, finally, a stable and hierarchical regime is established under the rule of the laws. Mentor is the new Sévarias. He is the sage who "regulated the clothes, the food, the furniture," decided which arts could subsist, and divided everyone into seven distinct classes, as a result of which "no change was ever [suffered]."[41]

The first important element in the preceding utopias is the frequent presence of a legislator who reforms past abuses or founds a new civilization. Subsequently, he fades into the background or dies, but his work remains intact because, as Fénelon says, "it is the law & not the man who must reign."[42] This second element is a constant of these texts. The princes hardly intervene in the lives of their subjects. They do not rule. Magistrates ensure that society functions by obeying, not a set of superiors, but a body of laws that gives it structure. In addition to the ideal of stability, the third major element to note in this literature is the role conferred on the state as a disembodied and all-powerful entity. Louis XIV was regularly accused of tyranny in the sense that he blurred the line between public and private property and exercised violent oppression on a wide spectrum of his subjects. However, if we compare the state of Louis XIV with the states of previous utopias, the former appears to be mild and far from intrusive. The problem, then, lies not in the means—the use of force or coercion—but in the objectives pursued. Private liberties are almost nonexistent and punishments terrible in the utopian imagination of the period, but, unlike in the France of the Sun King, the socialization of wealth does not serve the glory of the monarch. If the state appropriates everything for the benefit of everyone's material well-being, this is acceptable. In kingdoms that are generally isolated or at peace, it is (as in the work of Boisguilbert and Vauban) the material well-being of populations that these utopias insist on. The social and economic organization of societies becomes the alpha and omega of politics.

Alongside these established ideal societies, of which one of the central criteria is that they are based on reason, other utopias of the period are not pervaded by statism. Certain texts or stories within the same text reject economism à la Boisguilbert-Vauban and the hierarchical and organized society of Vairasse and Fontenelle. This is the case, for example, with *Les avantures de Jacques Sadeur* (1676) by the defrocked monk Gabriel de Foigny (1630–92), or when Fénelon evokes the province of Bétique, or the *Voyage et avantures de François Leguat et de ses compagnons* (1708). In these kingdoms or spaces, all people are free and equal, everything is held in common, and there are neither laws nor coercive force. In the *Voyage* of Leguat, which is in part an authentic account of Huguenot emigrants in the Indian Ocean, Rodrigues Island becomes a veritable Garden of Eden where the animals, which have not experienced the presence of human beings, do not flee from them and everything is found in abundance. It is "the Earthly Paradise": the generosity of nature invites man to idleness since subsistence abounds without any need for work.[43] Fénelon, for his part, transposed into Bétique the customs of the American Indians as they were described in other travel accounts of the period. The myth began in France with the narratives of Jean de Léry (1536–1613), who participated in the French colonial adventure in Brazil, and with the philosopher Michel de Montaigne (1533–92). The "savages" became, under their feathers, strong and robust men, innocent and cheerful, without concern for material goods and ignorant of religion, property, and money. It was largely in this guise that the peoples of the St. Lawrence Valley were described by the traveler Louis-Armand de Lom d'Acre, Baron of Lahontan (1666–1716). What characterized them and marked a break with other civilizations was the absence of "laws." Ownership of goods was unknown to them; they had "neither yours nor mine." They also rejected any subordination to others, and, "living as they did in a kind of equality in accordance with the feelings of Nature, thieves, and particular enemies are not to be feared among them, which means that their huts are always open by night & by day." In his famous *Dialogues* (1704) with a native, Lahontan presents a picture that, though not idyllic, is quite desirable. It evokes the great freedom, the liberated sexuality, and the good faith that reigns among the Amerindians and the perfect health that they enjoy.[44]

Lahontan's *Dialogues* were a great success in the Age of Enlightenment thanks to the expanded edition issued by Nicolas Gueudeville (1652–1721), a journalist, pamphleteer, and historian, in 1705. This former Benedictine monk who had taken refuge in The Hague is often considered to be one of the precursors of utopian socialism. He was above all a staunch opponent of Louis XIV, whose reign he considered to be the most monstrous and inhumane in all human history. He constantly denounces the misery, servitude, and suffering endured by the people and the atrocities committed against those wretches. But what is of particular interest is that he contrasts this excessive misery with the happiness that, in his view, the natives enjoyed. Gueudeville substantially modifies the dialogues of Lahontan to depict the condition of the savages as a real Eden. He insists in particular on the fact that "famine & hatred do not enter into such a Society; abundance & friendship are its two main bonds." He continually contrasts American prosperity with European *famine* and *beggars*, words and rhetoric not found in Lahontan's original *Dialogues*. Even more than the sexual freedom on which he also digresses, the utopian writer insists on the ease with which the so-called savages can meet their needs, unlike the hardworking people of the kingdom of France. In short, not only does Gueudeville make the savage condition even more desirable than Lahontan had; he actually seems to be urging the poor of Europe to become "savage" in order to free themselves from the yoke that oppresses them. However, we will see that in 1719 he participated in the System's propaganda in favor of Louisiana by reusing this corpus and this "American" utopian material.[45]

For now, I provisionally conclude by looking at the counterpoint to the society of Louis XIV presented by different imaginary constructions over the period 1675–1715. What unites them is the rejection of poverty, but this is the lowest common denominator. Many of these novels depict what are called *dystopias*, quite terrifying worlds closer to nightmare than to dreams, in which the state sacrifices everything, in particular individual freedoms, to order and material prosperity. The society described by Vairasse, which inspired a good number of utopias of the period, has been described as *state socialism*:[46] this is not a challenge to the Louis XIV model but, as in

Boisguilbert and Vauban, an observation of its ineffectiveness. Obedience to the supreme power must be total and the individual completely erased when this power organizes collective happiness. Others make the universal equivalent constituted by monetary wealth the quintessential "despotic" form. The social significance of these discourses most often lies in a strong hierarchical ideal, nostalgia for a mythical past where the demarcation of rank would be strict and stable. Finally, some writers advocated the destruction of society as a remedy for inequalities and oppression. Freedom, the absence of laws, and equality and abundance for all lay at the heart of these repressed desires. They expressed themselves in "natural" utopias as well as in the reveries of the priest Jean Meslier (1664–1729), and they found concrete practice in the golden age of "anarchist" piracy (1716–26) that followed the War of the Spanish Succession. In 1715, Gueudeville published a free French translation of *Utopia* by the famous philosopher and politician Thomas More (1478–1535), and in his preface he castigated "property, avarice [greed], and ambition, those three plagues of civil society, those three monsters that ravage the human race."[47] But in the same period, in that miserable kingdom that he both pitied and loathed, some men were imagining the exact opposite. According to them, it was greed and the free rein given to individual interests that were to lead to the prosperity of nations. We know what became of this new utopia, which was as good as the previous ones.

The Liberation of Individual Interests: A Cure Worse Than the Sickness?

At the end of Louis XIV's reign, it was not only tax pressure that came under fire from critics but more broadly state interventionism in economic matters. There were voices calling for a reconsideration of the customs policy that stifled international trade and the removal of privileges and regulations that prevented competition. The ensuing debates produced many innovations in the political practices, ideas, and language of the coming century. New hopes and fears were emerging during a period in which Colbert's management of affairs was opposed by some, defended by others.[48]

From 1661 until his death in 1683, Jean-Baptiste Colbert (1619–83) was Louis XIV's principal minister, and his influence on the reign was decisive. I shall not here retrace his economic action in detail, let alone attempt to take stock of it, but simply recall a few important elements. First, it should be noted that the minister's ideas for trade management were not innovative when compared to those of his predecessors. Colbert merely implemented them with a consistency and constancy never seen before. It should be noted, then, that he shared with most of his contemporaries a desire to increase the quantity of cash in the kingdom. If, as the minister believed, all parts of the world have been discovered and world trade was stable, each time one nation gained market shares, another lost them. The objective was, thus, to reduce the inflow of foreign products (outflows of precious metals) while promoting the outflows of finished or processed domestic products (inflows of precious metals). Such a conception of prosperity finally led to an aggressive commercial policy on the external level (the construction of a powerful navy, colonial expansion, the creation of monopoly companies) and a protective policy on the internal level (granting of privileges, taxes on foreign ships, and, above all, an increase in customs tariffs, such as that of 1667).[49]

While all these canonical elements are true, we must still beware of caricatures. We now know that Colbert was much less protectionist than his great rival, the minister of state François Michel Le Tellier de Louvois (1641–91), whose principles dominated from 1682. He was in favor of the free movement of goods in the kingdom and, therefore, sought the removal of many tolls and internal customs duties. From a foreign trade perspective, the 1667 tariff did not bring an end to imports from abroad, mainly because it concerned luxury goods that the upper classes were unwilling to do without. Better still, Colbert approved the Treaty of Nijmegen (1678), which exempted several essential Dutch goods, including textiles, from the customs tariffs of 1667, and he seemed to conceive of customs protection as a temporary measure. However, it was this same Treaty of Nijmegen that was to lead to a sharp increase in imports and the decline of many French manufactories and, consequently, to the establishment after Colbert's death of customs legislation so harsh that it would bring a drastic halt to foreign trade.[50] Although Colbert may not have been the interventionist and protectionist we have long imagined, this is, nevertheless, the distorted image that his immediate posterity bequeathed us.

The authors of *Les soupirs de la France esclave* produced an overall negative assessment of the minister's action. Colbert had turned a blind eye to the "rigors" and "cruelties" inflicted by the "Customs farmers [*fermiers des douanes*] on the merchants." He had encouraged "monopolistic trade . . . to exclude all others, which [has ruined] an infinite number of people." As for the "ban on foreign goods," this had destroyed French foreign trade since other European nations had retaliated by refusing to buy anything from France. In the same vein, Gatien de Courtilz de Sandras (1644–1712), a novelist, journalist, and polemicist, decided in a famous pamphlet that people must be careful not to "follow the maxims of M. Colbert." Indeed, "under the pretext of doing without a lot of things that used to come from foreign countries," they had "deprived the kingdom of the sale of its wines, & of its other foodstuffs." According to these texts, customs prohibitions had prevented "reciprocal trade" between nations, the only source of prosperity.[51] The Treaty of Ryswick (1697), which put an end to the Nine Years' War (1688–97), seemed to take note of these observations, and, even more than in 1678, it opened the French ports wide to Dutch merchants. Sometimes considered as a real turning point in Louis XIV's trade policy, it sharply reduced customs tariffs for dozens of products from the Netherlands, Dutch ships were exempted from access rights in ports, and Dutch traders were treated on an equal footing with their French counterparts.[52] The period was a favorable time for this experiment because it saw the emergence of two major—but quite different—conceptions of freedom of trade.

The first conception was based not on a metaphysics but on the practice of merchants. It did not set out timeless general principles valid everywhere and at all times. It envisaged commerce as a means of enriching oneself but also as needing to be attentive to the "public good." The latter was defined as supplying the royal treasury and giving subjects everything they needed in quantity and at low cost. This conception was embodied in the principle of "freedom and protection," which was overwhelmingly defended by traders within the Council of Commerce, created in 1700 by Pontchartrain. The council was an institution that brought together administrators, manufacturers, and merchants to collect data, investigate legal proceedings, and enforce economic regulations. Its function was also to consult economic actors on changes in trade policy in general. And this is how we know of a collection of memoirs commissioned by Pontchartrain and sent by deputies from major ports and major manufacturing towns when the institution was set up. So long as we refuse to apply inapplicable categories (mercantilism/liberalism) to these texts and realize that there are slight differences between them, all nonetheless defend the principle of freedom and protection.[53]

These memoirs begin by attributing the weakness of French trade to excessively high customs duties and the vexations caused by the clerks of the General Farm while advocating freedom of trade.[54] They then seek to put an end to the monopolies granted to certain ports in traffic with foreigners and castigate "exclusive" trading companies and "privileged" manufactories. According to them, the latter tend to produce and deliver too few goods and slaves. They are prone to indolence, pay too much income to their owners, and are poorly managed by Parisians who do not understand business.[55] Finally, these memoirs demand the "protection" of the income of the king and the merchants, in other words, customs duties (albeit moderate) and regulations (albeit intelligent). Far from wanting to eliminate tariffs, they consider that trade fully needs to pay attention to the public good and, therefore, to state financing. But they want a clear distinction to be drawn between the big "merchants" (*négociants*), so useful to the public good, and the despicable little "traders" (*marchands*), with whom they do not wish to be confused.[56] This principle of freedom and protection was shared by men like Charles Hurault de l'Hôpital, Seigneur de Belesbat (d. 1706), and Jacques-Joseph Duguet.[57] But, at the same time, several theorists were defending a rather different approach.

The second conception of free trade was based on the idea that there is a providential or natural equilibrium that allows the true prices of goods to be determined. According to this conception, there are immutable and ahistorical laws of commerce, and any state intervention in the latter would disrupt the wealth of nations. On the contrary, by allowing the desire for personal enrichment to be expressed freely, the material prosperity of human societies would be ensured without the public power intervening in the least respect. The beginnings of this last utopia can be found in the Jansenist theologian Pierre Nicole (1625–95).[58] Thus, in 1670, he describes the good results of greed in these famous words:

> [W]e must consider that men, being empty of charity by the disorder of sin, nevertheless remain full of needs, & are dependent on each other in an infinity of things. Greed has therefore taken the place of charity to fulfill these needs, & it does so in a way that is not admired enough & where common charity cannot succeed. For example, if we go out into the countryside, we find almost everywhere people who are ready to serve those who pass by, & who have lodging fully prepared to receive them. We can make use of this as we desire. We command them; & they obey. . . . Who would be more admirable than these people if they were animated by charity? It is greed that makes them act.[59]

No doubt the prince must distribute rewards and punishments to guide and sometimes suppress this greed, but Nicole invites us to admire its positive effects. Boisguilbert radicalized and popularized this idea:

> There is a reflection to be made that all the commerce of the earth, as much wholesale as retail, and even agriculture, is governed only by the interest of the entrepreneurs, who have never dreamed of being of service nor of obliging those with whom they contract through their trade; and any innkeeper who sells wine to passersby has never intended to help them, nor have the passersby who stop at his house while traveling acted so for fear that his provisions might be wasted. It is this reciprocal utility that brings harmony to the world and the maintenance of states.[60]

Except when acting against violence, the state should never intervene in society. We just have to "let nature take its course." In his *Dissertation* (1707),

Boisguilbert explains: "[P]olicing is needed to ensure that concord and the laws of justice are observed. . . . But it is for nature alone to impose this order and maintain peace; any other authority spoils everything when it tries to interfere, however well-intentioned it may be." Without customs duties, without tolls, without manufactory regulations, without privileges and monopolies, "all commodities [will be] continually in equilibrium, and [will retain] a price in proportion to them and to the costs that have been needed to establish them." In other words, neither high prices nor low prices can be maintained since the merchants will have complete freedom to produce and transport goods where they are lacking and to change activity and remove goods when they are overabundant. The "equilibrium" is embodied in these "proportional prices" that "all maintain night and day, by their particular interest, and at the same time shape, although this is the least of their concerns, the general good." However, it is competition alone that will allow things to remain in this "equilibrium" because "there is no other resource for enriching oneself . . . than to outdo one's neighbor by work and skill, not to deceive him by trying to get his food at a low price, but to get ahead of him by cunning."[61] The absence of any obstacle to the free movement of goods matters more to Boisguilbert than their actual movement. What counts is an abstraction, that of the "market principle." In the eighteenth century, supporters of this principle thought that there were natural laws, often of a providential nature and prior to forms of social organization; they included private property and freedom of trade, which were inviolable in all circumstances. If these laws were not subject to any restriction, especially by the government, then supply and demand would naturally balance themselves out.[62] Or, rather, the market principle would be, through the unintentional (positive) results of individual (greedy) interests, the new principle of social organization. This was a revolutionary idea that was sure to arouse broad opposition from the moment it was formulated.

In 1715, the Académie française decided to award its annual prize for eloquence to the dissertation of a certain Monsieur Roy, who had answered the question set in the competition on the "drawbacks of wealth." In this piece, the author strongly condemns greed and self-interest. The pursuit of enrichment is presented as a misguided way of consuming one's existence, "a fever of the soul." The willingness to consume and spend one's money, especially on luxury goods and services, is castigated as an oppressive enterprise. It leads the poor to "dependence" and "enforced obedience" to the rich. The latter "despises men": "Superior to them, he tyrannizes them. He considers them as victims forced to do nothing but work, he chooses them, he pays for their slavery." The only Christian way to support the poor is charity, not spending money to make them work. But, "as greed increases, charity decreases." Accordingly, Roy does not hesitate to describe "greed" and "luxury" as "plagues more dangerous than war."[63] An important speech entitled "Love of the Fatherland [*Patrie*]" was delivered on November 15, 1715, in the *parlement* of Paris by the man who was still only its attorney general, Henri-François d'Aguesseau (1668–1751). He uses a lexical field close to Roy's.

D'Aguesseau worries: "[A]s the zeal for the public good dies in our hearts, the desire for our self-interest is kindled. It becomes our Law, our Sovereign, our Fatherland. . . . Thus slips into each of us the deadly poison of society, that blind love of oneself which, distinguishing one's fortune from that of the state, is always ready to sacrifice the whole state to its own fortune." D'Aguesseau insists that, in his view, everyone in his condition now seeks to "distinguish between the interest of his state & that of his person; & the common good is so forgotten that all that remains in a Kingdom are self-interests, which through their struggle form a kind of civil war." In "a Fatherland subjected to the greed of its Citizens," the bonds of society have been severed, everything seems to "bring us back to this ancient state that preceded the birth of Republics & Empires, where man never had any greater enemy than man himself."[64]

In this important passage, the attorney general reduces the clash of individual interests to the war of all against all, as in the state of nature in Thomas Hobbes. According to d'Aguesseau, the material prosperity of a society cannot emerge from the greed of a multitude of individuals. On the contrary, the result of such a confrontation can be only a presocial chaos in which the bonds between men are broken and the advantages of living in society destroyed. Predatory behavior thus leads to another internal war. This is the second war that we meet, after the tax war, and they are of different natures. Boisguilbert and Duguet were alarmed that, in the process of building and maintaining the state, it was at the same time being destroyed as the wealth of the kingdom was ravaged. They saw this as a break in the social bond, but everyone knew who the enemy was and how to fight him. D'Aguesseau, on the other hand, thinks of an enemy lurking in the depths of people's hearts. Each individual becomes his own adversary since, merely by wanting to be satisfied, he harms society. This marks a change of scale. It is no longer the state that is in question, or politics, but the individual and morality. And d'Aguesseau describes the few people who have remained outside this warlike greed as having built a separate world, a private life of "leisure" that leads them to lose interest in public life. On the one hand, then, we have civil war and, on the other, an uncivic apathy. What is left in France? "A numerous population, & almost no citizens remain." Justice alone—in other words *parlements*—can, to d'Aguesseau's mind, attempt to redress the situation by bringing "the fatherland back to its true principles." What are they? D'Aguesseau is faithful to the tradition of the scholastic theologian Thomas Aquinas (1224–74). He argues in terms of the social body, in the sense that all individuals contribute to a common good that transcends them. They do this both out of natural sociability, for men in the state of nature love one another, and through the authority of the sovereign who must contain—"in an exact discipline for the maintenance and good order of the body politic"—the "passions & natural appetites" of the subjects.[65]

In the organicist conception of society as it is found in Thomists such as d'Aguesseau, the parts of the whole that constitute society cannot follow their own path independently of one another. They work, not for themselves, but for the survival of the body politic as a whole. The *commissaire* Nicolas Delamare (1639–1723) sets out quite similar views in his famous *Traité de la police*: "Each state must be considered either as a single body, all of whose members owe each other mutual aid, or as a large family that cannot be preserved for long if all the parts that compose it do not unanimously contribute to the common good." So, for Delamare, if "freedom is the soul of commerce," it must not degenerate into "license." In other words, the circulation of goods is possible and even desirable, but the "self-interest" of merchants must not lead them to enrich themselves at the expense of the subsistence of others. This is why "the father of this great family," in other words, the king, must restrict "free trade" in "well-disciplined states" by controlling merchants, the flow of grain, etc.[66]

One of the kingdom's most powerful administrators under the Pontchartrain ministry, the director general of commerce Jean-Baptiste de Lagny, agreed. Fundamentally opposed to the Dutch-friendly clauses contained in the Treaty of 1678, de Lagny was a convinced protectionist who fought—unsuccessfully—to ensure that the Treaty of Ryswick did not grant any commercial advantage to foreigners. In a long manuscript of 1696 he set out in detail his point of view, one that was highly unfavorable not only to giving free rein to greed but even to the principle of "freedom and protection":

> It is said that, to make trade abundant and profitable, there is no need for regulation, but full freedom, and strong protection. These are the two big words by which general policing is defined. It is not easy to understand what is meant by freedom in commerce to make it more advantageous, for usually this word freedom signifies a natural situation in which one exercises the movements of one's will; and if one does not suppose an enlightened will, one subject to the prescribed rules, this liberty is a form of libertinism, or at least an exercise of the power to live as one wishes. Indeed, this is the meaning given by those who ask for this freedom: let us pursue, they say, our trade as we see fit; if we lose

> on the purchase or on the sale of such or such merchandise, we do not need to be protected, we will simply stop trading. But the subjects of a state are to that state what children are to their families. The former are obliged by divine and human laws to work together for the good of the state, for which many laws are established; children are by the same laws obliged to contribute to the benefits of their families.[67]

The sole purpose of trading is not to enrich merchants—that goes without saying. But, beyond this idea shared by many representatives of trade, de Lagny is expressing something else. As the father of his children, the king must control their "timetable" and their "industry." They cannot "play" as they see fit. He can, thus, prevent a situation in which, "by whim, by fancy or ignorance, [the merchants] carry out a trade that vainly uses their time, that absorbs their fortunes, and stultifies their industry by the misfortunes that their imprudence would inevitably entail." The ruler must use trade to collect dues and, thus, ensure that his state functions, but he also has to tell traders what to do and where and how to do it. Traders are instruments of power, and they should not have the freedom of their actions. What de Lagny envisages is, therefore, a centralized management of the creation, circulation, and distribution of wealth. He takes a very dim view of the creation of the Council of Commerce, a body in which traders and manufacturers will be able to assert their points of view.[68] This state management of French commerce lies at the heart of the proto-Systems and of the System itself, in a post-Colbertist dynamic where debate rages on.

Bringing Trade under State Control?

The years of impoverishment at the end of Louis XIV's reign were not poverty-stricken for everyone. As commercial rivalry became a crucial part of the balance of power in Europe, the early eighteenth century marked the beginning of prosperity for the major French ports. In the aftermath of the Treaty of Ryswick, Atlantic merchants invaded Spanish America but also the Pacific and China. Many private companies were created, and, though the risks were high, successful campaigns generated gigantic profits. The net profit of Saint-Malo merchants in Asian commerce alone amounted to some 18 million livres between 1708 and 1719, or nearly 15 percent of France's annual tax revenue. Thus, the period 1690–1720 was marked by the construction of large mansions and the famous *malouinières* of the shipowners of the great Breton port of Saint-Malo.[69] From the end of the seventeenth century up to 1730, the value of shipments returning from Brazil increased sixfold, and French companies actively participated in this trade, especially during the War of the Spanish Succession. The French tonnage to Asia also grew steadily from 1660 and exceeded that of Portugal by the turn of the century. Thanks in particular to the wool of Languedoc, trade with the Levant rose from 6.7 million livres in 1685 to 14 million in 1717. And, even if the gross margin of the large trading companies fell between the beginning of the seventeenth century and the 1770s, there was a resurgence in their profitability precisely around the first decade of the eighteenth century, with a ratio of about 3:1 between the buying price in Asia and the selling price in Europe.[70] Surely this growth would whet appetites and above all that of the state. An old-fashioned mercantilist paradigm describes a mutually fruitful collaboration between trading companies and the monarchical state. Whether or not they were encouraged by the government, whether or not they benefited from a monopoly, those companies that brought together several large traders with the aim of trading from afar contributed to the building of nation-states through a give-and-take policy: protection and opening of markets for some, tax revenues on imports and national industry for others. But, of course, things were not that simple.

For the past fifteen years or so, researchers have seen the monarchies of the early modern era less and less as centralized and absolute entities and more and more as fragmented spaces within which competing and hybrid institutions clashed and joined forces. In this configuration, the state was only one actor, admittedly a more powerful one, among others. Thus, like the provincial states, trade guilds, or cities, trading companies were "in both alliance and tension with the national state and its claims to coherent and central power." As political bodies often endowed with the attributes of sovereignty (in the event of conflict), and as profitable enterprises, companies represented both resources and competitors for the state.[71] The latter could, therefore, be tempted simply to incorporate them into itself, transforming merchants into the royal administrators of a trade carried out by and for the central power. Things would have the merit of being clear: instead of merely taxing trade and sometimes using it for sovereign causes, they could socialize the profits and make them an instrument of power equivalent to sovereign forces. Here was a radical project, well worthy of the dystopias of the turn of the century but also of the System and of some other more or less coherent plans that preceded it or were contemporary with it.

When he published his *Oeuvres complètes* of John Law in 1934, the historian of ideas Paul Harsin included a long memoir entitled "Restoration of Commerce (September 1715)" that took up most of the second volume. However, this memoir cannot be attributed to Law,[72] and this is precisely what makes it very interesting. We know of several versions of the "Memoirs concerning the Commerce of France and the Means to Restore It,"[73] whose author was a former civilian lieutenant general of the Admiralty of Flanders, Jean Pottier de la Hestroye. The first version of this text dates from the very end of the seventeenth century, probably 1699–1700. Shortly before the Peace of Utrecht, probably around 1711, Pottier substantially modified it and included new elements. The manuscript wrongly attributed to Law and published by Harsin unfortunately disappeared during the Second World War, but in all likelihood this was the last version of this work. The date of September 1715 is quite plausible. The author in fact refers to the regent and to the "royal council of the navy" (set up on September 15), so what he is proposing must begin "on next October 1, 1715," and the projections (of reduction in taille, distribution of dividends, etc.) start from 1716.[74] Most of the elements of the original text of 1698–99 and of the intermediate version of 1711 are present, sometimes out of order, in 1715. The author sometimes changes words (*Ryswick* is replaced by *Utrecht*) and sometimes makes cuts, but above all he includes important additions.[75]

Basically, the different versions of Pottier's text always begin the same way: "There are ordinarily in commerce two interests that at first seem to be the same and that nevertheless are always different and strongly opposed, and this is what must be disentangled: the particular interest of the merchant and the general interest of commerce. The first is often false and contrary to the good of the state, and the second is real and has as its object only the general good and that of the state." The merchant wants to get rich—that is his only goal, and it does not matter to him "whether the state profits through his trade or not." This is a real problem because the state's mission is "to relieve the country of the superfluous food and merchandise it produces . . . and to extract from foreign countries the things necessary for life," on the one hand, and "to enrich the state at the same time as individuals," on the other. In short, it is not enough for traders to earn money; it is also necessary for the state to receive it and for the subjects of the kingdom to have whatever they need. Here is the "protection" side of the principle of freedom and protection.[76]

Once these elements have been established, an important first line of Pottier's argument concerns the question of the distribution of wealth. "[W]hat does it matter," writes the author as early as 1699–1700, "where the riches may be, or which subjects possess them, provided that it is all within the Kingdom, and that people in general or the state can enjoy them." He insists on this subversive idea: "The greatness of a state is not to have individuals distinguished by their wealth: all subjects must be rich without distinction." What matters is that the money circulates and that it puts traders, artisans, and farmers to work:

> The very rule of charity is that the richest share their property with the poor. Does it matter whether this is for free or by making them work at unnecessary or superfluous expense? It always means sharing their property with them. Too bad for those who engage in unnecessary expenditure beyond their power; this is a vice that does not affect the state, for, far from the state losing in the process, it wins.

Pottier is highly favorable to fashions, luxury, and all "superfluous" expenses, and he responds to his own objection about the ruin of families, the confusion of ranks, and the necessities of which one deprives oneself with such reckless spending. He does not care since consumption—especially disorderly consumption—makes people work and generates tax revenues, and, therefore, "the interest of the individual is of no concern."[77]

The same goes for the interests of the merchant, of which Pottier is wary, and this is the second important line of argument, which brings him closer to Jean-Baptiste de Lagny. In his first memoir of 1699–1700, Pottier castigates the advice given Colbert by the merchants, who "deceived the Minister." In 1711, he became angry with the representatives of trade, "focused only on what concerns them," as they "always prefer their particular interest to that of the general population of the state for which they show little concern." He criticizes their "ridiculous proposals" and develops the idea of an alternative council organized vertically from Versailles. Headed by the king, the chancellor, state councillors, and "commissioners general" in the provinces, it would be responsible for producing information and providing advice on trade and manufacturing matters.[78] Merchants would have no place there.

As a great admirer of Colbert, Pottier revealed himself in the 1711 version to be a resolute supporter of the great trading companies. He wanted to expand them and, with this aim in mind, to imitate the English and the Dutch, who, alongside the main shareholders, admitted "subassociates, that is to say that everyone is allowed to subassociate, or have an interest, for whatever sum pleases them; they will share in the profit, or in the loss that the company makes, in proportion to what each has put back into the fund, but without having any share in the government": "[T]his arrangement would be favorable to all subjects, beneficial to the state, and useful to these companies." The development of mainstream shareholding would at once provide "considerable" funds to companies, enrich a "host" of subjects, and strengthen state power overseas.[79]

Companies that were created not only to develop trade but also to establish or strengthen colonies must, according to Pottier, enjoy exclusive privileges and monopolies. Those that were intended only for the "trafficking" of goods did not need so much protection, but that did not mean that they should be abandoned—quite the contrary. The most important, the one he discussed first, was the Compagnie française des Indes orientales (the French East Indies Company). He thought that it had not adequately served its purpose, but, far from proposing to replace it with a free trade of individuals, he envisaged its nationalization: "[I] do not believe that the state has hitherto obtained any advantage from its establishment, that it would have done better if His Majesty, without leaving it entirely to the conduct of those concerned, had acted by himself." If it is ever to be restored, it will require the full authority of the king. Pottier's idea is complex and not completely clear, but it is basically a matter of establishing a sort of sovereignty over all Indian trade through a state-run parent company, which will be in charge of its daughter companies under the leadership of the merchants. He then criticizes the companies from Guinea and Senegal, which never brought enough slaves to the French West Indies. Pottier wants to suppress them "and establish others." While he sees them as private companies, they will be closely supervised by the government, which will determine their capital, the number of vessels, the quantity of slaves to be sent, etc. They will have to report on their activities by bringing certificates to the secretary of state for the navy, who will not hesitate to resort to fining them for anything they fail to bring to the islands.

Pottier agrees with de Lagny that the few overtures made to the Dutch by the Treaty of Ryswick are a real scandal. He wants to ban freight to all foreigners in French ports, establish new privileged companies, in particular for the North Sea trade, and, above all, create a vast public industrial sector. With the rise of a Bourbon to the throne of Charles V, Pottier believes the time has come to take over Spanish-American commerce. To do this, he envisages the creation of numerous "fabric," "silk," and "wool" factories in France so as to flood the Atlantic markets to the detriment of the English and the Dutch: "The King could entrust the care of this business, which he would carry out on his own behalf, to skillful and faithful people." In 1711, Pottier envisioned public factories whose profits would be used to "create cash" and even "to pay the debts of the King and the state, something which His Majesty could do by this means without taking anything from his subjects." Even though there were a few state-owned factories at the time, this idea of establishing state-owned enterprises whose profits would be used to pay off the public debt—perhaps by suppressing taxes—was quite different from the existing one; it is very interesting for our purposes, but it was not the whole story. In keeping with the logic of putting the poor to work prevalent since the Middle Ages, but also with a view close to certain dystopias at the end of the seventeenth century, Pottier wanted "to force all beggars and lazy people to work." Indeed, the constraint of an economic Leviathan looms throughout his work. The state should force landowners to sow their fallow land, "on pain of losing their ownership to its own profit," and should force plowmen to supply a certain amount of wheat to the public granaries. These stores would be run by the state, which would be tasked with maintaining a year's store in the kingdom and, in a way he does not specify, always keeping grain "at a reasonable price."[80]

In 1712, the prelate, scholar, and academician Pierre-Daniel Huet (1630–1721) published *Le grand trésor historique du florissant commerce des Hollandois*. If the author is to be believed, "states have flourished only insofar as they have cultivated trade," which was the case with England and Holland but much less France, which had "lacked an experienced leader . . . , able to protect those in his business, & the commissioners in whatever places they may be." The model to follow was that of the Netherlands, where this "leader" was embodied by the Dutch East India Company. If one is to believe Huet, the Dutch, like the French, remained weak for a long time because their trade was dispersed in various small companies, "until the year 1602 when the Estates General judged it right to bring them together, so that they would be better able to resist the damage inflicted by the Spanish & Portuguese": "Subsequently, the Company's trade grew wonderfully, and in a short time it became the largest in Asia."[81]

It is quite probable that Pottier read Huet's work before writing the last version of his memoir,[82] in which he writes: "Having seen from several experiences that particular companies have always succumbed, as they were unable to recover from the accidents that happened to them either by the division of the interested parties or by the lack of application, economy, and strength they had to support each other," he had proposed to the regent the establishment of a "General Company" that would bring them all together under the aegis of the state. This company should be "privileged" as were the previous ones; in other words, it should have a monopoly on French foreign trade. Each of the subjects could be accepted as a shareholder in it, including the nobles, because it was "absolutely necessary that the whole public contribute . . . according to the faculty of each individual." The company was to be conducted "under control," that is, under the aegis of the minister of the navy, by directors appointed by the king from "the principal and most able merchants of the kingdom." The "public" could, thus, consider "that it will be itself that carries out the operations through the ministry of the directors, who will have at heart only the public interest; it will be a unanimous company of the whole state, and no one in it will benefit except the public alone, since it is for their advantage that it is established." The shares, costing from 400 to 1,000 livres, were also to function as currency since it would be possible to buy company goods with it and probably make other payments. Finally, the large number of vessels that the company would need to build at its expense in the king's arsenals could be used alternately for war and for trade. Clearly, what was involved here was the constitution of a vast monopoly, half public and half private, that would bring all trade under the control of the monarchy and place new resources directly at the state's disposal: fiduciary currency, ships, and capital.[83] And that was not all. While the period 1702–15 saw dozens of plans for banks—private, business, and "royal" banks—submitted to the Control General of Finances, the 1715 memoir ends with a different project, namely, the establishment of "a bank to discharge the debts of the state." The idea was to offer holders of rentes an opportunity to exchange them for shares in a public bank whose capital was to be limited to 900 million livres. The king was then to provide this bank with a sum of 45 million livres per year for twenty-five years. With these 45 million livres, the bank was to reimburse shareholders gradually up to the level of 900 million livres.[84]

A memoir addressed to the Duke of Orléans at the outset of the Regency starts from the same observation as that made by Huet and Pottier de la Hestroye about Holland and concludes with a proposal for the socialization of trade that is not unrelated to the previous one. This memoir, of which several handwritten copies have survived, was printed with others in 1727 under the name of the former soldier, scholar, and astrologer Henri de Boulainvilliers (1658–1722). This attribution is uncertain, but it hardly matters. What is interesting is that the "Memoir to make the State powerful & invincible, & all the subjects of this same State happy & rich," explains that the creation of the Council of Commerce may have been a good thing but that this institution was quite inadequate to bring about the material prosperity of the kingdom. The council was not in a position to "provide money" for manufacturers, plowmen, or farmers to improve their production. Nor was it the council that would stock up and store grain: "Therefore, a general establishment is necessary that will play an active role so as to arrive at this point of view, which by its direction, its trade & participatory commerce, can unite in the same spirit all the merchants of the kingdom, without nevertheless monopolizing the inclination of each in particular, or preventing them from acting according to their particular views; & at the same time opening up an assured means for all the subjects of H.M. to carry out wholesale trade without derogation, or having their money accepted in trade without usury & with security." The establishment was to be a joint-stock "Trading Company," both merchant and banking, in which all subjects in the kingdom could invest. It was to be steered in Paris by six treasurers who would ensure the "general direction of commerce," with branches in the provinces, called "chambers," managed by "bank agents," in charge of collecting taxes, lending money to merchants and traders, and making deals with the latter. The merchants and traders would, "by handing over to the said agents commodities & merchandise," "easily find the money they will need by means of these agents." In other words, the agents would be public intermediaries whose function, with the income from taxes, was to buy, centralize, store, and then resell a large part of national production: "[They] will, to the exclusion of all others, ensure the sale of foodstuffs & merchandise that will be stored in the markets, ports, quays, merchant offices, and arts & crafts communities." Merchants and manufacturers were to "put all their money in this treasure," that is, the proposed company, and withdraw or borrow it as they needed. If the author is to be believed, nothing was more to be desired than such an establishment that "voluntarily unites different geniuses, without preventing them from acting according to their will." The agents of the company-bank would also be tasked with supervising the harvests, keeping two years of grain, giving money to the peasants in case of need, providing "for the education & food of the children, & relieving and feeding the poor decaying, sick, & crippled people, so that there are no beggars." In a luxury of detail that makes this memoir a kind of nonnarrativized utopia, the state is once again the great Leviathan that socializes a part of what is produced and traded, to then redistribute it as it sees fit.[85]

A fairly similar project is set out in a curious work by the engineer and treasurer of extraordinary war expenses Étienne Lescuyer de La Jonchère (1690?–1740?) entitled *Système d'un nouveau gouvernement en France* (1720). To add to his point, the author begins by praising Boisguilbert's *Détail de la France*, which, he says, "perfectly demonstrates the misery of peoples, and what causes it." With the aim of reforming this disastrous situation, La Jonchère proposes "to unite, by considering the way they share the same interests, all the different states of the kingdom." To do so, he imagines that it will be "necessary to form a company, whose income will be dependent on H.M. & which he can dispose of." Entirely managed by the state through a highly hierarchical administrative organization, it would leave to the regent and the king only questions of religion, justice, and war: "So from now on there will be only one king, one law, one religion, one *parlement*, one company." Its capital was to be made up of interest-bearing shares, obtained by all the individuals who wished, including nobles, in exchange for securities on the public debt (rentes). Thus, this debt would be annulled, and the prosperity of the kingdom of France would be unparalleled.

The scope of the prerogatives of the planned enterprise was immense: it was to collect taxes, maintain the troops on land and sea, manufacture ships, dig canals, make roads, create public transport, build stores and factories, erect hundreds of buildings, deal with the mail, give credit to the state and individuals, and support the poor, among other things. The company had to leave nothing to private initiative, or almost nothing since it was to "reimburse," in other words, nationalize, "all the factories, companies, and enterprises of whatever kind" that it would need as well as "reimbursing the owners of the lands, woods & effects that it will seize." The company would be responsible for most of the kingdom's commerce, both internally and externally. La Jonchère thus imagines that, by taking a tenth of the harvest of grain, wheat, salt, and hay, it could ensure it had a monopoly on the resale of these goods in the towns. The prices would have been fixed, except in the event of war, even for manufactured goods. The payments could have been made first in gold and silver currencies; then the company would have substituted paper money for them. Fully in agreement with Pottier on the logic of spending and the necessary circulation of wealth, La Jonchère believed that it was against "the public good to allow an individual to have too much wealth." It was necessary to prevent hoarding and even to set by law a maximum that individuals could own, "with a prohibition on transgressing these regulations, on pain of death."[86]

The organization of the company would be military in nature, the punishments of those who did not respect its rules would be appalling, and the social control over the populations would be total, as in the case of peasants who were strictly forbidden to come to work in the city. Architecture and decoration also played an important role in this project. The designs for building the houses and embellishing Paris were presented with a wealth of detail. Better still, the engineer described very precisely how to build and furnish the future headquarters of the company at the Place Dauphine in Paris. The "hôtel du commerce" was to contain an allegorical representation of the new monarchical form, with a statuary group made up of "His Majesty [who] will hold the scepter in one hand, and the Statutes of the Company in the other, & H.R.H. Monseigneur the Duke of Orléans, will pour a cornucopia on the people. At the four corners of the pedestal will be represented in Bronze four chained figures: one will be Idleness, the other Misery, the third Injustice, & the fourth Discord."[87] Thus, the monarchy was, henceforth, to be intimately linked to this other institution, the company. Which was to absorb the other? The answer to this question would remain open. What is certain is that an economic Leviathan was described by the engineer, who moreover saw fit to clarify things in an explicit reference to the current System of Law:

> Without going into any detail about the system that we are currently following, as I believe it is very different from mine, I will not stop proposing it [his own plan], in the hope that by joining my ideas with those of enlightened people who contribute to the happiness of the King & that of the Nation, & by taking what is best from both, a way will be found to form a just, solid, & eternal government.[88]

In the preface to his book, La Jonchère says that he met the regent twice to explain his plan for government to him, the first time in 1715 and the second at the start of an undetermined year. He says he was criticized for the lack of "demonstrative evidence" at this last meeting. He then decided to present his project to the public. But the printer's negligence meant that he had to reprint the last three volumes, which delayed the publication of the book. What the engineer seems to mean is that he would have devised his plan, if not before, at least independently of Law's. A nineteenth-century historian, Alphonse Callery, asserts that, while La Jonchère's work is dated 1720, all four volumes were "printed in the course of 1718 and 1719." The same writer does not hesitate to accuse Law of having appropriated "a large part of the La Jonchère project."[89] All hypotheses remain open. However, whether the engineer inspired the System implemented by the regent, Law, and a few others, or whether, on the contrary, it was La Jonchère who developed his ideas in contact with the first measures implemented under the System, or whether similar plans were imagined independently does not matter. The same applies to the memoirs attributed to Pottier de la Hestroye or Boulainvilliers because what I am trying to highlight is an impetus that goes far beyond the question of people. More precisely, what matters is that there were several types of response to the Louis XIV model, which many contemporaries considered a bitter failure: tax reform, a natural utopia, the market principle, and, also, a totalizing and statist solution. This intense focus on utopias around 1700 found expression in several government projects of the years 1715–20. In many ways, the plans of Pottier, the memoir attributed to Boulainvilliers, and the one by La Jonchère were dystopias in the same way as those of Fontenelle or Vairasse. But this was the Regency, speech was freer, and the field of possibilities had opened up, so another form of writing could be employed. These projects were sometimes even implemented, including the System attributed to Law.

Faced with the ambiguous attitude of contemporaries toward finance, the System constructed a figure, the shareholder, who was supposed to have the positive attributes of financiers and none of their flaws. By this scheme of things, even lackeys and the poor could really get rich; their desires for wealth, social advancement, marriage, and sex were genuinely satisfiable but without these benefits coming at the price of oppressing the productive classes. Following the theologians, magistrates, and economists who, from the seventeenth century on, had associated supposedly innocent and legally constituted rentes with several serious social ills (including misallocation of capital and oppressive taxation), the System of 1720 sought purely and simply to abolish the rentier class and taxes. It aimed to put an end to the divisions in the kingdom and to the low-level civil war denounced by men such as Boisguilbert and Duguet. By definitively relieving debtors, the experiment was meant to assist those Vauban had described as "burdened by debts and lawsuits." By proposing a socialization of wealth and total control of the central power over trade, the System also sought to ward off the consequences of individual interest, freedom of trade, and competition that d'Aguesseau, de Lagny, Pottier de la Hestroye, and many others had deemed deleterious. The Compagnie des Indes was the spearhead of an immense economic Leviathan with which the state would take control of trade and prices, eliminate many trading mechanisms, bring the interests of the kingdom's inhabitants into alignment, redistribute private property and wealth, create public factories, cancel debt, promote luxury and consumption, turn stock shares into a form of currency, and restrict economic freedoms, all in the service of reshaping society for productive ends. These elements had all been present both in the dystopias of the period and in several more or less successful projects developed by public or semipublic companies before or during the Regency. In this sense, the System was anything other than an accident. It was not the fruit of a single brilliant and unique mind but the product of an intellectual and cultural dynamic that had begun to take shape in France twenty years earlier. The following chapter will provide evidence for this point by analyzing the colonial, scientific, and literary networks in the kingdom, the colonies and abroad that laid the groundwork for the experiment of 1717–20.

2

Colonial Competition, Imaginaries, and the Moderns

Since the end of the seventeenth century, several ideas had metamorphosed into a movement in favor of radical reform of the French monarchy. This upheaval was made possible by a set of networks and a specific rhetoric. One of the important elements in understanding what crystallized during the System is the commercial and colonial competition between European powers. The War of the Spanish Succession clearly demonstrated Franco-English rivalry in Atlantic trade, with the Castilians increasingly playing a walk-on part in this theater. The conflict had its origins in the question of the balance of power and fear of French domination of the continent, but its duration and the difficulties in reaching a peace agreement revealed its significant commercial dimension. The hegemony of French traders in Spanish America from the end of the seventeenth century was a matter of major concern to the British. It was also, in their view, the factor that explained why Louis XIV was able to withstand such a long and costly war.[1]

The Treaty of Utrecht (1713) profoundly changed the situation. The English obtained commercial privileges from Spain previously in the hands of the French, and their South Sea Company, founded in 1711, then assumed its fullest extent, particularly in the slave trade. French commerce in the Americas was struggling,[2] which is why the Compagnie d'Occident, founded in 1717 in the wake of the System, was seeking a new and lasting establishment on this continent. This rivalry was portrayed by contemporaries in a very interesting way. The South Sea Company was conceived in response to the French successes of the 1700s, and the later Compagnie d'Occident was itself a response to English successes after 1713. Both also had a financial dimension as they were meant to settle part of the public debt in addition to implementing long-term trading. To promote these commercial and colonial adventures, writers, cartographers, travelers, and scholars reactivated the phantasmagoric imagination dating from the Spanish conquest, with its legendary anthropology and geography, not unrelated to the utopias being developed at the time. Public credit was also the subject of an abundant allegorical and "marvelous" treatment by the novelists and poets of the time. So we need to explore the relations of travelers, of the men who described the fabulous trade (with the North American Indians but also with Asia), the abundant precious metals, the freedom of manners, and the infinite natural resources of Louisiana. This American dream could be found in more or less identical form in England at the time of the deep financial and political crisis that led to the South Sea Company project. Regarding this enterprise, the issue here is less to understand power relations and financial techniques than to see how this scheme was presented and sold to English opinion. Famous authors wrote about how important it was to move into the South Seas so as to counter, abroad, the hegemonic projects of the French and to try, at home, to put an end to the scourges of debts and credit. They also expressed their fascination with these distant lands, allegorizing credit as a female figure, by turns desirable and repulsive, firm and unstable.

The rhetoric used by the propaganda team at work in England was replicated in France by the Modern writers. Their network was marked by various great figures of the Regency, who joined forces in various literary and worldly practices and in a certain way of thinking about politics. Whether it was fictions, theoretical letters, a mixture of the two, marvelous stories, poems, or songs, the dozens of texts they published to the glory of the System revealed a convergence of interests but also an aesthetic and convictions shared with the authorities. Ultimately, the so-called Law experiment was a collective endeavor, and it was the fiction produced in the moment in order to publicize it that allowed it to reveal all its mechanisms and possible meanings.

The American Dream

While the French expeditions led by the explorers Robert Cavelier de la Salle (1643–87) and Henri de Tonti (1649–1704) did not give rise immediately to the establishment of a permanent colony at the mouth of the Mississippi River, they did lead to a French presence in the region. This presence comprised an informal network of woodland traders, adventurers who married into Indian tribes, and itinerant Jesuit priests, until Minister Pontchartrain decided to launch three new expeditions between 1698 and 1702. Undertaken by Pierre Le Moyne d'Iberville (1661–1706), they resulted in a small but continuous French settlement in two locations: Fort Maurepas (also known as Fort Biloxi) and Mobile Bay.

Between the makeshift wooden constructions, the few dozen people who lived and mostly starved there, and the bleak reports sent back by d'Iberville, the image of the country during those early years was anything but glorious. Pontchartrain, however, firmly believed the region held deposits of precious metals, as was the case in Spanish Mexico, and demanded that further expeditions be organized to locate them. He also sought to halt the spread of British settlement south of the then-extant twelve colonies and to cut off the possibilities for British merchants to trade with Indian tribes living in the center of the continent.[3] As secretary of state for the Maison du Roi, Pontchartrain was also at the head of the Académie royale des sciences de Paris. This prestigious institution hoped to coordinate research around the Mississippi, spurred on by cartographers, historians, and geographers such as Guillaume Delisle (1675–1726) and his father, Claude (1644–1720). The latter had been tutor to the Duke of Orléans, who maintained very close ties with the Delisle family. His son Guillaume was a student of the astronomer Jean-Dominique Cassini at the Académie (1702), then *adjoint* (1716), and, finally, *associé* (1718), receiving in August of that same year the title first geographer to the king. He was a man by whom the all-powerful Abbé Jean-Paul Bignon (1662–1743), Pontchartrain's nephew, director of all the academies of the kingdom and editor of the *Journal des savants*, set great store. These various elements led to a certain interest in Louisiana on the part of the French academic world during the short respite between wars at the turn of the seventeenth and eighteenth centuries.[4]

These efforts were, however, set back badly by the War of the Spanish Succession (1701–14), which proved a disaster for the French settlers in Louisiana. With hardly any supplies, too small a labor force, and trading difficulties, they experienced famine, disease, and desolation. As a result, Pontchartrain decided to put French affairs in the region in the hands of a private company. He succeeded in doing so only in September 1712, when the king granted the financier Antoine Crozat (1655–1738) a fifteen-year trade monopoly in Louisiana. Crozat was commissioned with sending at least two ships a year carrying food, seed, livestock, settlers, and ammunition as well as exploiting the country's wealth and establishing factories and warehouses for trade. During the first months of the Regency in 1715, however, the "Crozat regime" did not achieve much success. Indeed, the civilian and military population together totaled no more than 250 souls, desertions were common, and neither of the two settlements could boast stone fortifications. Crozat's monopoly actually did more harm than good to the colony. The prices at which he purchased skins and tobacco were very low, while those he charged for foodstuffs imported from France were exorbitant. Discontent among the settlers grew. A system of free trade was demanded, in other words, the right to buy and sell with other traders and nations, but Crozat systematically refused to implement it.[5]

Between 1715 and 1716, the Naval Council established by the Duke of Orléans decided to intervene in order to compensate for the shortcomings of the Crozat monopoly, even while continuing to work with the financier. The unjust price system was reviewed, and the council negotiated with Crozat to send more troops led by skilled officers as well as a fortifications engineer. Unfortunately, lack of funding and Crozat's resignation in early 1717 following his conviction by the chamber of justice did nothing to improve the fate of the French settlers in Mississippi or carry out the proposed construction. What is crucial, however, is that these negotiations between Crozat and the Naval Council in the early years of the Regency, when John Law was as yet playing no part in the affairs of Mississippi, laid the foundation for the future System in several respects.

In the reports he drew up for the Council between 1716 and 1717, Crozat again suggested entrusting Louisiana to a chartered trading company. He was supported in this endeavor by his brother-in-law Joseph Le Gendre Darminy, one of the shareholders of the Compagnie de Saint-Domingue and adviser to the regent, and by their friend Jean-Baptiste Duché, a finance administrator from La Rochelle, then director of supplies at Rochefort, who himself in 1707 proposed a plan to develop Louisiana. These men suggested the creation of a joint-stock company, the capital of which could be formed by banknotes from the floating public debt in circulation (the *billets d'état*), and to which some of the receipts from the General Farm could be added. These were all elements that would be found on a completely different scale in the System but whose foundations would be those of the Compagnie d'Occident and the Compagnie des Indes, in which, moreover, Duché played an important part since he was to become one of its directors. Crozat, Le Gendre Darminy, and Duché also developed some essential principles for establishing a real colony in Louisiana. These principles primarily concerned the important issue of emigration, followed by mining issues and then trade within the American continent and the balance of power with Great Britain. In Crozat's opinion, it was a lack of population that had impeded the prosperity of the colony up to that point. To compensate for this, he suggested the implementation of widespread forced emigration from France.[6] Until the death of Louis XIV, Pontchartrain had opposed this policy. The Count of Toulouse, the head of the Naval Council, had fewer qualms. In addition to deserters, foundlings, and "young libertines," in 1716–17 he included among those forced to emigrate *faux-sauniers* (prisoners arrested for smuggling salt), the female orphans of the General Hospital of Paris, and "a group that included plowmen, day laborers, and craftsmen, all in the prime of life," taken from various jails throughout the kingdom in 1717, steadily increasing the numbers of immigrants.[7] This policy was, however, still not enough to make up for the lack of skilled labor in the colony, nor would the timid beginnings of voluntary emigration originating out of Rochefort (only a few individuals) prove enough to reverse the trend. This phenomenon was due to a general lack of knowledge about Louisiana outside scholarly circles and the circles of power. However, it was during these years preceding the System that a discourse and propaganda strategy concerning the Mississippi began to be implemented.

To begin with, the Naval Council and the Académie des sciences returned to the project of mapping Louisiana begun by Pontchartrain before the War of the Spanish Succession. In 1717, an officer and several instruments were sent to the Mississippi delta with a view to producing survey sketches that, along with others, would serve as preliminary work for the map ultimately published by Guillaume Delisle in 1718. It would become one of the major pieces of government propaganda in favor of the System. But, besides mapping, the council and the Académie wanted to learn more about the natural history, the mining resources, and the inhabitants of Louisiana. In this undertaking, Bignon and Delisle were able to count on the unwavering support of two priests. The first, Father François Le Maire (1675–1748), was a missionary who, when not traveling on the river or on an expedition to Mexico, resided in the Mississippi delta. The second, Abbé Jean Bobé (1654–1735), was, during the Regency, a Vincentian priest in the king's chapel at Versailles. Having served a few years before at La Rochelle and Rochefort, he was particularly familiar with the context of American colonization. Through his family, he was also related to several administrators of the navy and intendants of New France, especially the Raudot family, which was itself linked to the Pontchartrain clan. In 1717, Antoine-Denis Raudot (1679–1737), a close friend of Bobé's and former intendant of Canada, was appointed one of the three directors of the new Compagnie d'Occident founded by Law. It was Bobé who introduced Delisle to Raudot and who was also in constant contact with Le Maire. Both ecclesiastics consistently promoted the colonization of Louisiana by providing concise maps, travel narratives, and details about the local wildlife, the customs of the inhabitants, and especially the mining and commercial wealth of the region.[8]

Le Maire and Bobé voiced strong opinions concerning the first point of Crozat's program, namely, emigration. While they were not supporters of forced emigration, they did insist on the priority, in their opinion, of sending significant numbers of *filles* to Louisiana. In a report of March 1, 1717, Le Maire argued against the enslaving of Indian women, which he considered detrimental to the establishment of a permanent white settlement in the region. In doing so, he painted an unwittingly attractive picture of the country's sexual practices. Despite emphasizing his disgust, he pompously highlighted the fact that, while "polygamy is mostly rare among them [the natives]," "they regularly change wives, which amounts to the same thing." He particularly noted that all the French settlers, "even the soldiers, buy girl or women slaves to serve as their concubines; which prevents them from settling down through legitimate marriages, and consequently prevents the Colony from increasing because more than half of the children conceived from these illicit unions perish before birth, by abortions obtained through a thousand evil means." This last point was not all that surprising given that "there are in this country countless medicinal plants." Thus, Le Maire described the nascent colony as a "real Babylon."[9] Were these remarks disapproving? In other words, was Louisiana seen as a place abandoned by God, ruled by immorality rather than by good morals and the sanction of the law? There was a strong ambivalence in Le Maire's discourse that actually reinforced, no doubt on purpose, the utopias of Lahontan and Gueudeville. His depiction of the customs and manners of the settlers in Louisiana was, indeed, a kind of de facto validation of the sexual liberation of men (because women were exploited here), authorized by an American "elsewhere." There is no doubt about the dimension of advertising involved. This depiction was also not unrelated to the customs of the Louvre and the Palais-Royal at that time, which were much freer than they were at Versailles at the end of the reign of Louis XIV. The American fantasy and the sexual practices of the upper class clearly echoed one another here.

In addition to the need to populate the colony, Crozat, Le Maire, and Bobé focused on mining and trade issues. According to Crozat, Louisiana offered "what remains of the [unexploited] mines in America not held by the Spaniards and the Portuguese, and including a large number of Gold, Silver, Lead and Copper Mines, which have been recognized for being located in the same Mountain Chain as those of Mexico, and which . . . are scarcely 12, 15 and 20 *lieues* from the Mississipy River." For Crozat, it would be easy "to penetrate the Mines of New Mexico" from Louisiana and thus take possession of an infinite source of precious metals that were just waiting for French ingenuity and enterprise.[10] Le Maire insisted on this point from the beginning of his report and kept returning to it:

> It is a constant Truth with which even the Spaniards are in agreement, that all the Country West of the Mississipy at 37, 38, 39 and 40 degrees latitude is full of Mines as abundant as those of Old and New Mexico. . . . Let none tell me that, were there Mines in these cantons, the Spaniards would not have failed to spread and settle in these parts. The Spaniards cannot occupy all the Land; and if they have not penetrated as far as the Mines of which I speak, it is both the distance from Mexico at which they are found and the War with the

> Indians in these Regions . . . which have prevented them from doing so, and continue to prevent them today.

Le Maire spoke of the "huge profits" it would be possible to make from mining, his account filling the mind with images drawn from the reports of the initial Spanish conquest. "We have learned from the most remote nations of Missouri that, at certain times, small caravans of Spanish adventurers ford the river to its source, with several horses, and that they trade yellow iron (to quote these savages) with some of the nations to the West. Now, that yellow iron can be none other than gold; for only this metal has this color when mined." Le Maire believed that "great cities" existed in this region, where there was "a great salt sea," which he called "Cibola."[11] In 1717, when he read a report to the Naval Council on the possible existence of an inland sea west of Missouri, Guillaume Delisle, on the strength of Le Maire's writings, put forth his own conjectures on the existence of the mythical cities of Cibola and Quivira. He mentioned them by name more than a dozen times in just a few pages and placed them on his map (fig. 2.1) only a short distance from the Mississippi on the shores of the so-called Western Sea. Cibola and Quivira had, in fact, belonged to the mythical Seven Cities of Gold that Francisco Vásquez de Coronado (1510–54) sought for in vain during his expedition of 1540–42.[12] Delisle doubted neither Coronado's testimony nor the presence in the ports of these cities of numerous vessels that "had golden spars & silver bows; which were loaded with merchandise, & which were said to hail from Cathay, or China."[13]

The narrative systems used by Crozat, Le Maire, and Delisle proceeded not only by extrapolation from established geographic and historical knowledge but also by a process of suggestion. If mines existed in the mountain ranges of Mexico and New Mexico, why should they not also be found in those of Louisiana? Moreover, would the "Western Sea" not allow the French access to the mines of Spanish America? Better yet, would it not represent a route to Asia via the Mississippi and Missouri Rivers? *Cibola* and *Quivira* functioned as very clear signifiers. As noted by Paul Mapp, if "New Mexico" "meant wealth" for Europeans of the seventeenth and eighteenth centuries, the Seven Cities of Gold were connected to a magical notion of even greater wealth. This idea of gold that was "both loot and wonder" possessed the Western imagination until the early eighteenth century.[14] The work carried out by Le Maire and Delisle received significant attention from the regent and the Naval Council, who were of a mind to launch expeditions in search of this "Western Sea." However, while encouraging a much greater interest in Louisiana, their work contributed to more than just a colonial policy.

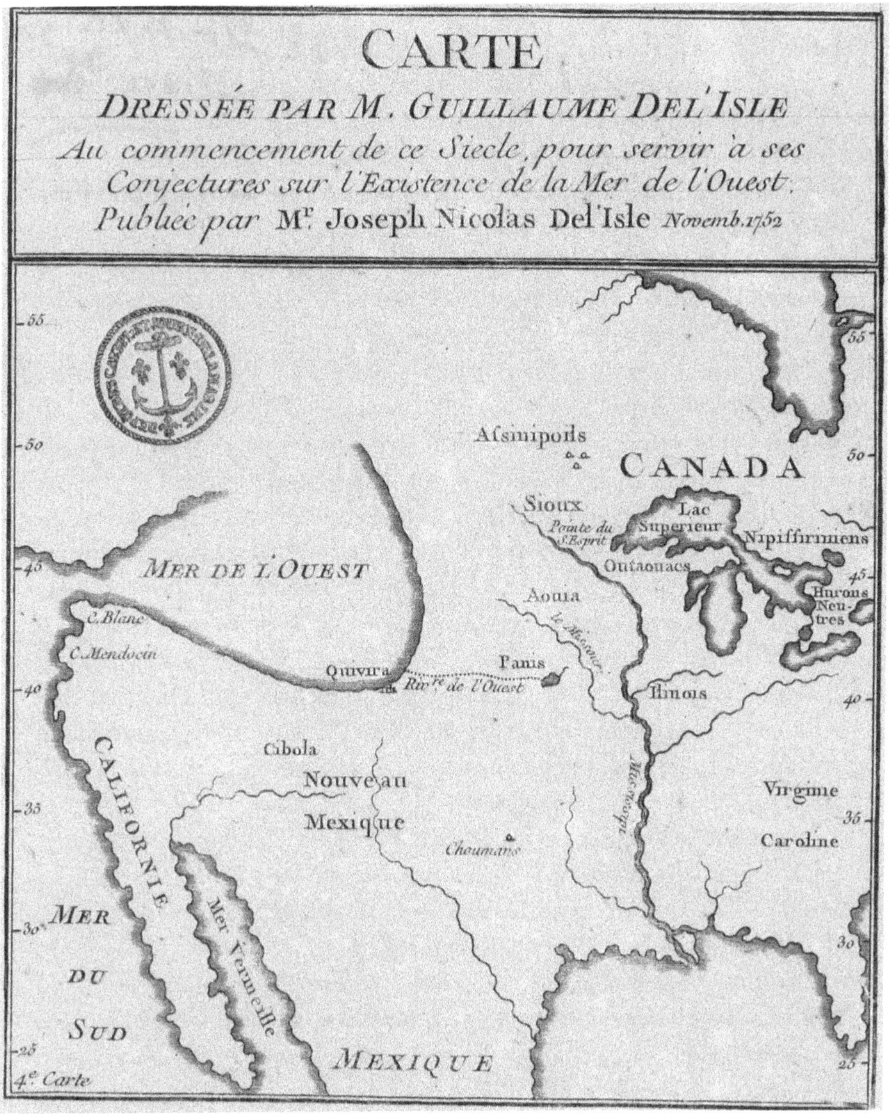

FIGURE 2.1. *Carte dressée par M. Guillaume Delisle au commencement de ce siècle pour servir à ses conjectures sur l'existence de la mer de l'Ouest, publiée par Mr. Joseph Nicolas Delisle* (Paris: Delisle, 1752). Courtesy Bibliothèque nationale de France, Département des cartes et plans, GE SH 18 PF 172 DIV 2 P 5/5 D. Concerning this map, see Marcel Giraud, *Histoire de la Louisiane française*, 4 vols. (Paris: Presses universitaires de France, 1953–74), 2:20.

Indeed, this mining fever was also at work in metropolitan France and under the aegis of the same actors. In 1717, Le Maire dispatched metal samples mined from the Mississippi delta to Abbé Bignon for analysis.[15] The latter, who served as director of the Académie des sciences, included this shipment within the scope of a much larger program that had been launched by the Duke of Orléans only a few months after his accession to power, namely, the famous *Enquête du régent*.[16] Carried out between 1716 and 1718, and coordinated jointly by the Académie and the regent himself with the support of the intendants of the provinces, the survey had as its main purpose to take an inventory of the mineral wealth of the kingdom.

The regent's interest in the sciences in general and chemistry in particular was well-known. Philippe had had his son, the Duke of Chartres, attend the public sessions of the Académie des sciences between 1701 and 1702 and, in the laboratory he had built at the Palais-Royal, himself took private lessons with the renowned physician, botanist, and chemist Wilhelm Homberg (1652–1715). Homberg was a diligent and prolific researcher, recruited by Bignon.[17] Along with Fontenelle, who praised him in 1715, he shared the idea that knowledge should have useful applications. From this perspective, geology and minerals were of crucial importance. "Metals," said Fontenelle, "have particularly piqued Mr. Homberg's curiosity," and, more than any other person, it was Homberg who convinced the regent shortly before his death to use the Académie to develop the relationships between science and the arts and crafts. The *Enquête* was a first step in this direction.

At the end of 1715, Bignon wrote a letter to be circulated to the intendants specifying his information-collection methods and the chain of communication. The Académie des sciences expected samples, reports, and maps from the intendants, who, to this end, were to consult a wide spectrum of persons and institutions, even "private individuals, miners, priests, soldiers, artisans, and fishermen." Bignon was very clear: mineral wealth and industrial establishments should be the top priority for those responsible for carrying out the *Enquête*, in France and elsewhere. Indeed, he specified in his letter: "The French citizens who travel and those who for their office, their trade, or other reasons establish themselves among the other peoples of the world, shall provide the regent with the very best proof of their loyalty and zeal, by sharing these matters with him, in accordance with the following articles."[18] This passage can be understood as a direct reference to the works of Le Maire and his intermediaries in Versailles and Paris.

Several hundred people participated in this vast enterprise of scientific-information gathering, and the *Enquête* aroused general interest on the part of metal manufacturers and mine operators. Indeed, like other European nations, France had in the early eighteenth century begun the transition from using organic matter to using minerals as sources of energy.[19] But the *Enquête* had a much broader scope. It conveyed and supported a systematic reflection on the way in which the productive forces of the kingdom should be organized. In particular, the reports by the intendants stressed how little connection there was among French industries, each of which seemed to exist in a semiautarkic state at the local level: "[O]ne gets the impression of a country of 'nuclear' manufacturing industries, working independently and wary of alliances with other producers." However: "In highlighting certain barriers encountered by the arts and manufactures in France, the *Enquête* provided evidence that the application of scientific knowledge to the arts and manufactures . . . would be possible only insofar as it was managed at the national level. And who should implement this strategy? The state and its agents, in collaboration with the Académie des sciences." The *Enquête* therefore not only required the all-out mobilization of the resources of the kingdom and its colonies; it also opened the way for a new state centralization policy.[20]

The *Enquête du régent* also represented an opportunity for many scholars and administrators to justify their efforts by reference to France's growing rivalry with Great Britain, Spain being considered less and less a serious geopolitical competitor.[21] In the American colonies, Crozat was concerned that the British had cornered the gold trade with Brazil since the end of the war in 1714. If France did not take advantage in Louisiana, "all the savage nations will return to the English side": "[T]he first thing they will do will be to descend the Wabash River to the Illinois Country with its Mines of Gold and Silver, Copper and Lead, of which they have knowledge, whereafter they will spread throughout the Mississipy River, to the sea, and when they have spent two or three years setting up their establishment, they will then enter Mexico by the same River." The situation was serious because, according to Crozat, "the increasing power of England in Europe is especially due to the Trade of its Colonies." Le Maire was in agreement. He considered it essential for the French to settle along all the region's navigable rivers in order to eliminate the possibility of the British reaching the mines in the South and the West first and putting an end to their trade with the Indian nations.[22]

Le Maire described in detail the competition that existed between the British and the French around the commerce in animal skins. He also stressed the infinite resources available in the region and insisted that they should not be left to the British settlers. He was of the opinion that the country enjoyed an "excellent" climate. All kinds of game, fish, deer, and "wild oxen" could be found there as well as all the fruits of Europe, "the whole land" also being "covered with wild vines." And, while grain did not grow well in "Lower

Louisiana," "Upper Louisiana" was a land flowing with milk and honey: "Everyone is in agreement that it contains vast fields and prairies, where one has but to install his plow, to produce all kinds of grain." Le Maire continued on in this same biblical and metaphoric vein: "In a word, the whole country watered by the Missouri is a land so fertile, so beautiful, and so temperate, that it may be regarded as the Heaven on earth of North America." In a place that God had so richly blessed, where the natives "are gentle and keen to Trade with us," violence could be the result only of British maneuvers.[23]

Indeed, the thirteen colonies—and especially the province of Carolina—quickly recognized the dangers of French settlement around the Mississippi. From 1699–1700 on, both the British and the French engaged in intimidation tactics via native intermediaries. While the conflicts increased with the start of the war between England and France (May 1702), they did not involve large numbers of regular troops. Neither party had either the means or especially the will to control the other's territories, the true weakness of the French colony being most likely not precisely known to the British. What was at the heart of the conflict in North America was, therefore, not territorial conquest, but rather a struggle over areas of commercial influence. In 1712 and 1713, the establishment of Crozat's company generated strong opposition from Great Britain.[24] In reality, British fears began at an even earlier date. If they reached a climactic point during this period, it was because Crozat's monopoly clashed with a project that had very similar aims to those of the French company: the famous British South Sea Company. Along with the propaganda surrounding it, this project formed at least as much a part of the background of the future System as the fantasies the French had entertained about Louisiana since the end of the seventeenth century.

The British South Sea Company: Rivalry and Propaganda

From 1706, there was concern in Great Britain over a possible French domination of trade in America. What was believed to be a growing French settlement in Mississippi, on the one hand, and the new alliance between the courts of France and Spain that opened up South America to French traders, on the other, quickened fears of the advent of a "universal monarchy" under Louis XIV. Several pamphlets called for Great Britain to react to these threats and, specifically, to create a monopoly company capable of competing with the French in the Spanish-American trade. Two of these pamphlets, published in 1706 and 1707, envisaged the creation of a British colony in the Gulf of Darién, in the north of present-day Colombia, explicitly linking the mining issue and the French domination:

> In order to prove the One thing Necessary then, *It is humbly Proposed,* The *Spanish West-Indies* in *America,* is the only Fountain of *Gold* and *Silver*; and should the *French,* whose Ambition is well known to all Men, keep the Possession of the *Spanish West-India* Trade, which they have of late Surprized, it cannot be but they must be Masters of all the Current *Gold* and *Silver,* and they will thereby Ingross to Themselves the Trade of the Whole Universe; and it is very likely that all Ballance of Power, will unavoidably in the End, be the Consequence of their being Posess'd of all the *Material Treasure* in the World.[25]

The idea that France was in the process of seizing all the precious metals to be found in Peru, Mexico, and "Nova Mexico" seemed to explain why it was able to support so costly a war. This situation had, therefore, to be remedied through the establishment of a "body of Merchants, that shall Entitle Themselves by Subscriptions to Carry on a Trade with the *Spaniards* in those Seas."[26] These projects preceded and prepared the way for the creation of the South Sea Company in August 1710 by Britain's new strongman, Robert Harley, First Earl of Oxford and Earl Mortimer (1661–1724).[27] Like France, Great Britain was undergoing a full-blown financial crisis in the period 1709–10. Trust in the national debt fell so low that the government had to offer extremely high interest rates in the hope of raising new funds. It was feared that the state would be unable to support a protracted conflict financially. This situation led to the political crisis that would bring Harley to power. The latter decided to combine the problem of the national debt with the issue of trade with Spanish America.

The discussions he initiated in the fall of 1710 led to the creation of the South Sea Company in May 1711. The main lines of this plan were relatively simple: British public debt securities owned by private individuals would be exchanged for shares in the new trading company. The transaction was expected to clear the market of short-term, unconsolidated securities "issued by the Royal Navy, Army, munitions, and troop carriers." These securities carried very high interest rates and, therefore, were expensive for the public purse. They were also due very quickly, and the risk of bankruptcy was, therefore, real. Converting them into shares made it possible to consolidate the debt, in other words, to lower the interest rates paid and not to have to repay the principal (the state would never have to buy back all the shares from their owners). The government encouraged this exchange both by promising high dividends paid out on the company shares and, at the same time, by arbitrarily announcing a drastic decrease in the interest rate paid out on the securities themselves. The state thus transferred part of its financial burden to the new monopoly company, the trade activities of which were expected to pay dividends promised to the shareholders in lieu of their return on their previous securities.

There was, of course, alongside these financial questions, a strong political dimension to the creation of the South Sea Company. Even though he was a moderate himself, Harley had after all been brought to power by the Tories, defenders of landowners and supporters of a strong king vis-à-vis Parliament. The Tories accused their opponents in the Whig Party, the representatives of banking and finance, of having made a great deal of money thanks to government loans since the start of the conflict. The South Sea Company was, thus, thought of as a counterweight to the Bank of England and the East India Company, both in the hands of the Whigs. What was at stake in Harley's project was, therefore, a factional struggle over credit, taxation, and the aims of the British monarchy. So Harley initially turned the management of the company over to the Tories in an attempt to convert the latter to a public credit that would be in their hands against the Bank of England. He then sought to secure the support of land interests by using the income from trade, in lieu of taxes on the land, to pay the interest on the English debt. Finally, whereas the Whigs' interests were oriented toward the European continent, the Tories' interests were oriented toward the Atlantic and Pacific worlds, and the project reinforced their imperial aims.[28]

While the exchange of government debt securities for shares in a monopoly trading company was to form the basis for the System, implemented just a few years later in France, this technical and financial issue is not of direct relevance to the subject at hand. This chapter examines the propaganda around the launch of the South Sea Company and its consequences. Two kinds of discourse were at work here, both providing an arsenal of arguments for the journalists, pamphleteers, poets, songwriters, and engravers who would later promote the French System. On the one hand, Harley's men used educational methods to try to justify the semiauthoritarian exchange of debt securities for shares in the new company. On the other, they imbued their vocabulary with an element of the fantastic when speaking of the amazing American continent and of credit instruments that were every bit as wonderful. This propaganda project involved both anonymous individuals and some famous men of letters, notably the authors Daniel Defoe (1660?–1731), Jonathan Swift (1667–1745), and the Huguenot emigrant Abel Boyer (1664–1729). They also included Herman Moll (1654–1732), the renowned geographer, cartographer, and illustrator of some of the novels by Defoe and Swift.[29]

The South Sea Company was not just a financial enterprise for reducing the public debt but a fully fledged company that was active—very active indeed—from 1713 to the end of 1718. On the signing of the Treaty of Utrecht in March 1713, England obtained from the Castilians the *asiento*, in other words, the right to carry on the slave trade in Spanish America in return for financial recompense. Now, the South Sea Company accounted for between 20 and 25 percent of the English slave trade over the period under consideration, a far from negligible amount.[30] It was this trading activity that the propagandists of Harley's scheme sought initially to emphasize. Published in 1711, *A True Account of the Design, and Advantages of the South-Sea Trade*, whose author is uncertain,[31] began by recalling the financial ruin Great Britain faced before Harley came into office. After two very expensive wars and a national debt that was quite simply unbearable, the ministry and Parliament decided to proceed "like able Physicians, to probe the Wound." This consisted of "Incorporating the Proprietors of the said Debts to carry on a *Trade to the South-Seas*," thus "enabl[ing] her [France] to arrive at Universal Empire in *Europe*." Indeed, since the seventeenth century, France had started "to lay a Foundation to engross the Trade thither, by Means of a Communication between the River *Canada*, and that of *Mississippi*, which empties itself into the Gulf of *Mexico*." The goal of the South Sea Company was therefore to counter France's power in North America.[32] After briefly discussing the trade in enslaved people, the author then went into great detail describing the British products that could be traded for precious metals in Spanish America and ended by addressing the concerns that had arisen during the implementation of the debt-for-shares exchange project. He mentioned "the *Compulsion* put upon the Proprietors of Publick Debts," who were more or less forced either to accept the exchange or to retain only a paltry rate of interest on their old rentes. The author first highlighted the patriotism that should animate all good Englishmen wishing to "[d]islodge the French out of the Spanish West-Indies" and then justified the authoritarian coup that governed Harley's grand plan:

> Now, if ever *Compulsion* can be justify'd, (and no Government can subsist without it) it is certainly in a Case not only of Necessity, but Visible Benefit. The Forcing therefore the Proprietors of Publick Debts, that is, a Multitude of Persons of different Humours, Interests, and Views, to agree and meet in one Common Center, *viz*, the Publick Good, and their own Private Advantage, is certainly a very happy and commendable Violence. Not but that such a Compulsion may occasion Inconveniences to several particular Persons: But as *Salus Populi Suprema Lex*, so *Private, ought to yield to Publick Considerations.*[33]

The fact that the pamphlet justified a use of arbitrary authority in this operation is important. The idea that the French Mississippi Company was a "center" that combined both private and public interests through a form of "happy violence" would become one of the leitmotifs of the propagandists of the System in France a few years later. In *The True State of the Case between the Government and the Creditors of the Navy* (1711), Defoe used similar language to address the same issue. Given that a "Publick Disease" threatened "the Health of the whole Body," the complaints of those who refused to exchange their debt securities for shares were, he explained, unjustified. Without Harley's project, there would have been no more interest payments anyway thanks to a state bankruptcy. Moreover, it was quite simply the case that "you are not bound to subscribe at all."[34] Defoe returned more fully to this issue in 1712 in his pamphlet entitled *An Essay on the South Sea Trade*. Summarizing once again the "Clamour" surrounding the alleged violence toward public debt holders, he asserted that "seeming Force" was the only way to define a process that was necessary for the good of the country at the same time as it enriched individuals.[35]

Fascinated by the South Seas, Defoe saw in Harley's project an adventure that was not only commercial but also colonial. More than the financial plan itself, it was the vision of a British South America complete with a network of trading posts, cities, and depots that caused him to support the project. He too, in fact, gave free rein to fantasies of an America overflowing with precious metals and simply begging to be developed by an industrious nation. In a letter dated July 20, 1711, the celebrated English writer suggested that the emphasis in the propaganda needed to be placed on the fact that the English colony would lie amid American gold and silver, resources that had greatly enriched the Spanish and that the English would be much better placed to develop thanks to their powerful navy.[36] In the pamphlets he wrote in 1711 and 1712, he even seemed somewhat hostile toward those persons of independent means and other financiers who held public debt securities. This tendency would continue over the course of the following years, which is interesting for two reasons: first, the notion of the extinguishing of public credit in the classical sense, that is, that of the government borrowing from individuals, and, second, the discussion of public credit in a language replete with images of fantasy and myth.

By 1717, the problem of the British debt resulting from the wars against the France of Louis XIV had still not been settled, the South Sea Company having provided only a fleeting respite. When Robert Walpole (1676–1745) was appointed first lord treasurer in October 1715, he tried to convince the holders of debt securities to accept a lower interest rate. Defoe participated in this campaign with his famous pamphlet *Fair Payment No Spunge* (1717), in which he expressed the full extent of his resentment toward forms of investment similar to rentes. Right from the introduction, he denounced the "stock-jobbers, *Gens d'affaires*, as the *French* call them," and later strongly attacked the rente holders of the state, who were guilty of having practiced

"Usury and Extorsion for above Twenty Years" and of putting the British nation "in Slavery to Creditors." Now, "the Oppress'd labouring and Trading People" were seeking justice against the financiers and rentiers, the latter having consistently enriched themselves at the expense of the former, receiving in interest and dividends the unjust taxes and levies that the kingdom was forced to bear. The most numerous were also "in many Respects the Strength, the Life, and the Soul of the whole Body," those who "support the whole," who pay for the least useful "an extravagant Interest for Loans!"[37] He called for a drastic reduction in the interest rate to promote trade and a fairer distribution of taxes to improve tax revenues while relieving the poorest.[38] By avoiding wars and following this wise policy, the state would be able to put an end to the scourge of public credit. On January 10, 1706, he had proposed in his weekly newspaper *The Review* a gendered metaphor that was also a form of genealogy:

> Money has a younger Sister, a very useful and officious Servant in Trade, which in the absence of her senior Relation, but with her consent, and on the Supposition of her Confederacy, is very assistant to her; frequently supplies her place for a Time. . . . Her name in our Language is call'd CREDIT.[39]

The same year, Defoe suggested another genealogical form in his *De jure divino* and specified what the "credit" character could do "from Paper and from Air":

> Funds perhaps may fail,
> And Streams may stop, but Credit must prevail:
> Credit's a Bank no Mischief can undo,
> She's Sister to *Potosi* and *Peru*;
> She'll out-do Nature, Mines of Gold prepare,
> And Fleets of Coin, from Paper and from Air;
> New Species forms, anticipates the Oar,
> Extends a little, and then can wait for more;
> The vast equivalent that she supplies,
> Our mighty boasted Poverty defies,
> And mocks th' abortive Hopes of *England*'s Enemies.

Defoe used powerful signifiers here, such as the proper names "Potosi" and "Peru," but he also assimilated "credit" with the supernatural in this elegy. He returned to the idea in 1709 in *The Review*, treating "credit" as a "nonentity" that "seems to have a distinct Essence (*if nothing can be said to exist*) from all the Phaenomena in Nature": "[T]he greatest Alchymists could never fix its Mercury, or find out its Quality; it is neither a Soul or a Body . . . it is a Being without Matter, a Substance without Form. A perfect free Agent acting by Wheels and Springs absolutely undiscover'd."[40] This mysterious character that had so many beneficial effects, notably in "paper" form, became "Lady Credit" in 1709.

By transforming the metaphor into an allegory, and by making the character of "credit" more complex and likening it to a "Lady," Defoe helped bring about a change in the meaning of the word *credit*. In place of the miracles previously attributed to "credit" and its "paper," there appeared a more ambiguous, fragile, and hazy character whose effects were more uncertain. Catherine Ingrassia and Laura Brown have extensively studied the similarities between the hypochondriac and hysterical female figure of Augustan literature and Defoe's "Lady Credit." She could be delightful, desirable, generous, and forward or, alternatively, timorous, ailing, susceptible to excess, and dismissive of advances.[41] In his *Machiavellian Moment*, Pocock had already stressed this instability: "Defoe is describing Credit in precisely the idiom employed by Machiavelli to describe *fortuna* and *occasione*, and we may also appropriately recall that *fantasia* of whose supremacy Giovanni Cavalcanti had been convinced by the triumph of manipulative politics at Florence a hundred years earlier still. Like all these goddesses, Credit typifies the instability of secular things, brought about by the interactions of particular human wills, appetites and passions."[42]

Thus, according to Defoe, "Lady Credit" had been completely happy during the first decade of the eighteenth century, producing wonders of generosity for both the state and individuals. But, from 1709–10 on, she became ill, which led the author to propose a second change in meaning. "If Credit is an Augustan Fortuna, she is also a courtesan," as Sandra Sherman puts it, and she would soon become "a whore" in tatters.[43] The constantly renewed loans destroyed all trust in the government's ability to repay its debts. "Lady Credit" was raped in 1710, becoming, "not only a woman with a past, but a woman whose reputation is on the way down."[44]

The statesman, poet, and journalist Joseph Addison (1672–1719) also used the allegory of Lady Credit in the March 3, 1711, issue of his journal *The Spectator*. During a "dream," the author visited the Bank of England, where he saw a marvelous goddess called "Publick Credit" "seated on a Throne of Gold." Then there appeared "the most hideous Phantoms"—"Tyranny and Anarchy," "Bigotry and Atheism"—and suddenly the bags filled with gold behind "Publick Credit" changed: "[T]he Bags that were really filled with Mony, had been blown up with Air, and called into my Memory the Bags full of Wind, which *Homer* tells us his Hero receiv'd as a Present from *Aeolus*. The great Heaps of Gold; on either side of the Throne, now appeared to be only Heaps of Paper, or little Piles of Notched Sticks, bound up together in Bundles like Bath-Faggots."[45] Order was restored only with the return of "Liberty," "Monarchy," "Moderation," and "Religion." The "Heaps of Paper" changed back into "Pyramids of Guineas" once again.

Different actors were, thus, able, depending on the circumstances and the interests that occupied them, to seize the gender allegory of Lady Credit, as the promoters and slayers of the System in France will do. But what matters to us at the moment are the virtues of the marvelous of allegory proper. Thus, in Defoe commerce becomes a mysterious force driven by the imagination outside the rules of reason and logic.[46] In the anonymous pamphlets of 1711 and 1712 in favor of the South Sea Company,[47] inaccuracies very quickly slipped into pure fantasy. The geographic ambiguities, in particular, remind us of the literary devices of utopia. The commercial and colonial competition between European nations found both an expression and an embodiment in those more or less fictional reveries. We can give a few examples. The French were thought to have a mysterious "Plantation in a convenient Place in the *South-Sea* to secure their Ships": "[T]hey have sent . . . 500 Families to settle there, where they have built Houses and a Fort to have there some Haven." No geographic indication was given, but a pamphlet of a perfectly identical nature dating from 1712 and signed by one Robert Allen stated that, "[a]s to the trade of *Mexico*, the *French* have made a considerable Settlement near that Coast, at a Place call'd St. *Bernard*, or St. *Lewis*'s Bay, and from thence drive a very great Trade with the Mexicans," followed by the entire Caribbean and South America.[48] This time, the details were a little more specific, the bays in question corresponding to Mississippi River delta. Given the dismal state of the French colony in Louisiana in the period 1711–12, it is hard not to be amused by these ramblings on the number of settlers and the extent of the trade carried on there.

These same pamphlets described at length the "golden Continent of America," where the "Hills are thought to be full of Mines" and the rivers full of gold and silver, always extending the metaphor of the "inexhaustible Fountain of Those Treasures."[49] Moll's *A View of the Coasts, Countries and Islands within the Limits of the South-Sea Company*, published in 1711, contained a detailed map (fig. 2.2) of the trading posts from New Mexico all the way to Tierra del Fuego. The geographer emphasized the fertility of the soil, the different plants and animals, and the mineral resources (obviously) as well as the possibilities for trade with the indigenous inhabitants. The latter were portrayed as innocent and naive partners, the Spanish being reported as exchanging all kinds of metals and precious goods for "some light Stuffs" or

"Trifles and Toys."[50] As Carl Wennerlind points out, Moll produced a selective narrative likely to resonate with the expectations of the investors.[51] He was not afraid to border on the fantastic in his descriptions, in the same vein as Le Maire or Delisle. The country in question was, after all, located very far away, and the precise positions of authority held by those who described them were obviously unverifiable.

Addison theorized this relation to fantasy, fairy tales, and fables in a manifesto published between June 21 and July 3, 1712, in *The Spectator*. "The Pleasures of the Imagination have this Advantage, above those of the Understanding, that they are more obvious, and more easie to be acquired." Especially, they "disperse Grief and Melancholy, and set the Animal Spirits in pleasing and agreeable Motions." Mankind is sensitive to distant narratives, even more so to extraordinary stories that recall the fairy tales of childhood, and is, therefore, naturally inclined to pay attention to them:

> Men of cold Fancies, and Philosophical Dispositions, object to this kind of Poetry, that it has not Probability enough to affect the Imagination. But to this it may be answered, that we are sure, in general, there are many Intellectual Beings in the World besides our selves, and several Species of Spirits, that are subject to different Laws and Oeconomies from those of Mankind; when we see, therefore, any of these represented naturally, we cannot look upon the Representation as altogether impossible; nay, many are prepossest with such false Opinions, as dispose them to believe these particular Delusions; at least, we have all heard so many pleasing Relations in favour of them, that we do not care for seeing through the Falsehood, and willingly give ourselves up to so agreeable an Imposture.[52]

But Addison went even further. To make his discourse intelligible and capable of leaving a mark on the readership to which it was addressed, it was necessary that he introduce a dimension that spoke directly to the imagination.[53] He does not reject the criticisms that the philosophers of the seventeenth century addressed to the use of superstitions or exaggerations in literature. In a way, he makes them his own, but he wants to transform them into a useful pleasure.[54] Indeed, fantasy constituted a force that could be made use of, even in serious undertakings. On the subject of the pamphlets and newspaper articles concerning the South Sea Company, Wennerlind notes: "Defoe and Swift used similar literary styles to those they would later employ in their successful fictional writings, such as *Robinson Crusoe* (1719), *Captain Singleton* (1720), and *Gulliver's Travels* (1726). The continuity between their propagandistic pamphlets and their novels has not gone unnoticed."[55] Precisely the same phenomenon occurred in France between 1718 and the 1730s.

FIGURE 2.2. This map of Central and South America from Herman Moll, *A View of the Coasts, Countries and Islands within the Limits of the South-Sea Company* (London: Morphew, 1711) served as propaganda for the new English South Sea Company. Courtesy New York Public Library.

Here, a generation of men of letters played an active role in the propaganda surrounding the System and afterward undertook or continued literary work in the same style, namely, that of imagination and fantasy.

A Team of Moderns

The figurehead of the circle was Jeanne-Baptiste d'Albert de Luynes, Countess of Verrue (1670–1736). Sharing the same Christian names as Colbert, who had been present at her baptism, the countess married in 1683, when she was not fourteen, a Piedmontese aristocrat, Joseph de Scaglia, Count of Verrue. The couple lived in Turin, where the countess very quickly became the mistress of Victor-Amédée II of Savoy, with whom she had two children. Showered with blessings by the prince, it was in Piedmont that she began to take an interest in the arts, regularly bringing in antique dealers and merchants from Rome. She is also known to have been closely involved in politics at this time. By seeking to promote a rapprochement of the duchy with France, she alienated the Austrians, who were very influential at the court of Victor-Amédée. A typical adventuress, she decided in 1700 to leave Turin for Paris on the sly. Her husband, the Count of Verrue, died in the war in 1704; she was then a little over thirty years old and enjoyed a considerable fortune. From that moment on she would lead a free and independent life in France. Shortly after arriving in Paris, she met Léon de Madaillan de Lesparre de Lassay (1681–1750), a soldier who became and would remain her closest friend until her death. During the War of the Spanish Succession, Lassay commanded an infantry regiment in which there served Captain Jean-François Lériget de La Faye (1674–1731), a future diplomat and man of letters; he became Madame de Verrue's lover. Two other characters were intimates of the countess and the closest friends of Lassay and Lériget. They were the magistrate and industrialist Jean-Baptiste Glucq de Saint-Port (1674–1748) and his partner, the manufacturer and painter Jean de Julienne (1686–1766).

All had close links with the System, but they were not, strictly speaking, speculators. Lériget de La Faye, Glucq de Saint-Port, Lassay, Verrue, and a few others attached to the countess had a real faith in the importance of long-term trade and bought many shares in the Compagnie d'Occident, which had become the Compagnie des Indes. Most of them kept these shares after the fall of the System, and they invested in a concession in Louisiana. The Glucq and Jullienne families specialized in linens, cloth, and dyes and, therefore, had an interest in maritime and colonial trade for both their supplies and their markets. They were also in contact with the shipowners and manufacturers of Saint-Quentin who were at the head of the Compagnie du Sénégal.

It was, therefore, not surprising to see the Glucq family invest considerable sums in the Compagnie d'Occident from September 1717 on.[56] They remained shareholders for decades, Glucq de Saint-Port becoming the Compagnie's *syndic* (shareholder representative) in 1745. Léon de Madaillan de Lassay also held this position. His father, Armand, a friend of Law's, was named honorary director of the Compagnie in 1717, a position he continued to hold at the downfall of the System and until his death in 1738.[57] These men and women were also art collectors and amateurs of *belles lettres*. The Countess of Verrue, in particular, spent a fortune on paintings, engravings, curiosities and books. Her collections of paintings and her library were considerable, even exceptional. The latter included all the contemporary authors, the old classics and many science books, but especially novels, travelogues, Oriental literature, tales and fables.[58] The countess did not keep a "salon" strictly speaking, in the sense that she had not established a fixed day of the week on which she brought together a chosen group in her private home, but she maintained a similar network of sociability. This point is of great importance with respect to the System.

Indeed Countess of Verrue's circle was in direct contact with the high aristocracy and those in power. The countess had placed her friend Jeanne-Agnès Berthelot de Pléneuf, marquise de Prie (1698–1727), as mistress of the Duke of Bourbon and Lériget as private secretary to the latter. Lériget is said to have had a lot of influence on the young duke. Bourbon was a considerable figure, head of the Regency Council, future prime minister (1723–26), an intimate of the Duke of Orléans and John Law. As for Lassay, he was close to the Condé family, the Duke of Bourbon, and the Duke of Orléans. The circles of the dinner were also the rendezvous of some of the greatest minds of the time. Among those who regularly attended were the scientists and metaphysicians Bernard Le Bovier de Fontenelle, Jean Terrasson, and Jean-Jacques Dortous de Mairan (1678–1771) as well as writers, playwrights, journalists, and songwriters such as Antoine Houdar de la Motte, Jean-François de Pons (1683–1733), Jean-François Melon (1675–1738), and Charles Dufresny. Some of these scholars and men of letters, such as Terrasson or Melon, were close friends of the Countess of Verrue: they were received several times a week, received presents, had rooms in her country house, and inherited valuable objects on her death. These writers and aristocrats visited each other assiduously, as reported by the wealthy president of the *parlement* of Paris Charles-Jean-François Hénault (1685–1770). At the start of the Regency, the latter "spent his life" with Fontenelle, Houdar de la Motte, Lériget de La Faye, Dufresny, Terrasson, de Pons, and a few others.[59] Although not as well connected to the countess as the latter, the artist, playwright, and poet

Charles-Antoine Coypel (1694–1752) was a close acquaintance of Lériget de La Faye and Dufresny. Coypel was also a protégé of the House of Orléans, becoming first painter to the regent and the "guardian of the King's drawing and painting" in 1719.[60] Furthermore, Coypel regularly collaborated with François-Gérard Jollain (or Joullain) (1660–1735), an engraver and seller of engravings and almanacs. Both men worked on the illustration of the main scenes of Molière's comedies, and, according to Coypel, Jollain engraved the portrait of Dufresny and those of the children of the Duke of Orléans.[61] Jollain also worked for Jullienne and participated in the latter's enterprise concerning the engravings of works by his friend the painter Antoine Watteau (1684–1721).[62]

In the arts, the Countess of Verrue and her friends were great defenders of the new rococo movement and style (especially the works of Antoine Watteau) and, in the literary field, of novels, stories, and fairy tales. As such, they were undoubtedly members of the Moderns party as opposed to that of the "Ancients." It can even be argued that, under the Regency, the countess and her circle represented the epicenter of the former group in its quarrel with the latter. This point is of major interest, given that a whole area of the System fell within the scope of this famous quarrel. Having originated in the 1680s, and continuing until the mid-eighteenth century, the dispute ostensibly concerned canons of beauty and truth in art, literature, and science. On the surface a debate about whether classical works were timeless and should forever serve as models against which modern works should be measured, the dispute actually concerned much more deeply opposed views of culture and society.[63] And, in reality, both the Ancients, led by the poets and playwrights Nicolas Boileau (1636–1711) and Jean Racine and, later, Anne Dacier (1645–1720), and the Moderns, led by the poet Charles Perrault and, subsequently, Fontenelle and Houdar de la Motte, all agreed on the distance that separated the turn of the seventeenth and eighteenth centuries from antiquity. Both parties also recognized how much progress had been made since then, in science as well as in the arts.[64]

So what was it that really separated them? To begin with, there was the idea held by the Moderns that the age of eloquence, tragedy, and lyric poetry was past. For them, prominence now needed to be given to the novel, the opera, and, especially, the fairy tale and its associated elements of the fantastic. They were also divided on the question of literary criticism. While the Ancients called for a form of presensationism in the understanding of artistic works through individual taste, the Moderns developed the idea of a universalist and rationalist critique of art within an explicitly Cartesian perspective. Finally, the two groups also divided over their judgment of the morals of ancient times. The Moderns claimed to be "horrified" by the practices of the heroes of antiquity and were in favor of generating wealth through trade. The Ancients, on the other hand, prized frugality, simple manners, and heroic passions and found the modern world wanting in these qualities, which the ancient world had cultivated so assiduously. The death of Louis XIV saw "the victory of a coterie which for years had revolved around the Duke of Orléans," that of the Moderns.[65] It included Fontenelle, of course, who lived in the Palais-Royal, and especially Houdar de la Motte, Dufresny, Melon, and Terrasson, all four of whom were to play a decisive role in the history of the System.

Antoine Houdar de la Motte had been taught by the Jesuits and studied law before beginning an early career in literature. His opera-ballets, comedies, and poems met with resounding success in the late seventeenth century. He later had artistic triumphs with his tragedies, notably *Inès de Castro* in 1723. An admirer of Fénelon, elected to the Académie française in 1710, he was a close friend of the Abbé Guillaume Dubois (1656–1723), the regent, and the famous salonnières Madame de Tencin and Madame de Prie. At the head of the Moderns party along with Fontenelle, Houdar worked with Fontenelle to effect a rapprochement between literature and science. A specialist in the genre of the ode, he published in 1707 his *Odes avec un Discours sur la poésie en général*, which met with instant success.[66]

Houdar was at the height of his fame under the Regency. He led the Moderns in a literary controversy over translations of the *Iliad*,[67] and it was at this time that he published his *Réflexions sur la critique* (1715) and his *Fables nouvelles, avec un discours sur la fable* (1719), in which he renewed his endorsement of the genre of fantasy: "Let us introduce as we choose Gods, Genies and Men; let us give voice to the animals and the plants; let us personify Virtues and Vices; and let us animate all beings according to our needs. . . . The less used & the most bizarre of Actors become natural, & even deserve preference over others, as they are the most apt, either by consent or by appropriateness, to represent the truth of a matter." Often accused of improbability in his fables, Houdar was sometimes coarse and overfamiliar in his descriptions. He was the author of numerous songs (some of them quite bawdy) as well as riddles, logogriphs, and rhymes published in the newspapers of the time or sent to his friends.[68] Blind in later life, he died covered with honors in 1731.

While we know very little about the first decades of the life of Charles Dufresny, we do know he became an artist and painter in the gardens of Versailles at the start of the eighteenth century. He also made his debuts as a songwriter, playwright, and storywriter during this same period. With his interest in comedy, and as a good Modern, he "introduced the theater to the magic of fantasy, with elements suggested from the fashion of the time for fairy tales."[69]

In 1710, Dufresny obtained the *privilège du roi*—exclusive authorization from the king—to publish the semiofficial government periodical then entitled *Mercure galant*. Houdar de la Motte and all the Moderns actively contributed to this publication, thereby guaranteeing its success. It included all sorts of topics, from the more serious to the more lighthearted, and also many songs, puzzles, and anecdotes. There were also numerous articles of a "scientific" nature. Dufresny produced genuine "documentaries" from the Académie des sciences that he published in the gazette (not without humor), thereby inaugurating a new journalistic genre.[70] After the death of Louis XIV, Dufresny showered his patron, the Duke of Orléans, with praise and enjoyed a significant level of influence in the literary world until his death in 1724.

Jean-François Melon had published nothing before the downfall of the System but belonged to the same circle as Houdar and Dufresny. After studying law, he was appointed inspector of the United General Farms in Dax in southwestern France in 1708. At the beginning of the Regency, Melon worked in the ministry of foreign affairs with Abbé Dubois before joining the Finance Council. He was appointed first secretary to John Law in 1718, then secretary to the Duke of Orléans at the downfall of the System. The two men were friends, and, at Philippe's death in 1723, Melon became secretary to Louis XIV's grandson, the Duke of Bourbon.

Melon presented several scientific papers to the Académie de Bordeaux, of which he had become a member, like Montesquieu, in 1713. He was also a very close acquaintance of the Countess of Verrue and a regular visitor to her house in Meudon. Besides his veiled reference to her in the preface to one of his works, we also know of a letter dating from 1736 in which he extolled the countess's luxury spending practices.[71] Glucq de Saint-Port was the executor of Melon's will and one of his universal legatees. Houdar de la Motte and Abbé de Pons were close friends with whom he frequented the Café Procope. Moreover, Melon also edited some of the latter's works.[72] He was, therefore, resolutely a Modern, not only because of his associations, but also because of the literary genres of which he made use several times during the 1720s and 1730s. His first book, *Mahmoud le Gasnévide*, was both an Oriental tale and a novel of good government along the lines of Fénelon's *Les avantures de Télémaque*. He published another book in 1734, *Essai politique sur le commerce*, a "rational" and "serious" treaty that included a fable in the tradition of Defoe, Addison, Dufresny, and Houdar de la Motte. In both cases, the fantasy genre allowed him to discuss an experience with which he was very familiar, namely, the System. These works were, however, published after the fact, and we will see how they helped construct the myths surrounding the System.

Within the circle of the Moderns, however, it was unquestionably Jean Terrasson who played a key role in the dissemination and promotion of the System. A scholar and a man of letters, Terrasson embodies the alliance between science and fiction of the seventeenth century and the early eighteenth.[73] He judges indeed that scientific investigation sometimes needs the *merveilleux* register to be embodied, to produce knowledge, and to convince when there is something inaccessible to the understanding and to reason. Voltaire considered Terrasson as an "apostle of La Motte and of Law."[74] Educated by the Oratorians, Terrasson was admitted to the Académie des sciences in 1707 thanks to the support of his mentor, himself a former member of the Congregation of the Oratory, the omnipresent Bignon.[75] He not only worked with the latter; he was also the protégé and a collaborator of Fontenelle's. He held no specific role in the Académie until 1716, when he was appointed assistant engineer, then *adjoint* in 1718, and, finally, *associé* in 1719. He was also a scholar and a writer, holding the chair of Greek and Latin philosophy at the Collège royal (later the Collège de France) in 1721, and joining the Académie française in 1732. He also frequented Madame de Tencin's salon along with Houdar de la Motte, Dufresny, and Fontenelle, and there he came into regular contact with Dubois, Law, and the regent.[76] Originally from Lyon, Terrasson lived in Paris with one of his cousins at the beginning of the century before moving to an apartment near the Countess of Verrue in 1719, and for many years he had his own room in her residence in Meudon.[77]

Terrasson published little during his lifetime. In his first book, *Dissertation critique sur l'Iliade d'Homère* (1715), he roundly criticized the supposedly barbaric customs of antiquity and denounced the age of Louis XIV, whose "reduced & lost taste" stemmed from its long-running wars and general "tyranny." His other great work was an Oriental novel explicitly built on the model of *Télémaque* and entitled *Séthos* (1731).[78] This book employed both prosopopoeia—Terrasson claiming to have found a manuscript in a foreign country and telling the story in the words of fictional narrators—and Menippean satire in the sense that the literary theorist Mikhail Bakhtin gave this genre,[79] that is, a book written in many voices, sometimes discordant, and with digressions on several topics interrupting the narrative. Two texts were published after Terrasson's death. The first, which appeared in 1754 under the title *La philosophie applicable à tous les objets de l'esprit*, was a compilation of philosophical reflections written throughout Terrasson's lifetime. It praised the works of Descartes, Fénelon, and Fontenelle, the beneficial role played by the Académie des sciences, and the importance of a peaceful government attentive to the happiness and well-being of its subjects. It contained a preface by the famous mathematician Jean Le Rond d'Alembert (1717–83), the son of Madame de Tencin, and a letter from the poet and writer François-Augustin Paradis de Moncrif (1687–1770). The latter mentioned another work by Terrasson, the *Traité de l'infini créé*, which was supposedly lost. This book, written by Terrasson in the late seventeenth century or the early eighteenth but before 1715, circulated in manuscript for decades before being finally published by Marc-Michel Rey in 1769. At that time it was attributed to the Cartesian philosopher Nicolas Malebranche (1638–1715), and only in 2007 did Antonella Del Prete prove that it was undoubtedly by Terrasson. The *Traité* was an ambitious metaphysical treaty on the plurality of inhabited worlds, the infinity of the universe, and the eternity of matter that displayed a certain indifference with respect to the principles of the Christian religion.[80] Several elements of these four works deserve attention.

Terrasson did not believe in any established principle, whether in science or in the arts. For him, nothing was stable, nothing was accepted, and, "far from subjecting themselves to ancient rules, nor do real Physicists subject themselves to modern rules." And he himself, although an advocate of Descartes, abandoned the latter's ideas in several parts of his work. He more generally considered that the eighteenth century was striving to overcome all "prejudices" through a "spirit of examination and discussion," the results of which had begun to be organized into "a constant and general system." The term *system* recurs again and again in his writings. The Ancients wrongly admitted "no general system," for "nothing marks scope and genius more than the talent of systems." In *La philosophie applicable*, he employed the uppercase. The "Systems" of nature or of art (Copernicus, Newton, Descartes, Perrault) represented the mark of the progress made in the modern world. But, since nothing was established, Systems were destined to follow one another, each having its moment in history. For Terrasson, fiction was an education, the new novel a form of legislation. For instance, he believed that "envy, avarice, & the other loose passions" were factors that could only "poison the present and the future." Good fiction should praise "generosity" and "superfluities" because "how many Workers find their livelihood in the spending by the Rich!": "What a source of growth for the Fine Arts & for public Decorations!"[81] As Larry Norman points out, a form of universalism was at work here. For Terrasson, "general laws of morality" had existed since time immemorial, and the role of fiction was to portray them for humanity as a whole. In his writings, this idea often took the form of an eschatological and Manichaean struggle. His *Traité de l'infini créé* gave pride of place to this question, discoursing at length on the new man that would arise following the decay of the body. Terrasson explained the fate of the righteous and the wicked, that of the heavenly Jerusalem, and the battle of the archangel Michael against the dragon in the book of Revelation.[82]

This last point is not unrelated to the role of the "fantastic element" and how governments should conduct world affairs. For Terrasson, "fantasy" could be used as long as it followed "the thread of nature." Thus, as was the case with Addison, Houdar, Dufresny, and later Melon, it was sometimes necessary, in fiction, to sacrifice the accuracy of the facts in order to embellish the discourse. Fantasy was not just possible; it was especially useful. And, even if they were perhaps a little less so than their neighbors, "the French, like all other peoples, are subject to seduction and illusion." For Terrasson the statesman, it was sometimes useful to play on that fact and even to maintain popular superstitions or prejudices "when they contribute to the good of the State."[83] In the same vein, d'Alembert specified how Terrasson was suspicious of the right of just anyone to judge works of art or of the mind: "He responded with a more energetic than studied comparison, that *the mind of a nation resembles Gold leaf, which becomes thinner the more it is stretched; & what it generally loses in depth it gains in surface area.* He feared above all that these Tribunals without law & without title . . . should seek through this usurpation to become the plague of good Books & the asylum of bad taste." With the exception of men of letters, rulers, and the great, those whom Terrasson referred to as "the People" were not entitled to judge what was offered them. With them it was possible to use "tricks of the imagination," to seduce and even deceive if it was for their own good.[84] This last point is important with respect to how the Moderns would invest themselves in the propaganda surrounding the System.

The Team of Moderns and the Propaganda Surrounding the System

In November 1716, the *privilège* for the semiofficial government newspaper the *Nouveau Mercure galant* (1714–16), run by Hardouin Le Fèvre de Fontenay (1686?–1736?), was revoked. The exact circumstances of this matter are not known, but it would seem that a combination of factors was at work. The content was considered dull, with few, if any, interesting contributions. Matters were not helped by Le Fèvre's disagreement with both the Ancients and the Moderns and his repeated attacks on the actors of the Comédie française and his fellow journalists as well as some figures of very high rank.[85] Whether or not these factors served as a pretext for ousting Le Fèvre, everything does seem to suggest that the Orléans-Fontenelle-Bignon trio was intent on taking over the kingdom's main information channel.

As censor of the Chancellery in 1716, Fontenelle had the final word on a lot of what was published in France. As for Bignon, he was obliged to give up running the book trade and the *Journal des savants* on the resignation of his uncle and protector Pontchartrain in July 1714. He continued, however, to maintain control over the royal academies, and the Duke of Orléans was quick to appoint him king's librarian as soon as the position became vacant in 1718.[86] In 1711, Bignon became directly involved in the awarding of the *privilège* of the *Mercure* to Dufresny, and he, a man whom François Moureau called the "Minister *sans portefeuille* for culture," exerted considerable influence in the literary world throughout his entire life.[87] In 1717, the actual running of the periodical was entrusted to a man who was both at the heart of the information channels of the power in office and in direct contact with the Modern party: Pierre-François Buchet, known as "Abbé Buchet," who renamed the gazette the *Nouveau Mercure*.[88] A journalist "of the French official press," Buchet employed five or six copyists to distribute, twice weekly, a handwritten gazette to a happy few of about twenty people, with the permission, although not the cooperation, of the police. The other *nouvelles à la main* (handwritten and secret news for a limited audience) authorized by the authorities tended to take most of their information from Buchet.[89] As an example of his skill, he published an *Abrégé de l'histoire du Czar Pierre Alexiewitz* during Peter the Great's visit to France in 1717, a work that drew heavily on official sources and from which all other gazettes and newsletters took inspiration. Furthermore, the very precise references to the tsar's visits to the Académie des sciences and his exchanges with Abbé Bignon suggest regular collaboration between the latter and Buchet.[90]

The censor of the *Nouveau Mercure* was none other than Jean Terrasson, who served in that position from January 1717 to May 1718, at which point he became one of the *Mercure*'s contributing journalists. It was clear from the outset that the *Nouveau Mercure* was the "headquarters" of the Modern movement, the "instrument" of Fontenelle, Houdar de la Motte, and Dufresny: "Their coterie, into which Marivaux appears to have wormed his way early on, . . . , could do all . . . thanks to La Motte, who was at its head."[91] The mention of the name of the famous novelist and playwright Pierre Carlet de Marivaux (1688–1763) is significant. Close to the Moderns, Marivaux was a regular contributor to Buchet's *Nouveau Mercure* and copied the gazette's style in his periodical, the *Spectateur français* (1721–24), the title of which was directly inspired by Addison's. It should also be noted that the columns of the *Nouveau Mercure* quickly started including translations and discussions of works by Defoe.[92] The propaganda for the System that appeared in the *Mercure* was clearly situated at the confluence of all these elements: official journalism, the network of the Moderns, rational reasoning, the element of fantastic fiction, and, finally, the "peculiar." It took two major forms.

That propaganda comprised, on the one hand, works of fiction (poems, songs, riddles, fairy tales, and prose theater) and, on the other, letters, articles, and stories that were intended to be both informative and rational but still encouraged a form of fantasy and imagination. Many were anonymous, but it is possible by a process of elimination and analogy to determine their authors. The pro-System fictions were produced mainly in the period between July 1719 and April 1720. They are too numerous to be studied in detail here, but I will take a brief look at the most interesting of them. The greatest poets of the time were involved, starting with Dufresny, who rarely missed an opportunity to praise the virtues of his patron, the Duke of Orléans. At the time of the System, he published in the *Mercure* a "petition" (*placet*) representing a tribute to the newfound prosperity of the kingdom. Another work of prose entitled *L'actionnaire bigame, avanture* was very likely by the same author. Indeed, it contains the same vocabulary and characters that were common in Dufresny's *nouvelles historiques*: the Widow, the Cavalier, the Marquis, and a noble character. The plot, moreover, is similar to that of his short story "Les dédits" while at the same time being anti-*Turcaret*.[93] *L'actionnaire bigame* is a lengthy moral story expounding the new values embodied in the System and echoing numerous texts by John Law and Jean Terrasson that were intended to be more "serious." Coypel published a long allegorical poem to the glory of Law in the *Mercure* of December 1719.[94] The very enlightening "Ode to the Regent," published in the same issue, was penned by Houdar de la Motte. And the latter, who flattered the financial genius of the Duke of Orléans under the pseudonym Michel Bohm in the introduction to a new edition of Pierre Bayle's dictionary in spring 1720, was likely the author of several "riddles" and other "logogriphs" to the glory of "paper," again in the *Mercure*. Published in January 1720, the fable entitled *L'amour et la fortune* is of great importance when placed in relation with other texts. This fable, probably by Houdar de la Motte or the actor and playwright Marc-Antoine Legrand (1673–1728), is written in the marvelous style: it explains the System and the good behavior one needs to adopt to play a part in it by bringing several goddesses to intervene in a fabulous world.[95] Other interesting elements can be found in the gazette: verses by Legrand, one of Nostradamus's prophecies, a one-act vaudeville in verse by another playwright, Denis Carolet (1696–1739), performed on November 21, 1719, at the Comédie française, and several anonymous poems and songs.[96] All developed the themes of how prosperity had returned to France since the arrival of the regent and Law, the possibility of enrichment for the poor, and love, now to be found all along the cobblestoned rue Quincampoix. Engravings published by Jollain and plays presented in other official venues, such as the Théâtre-italien, complemented this propaganda in the register of the marvelous, such as Legrand's *Plutus* (1720), a highly interesting variation on the play by Aristophanes that describes the benefits of the System and the good behavior it promotes.

Alongside these fictions, the *Nouveau Mercure* published several letters and articles, in different forms, between 1717 and spring 1720 in favor of the System. Chronologically, the travel narratives appeared first. In September 1717, the *Nouvelle relation de la Louisiane* appeared, and, in February 1718, an alleged "Naval officer" published the *Lettre touchant la Louisiane, autrement dit le Mississippi*, written in the same tone as that used in Le Maire's reports while including an even greater element of fantasy. Another similar letter was published in March 1719, while the gazette frequently inserted advertisements on the equipping of ships sailing to "this enchanted land" or short cryptic phrases on the gold mines and the great numbers of emigrants leaving from La Rochelle.[97] "Fugitive Facts," also very short, employed the same themes and images. So, in October and November 1719, Buchet inserted in his journal ever more implausible stories about the enrichment of individuals from humble backgrounds.[98]

A coherent set of nine texts constitutes one of the main ways of getting into the System's deep expectations. Of these nine texts, one remained as a manuscript during the time period the System was in operation; this was the *Idée générale d'un nouveau système des finances*, of which several versions have survived. Another was published in 1720; this was the *Mémoire pour justifier la Compagnie des Indes contre la censure des casuistes qui la condamnent*, by Terrasson, which does not seem to have attracted the attention of commentators until today. The other seven were published in the *Nouveau Mercure*. First, these were two very long articles aimed no longer at distilling information but at explaining the general functioning of the System. The first was the *Abrégé historique de l'établissement & du progress de la Compagnie des Indes en France*, published in January 1720. This was by Buchet, occasioned, as he announced in the preamble, by the fact that, as director, he was assailed by letters from the provinces asking for an explanation of what was happening in Paris. Buchet did the same thing again the following month with the *Histoire abrégée de la banque*. In these bravura pieces, the overt pedagogy constantly gave way to propaganda and fabulous subtexts. Then, we find in the *Nouveau Mercure* issues of February, March, and May 1720,[99] three long letters by Terrasson in favor of the System that historians long attributed to John Law himself. The information they contain testifies to the close relationship between the author and the Scottish economist and his views, but Terrasson's style and major ideas are easily recognizable. These letters were, in fact, published independently in spring 1720 under Terrasson's name, and his immediate posterity attributed them to him. They were supposedly addressed to a provincial correspondent. This was a classic strategy, but in this particular case it was not wholly fictional. Between the March and May letters, an anonymous reply appeared in the April issue. The diarist Mathieu Marais specifies that the latter was the work of a certain "Monsieur Panier,"[100] a character praised in the fable *L'amour et la fortune*. "This beautiful mind to which all Paris pays attention" was Jacques Pannier d'Orgeville, who, like Terrasson, came originally from Lyon and had received a religious education. Marais called Pannier a "speaker for the Company." While his relationship with trade affairs in Louisiana is difficult to establish, we do know that he was in business with Glucq de Saint-Port in 1717 and that, in 1753, his widow married a *syndic* of the Compagnie. His wedding with Mademoiselle de Saint-Hermine in the marquis de La Vrillière's house in Montrouge shows to what extent Pannier was close to the powerful in 1719. He became a magistrate in the *parlement* of Metz and *maître des requêtes* in 1720, then intendant of Martinique from 1727.[101] He had come to prominence in 1719 by winning the eloquence prize of the Académie française with a dissertation entitled *Le trône du roi qui juge les pauvres dans la vérité sera affermi pour toujours*, from which some excerpts were immediately published in the *Mercure* in August of the same year.[102] This short opuscule was actually an implicit commendation of the System, an apology for expenditure that told the same story (but in a different argumentative register) as many of the poems and songs published around the same time in the *Mercure* by the Moderns. But what relationship did these men and these texts have with their worldly friends and with power? What was the role of this literature within the System? This is the last point to consider before coming to the experiment itself.

Relations between the Moderns and their rich and powerful friends were now only partly an aspect of the patronage practices of the seventeenth century. Of course, the social recognition of authors and artists always involved a bond of subordination and protection with the powerful, not some chimerical independence from them or any confrontation with them. Their relations were always asymmetrical, but, in many ways, the practices of Verrue and the Moderns foreshadowed the salon of the Enlightenment. We thus find several of the main characteristics of this worldly practice being anticipated.[103] Their feasts and their meetings took place on a very regular basis and tended to transform all the guests/participants into men and women of the world.

Thus, their reciprocal relations were more complex than they had been in the past. Neither Fontenelle, nor Houdar de la Motte, nor Terrasson were they ornaments of an illustrious family. They were academicians, which naturally bound them to the state but also gave them a prestige that meant that they were sought after by aristocrats. The Countess of Verrue, Lassay, and Lériget de La Faye, art lovers and muses, had an interest in frequenting them, especially if, like La Faye, they nursed literary ambitions (the latter was to be elected to the Académie française in 1730, received by Houdar de la Motte). If Dufresny and Coypel seemed to be more dependent on the House of Orléans, they could in no way be considered to be in its service. It was no longer a question of aristocrats maintaining artists in the strict sense or of the latter serving permanently as panegyrists or defenders of patrons. Increasingly close ties bound them, and their meetings were at the same time places of literary discussion and places of political intrigue. The distances were reduced, without disappearing entirely, including from a geographic point of view.[104] The Moderns did not directly expect recompense for their contributions to the regent's policies in general and to the System in particular. Reciprocal relationships were more complex than before. The growing proximity between men of power and men of letters turned their encounters into forums for literary discussion and political intrigue. During the Regency period, this circle of Moderns therefore offered a new venue for recruitment, information, innovation, the sharing of tastes and interests, and the determining of strategies concerning political actions to be pursued: "Political interests and worldly interests constantly mingled and were usually expressed in the same language of friendship, protection, and gratitude. . . . The politics of worldliness lay both in the political efficacy of society talents and in the salons' ability to reformulate political interests in worldly language."[105]

It is precisely in terms of this notion of shared space that the System can be understood and grasped as a collective enterprise. It was a moment of concatenation in which several networks converged and interpenetrated before each resumed its own path after 1720. The first network, that of the rich and noble friends of the Countess of Verrue, really believed in the potential of American trade and played a direct part in the management of the Compagnie des Indes and the colonization of Louisiana. Many of the aristocrats in this circle had access to the great figures of the state, with whom they could act. The second network, that of scholars and men of letters, less wealthy and socially more distant from the powerful, was involved in theorization, explanation, and propaganda and, thus, participated in the intellectual construction of the System. The third network was that of cartographers, clergymen, and administrators who sought to encourage colonization and trade.

Through their works and their enthusiasm, they publicized certain aspects of the experiment, drawing its outlines while working with but also deviating somewhat from and going beyond Law and the regent. The years during which the System was in effect were, thus, a time when the principles that governed access to the mysteries of government at the court of Louis XIV were no longer operative. During the experiment of 1717–20, the roles changed as writers and subordinate figures sought and succeeded for a time in sharing power. And, finally, this interwoven fabric of actions and discourse contributed to the meaning that contemporaries and history gave to the System, but in different ways.

It is, thus, necessary to distinguish several levels of publicity and propaganda, of the authors' involvement and relations with power. Let us start by looking at the instrumental part of the question. In 1739, the speculator and man of letters Barthélemy Marmont du Hautchamp (b. 1682?) mocked what was in his view shameless and vain propaganda on behalf of the Moderns: "People were forever publishing the most exaggerated eulogies to exalt the System & its author. I do not know if these writers have been rewarded for their zeal, but I doubt it. I have known several of them, & apart from one or two, all the others have remained in a state of want."[106] A first level of involvement concerned the pieces of praise and thanks inserted by the Duke of Orléans's clients such as Coypel, who at the same time rose to prestigious positions thanks to the regent. Dufresny also owed a great deal to the latter, but he was also a kind of "official" journalist, one of the patrons of the Modern clan, and as such collaborated with the *Nouveau Mercure*. His friend Buchet, the editor of the periodical, supported the System for obvious reasons. If he sought to keep his privilege and obtain firsthand information, he had every interest in collaborating with the authorities. The cases of Houdar de la Motte and Legrand are a little different. Both belonged to official institutions, one to the Académie, the other to the Comédie française. Their participation can be interpreted as loyalty to the state that supported and protected them but also as kindness to their shareholder friends. They did not expect any direct reward; this was, rather, an exchange of good practices. Finally, we have to reckon with that exhilarating moment of euphoria, namely, the years of the System, when people believed they could change everything. Some of these men of letters and these artists may well have been animated by a sincere enthusiasm, by the feeling of participating in a completely novel experiment.

The fabulous tales and fanciful maps of Louisiana came from the Le Maire–Bobé–Delisle network, which had a direct link with the Raudot clan, with Jean-Baptiste Duché and, therefore, with the navy and the Compagnie des Indes. There is no doubt that Le Maire was a passionate adventurer and that Bobé was keen on science and cartography. These clergymen, already elderly, did not really seek to obtain prestigious positions, but they felt that, with the System, they could reconcile their enthusiasm and the interests of the state. Conversely, Delisle had good instrumental reasons for promoting colonization across the Atlantic, and this worked perfectly for him from a professional point of view. Terrasson and Pannier d'Orgeville had a different relationship to power and its propaganda. The latter was unquestionably enriched and was able to make a career thanks to the System. The former was a special case. He was a famous academician with only a mediocre fortune; legend has it that he enriched himself somewhat, then lost everything with the fall of Law and felt a sense of relief at this. "Now I am out of the woods," he is supposed to have said. "I will again live on little; that suits me better." The great, indeed, the essential contribution that Terrasson made to the System had no instrumental motives if we are to believe d'Alembert and Paradis de Moncrif: "[He] had the courage to stand up for [the System]; because, having considered it with a philosophical eye, he considered it useful, & separated the principle of it from what was merely accessory. . . . & today, when minds are no longer heated on this matter by a present and personal interest, the opinion that he defended would perhaps not lack enlightened supporters." The letter that his friend Moncrif published following d'Alembert's reflections is more precise. He explains that, in the days of the System, Terrasson, "intimate with people of a higher credit," turned all his ambition "toward pointing out principles that spread wealth through their circulation, banished idleness & greed, two pernicious scourges to society"—scourges that the abbé wished to combat.[107]

These reflections lead us to a second level of analysis of the relationship between power and the propagandists. It would be wrong to believe in the verticality of propaganda. It is unlikely that it was permanently organized in the higher echelons of the state, that it was an implacable and Machiavellian machinery of which the Moderns were merely the executors. It would also be wrong to reason only in terms of material reward: it was not, or not solely, the lure of profit and the search for social position that guided these writers. To consider propaganda in a hierarchical and pecuniary manner would be to deny these men their agency, their capacity to act in the world according to their own intentions. So alongside the services rendered—loyalty, the quest for well-paid positions, etc.—we must take into account shared convictions. The historian Christian Jouhaud has theorized this idea in *Les pouvoirs de la littérature* (2000). Writers who serve the state "are able to conduct a policy of writing in harmony with the political practices of those who protect, honor, or pay them, without giving up their self-esteem." For a political event "finds its meaning, and its greatest power, in the action of writing that represents it and presents itself as marked by its imprint." A common belief animated both those in power and the Moderns. There was a shared identity between their aesthetics and the System. The style of the Moderns—the *merveilleux*—served to publicize Law's experiment, but it was also the product of the effects of the experiment, in a constant feedback loop. Newspaper articles, letters, travelogues, poems, plays, fables, and songs are all performative. They produce acts and other ideas that cannot be evaluated in terms of truth or falsity. On the one hand, literature is a way of "fictionalizing politics and politicizing fiction to produce persuasive effects." On the other hand, it strengthens the state by confining "the authority of the learned: scholars, jurisconsults, orators, while delivering lessons of pleasure and good taste in society."[108] This is how the fictional and marvelous literature constructed for and about the System broadened the meanings that could be given to the experiment. It gave it a greater scope than theoretical and administrative texts could. It revealed its hidden and implicit mechanisms. It still combated or mocked those famous "learned men" of whom Jouhaud spoke: the theologians of the Sorbonne and the jurisconsults of the *parlement*, all in the name of strengthening central power, the omnipotence of the state. This dimension is central to the next chapter, which considers the System as a totalizing Leviathan, promoting a new form of monarchy.

3

Refounding the French Monarchy

"Absolutist" thinkers such as Thomas Hobbes, Jean Bodin, and Jacques-Bénigne Bossuet prescribed a political construction rather than describing a reality unfolding before their eyes. The emergence of the central state and such related processes as debt and taxation concurrently strengthened the powers of a wide range of traditional elites and made local specificities more important. Furthermore, trading companies, in theory dependent on this same central power, often proved to be in competition with it—or at least to be serious obstacles to the realization of the fiscal-military structure of the great monarchies.[1] The System aimed to impose Hobbes's prescription of a central power that would rule unchallenged. Its goal was to put an end, once and for all, to intermediate bodies and rivals acting as tenacious parasites on the government apparatus. The System was a product of the critique of how the French monarchy had been constructed for a century. For its supporters, the strengthening of taxation and the increase in the public debt had been merely a machine that increased inequality. Traders and merchants could have been used much more effectively. They had been left too free to grow rich on their own behalf, and trade and colonies had been insufficiently promoted. In fact, the problem was that the state had been established for itself alone; it sought, as was its nature, only to reinforce its own power. The purpose of human beings living in societies is self-preservation and the improvement of welfare, but the state had now thwarted this goal by destroying the wealth of the subjects that fed it. Therefore, something else was needed.

The System was a combination of the utopias and state-controlled trading projects imagined since the end of the seventeenth century; it was a single body, all-powerful, omniscient, and benevolent, that had merged with the central state in order to organize the entire creation and distribution of wealth. To implement this, the aim was nothing less than destroying the former fiscal system and even all forms of taxation, removing rentes, public debt, and *parlements* and every kind of counterpower and controlling prices and supplies, gathering cash into a bank belonging to the king, and nationalizing the profits of foreign trade on behalf of a trading nation. Such a revolutionary policy would lead to a refoundation of the divine right hereditary monarchy and a redefinition of the beliefs of its individual members.

This chapter begins by describing the general purpose of the System, theorized by Jean Terrasson and various others in 1720, as placing all the greedy forms of self-interest in the service of a great economic Leviathan, thereby forcing the subjects to contribute, with or without their consent, to public welfare. The conceptual framework was both Hobbesian and Ludovican; it implied an authoritarian power that could modify private property rights and force subjects to make a productive use of their possessions. However, it was a matter not merely of the state relying on the material prosperity of its subjects (by taxing or depriving them) but of enriching the public authority, which would then shift the wealth accumulated in society downward. This chapter then studies the practical way in which this project was implemented. It unveils how the Compagnie des Indes became a giant conglomerate, a heart, in Terrasson's metaphor, that constantly absorbed and circulated cash to boost a great imperial project. Actually, the undertaking did not have a solely financial agenda—far from it. Now intrinsically linked to the state, the Compagnie des Indes pursued a huge mobilization of resources to create a trading power and simultaneously a military maritime force. The Compagnie mobilized foreign workers from England, created public manufactures, increased Asian trade, supported agriculture, and strengthened the Louisiana colony. The System transferred resources beyond supply and demand mechanisms, prevented competition, set prices, and even attempted to cartelize European trading companies.

In transforming trade into a public, stable, unchanging, risk-free activity, the aim was to turn the shares of the Compagnie des Indes into a kind of rente. The French nation became "a body of Merchants," peaceful and hardworking. The idea was not to transform all the subjects into practitioners of trade, in other words, traffickers in goods or money, but to unite all wishes, all interests, and all capital in a "body" that was at the same time very real (the Compagnie) and metaphoric (the System) and that made subjects conspire to the same end, the creation of wealth. I detail the political and social implications of this mystique of the negotiating body, which took the place of the king's body, which was deemed incapable of bringing his subjects together and drawing them toward a common will. The chapter concludes with a discussion of how the state as it had been built since the fifteenth century was to be cut down in order to make way for a kingdom that lived without taxes, without war, and without magistrates and derived its sole glory from trading. Returning to the critiques of rentes and taxation, the promoters of Law's experiment sought to deconstruct the interpersonal and hierarchical relationships of the society of social orders so as to imagine a new form of monarchy.

The Social Contract and Property Rights

According to the thesis of the "universal royal direct" (*directe royale universelle*), developed between the end of the sixteenth century and the beginning of the seventeenth, all the properties of the kingdom had once belonged to the prince: "[T]hey had been attributed only conditionally, and the king could revoke them and reunite them with his domain [whenever he wished]." Louis XIV brought this thesis back into force with his edict of August 1692, which proclaimed the right of the monarch to tax lands previously considered "free" (in *franc-alleu*, in other words, freehold). It can be supposed more generally that Louis XIV tended not to differentiate between taxation and tribute and "confused his eminent domain with real property."[2] These practices were denounced as tyrannical by the opponents of the Sun King but above all as ineffective and even counterproductive by men such as Boisguilbert and Vauban. The anonymous author of the *Histoire des finances pendant la Régence*, written after the experiment by an ardent defender of the System, had captured this idea clearly: "By means of the previous administration, the interests of the King and those of his people were separated and united only by common misery."[3] In this sense, the state and the reason of state had failed: they had brought about the material prosperity of neither the subjects nor those in power.

So it was not this constraint that needed to be employed, though this did not mean that the thesis of the universal royal direct should be abandoned. If the latter were true, then one could imagine doing what Pottier de la Hestroye had envisioned around 1711: bringing under state control all the individual properties that the state considered as misused (i.e., not productive enough). Clearly, there was no longer any question of impoverishing subjects through oppressive taxation in an attempt to increase sovereign power. But was the aim, from a Boisguilbert-Vauban perspective, to allow these same subjects to enrich themselves at will so as then to draw abundant resources from them via light taxation? Not really. What the proponents of the System had in mind was socializing some of the wealth of large-scale commerce and perhaps the church and then circulating it back to the subjects of the kingdom. The tension between individual freedom and the material well-being of statist dystopias was again at work here. The state was to violate property rights no longer for its own benefit, no longer to strengthen its apparatus and prerogatives, but for a so-called collective prosperity, that of all individuals. Constraint was necessary "to save men from their own hands." Sometimes "one had to resort to authority to engage people to contribute to their own happiness."[4]

This last quotation comes from one of the most important texts in the corpus of the System, the *Idée générale d'un nouveau système des finances*. This is an anonymous report, the two versions of which known to have survived exhibiting fairly significant variations.[5] From the information it contains on the events of the day, we can date it to the first weeks of 1720. Harsin attributed the report to Law, but it is very probable that Terrasson and Pannier d'Orgeville contributed to it since it appears to be a preparatory work to the four letters subsequently published in the *Nouveau Mercure*. In one of the versions, the author or authors presented the general principle of the System as follows:

> The new System does nothing to increase the wealth of the French people than that which the first legislators undertook in the establishment of civil societies. By uniting all parts within a single body, each member of this body benefits from all the others as his protectors. . . . Similarly, by bringing together all competing interests, all specific credits and segregated funds, the new System increases the wealth of the French nation. It is this unity that establishes both the wealth and the power and strength of states. All parts support each other, all conspire to the same end, each individual part serving the whole and the whole serving each individual part. It is by this mutual union that common wealth and power increase.[6]

The text establishes a homology between the principle of the System and the social contract theories of the seventeenth century. Implicitly, it highlights the incomplete nature of the social pact, which, after its establishment, did nothing to guarantee an increase in "common wealth and power." In other words, it was not enough for men to come together and decide mutually to defend themselves and their property in order to ensure the material prosperity of civil society. This was precisely the issue that the System was intended to address and correct.

For Thomas Hobbes and, later, John Locke, the fiction of a man who was free but surrounded by dangers and incapable of ensuring his self-preservation in the state of nature led to the birth of a contract. Individuals decided to submit their freedom to a government in order to find relief from this precarious and dangerous situation. The social contract therefore promised, first, the protection of the individual and, subsequently, the guarantee that said individual would be able to enjoy the use of his property. In the

Lockean tradition, this property was deemed to have been acquired through work. But, since society inherently comprises both industrious individuals and others who are less so, inequalities in the distribution of real and personal property arose after the establishment of the social contract. Society nevertheless worked, Locke imagining an agreement between rich and poor that authorized the former to own more land and property than the latter.[7] Locke also set the stage for the idea that differing self-interests led to a positive unexpected result. The material prosperity of individuals in civil society required a laissez-faire regime tempered by sanctions and encouragements on the part of the state, in other words, good laws that guided self-serving behavior.[8] Hobbes, however, set the stage for something different.

Among the state theorists of the seventeenth and eighteenth centuries, Hobbes was the first to pose the problem of the relationship between individual interest and public welfare clearly. On the one hand, self-interest and even greed were powerful motives for Hobbes, useful to society. It was desirable that individuals should enrich themselves and prosper materially. On the other hand, the philosopher saw interest as a potentially destructive force in society as the rich generally sought to break free from common rules, something that did not fail to undermine sovereign power. As a thinker shaped by the English Civil War, Hobbes explained that public welfare was first and foremost a question of civil peace: "[A]ll the duties of the rulers are contained in this one sentence, the safety of the people is the supreme law." For this public order to be ensured, the state was required to enforce property rights while at the same time giving free rein to self-interest. Hobbes's Leviathan state did not "replace the contractual freedom of individuals" when sovereignty was not at stake, the prosperity of these individuals being that of the state as well.[9] But, if the accumulation of wealth in the hands of a few individuals or institutions was to prove a threat to the government, the state could remove this wealth from them: "Hobbes places the necessities of state power ahead of the rights of private property."[10] Property rights were only conferred on individuals by the state institution. And what the state had given, the state could also take back.[11] It was, therefore, essential that self-interest be continually subordinate to the preservation of the body politic. While the Hobbesian state did not direct economic relations, except in cases of force majeure, it did play an important role in the circulation of wealth. Using an analogy to the circulation of blood, Hobbes explained how tax collection led riches to the heart, which then sent them back via the arteries to the different limbs of the body through public spending. The tax issue was, therefore, of critical importance to him, and the power of the Leviathan was unlimited in this field. Indeed, the king could change property rights and decide taxes depending on what he considered necessary for the proper functioning of the kingdom.

The proponents of the System put forward the problem of the relationship between the state and civil society in Hobbesian terms. The *Idée générale* specified: "[There is] but one spirit that moves all men, and that is interest."[12] It was therefore necessary to draw on this motivation to lead them, as Terrasson stated: "The characteristic of the statesman is to lead the multitude without the latter being aware of it; or (to put it in other terms) you will be able to lead the multitude to accomplish your goals only by playing to their inclinations, or through the appearance of their interests." If Terrasson displayed a hint of cynicism here, he went even further in another passage, not hesitating to write: "The general view of Nature, as a Physics, appears to be to preserve the species, without caring for the individuals. Thus is Moral Policy designed to do good to the many, without worrying about the few, & this even at their expense, if it is so forced." In 1770, the philosopher Jean-Baptiste-Claude Delisle de Sales (1741–1816) described this passage as "thinking worthy of Hobbes and Machiavelli," and it is true that Terrasson was following in the footsteps of (at least) the former.[13]

Terrasson believed in the authoritative experience of antiquity: the cruelty of the republican regimes of Athens and Sparta and their continual internecine struggles were born of "the necessary contradiction of interests, opinions, and passions of those who framed them." This explains why in the following centuries monarchical regimes were preferred, being much more favorable to "public order." The *Idée générale* was written in the same vein. It criticized weak states that were "governed by the many" and considered individuals separated by "their conflicting interests" a permanent concern. Hostile to any form of counterpower, and in favor of a hereditary monarchy, Terrasson summarized the characteristics of a sustainable government in the following terms: "Much submission to the public authority, much affluence [*aisance*] in the lives of Individuals; much reflection by the Heads of the Republic, very little by Individuals."[14] And, for this "ease" to happen, subjects can be forced to be productive. In a passage from a letter published in the *Nouveau Mercure*, Terrasson explains that the prince has the right to change the species of gold and silver in any sign of transmission: "The Prince could exercise this right even over the property that you own outright, & he can require you to sow your land, & to repair the houses you have in a Town, under penalty of being stripped of them; because ultimately your property belongs to you only on the condition that you make a suitable use of it for society." We can read very similar remarks in the *Idée générale*: "Land is useful only for cultivation. . . . Anyone who cultivates only as much land as he needs for his livelihood, and who prevents others from working on it, is an enemy of the fatherland. . . . [The sovereign] can oblige them to cultivate the land, when they neglect it out of indolence. This authority can hamper the ill intentioned; but it is useful to the state, and therefore it does not deserve the name of violence."[15]

These two passages offer a secularized version of the medieval Christian conception of property. From the eleventh and twelfth centuries onward, theologians developed the idea that the true owner of earthly goods was the heavenly *Dominus*. Men, and even high-ranking clergymen, were only its administrators, temporary owners, or ephemeral guarantors. These goods did not have an individual purpose or even a collective purpose in a restricted sense (i.e., the sense of a specific community). They were at the service of Christian society as a whole, a whole that was more than the sum of its parts. They were to be used in a way that guaranteed the divine plan. However, anyone who did not respect the ends of the providential order, who, for example, enriched himself for his own sake without regard for the community, might see goods he had hitherto quite wrongly believed to be his own being taken from him. In late scholasticism, and among jurists in the service of the French monarchy of the sixteenth and seventeenth centuries, the earthly prince tended more and more to embody the possessor of the general dominium. He was the master of all the goods of his kingdom, of which the subjects had only a precarious and temporary possession. The king owned a "high domain" (*haut domaine*) over all land and buildings and was, thus, able to change the distribution of individual properties as he saw fit. It was to this doctrine of the high domain, which he distinguished from and placed above the "direct domain" of individuals, that the anonymous author of the *Histoire des finances* referred to justify Terrasson's words a posteriori.[16] But what was interesting about the latter and the quotation from the *Idée générale* was the reference to what was "suitable" for society or "useful" for the state. The propagandists of the System seemed to operate a sort of return to basics by reactivating a doctrine of property that was more Christian than monarchical. According to them, the prince was entitled to distribute goods differently, but it was not his own power that was at stake. It was not a question of producing more in order to tax better and enrich the sovereign since the king was not the state and did not embody the gathering of his subjects into a mystical body. The be-all and end-all here was the System, which merged with the central state to become a vast commercial public body whose task was to manage the production, transport, and consumption of wealth completely. If the king could modify property rights, this was to ensure that body's proper functioning, as in many utopias and in the work of Pottier de la Hestroye. The lands, houses, and trading companies needed to contribute to the creation of wealth by and for the System, which would then make that wealth flow back to society. The principle was to apply to ecclesiastical property, if we are to believe the rumor that circulated at the beginning of the year 1720:

> There is talk of a decree that will supposedly be issued shortly, to take from religious & ecclesiastical communities all the property that they have acquired since the year 1600, in order to put it back into ordinary commerce: It is said that this decree, if it takes place, will be passed in favor of the laity, who cannot find enough land to use their money, & whom the Compagnie des Indes is offering to reimburse, at its own expense, for all these acquisitions.[17]

This is a decree that would have been revolutionary in the literal sense since it would have anticipated the confiscation of ecclesiastical property in 1789. If I correctly understand the *Gazette d'Amsterdam*, which published the news, the Compagnie des Indes would have acquired part of the lands of the church (it would have needed, of course, to "reimburse" the religious communities); then it would apparently have had the task of reselling these lands to individuals (putting them "back into ordinary commerce"). To prevent too many stocks or banknotes from being converted into metal currency, this was a smart solution. The paper millionaires could have bought up formerly ecclesiastical estates in the same way that people such as Balzac's rapacious Père Grandet, in the eponymous novel, did at the end of the eighteenth century. From the utilitarian point of view, which was Terrasson's point of view, this confiscation could also be fully defended since it could be held that the church contributed only partly, or not at all, to the material prosperity of society as a whole (it privatized large land revenues for its sole use). These factors remind us of what we have seen in certain utopias and in Pottier de la Hestroye and La Jonchère. If the goal of the social pact was not only self-preservation but also the material prosperity of individuals, there was a problem because no force led to this end spontaneously. The sovereign needed to make up the shortfall, but by a method other than the Ludovican principle of the counterproductive fiscal heart. The idea of Terrasson and his friends was to reconfigure properties (in particular, commercial property, but not only that) to force individuals to get rich in a way fixed by the System and then to invite the king and his subjects to put their money in a single shared entity, both financial and commercial in nature. In this way, all would participate, mediately or immediately, in trade and its profits, henceforth directly managed by those in power, then redistributed by them throughout society. In a concise phrase, the author or authors of the *Idée générale* reversed the perspective of Boisguilbert and Vauban: "It is the wealth of the state that will create the wealth of the subjects."[18]

State Control over the Economy

In May 1719, all the French trading companies merged into a gigantic state-run conglomerate that took the name of the Compagnie des Indes. After having obtained the monopoly of the sale of tobacco in 1718, it took control of the collection of indirect taxes after the cancellation of the lease of the General Farm in the summer of 1719; in December, it obtained the monopoly of the manufacture of cash in the kingdom. The Compagnie absorbed the bank in February 1720, and it added other elements, such as an insurance company and even a fishing company, if we are to believe certain decrees passed in the spring and summer of 1720.[19] In short, if we summarize what was happening and take a Hobbesian point of view, a new heart was being set in place. It could not be compared in size to the solely fiscal heart of Louis XIV's monarchy. How was it supposed to work? The crux of the plan involved a constant flow of cash to the Royal Bank, which became the Compagnie's cash desk:

> The Royal Treasury, in any jurisdiction whatsoever, being the main source of the money that is used throughout the Kingdom; this source could not run dry without the furthest reaches feeling the effects. One has but to consider the prodigious number of bankruptcies suffered at the end of the last Reign by those who had the least to do with the King.
>
> What principle of government can prevent such a great evil? I will say, despite the initial scare this may arouse in the common man, that all monies must be brought to the King, not by way of loan, the interest being at his charge, nor by way of taxes, it being to his own advantage to do away with them; but by simple deposit in the Bank, to be withdrawn only proportionate to one's needs.[20]

Terrasson tried to explain that these principles were not as new as they seemed. When melting down coinage (*refonte des monnaies*), all the money of the kingdom had to be returned to the public authorities, the sovereign being the true owner of it: "Money carries the mark of the Prince, not yours, as a reminder that it belongs to you only through its circulation, & that you are prohibited from appropriating it in any other way." By these more or less convincing, if convoluted, arguments, Terrasson tried to justify the progressive prohibition of the use of gold coins by individuals, who would have been able to use only silver and copper coins and only for small transactions. Ultimately, the idea was probably that people would make payments only with paper money.[21] However, one thing must be noted: the fact that subjects could no longer use cash for more than small amounts did not mean that gold and especially silver had to disappear, at least not immediately. For now, the idea of the supporters of the System was to concentrate cash in the hands of the heart:

> The Bank is with respect to Finance the heart of the Kingdom, where all monies must return to restart the circulation. Those who would accumulate & retain money are like parts or extremities of the human body which would stop the blood that waters & nourishes them. They would soon destroy the principle of life in the heart, in all the other parts of the body, & finally in themselves.[22]

As Terrasson noted on the same page, the king must have all the coins "because he is the only debtor in cash [*argent*]." This discourse seems to have had a certain performative dimension because Jean Vercour, a broker from Liège and the founder of a banking dynasty who settled in France for business reasons at the time of the System and was in direct relation with the general manager of the mint (*monnaies*), now dependent on the Compagnie, said of him that "all the gold and silver of the kingdom pass through his hands."[23] Pannier d'Orgeville explains the ultimate goal of the operation:

> By how many different channels are gold and silver not usefully carried into the treasuries of the Compagnie? The trade in materials, which is permitted to the Compagnie alone, means that all the materials that enter the Kingdom from all sides pass through its hands. The Bank successively brings it all the money from trade; the finances bring into its coffers the immense treasures that were unnecessarily lodged in the king's coffers; and all this cash returns to it through the manufacture of coins. . . . [T]his prodigious quantity of money makes it master of all the trade it wishes to undertake.[24]

The more metal cash entered the heart, the more the money supply increased directly and indirectly through its conversion into banknotes, which was one of Law's goals. More importantly, the more cash the heart had, the more it was able to spend to strengthen the Compagnie's trade: "[The business] makes the major part of its payments in cash, in particular for fitting out, and to such an extent that the intendants of the navy complain about the competition they thus have to face, as they can only use banknotes. This cash contribution can only be explained by the advances made by the bank to the Compagnie. . . . Thanks to this financial base, which no previous company ever had, the Compagnie des Indes has given its trade such a strong impetus that it will be able to survive the liquidation of the System."[25] The drainage of cash to the heart thus had two essential purposes: to strengthen the confidence of subjects in the bank (by facilitating the conversion of shares and notes into metal currency) and to increase the commercial activities of the Compagnie. It is clear that, by allowing the Compagnie—and it alone—to pay in money (*argent*), the authorities intended to give it preference over any other activity and that the commercial and colonial project was, for Law and his friends, far from being a minor matter.

In the configuration envisioned by Pannier d'Orgeville, it was not because paper money had partly to replace metal coins that the latter became negligible: quite the contrary. In a self-sustaining phenomenon, it was necessary to strengthen international trade in order to bring in as many precious metals as possible, which were then used to promote the growth of this same trade and, therefore, of economic activity as a whole. Since there was a desire to eliminate taxes in the long term, and since confidence in paper money was still low and the activity of the Compagnie required purchases abroad, metal money was of great importance if the imperial capacities of France were to be enlarged. This is precisely what happened.

Indeed, the view that Law and his supporters had no vision of colonial development must be radically questioned.[26] One of the arguments put forward to support this conclusion is that of the low budget of the navy at the time of the System. But this argument proves nothing: the Compagnie replaced the navy—in the strictest sense—during the years 1718–20 and even a little later. The Compagnie des Indes participated with its own ships in several military expeditions, fitted out a veritable war squadron for the Pacific, and on its own launched an attack on the Spanish port of Pansa-Cola in 1719.[27] It became a true state within a state: the public infrastructure and the chain of command were put entirely at its service by the royal Naval Council.

In a strange, upside-down world, it was not the Royal Navy that chartered merchant ships, as was usual, but the Compagnie that requisitioned warships. We learn, for example, that the corsairs of Algiers took "the store ship the *Jeune Flore*, chartered by the Compagnie des Indes for the transport of salt," which the Royal Navy would like to have recovered, and that the Compagnie requisitioned "two large vessels [of war] that it needed to protect its trade in the [East] Indies" in the arsenal port of Brest in May 1720. The ships were not seaworthy, and the intendant of the navy, François-Roger Robert (1657–1736), received from the council the order to place the arsenal at the entire disposition of the Compagnie: he should work "as if the king were fitting out [the ships]," have sea biscuits made "in His Majesty's ovens by the bakers who are accustomed to working there," and provide "all the provisions that they will need." In November, when "the Compagnie informed [the council] that it [was] having two frigates built in Bayonne"—that is, warships, not merchant ships—and their manufacture was "languishing for lack of carpenters," the steward was asked by the council to "advance the construction of these vessels." The Compagnie did not hesitate to choose for itself and appropriate the sailors and Royal Navy officers it needed. When in September 1720 it planned to send one of its directors to the East for a vast operation to repatriate precious metals, Jean-Baptiste Le Gobien de Saint-Jouan (d. 1723), a native of Saint-Malo, was given a commission as "General of the French nation" with authority over all military officers. In June 1720, the governor of Canada, Philippe de Rigaud de Vaudreuil (1650–1725), learned that "the [navy] council has informed the directors of the Compagnie des Indes what you told me about the Illinois [people], so that they will give orders to the officer in charge there to endeavor to keep control of this nation." The council therefore went through the Compagnie to order the officers to enter into peace talks with the Indian tribes. As summed up in a letter received by Vaudreuil in April: "[T]he interests of this Compagnie cannot be separated from those of the state." The same terms are used for the governor of Cayenne's address. In the "Decree that subrogates the Compagnie des Indes to the rights of the company of Santo Domingo" of September 1720—another advantageous merger for the Compagnie—it was said of the Compagnie that "His Majesty regards [it] as the most important establishment in the state."[28] It was not beside the state, not an auxiliary, not an appendage; it was consubstantial with the state. It always had priority and always paid in cash.[29]

Through the archives, we understand that the Naval Council was constantly addressing the directors of the Compagnie on all matters relating to the navy and the colonies. For example, in March 1720, the council asked Law whether the Compagnie was willing to return to an officer of the Royal Navy the bales of goods that it had confiscated from him; in May, it wanted him to intervene in the war with the Illinois and, in September, to act in a lawsuit between a captain and his officers. In June, the council was supervising the fitting out of the two ships in Brest, after the Naval Council asked it "what side the Compagnie [would] take" with regard to provisions for these vessels. It also followed the affair of the frigates: in September, the council wrote Law to inform him that it had "expedited a decree to allow the Compagnie to take the wood that it [would] need for the two vessels that it [was] having built in Bayonne." In June 1720, the council asked the directors to arrest in Louisiana "the inhabitants of Canada who were traveling without permission from the Governor General." And it was the directors who were asked to undertake a transfer of prisoners from Belle-Ile "to Bordeaux and Nantes, where they [would] be embarked for the colonies" in September, and requested to provide the details of how many cannons were to be sent to Santo Domingo in October.[30]

Under the Regency, Pierre Grassin, director general of the Mint and as such subordinate to the controller general of finance and the Compagnie des Indes, bought the land of Arcis-sur-Aube, in Champagne. He then got in touch with Vercour, from Liège, to whom he advanced a large sum of money so that the latter could take over, organize, and expand textile workshops that were languishing in the village. The idea was to set up a real manufactory to supply the regiments.[31] Even better evidence is the fact that we know that John Law, his brother William, and an English watchmaker and businessman of French origin, Henry Sully, organized the sending of skilled workers to France to contribute to the commercial and colonial enterprise. Metalworkers, shipwrights, and shipbuilders were sent to Lorient at both Law's and the government's expense with a view to improving the French shipbuilding industry. The *Nouveau Mercure* of January 1719 explained at length how a clock factory was established "in the royal houses" in Versailles and "at great expense" on behalf of the state. Managed by Sully, this factory manufactured watches for individuals, but we also know that Sully worked on naval clocks, a crucial point of the Franco-British maritime rivalry. We also know that Law started to set up a foundry at Chaillot under the direction of "Gun" Jones and Charles Green, two English military steel specialists, that was to supply anchors and cannons for the Compagnie. It was "one of the great designs of M. Law," a "venture that was to amount to several millions." Law had expropriated land "under His Majesty's order" and in July 1720 obtained a council decree forbidding "workers to leave their tasks on pain of prison." Thus, a logic of vertical integration was being implemented by the supporters of the System so that the public monopoly would have high-quality infrastructure and instruments at its disposal. Law had embarked on a project of technology transfer and was, therefore, one of the architects of an industrial and commercial policy geared toward useful know-how and the practical application of knowledge.[32] But we know that Law was activating his networks for the benefit of his great imperial enterprise in yet another way. When colonization continued to drag its feet in 1718, he called on English and Irish emigrants to develop concessions in Louisiana. He created a small trading company with the economist Richard Cantillon, his brother Bernard, and another British investor and launched an expedition for clearing and development, comprising several dozen people.[33] In addition, on September 4, 1719, Glucq de Saint-Port, La Faye, the Countess of Verrue, Law, and a few others, in the presence of the notary Maître Gaillard, enacted a company deed for the foundation of another colony in Louisiana, in the Natchez area, to be precise. Named "Sainte-Catherine," perhaps in honor of John Law's partner, Katherine Knowles, it had a capital of 400,000 livres and was managed by the Swiss Jean-Daniel Koly (or Kolly), a former financial adviser to an elector of Bavaria, who invested in shares when the Compagnie d'Occident was created.[34]

Asian trade was not to be outdone. At the end of 1719, the Compagnie des Indes planned to set up a trading post in Canton and another in Moka and wished to restore those in Surate and Pondicherry. The directors of the Compagnie sought the seedlings of the main spices in the hope of acclimatizing them in Madagascar and the Mascarene Islands, an old dream that would take a few more decades to come true. Be that as it may, in 1719–20, the Compagnie sent at least eleven ships beyond the Cape of Good Hope, compared with only four in the period 1721–22. Three of them, the *Indien*, the *Courrier de Bourbon*, and the *Duchesse de Noailles*, made their way from Lorient to the Ile Bourbon (Réunion) and the Ile de France (Mauritius) in June 1720. Their goal was to seek enslaved people in Madagascar and Mozambique for the Bourbon coffee plantations and to establish an initial colony on the Ile de France. They arrived belatedly, in 1721, but put most of the instructions of the Compagnie into practice, and the colonization of the Ile de France, however tentative, began.[35]

To sum up, if, in the *Nouveau Mercure* of March 1720, the king invited "all his Subjects to collect their money to make advances in general trade,"[36] it was to give the Compagnie-Banque the means to fulfill its ambitions. And, indeed, it did build up a huge fleet by buying or building ships, including military vessels, in France and abroad (especially in England and Sweden): "Despite the short duration of the System—a year and a half—there was a considerable boost in the number of ships fitted out. From May 1719 to December 1720, there were fifty-seven. . . . Never before had large-scale French maritime trade known such activity. . . . Subsequently, the movement would rarely reach such a scale." For Louisiana alone, throughout the duration of the French presence, the highest number of convoys was reached during "the period of John Law (1717–20)": "Louisiana peaked with the arrival of 29 official ships in 1720. A few years later the colony was 'abandoned,' with an annual average of 6.6 ships recorded between 1723 and 1734."[37] The immense Leviathan that the Compagnie des Indes had become now truly lay at the heart of a global strategy, both commercial and imperial, driven and directed by and for the public power.

Another important element of this nationalization of commerce was the transfer of nonmarket resources for the benefit of the Compagnie. Thus, on December 29, 1719, a strange order issued by the Royal Council declared the "free trade" of hemp, the raw material used to manufacture ropes, throughout the kingdom. While the Colbertian notion of circulation was involved, this was still a far cry from free trade. Indeed, the same order prohibited the export of hemp (under pain of severe penalties) and, notably, established twelve warehouses managed by the Compagnie in various provinces to which hemp producers were to deliver their production, paid at a price set by the state (between 30 and 35 livres per quintal). These purchase prices were relatively high,[38] especially given that the Compagnie was to "provision His Majesty's Warehouses, at cost, in the Hemp necessary for his service."[39] One might think that such a policy would have resulted in losses for the enterprise. And, from a purely market-driven perspective, this would, indeed, have been the case. But, from the totalizing perspective of the System, the issue was elsewhere, and the example of hemp is, thus, paradigmatic. In the case of the fitting out of the two ships in Brest in the spring and summer of 1720, the Naval Council informed Robert on May 20: "[T]he Compagnie des Indes orders its correspondent in Brest to give you the hemp that it holds." The Compagnie delivered hemp to the intendant (from Brest and then from Nantes), having paid a high price to the producers for it, but it did not sell it to the arsenal since the workers, officers, and machines of the arsenal worked on behalf of the Compagnie. It subcontracted its activities and did not pay for the use of the infrastructure and personnel of the arsenal. The intendant, Robert, estimated the workmen's days and materials "paid by the king" for the fitting out of these ships at 35,249 livres. But, on September 13, when the vessels were ready, the Naval Council instructed him to settle "all that concerns this fitting out, without asking the commissioner of the Compagnie to pay this sum of 35,249 livres 8 sols because this part could be included in the accounts between His Majesty and the Compagnie, both for what it owes and for what may be due to it for the other supplies it has provided."[40] The organization of production by the System led different public entities—here the Compagnie and its stores, on one side, and the royal shipyards, on the other—to transfer resources without the mechanism of demand and supply intervening. The purchase prices of raw materials were set to increase hemp production. The inducement was apparently expensive, but only apparently. Peasants paid in cash would, in fact, be invited to take this cash to the bank, which would issue them notes. By supplying the ropes in question to a shipyard at cost—or even free, in this case—the Compagnie was losing money. But this was not a problem since it was the Compagnie that would use the ships thereafter for its trade or for its defense, and it was again thanks to the return of the profits of the trade to its coffers (the bank) that it would be able to consider new purchases thereafter and order ships. In this mechanism, institutions did not exchange goods and services according to a competitive principle that would dictate prices. They did not act in order to be profitable or to avoid incurring losses. In the example at hand, apart from the peasants who produced hemp, private initiative had no place. This was, indeed, a huge public sector that organized its supply chain to achieve goals decided by itself and for itself. In such a configuration, the heart decided the general price structure—the price of hemp but also the price of workers' daily labor, beaver skins, tobacco, etc. It did not matter that certain sectors worked at a loss since what was being maximized was not the profit of this or that branch of commerce but the capacity of the Leviathan to extend its empire, in other words, to achieve objectives by deciding the system of prices itself. The concept of price here took on a particular meaning. If it was still a signal that should make the actors react, the latter had no control over it since it was set centrally. It was the product of neither a concrete, geographically located market with physical actors nor an abstract encounter between ill-defined forces (supply and demand). It was an instrument at the service of the System.

Furthermore, the propagandists of the experiment did not hesitate to extend this principle, albeit in a slightly less dirigiste way, to subsistence. These men were largely hostile to a policy of low prices in agriculture. On the one hand, good harvests led to poverty among peasants owing to ridiculously low sale prices. On the other hand, the price of bread needed to remain affordable, and grain shortages in the kingdom had to be avoided.[41] The proponents of the System thought they could solve this squaring of the circle by means of a major public intervention. In the *Mémoire sur le denier royal* dated June 1719, it is stated:

> [The Royal Bank] has sufficiently considerable funds to make itself (through the opening of warehouses) mistress of the prices of commodities and goods, in such a way that the latter are always maintained at a fair value, neither too expensive nor too cheap; this is one of the greatest aids that the state can gain from the Bank, and which shall preserve the Kingdom forever from the misfortunes of famine and the inconvenience of too great an abundance.[42]

Terrasson returned to this idea in the same terms in his letter of May 1720.[43] During the ancien régime, the subsistence of the people was an essential preoccupation of the administration, for obvious reasons. During times of famine and, therefore, higher prices, the police could force the grain merchants and even the farmers themselves to supply the markets. They even had the authority to confiscate grain, which they did during the terrible winter of 1709. This was a fairly widely accepted breach of the principle of private property. But, regarding the prices themselves, it was not usually the police that fixed them, this situation being possible only as a last resort and even then only temporarily. But more than to the role of the police themselves the memoir of 1719 referred to a situation of intermediaries between the sellers and the buyers of grain. These intermediaries were the brokers.[44]

With the exception of a few years (1690–92), access to the profession was not regulated during the seventeenth and eighteenth centuries. Whether for flour or for grain, the broker acted as an intermediary between the merchants and millers, on the one hand, and the bakers, on the other. The merchants and millers were generally wealthier than their suppliers and, naturally, in a position of force with respect to their buyers, the bakers. As a result, they were often accused of raising and lowering prices at their convenience. The advocates of the System wanted to make the Royal Bank a kind of super-broker and not only for grain. The idea was not so much to increase market liquidity, that is, to facilitate transactions between sellers and buyers, as to hold a leading position in these markets. The bank-broker would be able to buy, store, and sell. Thanks to the huge amount of funds it held, it would also act as an arbiter, in other words, be in a position to counteract the tendencies of the followers, the private brokers. The bank could become a pricemaker, essentially making the market. Consequently, while the intervention was not as direct as it was in the example of hemp, where the prices were fixed by the public authorities, it was once again a case of the desire to remove the power of individual interests in deciding prices.

Viewed from the perspective of what Steven Kaplan has described as the "social contract of subsistence," the grain-consuming population subscribed to a pledge of "vassalage and docility" vis-à-vis the king; in return, "it would not be left to starve." The "prince as provider of food" became "the baker of last resort."[45] The System envisioned, not the end of this state intervention, but rather its strengthening. It promised to fulfill the old dream of public stores full of grain at moderate prices, thanks to the Compagnie-Banque. But what became of the father figure of the monarch in such a configuration? It was the omnipotence of the economic Leviathan that was brought to the fore. The talk was no longer of a discretionary, generous, symbolic policy, one that constantly reenacted the pact, but of a permanent, disembodied, rational organization. The danger was just as great as that of the liberalization of the grain trade, which broke the pact between the monarch and his subjects, the former seeking to free himself from the duty of feeding the latter. With the System, after all, why should people not end up wishing to do without a king who no longer served any purpose? There was a machine working at his side; an omnipotent power took power of everyone.[46] It will be seen that the adversaries of the experiment immediately understood the danger.

The propagandists of the System wanted to extend this incredible interventionist impulse to international trade. To understand this, let us follow the reasoning of Pannier d'Orgeville, who explains in the *Nouveau Mercure* that in his view large-scale French trade had been ruined by "the separate interests of individuals." The problem lay in the principle of competition. When a merchant sought to seize on a market in America, Africa, or Asia, his first instinct was to offer his goods more cheaply than his competitors offered theirs. He tended to slash prices. Conversely, when they bought products or human beings in those distant lands, the very same merchants were competing with each other and were generally in a weak position against a single seller, who pushed up the purchase prices. According to Pannier d'Orgeville, this was what resulted in all businesses eventually disappearing over the long term, the continual underbidding on prices inevitably leading to bankruptcy. In contrast: "[The Compagnie des Indes would] restore a Trade that the divided interests of Individuals have made ruinous . . . , the prices of the Goods, being in no way lowered by competitors, remaining steady. No longer shall the French destroy the French." Pannier d'Orgeville added: "[By] their reunion, the Compagnie no longer fears the inconveniences produced by the opposition of interests, so likely to diminish or even destroy the best deals." In the manuscript entitled "Project for Deliberation," indeed, we find the idea—expressed in appalling language when it is human beings who are at stake—that, with the monopoly of the Compagnie, the king was seeking "to reduce the price of Slaves, raised to excess by competition from the vessels of the kingdom's merchants."[47] Uniting the divided interests of traders and encouraging them to contribute to a common goal required founding a single company that forced them to cooperate and, thus, put an end to the continued and unchecked decrease in prices. But was it therefore a case of establishing a power capable of rivaling and even destroying foreign companies? Not exactly. Echoing Pottier de la Hestroye's arguments and the example of the Netherlands, Pannier d'Orgeville explained:

> [The monopoly] alone had created a thriving Nation, whose country is devoid of almost all the gifts of nature. Our alliance with it would be no less useful to it & to us in Asia as it is in Europe. . . . When united [the nations], their mutual aid makes navigation both safer & easier; their mutual forces protect them from the insults and affronts to which Foreigners are only too exposed in distant lands: the discoveries by some serve the others; the credit they extend

> each other increases their funds. Thus shall we join with the Trade in Asia that of Europe within Asia, & we shall bear the fruits of the Peace we enjoy here to the very ends of the world.[48]

Large trading companies, despite their exclusive privileges over buying or selling a particular product in a kingdom and its colonies, were in fact neither monopolies (sole vendors) nor monopsonies (sole purchasers). Smuggling and the existence of different companies with identical goals in each of the major European countries meant that many goods were supplied by different companies on competitive markets. The buying and selling prices were not determined unilaterally (except for delicatessens), but they resulted from what in economics is called oligopolistic competition, where a small number of players compete on the same market.[49] To put an end to this competition, which was no longer just national but European, the Compagnie des Indes tried to set up a cartel with its foreign counterparts. I will give an example of one such attempt in West Africa, in the slave trade.

The decree of the Council of State of September 27, 1720, gave the Compagnie des Indes the exclusive privilege "for trade on the coast of Guinea," "from the River of Serralionne [Sierra Leone] inclusive, up to the Cape of Good Hope." If the decree is to be believed, it did, indeed, result in "very great disadvantages" for free trade: the fall in the prices of goods offered by Europeans to "natives of the country" and the "outbidding" of enslaved people. From now on, the only body authorized to practice this appalling trade, the Compagnie des Indes, would have to transport "three thousand" captives per year "to the French Isles of America"; it would be exempt from almost all the taxes previously paid by individual merchants and would have to build forts and establishments that would belong to it and that it would manage in its own right.[50] But that was not all. In a handwritten memoir from the Compagnie's archives, undated but probably from the end of 1720, we read:

> No one can disagree that in relation to the interests of the state and that of the colonies & traders, we must have as an invariable principle . . . the fact that we must absolutely prevent the auctioning of slaves.
>
> No matter how hard we tried to imagine a solution, we found no other way than to have the Slaves traded in Juda [Ouidah in Benin], and in the other places where there are warehouses, by one and the same person; we have just experienced the efficacity of this expedient by the diminution to which M. Devighain has brought them during his short time in Juda. The reduction that M. Devighain has achieved does not come only from being the only Frenchman trading; it also comes from the fact that he had the prudence to come to terms with the English and Dutch directors by means of which the three nations have acted in concert, and managed to decrease the price of the

> Slaves in spite of the prodigality of the Portuguese, whom they will eventually bring to their senses, if the three nations continue to understand one another because they will combine their trades in such a way that they will have to conform to the others.

This price agreement between the French, the English, and the Dutch in the main site of the Atlantic slave trade was not without importance. We know how strong and even intense international competition was in this trade, "especially between merchants in the same port of departure." This was all the more true in Ouidah, where most European nations had trading posts but no strong military presence: "For their protection, the Europeans were dependent on the king of Ouidah. . . . So there was no possibility for one European nation to exclude others from trade here."[51] This situation resembled that described by Pannier d'Orgeville in connection with the places where traders were exposed to the "insults" of the native powers—hence the need, in his view, for an agreement between European companies. What was being attempted with the slave trade was a consequence of the analysis of the deleterious effects of competition at the level of merchants from the same nation. Pannier's analysis was economic but also political, and once again we can gauge how, far from being an anomaly coming from a single brilliant brain, the System was simply prolonging, in its own way, the intellectual dynamic of the Moderns.

Abbé de Saint-Pierre's projects to establish a "perpetual peace" in Europe were published between 1713 and 1718. By offering a league of defense among European nations, Saint-Pierre had in mind not only peace but also and especially the benefits of trade. In the Mediterranean, for example, this union would allow for more effectively combating piracy. Safer trade was seen as a consequence of political union. We know how pleased Saint-Pierre was with the negotiations conducted by his friend Dubois, the regent's plenipotentiary in London, during the establishment of the Quadruple Alliance in August 1718. This coalition between France, Great Britain, the Dutch Republic, and the Holy Roman Empire seemed to him to constitute a first step toward the "perpetual peace" that he so ardently defended. In spring 1719, he sent Dubois a paper entitled "Reflections on the Grand Alliance" to encourage him to take matters further. In this project, Saint-Pierre expected that a consolidation of the peace treaty between the European powers would allow for doubling foreign trade within only a few years.[52] Like their views on the shortcomings of the social contract, which guaranteed only the safety of civil societies, not their prosperity, it would seem that the propagandists of the System wanted to go much further than the mutual protection the treaty partners enjoyed.

Trading companies were considered by Pannier d'Orgeville as extensions of the public authorities, which in many respects they were. As such, they owed each other mutual aid, like the states of the Quadruple Alliance. But the example of Ouidah suggests that it was a question not just of a defensive alliance but of a real cartelization of European companies. They needed to trade their "discoveries" and lend each other their "credit" and even agree on prices to dictate their terms to buyers and sellers "at the ends of the world." This idea did not stop with the fall of the System. In 1752, one of the trustees of the Compagnie des Indes, Pierre-Claude Delaître, suggested the implementation of a treaty between the French company and its British counterpart. He said that the conflicts between the two companies had exposed them to vexatious interference from Indian sovereigns and the emergence of new European players. He thus proposed a sort of peace agreement, one that would guarantee the possessions of each of the companies even in the event of a conflict in Europe between France and England. Above all, it would commit them to not competing with one another for their respective market shares.[53] Even if this project were to fail, there was an important idea here, one that again differed from Hirschman's account, in which a supposed "spirit" (a "mentality"?)[54] predominant in eighteenth-century theorists made trade a factor of peace.

Law was not an "evangelist of *doux commerce*."[55] Under no circumstances did he believe that trade naturally sparked peace among individuals or nations. For the promoters of the System in general, far from having peacemaking effects, the self-interests of the traders were a constant source of discord and bankruptcy. The System's projects were not so very different from Saint-Pierre's. It was, indeed, the responsibility of the public authorities to build an environment that prevented individual interests and competition from expressing themselves. Whether at the individual level or between nations, it was necessary to create a common view politically as it was only then that lasting peace could be envisaged.

The propagandists of the System opposed the "market principle" logic. They did not believe that the abstract forces of supply and demand determined the "real prices" of goods, which themselves allowed the proper allocation of resources. The discourse around the System referred to a different logic. Through the creation of the Council of Commerce in 1700, Minister Pontchartrain's project was "to maintain institutional unity over and give single direction to commercial and manufacturing policy."[56] The System wanted to go much further. Against the industrial and commercial fragmentation revealed by the *Enquête du régent*, against the divided interests of the French traders, the System had to be the heart that forged a unity of the subjects around an ever more disembodied figure, that of a king who was no longer any more than the face of a machine beyond his control. The problem was that this ambition was entirely based on the Compagnie des Indes and, therefore, on trade. This involved nothing less than transforming the old warring monarchy into a trading nation.

The Trading Nation

When the Compagnie was established, its funds were very low at first and even incommensurate with its ambitions and spending.[57] Indeed, most of its shares had not been purchased with coins but acquired in exchange for *rentes sur l'Hôtel de Ville de Paris*, just as with Harley's grand plan of 1711. The Compagnie therefore received only the interest paid by the king on these rentes, which amounted to a very low revenues. But, as in Great Britain, the idea was first to shift the burden of state debt to a trading company, the profits of which had been socialized. Normally, at the end of the process, there would be no more rentiers receiving interest from taxes, only shareholders who would be paid dividends from the trading activity. The ambition of the System was also to make trading a national experiment, each individual, at his own level, required to play a part. For these two ideas to work, it was necessary to transform the concept of trading profit into a form of rente (a fixed income) and to make trade itself an attribute of the monarchy.

Regarding the first idea, Pannier d'Orgeville believed: "[Before the establishment of the Compagnie des Indes] the Merchants, Bankers, and Financiers never considered their business as a significant source of funds, or the profits they derived as a fixed income; because death, illness, dismissal or revocation, competitors and economic setbacks could remove, & indeed often did, the means that provided them with these profits; in a word, their trade & their employment were not a constant fund."[58] But what exactly was the definition of *profit* in the early eighteenth century? In the article dedicated to it in the *Dictionnaire universel de commerce* (1723), edited by the Savary brothers, *profit* was defined as an "advantage, gain, benefit resulting from trade, through either the purchase, exchange, or selling of the goods with which trade is conducted": "The sea trade offers tremendous opportunities; the risks are great, but the profits are sometimes huge, often greater than 100 percent." The same dictionary later notes that one of the important understandings among merchants who have organized themselves into a company is that they will share among themselves "all profits & losses that it pleases God to send [them]." The concepts of profit and gain were, thus, considered inseparable from that of risk. The 1694 edition of the *Dictionnaire de l'Académie française* had already associated "trade" with dangerousness, with an "adventurous" undertaking.[59] It was precisely this first risky and uncertain dimension of trade that had to be eliminated in the hope of convincing a broad spectrum of rentiers to acquire shares in the Compagnie.

The *revenu des rentes* "was characterized by its stable rate, and illustrated one of the major attitudes of society under the ancien régime with respect to the economy, namely the patrimonial concept of wealth." The rentier was "looking for a stable income, regarded as a sign of respectability." This idea of an income that was "moderate, regular, [and] consistent with morality" was diametrically opposed to the profit maximization of market activity. It was considered the "fair" remuneration for the individual who was anything but an immoral gambler. This traditional concept of rente came up against two problems. The first concerned the many faults and failings of the monarchy of Louis XIV with respect to the public debt and the reductions in the interest rates on the *rentes sur l'Hôtel de Ville*. The second concerned the discrepancy between the price paid to acquire a rente and the remuneration received. Over the period 1706–13, the hard-pressed French monarchy agreed to sell at very low prices rentes that had a very high interest rate (at least before the next rate reduction). At the end of the reign of Louis XIV, the government even accepted rente purchases partly in coins and partly in public papers that were practically or completely worthless. At the same time, certain individuals, finding themselves in dire straits, sold their rentes at ridiculously low prices on the secondary market to obtain some badly needed cash.[60] Thus, the ideal of stability and moderation in the rentier practice had been considerably weakened at the advent of the Regency.

The discourse of the System thus worked on two levels. The System presented itself both as a restorer of the stability of a former and largely fantasized order and as an experiment that made trade an activity that had nothing to do with the luck or chance described in the *Dictionnaire universel de commerce*. On the one hand, the shares would provide low but stable earnings. The shareholders would receive "une rente fixe" (a fixed income), which was "an income proportionate to their advances," in other words, a "fair remuneration [*une juste rémuneration*]."[61] Becoming a shareholder was meant in part to achieve an ideal—that of a protonoble and honorable life of leisure, conferred by the rente in the imagination of the monarchy of Louis XIV—and in part to support revenue-generating activities. One can imagine the difficulty of the conceptual shift that was needed. Indeed, on the other hand, for such an idea to be acceptable, it was necessary to change the very nature of trade. Income stability had to be able to rely on the stability of the activity underlying it. In other words, to avoid making the profits of the Compagnie a gain subject to chance and the dangers of trading, it was essential to eliminate any and all ideas of a hazardous undertaking. For the propagandists of the System, the new Compagnie des Indes was based on a risk-diversification insurance principle:

> Western trade promotes that of the East; the privilege of materials facilitates the purchase of foreign Goods; the Manufactures it supports provide the means necessary to procure the materials: the Slave trade advances the establishment of its Colonies; trading in its Shares maintains them at a fair price; Finance, Banking and Merchandise provide mutual aid, each one increasing thanks to the other.[62]

Here we once again find the ideas of the vertical integration of scattered activities and the transfer of resources outside market mechanisms. Especially, it was impossible that all the Compagnie's activities should suffer at the same time. If one was not profitable for a while, another was, however, and was thus "able to compensate for certain mishaps & financial setbacks." As Terrasson put it: "[O]ne fleet makes up for the loss of another, one year replaces another." Consequently, if the Compagnie had to "consider its profits as a fixed income," the dividends received by the shareholders would be such as well.[63] From this point of view, historians are wrong when they explain the setting of the share price by the public authorities in May 1720 only in terms of political circumstances or the will to deflate a speculative bubble. This intervention formed part of the ideological arsenal of the System, as did the Compagnie deciding in advance the dividends it would pay out over the following years.[64] The shares were "des actions rentières," to quote the propagandists of the System. The share value was indexed on the basis of a stable activity organized by the state precisely to ensure a nonrandom rate of profit. Consubstantial with the sovereign authority, the Compagnie des Indes was eternal: "[It] shall not die." Pannier and Terrasson were very insistent on this point: the System was unshakable because the monarchy could not destroy it without being lost along with it.[65]

This essential point is related to the assertion by Terrasson that the "Nation" would "become a Body of traders" with the introduction of the System.[66] But what exactly did that mean? The concept of nation was, at the beginning of the eighteenth century, starting to be the stake in a struggle between two very different meanings. The first, which we find in particular in Jacques-Bénigne Bossuet (1627–1704) and in Thomas Hobbes, was that of a mass of subjects whom the king embodied in his person. The monarch was not authorized by a so-called body of the nation to act on its behalf, for the nation existed as a body only through that of the monarch, who united in himself all individual wills. In this type of approach, the existence of the nation was not denied, but the latter could only express itself and derive its legitimacy from the person of the king. The second meaning, developed in particular by Boulainvilliers, then by d'Aguesseau, and taken up by the Jansenist *parlementaires* of the 1730s, was the complete opposite: it involved a nation quite distinct from the body of the monarch. The nation was the assembly of sociable beings endowed with rights and "privileges" that did not come from the authority of a king. They resulted from the application of other principles prior to the monarchical form (election by peers, natural law). Such a logic led to rejecting arguments that allowed the king to attack the properties and privileges of his subjects (of the high domain or universal royal direct type), and, more generally, this conception went against any pretense on the monarch's part that he alone expressed the general will. At the same time, the notion of body was less disputed. A social body implied order and unity. It was guided by a uniformity of feeling and will and acted to implement it. The bodies of the church, the *parlement* of Paris, and the corporations, for example, had heads that governed their limbs, in the name of a common goal. The parts of a body are one, and the body of the church is the most paradigmatic in the sense that, through the Eucharist, the body of Christ contains the bodies of all Christians. Now, in the first meaning of *nation*, the latter was itself a "mystical body": "The multiple wills of the multiple bodies that made up the French state had to be conducted in harmony by the king and his laws, and therefore subsumed in his single will."[67]

From the meaning of the term *nation* given by the theorists of absolutism, Terrasson retained this idea of the fusion of individual wills in a single body, in a single power. But he made one major replacement: the body of the king was to be replaced by a body of traders. This body was understood, not as an assembly of merchants large or small, but as the assembly of the subjects of the kingdom, whether they were shareholders, traders, merchants, peasants, etc., and of all their wealth into one and the same entity, the System. The latter directed individual wills toward a common end and enriched subjects through it and it alone. All became metaphorically traders because all contributed to the System, which was the universal trader. In doing so, the System's propagandists were being doubly subversive. First, it was not only Ludovican practices that were being called into question but also the entire political theory of the French monarchy. I return here to the incomplete social pact discussed at the beginning of this chapter: the inability of the monarch to inhabit the bodies of his subjects, the fact that the king was, in fact, incapable of translating individual wills into a single will and acted only for his person and his interests, which were not those of his subjects. In order for the wills of the bodies of the subjects truly to unite, it was necessary to create that great whole, the System, that all-encompassing entity that was meant to end the civil war of individual interests. The Compagnie-Banque fulfilled the mystical promise where the monarchy had failed to, and in this the *actions rentières* were, indeed, the new host (in the eucharistic sense) of a nation that had become a merchant nation. Second, the feat performed by the supporters of the System lay in the transformation of the glorious and bellicose body of the king into a peaceful and negotiating body. From an agricultural kingdom, the surplus product of which had for centuries been extracted from land rent, would they pass to another, one based on trade and commodities? Such a conception was extremely innovative, and it was not until the 1750s that it resurfaced in France. An almanac published in 1720 by François-Gérard Jollain (fig. 3.1), the engraver responsible for the visual propaganda of the System, illustrates this idea clearly.

The etching *L'auguste protection du roy accordée aux arts et aux sciences* depicts a scene of thanks that took place on May 22, 1719, at the Hôtel de Ville in Paris.[68] The character on the left holding his doctoral hat in his hand is the chancellor of the University of Paris, the Jansenist Charles Coffin (1676–1749). He is facing and addressing, to the right, the young Louis XV, seated on a throne that dominates the whole scene. They are surrounded by professors, painters, scholars, and craftsmen, one of whom is holding an armillary sphere, another a map, some paintings, others wool and metals. Coffin came to give thanks to the king for the income granted by the monarchy to the university professors, the latter no longer having to live off the fees paid by their students. But this benefit was in fact a repercussion of the System. Indeed, the universities were to receive part of the profits of the royal post and mail coach services, a lucrative business leased to a private company on the model of indirect taxes. The regent had initially assigned these profits to the payment of interest on the rentes owned by the Compagnie des Indes since the famous exchange of debt securities for shares. But, when Law obtained the monopoly of the sale of tobacco in September 1718, the regent decided that this would be a replacement for the profits of the post and mail coach services. This decision essentially meant that the interest on rentes would no longer be paid by the monarchy to the Compagnie des Indes, but this was of no significance since both entities were poised to become one and the same. The revenues of the post and mail coach services becoming tax free, the Duke of Orléans used them to offer free access to French higher education, an arrangement that continues to this day.[69]

The title of the etching includes a phrase from a sentence of Coffin's speech in which the word *roi* replaces the word *prince*.[70] It is, therefore, the monarchy itself that was concerned, as revealed by the elements surrounding the central

FIGURE 3.1. Engraving entitled *L'auguste protection du roy accordée aux arts et aux sciences pour l'avantage de ses sujets* (Paris: Chez Gérard Jollain rue St Jacques, 1720). Courtesy Bibliothèque nationale de France, Département des estampes et photographies, RESERVE FT6-QB-201(89).

FIGURE 3.2. Detail of the engraving *L'auguste protection du roy accordée aux arts et aux sciences pour l'avantage de ses sujets* (Paris: Chez Gérard Jollain rue St Jacques, 1720). Courtesy Bibliothèque nationale de France, Département des estampes et photographies, RESERVE FT6-QB-201(89).

scene and the accompanying text. This text places emphasis on what is found around the letter *B*, that is, the cartouche entitled "Missisipy" (fig. 3.2). On this subject, the art historian Darius Spieth wrote: "Curiously, Jollain's etching contains a cartouche floating above the reception scene in which French ships and trade on the banks of the Mississippi are depicted."[71] This point is actually anything but "curious" given that the purpose of the etching was to show how the monarchy now defined itself, how it and trading had become one. The text published by Jollain described it thus: "[U]nder the letter B we see Navigation and this Commerce that is so abundant and that enriches all its Shareholders, its reputation represented by Renown, Prudence by Minerva, all under the Royal authority as designated by its Crown. This glory is supported by two columns in bas-relief with a crown of laurels, representative of the Glory of the King."

There were, henceforth, two "glories" in the kingdom: one capitalized, that is, that of the king, and one lowercased, that is, that of the System. The two were intimately intertwined. On the one hand, the first protected and supported the second, the crown being above the "Missisipy" and the columns holding it up. On the other, the glory of trade was surrounded by conservative Minerva (stability) and by Renown. It was, thus, trade that increased and spread the glory of the king. Beside the natural glory of monarchies, military and divine, there therefore existed another form. The wishes of the merchants at the creation of the trade council in 1700 were granted. The decoration of the gallery—no longer in existence—of the Royal Bank in 1720 by the Venetian rococo painter Giovanni Pellegrini (1675–1741)[72] gives a deeper sense to Jollain's engraving.

The bank's premises had since 1718 been located between rue Vivienne and rue de Richelieu, at the Hôtel de Nevers, which adjoined the former palace of Cardinal Mazarin. In February 1720, the Compagnie des Indes moved into the old Hôtel Tubeuf next door. A symbolic first lay in having wanted to move into this place of power called the *Richelieu quadrilateral*. Above all, we know that "the main idea of this painting was to express the various advantages of the bank and to relate them to the glory of the King and Monseigneur the Regent." Thus, under their portraits, "a genius has been represented with wings and a helmet, he leads by the hand trade followed by wealth, security and credit." Next to the genius "France has been painted next to Hercules who holds a rudder with one hand and a club in the other to mark the strength of France both by land and by sea." Above are Jupiter and Juno, who "send Abundance to shed her wealth," and to the left of "Wealth is the River Seine which embraces the Mississippi River." To the right are vessels unloading goods from "Louisiana," and "below the sun are the provinces in the figure of women who are quietly enjoying such a beautiful day, that is to say, a government that provides them with all the advantages of commerce & peace through the advice of a minister filled with enlightenment and wisdom."[73] The monarchy had become peaceful and commercial while still being powerful and strong, by both land and sea.

The *Traité de la gloire* by the lawyer and academician Louis de Sacy (1654–1727), published in 1715, marked a profound shift in how the notion of glory was understood by the men of the time. At the end of the reign of Louis XIV, the nation, which had had its fill of hardship and misfortune, began to redefine the concept of a good ruler, whose main duty was to make his subjects happy. Thus, "[v]ery gently the notion of glory itself was detached from conquest" to make way for a "utilitarian notion of monarchy based on love between king and subjects."[74] Indeed, an important point of Sacy's argument concerned the role of trade in the glory of nations. Sacy, who socialized with Fontenelle, Houdar de la Motte, and Abbé de Saint-Pierre, was a great admirer of Cicero. In his "Historical Praise of M. de Sacy," d'Alembert even considered that the academician "wanted to imitate in everything this same Cicero," taking on the task of popularizing the ideas of the famous Roman orator. The *Traité de la gloire* was no exception. From the opening pages, Sacy explicitly referred to Cicero's *De officiis*, the treatise on duty, which "contends that the useful is inseparable from the honest."[75] Now, from the *Traité de la noblesse* (1678) by Gilles-André La Roque de la Lontière (1598–1686) up to the 1750s during the debate around the "trading nobility," what was witnessed was a reinterpretation of Cicero's concept of the useful and the honest. The starting point of these reflections (to which Sacy was no exception) was to distinguish retail and the *artes mechanicae* from (large) trade.[76] There was nothing servile or vulgar about the latter because one could "excel at it only in proportion to an increase in one's courage, spirit, & morals." Trade required a "reputation that can be acquired only through unfailing integrity." Sacy attempted to refute the idea that individuals engaged in trade for profit alone. This situation was true only within nations where it was despised. If, on the contrary, trade was honored as something useful and great, then everyone would want to engage in it, and the nation would flourish: "We must therefore admit that glory is very useful to a state, since it will never be powerful, neither in riches nor in allies, unless trade flourishes within it, & that it will flourish only to the extent that a sentiment of glory engages those who are the most likely to extend & maintain it."[77]

Trade was considered a means to an end for the warring king (Louis XIV), who would never have agreed to associate his power and his glory with that of business. Even for Colbert and his administrators, "while advocates of commercial expansion, the Controller general and his intendants duplicated the traditional view that saw merchants as fundamentally untrustworthy, morally vacuous creatures."[78] Only the fact that it operated under the control of or in the name of royal power, through regulations and large privileged companies, gave trade a form of legitimacy and dignity. But the System's propagandists had taken a giant step forward by making the glory of commerce an attribute of the French monarchy. The Compagnie des Indes was not just supported by royal power: it had merged with the state; it was itself the central power. Also, it was because it had become both royal (it belonged to everyone, to the nation as a body) and risk free (thanks to the insurance principle) that trade was now fully acceptable, moral, and valued. In one of the versions of the *Idée générale*, it is stated: "[I]t would be dangerous to make trade the sole object of the nation; but when most of the trade is done by a single company, supported and authorized by the sovereign, this way of trading can only be very useful." Were the military virtues and the traditional glory of the House of Bourbon and its vassals destined to fade? Certainly not. On the one hand, the propagandists of the System argued that the nobleman or ecclesiastic could participate in trade in a mediate way, by holding shares, "without violating canonical or civil laws" and especially "without dishonoring their condition and without abandoning their employment, whether in the Army, in the Church or in the Magistrature." On the other hand, these same propagandists argued that "[a]ll history teaches that the most warlike peoples have always favored trade." Although it was no longer the glorious king who made conquests, "a working and well fed people . . . is more likely to carry weapons in times of need than one that is lazy and hungry."[79]

The advocates of the System therefore considered that they had found the secret of the politics that legislators had been seeking since antiquity:

> Thus the new System, without weakening the royal authority, makes the interests of the Prince dependent on those of his subjects, and, without confusing rank, requires the great to protect the small. In this way, all members of the state being joined as one person; France has all the advantages that stem from the unity of the supreme power, without being exposed to the inconveniences caused by the absolute authority of the monarch and the elevation and loftiness of the lords. This is an expedient that the ablest legislators have thus far sought in vain in Carthage, Sparta, Rome and England, where the mixed government, by sharing in the sovereign authority, caused a perpetual struggle of contrary powers and, under a vain pretext of freedom, sparked popular seditions and civil discord among the citizens, these being the greatest of all evils.[80]

The System's incredible ambition—and that of Law himself, who ultimately considered himself a new Solon, a new Lycurgus—is here revealed. While we find the "common center" mentioned in English pamphlets of 1711 in favor of the South Sea Company, we can also note that the Hobbesian tone is very present in the preceding quotation, where what is feared above all is the division of the social body. This division was the result of conflicting individual interests, and the whole art of politics consisted in finding a means likely to reunite them. A system of opposing forces, like the British Parliament or, worse, the democratic systems of ancient history, far from achieving this aim actually contributed to the strengthening of the divisions of civil societies. "Powers" clashed in the state; they pulled in opposite directions and were also responsible for reducing or even nullifying the speed of decision specific to those monarchies where authority was not shared. But the sovereign should not have to suffer "the altercations and delays" of "the plurality of voices." The only way, then, to avoid abuse on the part of an absolute authority was to make the material prosperity of its subjects the condition of state power. Unlike Ludovican practices that ruined civil society by force and generated mistrust, and more generally contrary to the terror that the Hobbesian Leviathan state inspired, it was necessary to find a way to prevent the sovereign from violating the wealth of individuals. The best way to do this was to provide a single opportunity for individual interests to be expressed. Specifically, the subjects of the kingdom needed to be forced to enrich themselves, but only through the System. As Terrasson put it: "There is no other way to assert one's fortune than through trade."[81] The more flourishing the trade, the more coins would enter the heart, and, the greater the number of banknotes issued, the richer the king and his subjects would become. All forces must work together in this enterprise of general enrichment that had become the goal of the nation united in a body of a new and daring nature.

The System was basically a critique not only of the theory of the absolute authority of the monarch as found in Bossuet but also of the entire construction of the French fiscal state over the previous few centuries. Let me be more specific. For its supporters, the System needed to be all-powerful. It needed to be much more powerful than the state imagined by Bossuet and Louis XIV, but in a very different way. The alternative proposed by Law's experiment was basically the questioning of what has been called the *fiscal-military state*. France and England were representative of the joint and overlapping construction, from the fifteenth century, of an increasingly powerful fiscal apparatus and an exponential growth of land and sea forces. The whole was at the service of a central state that asserted itself not, as the sole institution, but as one that was the rival of other, less powerful institutions within a national monarchy.[82] Decades of experiences, of reforms, of revolts and violence, were necessary to expand the construction of the fiscal state and its counterpart, its immense military power, step-by-step. Replacing this construction, practically at the stroke of a pen, with the heart of the Compagnie-Banque was a very radical operation. To reverse the fiscal state meant to reverse the war that created it; it was to change the notion of glory and, ultimately, the whole monarchical form constructed since the Renaissance. Without taxes, and without credit in the sense of loans with interest, the System was the great trader that, now having become fully sovereign, no longer had any opportunity to oppress anyone.

What Is Credit?

Like Boisguilbert, Defoe uses the vocabulary of extortion to talk about the direct and indirect taxes that ruin the most industrious people and have led many families to begging. According to him, the tax that pays for rentes comes down to "robbing Peter *to pay* Paul." It "can never be call'd maintaining *Credit*"; it was "*a Chimera* of Credit."[83] Two years later, Law, Terrasson, and Pannier d'Orgeville used the same language: a form of credit needed to be found that put an end to credit as it had hitherto been known, namely, a tax system used in large part to pay interest on the public debt. If the state were simply freed from its debt, there would be no more financiers, no more taxes, no more rentiers, and even no more interest rates. The fantasy of the end of Louis XIV's reign had become a political program.

In the seventeenth and eighteenth centuries, "moral" credit and "economic" credit were not considered to be separate. What we distinguish between today, namely, the reputation or confidence inspired by a person, on the one hand, and financial debt, on the other, would at the time have been a case "of a unique phenomenon of influence and power," as Antoine Lilti has pointed out. Credit was both a "resource" based on trust and "a capacity for action, a power."[84] The distinction between these two meanings resulted from the intellectual struggles that started in the early modern period. In an organicist society, one in which everyone from the king to the humblest of his subjects occupied a specific place and was paid in this place by the principle of distributive justice (as opposed to the market principle), there could be no conflict between the two types of credit. The individual's power to act became indistinguishable from his financial position and his borrowing capacity. This was no longer the case with the emergence of the major financiers of the seventeenth century and the advent of the commercial society. Ordinary individuals—often commoners—were, henceforth, able to impose on the sovereign through their status as creditors of the crown. If credit was an implicit theory of power but the mechanisms of credit were no longer at the service of a pyramidal society governed by the order of dignities, then the traditional ruling classes could react in two different ways. The first was a "conservative" criticism like that of Fénelon or Saint-Simon, one that called for a reaction on the part of the nobles; the second was the creation of a "public credit." These various theoretical elaborations were part of "a European debate on the respective role of taxes and borrowing in the financing of public expenditure."[85] From this point of view, the beginning of the eighteenth century appears as a crucial stage, both in France and in England.

A consensus emerged during the years 1710–20 on both sides of the Channel, one that questioned the traditional bases of credit. The first theoretical effort consisted in rethinking taxation, as did Boisguilbert, Vauban, and Defoe. The *Projet d'une nouvelle forme d'asseoir les revenus du roy* (Proposal for a new form of establishing the revenues of the king), dated April 1718, and the *Mémoire sur le denier royal* of June 1719 presented an apocalyptic picture of the French tax system. Drawing on the same semantic field as the previous writers, the former maintained that direct and indirect taxes "already destroyed more than a quarter of the population and made the remaining three quarters less robust and less industrious." Moreover, if things were to continue in this way for a few more years, "the total ruin of the Kingdom" would, it was predicted, be "inevitable."[86] To prevent this disaster, Law proposed the abolition of all existing taxes, replacing them with a single tax on landowners, whether or not they belonged to the privileged classes, that would be collected by the state thanks to some one hundred employees. Such a project "upsets the form of Government and tends to abolish the oldest customs of the Kingdom," but that was precisely what he wanted to do. In typically Modern phraseology, he began by explaining that the seniority of a system was not necessarily a recommendation: "[T]o always prefer the traditional is weakness and superstition." If populations were in a deplorable state, it was essential to try something else. Regarding tax "immunities, privileges and exemptions," he considered them "abuses which cannot be too soon abolished." Whether concerning the provinces or individuals, Law demanded equal taxation and went even further: "Nothing is more important for the good order of a Kingdom than uniformity, and it should be hoped that it reigns in all laws, customs and taxes."[87]

In the first edition of the *Dictionnaire de l'Académie française* (1694), the terms *uniformité* and *uniforme* refer to something "that has nothing different about it . . . , all parts of which are similar." So, if the same laws were applied to all the subjects of the kingdom, in what way would these subjects differ? It was a question not of abolishing the nobility or the clergy but of emptying them of part of their substance. The idea was to leave aristocrats with only "honorary rights" such as, for example, "that only gentlemen are authorized to carry a sword."[88] Perhaps it was the English gentry that served as a model here. In England, this class of squires and knights was distinguished from the nobility in the strict sense, that of dukes, peers, marquises, and barons. The gentry had no political prerogatives and was not subject to the constraint of derogation (*dérogeance*)—through the exercise of trade, for example—unlike the aristocrats. It was a *nobilitas minor* whose members did not necessarily need the state's permission to declare themselves gentlemen. They could, however, display a coat of arms and carry a sword—symbolic elements that were important in social stratification.[89] The supporters of the System wanted at all costs to crush the political pretensions of the French nobility; they wanted to make all the king's subjects, without exception, potential merchants, in other words, individuals who exercised productive activities. They did not wish to abolish social branding and symbolic distinctions, which were anything but negligible (the bearing of arms was a right demanded in France at the time by certain categories of commoner). Above all, they hoped to reassure this new nobility by promising them an increase in income. The price of land owned by landowners—and, therefore, the price of the leases they received from their farmers—must rise sharply as the wealth of their "vassals"[90] improved. In short, these texts insisted that, with the System, all but the wealthy landowners would be exempt from taxation. But what mattered was to shift the tax burden from the productive classes to the idle classes (privileged or not) and, thereby, put an end, as Duguet and Boisguilbert wished, to the wars between the king and his peoples.

Even so, this was merely a last resort, given that the very principle of any public credit based on a tax system, however justified that system might be, was inherently flawed. This was the second theoretical exercise, one that involved imagining the disappearance of economic credit. Borrowing involved taxing. If the resources and the power of the sovereign lay in the wealth of his subjects, taxes would always tend to decrease. Taxing, in any manner whatsoever, was tantamount to reducing the well-being of the population and, sooner or later, the power of the sovereign. Thus, at the end of his pamphlet, Defoe called for the abolition *of all taxes*: "[I]f taxes were removed, Trade in general would encrease, Plenty and Cheapness make Families easy, and the whole Nation flourish." From that point on: "This would be the reviving the Halcion Days, and bringing the Golden Age once more upon the Earth. Then it would be no more a Proverb or by-Word among us, that there is nothing sure, but *Death* and *Taxes*." As Terrasson stated in his last letter, "taxes and loans" were a "resource as ruinous for the King as cruel for all state Orders without exception." On the subject of taxes, Terrasson explained that "its [the System's] greatest advantage is to do away with them." He therefore did not hesitate to affirm that the System, "whose soul is credit, the only source of circulation & abundance, reimburses the King by abolishing taxes."[91] It is less the question of the reality or feasibility of doing away with taxes that concerns us here than the theoretical background of the propagandists of the System.[92] By socializing the profits of foreign trade, and by monopolizing all coinage in the heart represented by the Compagnie-Banque, the king would, indeed, have no further use for taxes to finance his expenditure. Ultimately, the very concept of debt, followed by that of public credit, would disappear. Only moral credit would remain in the running, this power to act becoming infinite through the System.

Defoe asked his fellow citizens in 1717: "How much then does it behove us to put our selves out of the Danger of a Stop being put to our Credit, by putting an end to our general Dependence upon Credit at all?"[93] He wanted public debt to be extinguished and never again resorted to. The propagandists of the System spoke in similar terms. In a rather agreed way, the *Mémoire sur le denier royal* incorporated the accusations of usury against the financiers, whom the compared to "rats" in a granary.[94] The Royal Bank would have to put a permanent end to both their activities and those of the private bankers. In their own way, the apologues of the System contributed to the debate that had been raging since the seventeenth century in France and Holland on the subject of interest-bearing loans. As in the Jansenist circles, the question concerned not the "extrinsic titles" of late scholasticism (*lucrum cessans* and *damnum emergens*), but rather the final destination of the money lent.

Terrasson's first letter was almost entirely devoted to the deleterious effects of rentes. By implicitly endorsing the theological debates on the legality of interest-bearing loans, the former Oratorian stated on the subject of money that it:

> should be wished that it were always lent for nothing, or only to share with the borrower the profit made; this is the trade in which everyone can partake without being merchants, and it is also the only way to lend that is costly neither to the lender nor to the borrower. I have always looked with compassion on the yoke borne by the borrower in purchasing a rente.[95]

What mattered was not what the lender might have done with his capital. Terrasson did not justify the interest rate in terms of an opportunity cost. He did not question whether the lender could have won or lost less if he had been able to dispose of his money. What mattered to Terrasson was what the borrower would do with the amount loaned. The philosopher considered that most of those who borrowed in the form of rentes did so "to extricate themselves from an unfortunate situation." They were "unhappy" individuals, taken advantage of by "timorous and lazy men who think only of their personal interests." The poor debtors inevitably found themselves even worse off, which was why rentes had been regarded for centuries as a "tyranny" and a "public usury." The author of the *Idée générale* explicitly accused rentiers of being "idle" and "unnecessary" citizens. He pitied, like Boisguilbert, "the people, overwhelmed with taxes, who paid this interest [on rentes] to a small number of rich people who lived on usury with impunity." As with Le Correur and Defoe, the meaning of *usury* was broad: "And so it may be said that the natural idea of usury encompasses any loan that, in the guise of a kind deed, makes the benefactor more comfortable, and leads the borrower who is to be helped to his ruin." For Terrasson, it was clear that loans should be interest free whenever it came to helping a person in need. The situation was different where the capital loaned was to be used for a productive activity. When the borrower was a "merchant," he "only reluctantly reimburses the money he owes at maturity, because he would still enjoy the benefit thereof."[96] As far as the propagandists of the System were concerned, it was a case no longer of interest on money here but rather of cocontractors sharing the profits of a trading company. They defended a rather Thomist concept of interest: money alone could not produce money, not having the power to do so. Money needed to be turned into productive capital. It had to serve a commercial, industrial, or agricultural activity. In short, it had to be used to generate a surplus in order that something beyond the sum lent could be received. Here we find the distinction between a consumer loan and a production loan:

only the latter was considered legitimate, the former being nothing more than charity. In this logic, anyone who lent money to his sovereign, who borrowed for the purposes of war, a "consumption" activity, was, thus, a *usurer* (or *loan shark*) in Terrasson's meaning of the term, regardless of the interest rate. Such a person would make the borrower—his king—worse off and would not contribute in any way to an increase in public wealth.

The purpose of the System was to put an end to these practices. Terrasson could not have been more clear on this point, almost threatening: "practically no one any more is obliged to borrow," and the king "wants to inform his subjects that any borrowing at interest, however slight, is disadvantageous to the borrowers." He invites them to confine their ambitions and their enterprises to their present fortune; and by refraining from borrowing, they will be better able to rise in the future. The lenders, for their part, should, instead of seeking to burden the poverty-stricken or the imprudent, invest their money in the public Compagnie, which has just been established: in so doing, they will use said money in a way "that is inherently above suspicion of usury." The king discouraged borrowers and made it clear to lenders that they were expected to contribute to the profits of trade, thereby putting an end to the interest on money in the sense in which it had been understood up to that point. It was also necessary for the private bankers, who by seeking only their individual profit put "a kind of general taxation on trade," to disappear. Indeed, when a sum of money was deposited with them, they issued term notes that stipulated the payment of interest. When the person who possessed the term note returned it to the bank, he therefore received less than its face value. By instead issuing demand notes not subject to an interest rate, the General Bank—which in Law's words was not a "mercantile bank"—"emancipates trade and makes it stronger and more widespread."[97]

It was the same for the state. Under the System, there would be no more need to borrow. Nevertheless, should there be a need for "an advance of ten million," for example, this sum would be "found without interest in the Bank." The king lent to the king, using the coins that were constantly returned to him in the heart.[98] In this particular dream, there was, therefore, no more monetary debt: money as a whole would, henceforth, belong to the sovereign, who himself was a body that embraced the nation as a whole, a body without representatives and without representation, but one that held the monopoly on credit. In a civil society in which uniformity must prevail, in which intermediary bodies no longer played a role,[99] in which all participated in the same activity, individuals no longer had either economic or moral credit. Everyone had transferred this power to an entity that henceforth alone had the initiative of action. Individuals were "decredited" (*discrédités*) to the benefit of the state, which ensured their prosperity. The sovereign was once again in possession of the greatest power of action, a moral credit so powerful that he no longer needed to use his economic credit, or at least only with respect to himself.

A revolution of this nature could not be accomplished unless absolute trust was established in the great whole that was the System. For that, the latter had to rely on "trust" that was "not conquered" but rather "acquired over the course of time and through persuasion."[100] The philosopher Jean-Michel Rey has shown how essential this question of time was: "With the establishment of monetary credit in the early eighteenth century, . . . a new idea of time emerged throughout society: . . . the understanding of a collective time in which the threat of destruction played a prominent role; the perception of a time that was entirely under the primacy of the future." It would, then, take a will on the part of power strong enough to modify the beliefs of individuals about future times. But how was this to be achieved? In other words, how was this famous will to be expressed? Too dependent on the historiography of counterpropaganda, too focused on the issue of paper money alone, too trapped in a corpus limited to the works attributed to a solitary demiurge named John Law, most commentators considered it to be coercion and coercion alone that should impose new beliefs about the future on the public.[101] This canonical interpretation of the experiment, which takes for granted the way in which the dominant classes of the time described the event, has misunderstood the true foundation of the System.

In a mechanism of credit that was no longer based on interpersonal relationships, trust was "dependent on the stream of words and images that feed collective beliefs." This was something that the Moderns who gravitated toward the System fully understood. By making the experiment a "natural system," they offered a set of "beliefs" fueled precisely by this "stream of words and images." Was it a case of becoming preachers of a new religion? Was acceptance of the System considered an act of "faith"? This is what we might think following Jules Michelet. "The Middle Ages," said the famous nineteenth-century historian, "with faith, bread, a word, a breath, were able to make God. Law wanted only a little faith to deify his paper, turn it into gold, this God of the world, create a new Host." And he added that, for Law, "the wealth that is the daughter of credit, of opinion, is a creation of faith."[102] We know from Montaigne and Pascal that *faith* is distinct from *belief*. As noted by the historian Jean Wirth, the first term would gradually be reserved for "a transcendental truth claimed by the speaker faced with the *beliefs* of others." Faith became a private matter, an experience that was "inexpressible and incommunicable, free from critical discourse and manipulation." It was more than a set of beliefs. The latter fell within a "psychological phenomenon" that was the result "of submission to the power of the imagination, social determinisms, and conditioning through education." In the seventeenth century, the spiritual and elitist faith was condescending toward the beliefs of the vast majority of individuals, "who appear to be perpetually mystified, whether one attempts to maintain them in this condition or offers to free them from their superstitions."[103] Thus, the propagandists of the System could have faith, but it was not faith that they needed to "deify paper." As it was impossible to base the experiment on transcendence, by definition invisible, the System had to be embodied in a set of beliefs.

From this perspective, it is useful to examine the medieval concept of *fides*. This was neither exactly faith nor completely a belief but rather "trust" that was placed in something or someone. *Fides* was an adherence to the field of the probable, which differed from that of chance. It stood between science, "which consisted in accepting evidence," and opinion, which involved evoking nonevident suggestions "without assenting to them." In the Middle Ages, this adherence was an essential condition for the correct functioning of institutions. But it did not require knowledge; it was a question of the layman, not coming to know what was probable, but rather obeying and being faithful to the underlying social and religious system.[104] This is where a parallel can be drawn between the medieval *fides* and the trust that the propagandists of the System wanted to inspire, a trust based on a set of beliefs that were not to be questioned but simply accepted without discussion.

If we set to one side the rather unusual cases of the Convulsionaries of the 1720s, the end of the seventeenth century marked a decline in physical manifestations of possessions and cases of witchcraft. The disappearance of the devil, at least from human bodies, was, however, coupled with a concomitant withdrawal of God's presence. Following the work of Émile Bouvier, Jean Erhard and Tzvetan Todorov speculated that the advent of fantastic and fantasy literature at the turn of the seventeenth and eighteenth centuries represented a kind of manifestation of the repressed, a "compensatory compromise" in the face of a disturbing rise in rationalism.[105] This movement was accompanied by a fascination with the East, especially following the translation by Antoine Galland in 1704 of the *One Thousand and One Nights*, in other words, the premise of what Edward Said called *Orientalism*.[106] Fiction had taken over from religion and myths. Fictional stories, "[s]ituating their intrigues in a dreamy timelessness that renewed with the individual and collective past, with childhood, . . . could expect several benefits, among which those designated by Perrault: freedom from burdensome rules imposed by reason, the tyranny of meaning and value." Moreover, they served to "remove the text from the action of the law and in so doing transgress it."[107] The System had to take possession of this narrative mood to produce new beliefs—a form of transgression of values and liberation of desires—through the well-known educational value of the fable and the fairy tale. It was, thus, a case of submitting the subjects to a vast enterprise of conditioning, which relied on the power of the imagination and, more specifically, the fantasy fiction theorized by Addison in order to produce trust. As Terrasson had wanted, instead of reasoning, the subjects had to believe.

For the advocates of the System, free trade and competition were poisons and conquest a deadlock. Self-interest was a powerful and useful motive that led men to undertake great actions, but it had to be directed by the public authorities to ensure the prosperity of civil society. The System was the solution: it protected and supported the crown and was in return supported and protected by it in an indivisible package. The project was an alternative to the hierarchical society based on conditions, taxes, honor, and credit as interindividual relationships. Its totalizing vocation held society together in a body of a new nature, which managed to do what the monarchy could not do, namely, unite all wills toward a common goal, material prosperity. The nation was embodied in the Compagnie-Banque, which brought together all the individual bodies, and in which each participated at his own level in the creation of wealth, organized and distributed by the great economic Leviathan. Should we still speak of "subjects"? Maybe not, since a new sociological figure was to be born with the shareholder. The rentier was the traditional support of the monarchy (and its tax system); the shareholder became this atom of a society that no longer needed either a king, or a church, or intermediary bodies, a society that was no more than a collective belief. Public debt and rentes had technical dimensions, but above all they had political dimensions. The state, supposed to represent the public interest, could, if necessary, cheat its creditors to maintain itself because what did the interests of the latter represent?[108] This is the essential question to which there is no unequivocal answer, as everything depends on forms of indebtedness and political constitutions, but what is certain is that, in the case at hand, the liquidation of debt and the rentier class resolved the question of sovereignty. The System was no longer answerable to anyone. However, this result was potentially highly destabilizing. If rentiers disappeared, then a mass of people politically interested in maintaining the monarchical organization succumbed. The royal state might have fewer people to handle or to please, but who would defend it? On the other hand, if there were no more subjects but only individuals who sought to enrich themselves by enriching the System, then there was no more social taxonomy (even if symbolic distinctions remained). But was this uniformity of which Law spoke not opening the door to a war of all against all? Were these not the prolegomena of a new state of nature, a competition without rules and without referees? Was the fact that the System was based on trading—intrinsically risky, despite all the pledges its propagandists tried to give—not proof that all stability was definitively lost? Who indeed could count on a social bond as unreliable, as uncertain, as dangerous as trade? Was this not simply a way of programming the end of royalty, if not of all society? Far from defusing these fears, the propaganda continued to fuel them by producing a wonderful fiction. For this attempt to refound the French monarchy was accompanied by an intense endeavor to spread the belief that everything was now possible for anyone, at least in imagination. It depicted a fabulous universe, with virtuous heroes, villains, authentic goods, a new eschatology. The power of the storyteller, the performativity of his speech, mattered here more than its coherence or, indeed, its veracity.

4

Magical Politics

The dominant literary genre of the first decades of the eighteenth century has often been called *rococo* or *rocaille* by literary theorists. It is embodied in the fairy tale, the fable, and the "marvelous novel" (*roman merveilleux*). This genre refuses to guide the reader in a denunciation or an overly rational apology, contrary to the more overtly critical reason of the second half of the century. Considered too frivolous by the next generation, rococo works mix registers and deal with serious matters through pleasure, play, sensitivity, intimacy, the elsewhere, and the fabulous. They are marked by a presentism: the future, and especially the past, have little importance. The "variegation" (*bigarrure*) or "oddity" (*bizarrerie*) was described by Fontenelle as "a means of providing the mind with connections that it may not have noticed, and that always result in some morality."[1] Buchet, the director of the *Nouveau Mercure*, naturally made this aesthetic his own in the preface to his first issue in 1717; he stated loud and clear that he wanted to make his journal a variegated (*bigarré*) periodical in which poems, critiques, dissertations, factums, sacred discourse, public news, etc. would mix. The immense rococo work that is the *Nouveau Mercure* was to be an assemblage of pieces "curious enough to interest [the] reader." As Nicolas-Charles-Joseph Trublet (1697–1770), a friend of Fontenelle, Houdar de la Motte, and Madame de Tencin, stated in its pages, most men have "an inordinate love of the marvelous [*merveilleux*]."[2] It is therefore this literary register that the Moderns must use to interest readers in the new system of nature that they wish to promote.

Terrasson considered that it was always difficult to accept a new system, men being guided by what he called "the old prejudice," that is, the rejection of everything that seems new. Twice, the philosopher drew a parallel between the System and that developed by Descartes. When the latter published his discoveries everyone was against him, from the university authorities to the lowest classes of the people, and yet "philosophy has never stopped emerging through all these obstacles." But how did "systems" impose themselves? Science historian Simon Schaffer points out that for the philosopher and economist Adam Smith (1723–90), "'all the different systems of nature' had succeeded *not* because of 'their agreement or inconsistency with truth or reality,' but only through their ability 'to sooth the imagination and to render the theater of nature a more coherent, and therefore a more magnificent spectacle.'" He adds that "[b]oth David Hume and Adam Smith pointed out the intimate connection between the prevalence of deceit and what Hume, in his analysis of the authority of miracles, called the 'strong propensity of mankind to the extraordinary and the marvellous.'"[3] Thus, the Moderns counted on the System to provide a better "spectacle" of the functioning of human societies than what a few leaders had presented until that time. On the one hand, they translate and extend in their language and their aesthetic the wild hope that we have seen in the previous chapter. They reveal implicit aspects of the System. On the other hand, they give their own coloring to the experiment, making the System something different from the expectations of John Law and the Duke of Orléans. But all these elements are and make the System. They generate tangible effects.

The colonization of Louisiana was the first element of this propaganda campaign. New maps, so-called travel narratives, and engravings develop three identical features. The Mississippi valley was first depicted as a new Garden of Eden, a "wonderland" where everything could be obtained without effort. Louisiana was then a place where there were no dangerous animals, where the natives were innocent and good and their women promiscuous. The natives knew neither the value of goods nor European sexual taboos. Finally, the place abounded in mines and ores. All these were wonderful promises. We were wrong, until today, to mock them or despise them. The French Compagnie des Indes sought and found important deposits in the American continent. Social mobility, sexuality, and semiwild and adventurous independence were on the agenda of numerous settlers. The anarchist utopias of several travelers and men of letters such as Lahontan, Gueudeville, and Le Maire were performative.

After Louisiana came the question of secrecy and the (al)chemical references of propaganda. Several writings by Law, Terrasson, and Buchet described the System as moved by a mysterious force. The Moderns defended the use of secrecy in politics, so all this was perfectly normal, but, as we shall see, the projectors were also frequently seen and presented as being in possession of a trade secret unknown to other men. For the propagandists, Law and the regent had found the principles of true chemistry, the result of Louisiana metallurgy and the foreign trade of the Compagnie-Banque. Well versed in the occult sciences, they were also seen as akin to supernatural creatures. They were engaged on Earth in a Manichaean combat that was to see the victory of the believers who trustingly yielded to the System while the skeptics and those resistant to the new policy would be swallowed up by misery and misfortune.

The propaganda—in the shape of theological dissertations, plays, poems, and newspaper articles—encouraged followers of the System to overconsume: this was the third object of the marvelous. Unlike the proto-invisible hand of a writer such as Boisguilbert, it was not greed that made societies prosper but lavishness. As for wealth, it could and should now be reaped by anyone. But was this lottery compatible with the *actions rentières* of a company that was to merge with the state? Seen from the outside, perhaps not, but, in Terrasson's metaphysics, certainly—because it was a form of theodicy of the hidden harmony that he was deploying. The System distributed good and evil in a way that was not always understood, but there was a preestablished plan behind it. The nouveaux riches were spending more than their own purses could handle, but this was a blessing since they provided jobs for everyone. The rascals who sold their shares and invested in land or real estate seemed to harm the System when, in reality, they were driving up the prices of agricultural goods and houses and, thus, encouraging farming and construction.

Fortune, excessive spending, exoticism, sexuality: the propaganda of the System encouraged the liberation of desires. To this end, the *Nouveau Mercure* took on a literary register that the literary theorist Mikhail Bakhtin (1895–1975) termed *carnivalesque*. It thus published the prophecies of Nostradamus, poems employing a Rabelaisian vocabulary, and numerous improbable stories about poor people living in high style. This kind of literature mixed everything, from language registers to hierarchies and identities. But, of course, none of these reported events actually occurred. Servants and cooks did not become rich; aristocrats did not keep company with seamstresses any more than they already had. There was no carnival during the System, but there was a carnivalesque state literature that had to be performative. If the subjects behaved in accordance with the new beliefs publicized by the propaganda, then the fantasy would become reality. But this would be dangerous. The state legitimized what was, until the System appeared, repressed, forbidden, and impossible. The imaginary, that great historical force, had been liberated by power, the very same power that had been meant to contain the imaginary.

Fabulous Louisiana

At the founding of the Compagnie d'Occident toward the end of 1717, Father François Le Maire and Abbé Jean Bobé understood that Louisiana's moment had arrived. On the one hand, the duo had managed to spark, while not enthusiasm exactly, at least curiosity thanks to the report and the map of Mississippi, drawn up in partnership with the geographer Guillaume Delisle, that had been presented to the Naval Council a few months previously. On the other hand, Bobé saw his allies from the Raudot clan appointed to increasingly more prestigious positions. Indeed, Antoine-Denis Raudot, former intendant of Canada and chief clerk of the Maison du Roi, was appointed one of the directors of the Compagnie d'Occident in 1717, while his father, Jacques Raudot, became an adviser to the navy in 1719. Father and son were, henceforth, at the heart of the colonial policy of the Regency, and we know that, along with Le Maire, the Raudots and Jean-Baptiste Duché provided Bobé with much information on Louisiana of both a geographic and an ethnographic nature. Bobé forwarded this information to Delisle, who was continuing his father's mapping of America, and all these men worked together over the following months toward the drawing up of a new map, one much more ambitious than the last.

The advice and requests that Bobé addressed to Delisle are particularly interesting for the subject at hand. First, he encouraged Delisle to extend his map "as far as Mexico, and to Havana," because this would "make an even greater impression and be all the more pleasing, I do not mean to the scholars, but to countless people." Bobé was clearly implying that his patrons and friends from the Ministry of the Navy wanted the map to include a well-known and powerful fantasy. Next, he suggested that Delisle introduce more information and embellishments of a commercial nature: "Monsieur Raudot and Monsieur Duché [another director of the Compagnie] will be able to indicate those [trading posts for the fur trade] that are or will be established in Louisiana." Finally, Bobé wanted the map to bear the arms of the Compagnie and depict well-dressed natives around the edges.[4] This map was published toward the end of summer 1718 (fig. 4.1), and, while it did not by any means take into account all Bobé's remarks, it did contain numerous promotional elements taken from the reports drafted by Le Maire and Raudot.

Spanish America and its fabulous mines—because that was obviously what it was all about—are only partially represented in the map, but at the top left there is a quotation we know was taken from Le Maire's report. Delisle included neither the Western Sea nor Quivira and Cibola, but he did cite the "yellow iron" that the Spanish were known to be trading in with the natives somewhere around the sources of the Missouri River (top left). In the same vein, and somewhat symptomatically, it is not the trading posts that are noted on the map but the alleged mines, both French and Spanish, with assertions such as "This whole district is full of mines" to the left of the Mississippi River. Another map placed great emphasis on the same subject (fig. 4.2). Also

FIGURE 4.1. *Carte de la Louisiane et du cours du Mississipi par Guillaume Delisle* (Paris: Chez l'auteur, 1718). Courtesy Bibliothèque nationale de France, Département des cartes et plans, GE DD-2987 (8788B).

published in 1718, this update of older maps was carried out by the king's geographer, Nicolas de Fer (1647–1720). It largely represented the Spanish mines in Mexico, like San Luis Potosi north of Mexico City, as well as other "real de mines." New Mexico was likewise depicted in great detail, and the map also indicated "the Province of Quivira" at the sources of the Missouri River. Here are the arms of the Compagnie (top left) and a few well-armed natives with plenty of game. The map would had been prepared from the narratives of such well-known characters as La Salle, Tonti, Lahontan, and Le Maire.

At the same time, this cartographic propaganda was accompanied by alleged travel narratives concerning Louisiana, written by supposed officers and gentlemen. Indeed, as shown by Steven Shapin, in the seventeenth and eighteenth centuries knowledge in general and reported knowledge in particular had to be accredited and validated by men who were both financially and socially independent.[5] Thus, in September 1717, February 1718, and, finally, March 1719, the *Nouveau Mercure* published three long narratives supposedly written by men who held certain forms of authority, but without quoting their names. And the editorial career of these texts did not stop there.

FIGURE 4.2. *Le cours du Missisipi, ou de St. Louis, fameuse riviere de l'Amérique septentrionale avec environs de laquelle se trouve le païs appellée Louisiane: Dressée sur les relations et mémoires du Père Hannepin et de Mrs. de la Salle, Tonti, Laontan, Ioustel, des Hayes, Joliet, et le Maire &c, par Nicolas de Fer* (Paris: Chez l'auteur, 1718). Courtesy Bibliothèque nationale de France, Département des cartes et plans, GE C-5184.

The first narrative was republished in Amsterdam in 1719 under a slightly different title in the *Atlas historique* by Henri Abraham Chatelain and Nicolas Gueudeville.[6] After his rewriting of Lahontan's *Dialogues*, it is no surprise to see Gueudeville be interested by a fabulous narrative published in the *Mercure*. In the preface of the sixth volume of the *Atlas historique*, which contains America, he specifies that the texts and maps "were drawn up for the establishment of the Compagnie d'Occident": "One can judge by the care taken to gather all that is most reliable and most new, how much care was taken to make this work useful to the public."[7] It is necessary to underline the passage of Gueudeville on the "sure" character of these accounts, which in fact use the same register as his American utopia, and of which we will see in a moment the fabulous aspects. The long narrative dating from February 1718 was reprinted in 1720, again in Amsterdam, by the bookseller Jean-Frédéric Bernard. Bernard was a French writer in exile in Holland who had a strong interest in history and geography, and alongside the text of the *Mercure* he printed royal acts related to the Compagnie and Delisle's map (fig. 4.1). The European dimension of the propaganda is not denied because the same text as that of March 1719 appears abridged and translated into German in Leipzig in 1720. The latter was accompanied by a long poem to the glory of the System as well as a rough map depicting some mines and the arms of the Compagnie des Indes with a horn of plenty. At the same time, the German geographer Christoph Weigel (1654–1725) published a scaled-down and slightly modified version of Delisle's map with a cartouche containing a shareholder and a box full of gold. In this case, the fact that practically everything was left in French—with the exception of the annotations "This whole District is full of Mines" and "Country full of Mines," which had been translated into Latin—is very significant.[8] Finally, we can note two other texts belonging to the same corpus. The first is the "Description of Mississippi," which was published in 1720 by a certain "chevalier de Bonrepos" and was supposedly written for one of his cousins. The second is a bilingual French-English publication entitled *A Full and Impartial Account of the Company of Mississippi*, also dating from 1720, that contains the anonymous "Discovery of Mississippi, Otherwise Known as Louisiana."[9]

A handwritten report dating from 1717 seems to be the common denominator behind this literature.[10] What is striking is how all these texts place emphasis on the same three points: first, the fertility of the soil, often described in almost biblical terms; second, the docile nature of the natives, their innocence, and their promiscuity; and, third, the precious metals to be found in the region. This last point is also and by far the most developed in these various texts.

The 1717 report describes the country as being "one of the most fertile in the whole world, grain being harvested here two to three times a year . . . , the grapes, which grow naturally, are of extraordinary size and goodness." Everything in Louisiana was better and more abundant than it was in Europe, notably the wine, the fish, and the mammals. More importantly, everything there seemed to be a gift of nature. The anonymous author of the narrative published in September 1717 in the *Nouveau Mercure* wrote of Louisiana as being "a wonderland," a place where everything "grows marvelously well," with whatever sown there being "reaped a hundredfold." Moreover, all tools, supplies, land, and so on were provided free by the Compagnie to settlers. "Persons of quality" would be entitled to "own outright as much land as they wish, to be cleared by their servants, the Slaves, the horses, and the oxen that said Compagnie will provide free of charge." It would be the same for "women and girls," who would "also own concessions." And it went without saying that "no taxes are due there." In the long "Letter concerning Louisiana," the so-called officer saw fit to clarify for the lady to whom his correspondence was addressed: "You will find quite extraordinary things there, as to regard me perhaps in the same light as the Israelites regarded Joshua and Caleb, on their return after discovering the Land of Canaan."[11]

The wild animals were harmless in this Garden of Eden. Bears, reptiles, and leopards were reported to "flee before men and harm them not." And, just like the animals, the humans living there were no cause for alarm either: "The spirit of goodwill is such there that every man leaves his doors open, each one helping the other." Indeed, according to Bonrepos, there was "practically nothing savage" at all about the "savages." As stated in the report of 1717, the natives were so docile that they contributed to "help the French set up their establishments and provide them with all the meat and game they require, as well as pelts and other items in exchange for trinkets." These innocent souls were unaware of the value of money, and, regarding game, they "provide as much as is needed in exchange for very little." They also knew nothing of the sexual taboos of European societies. Writing of the native women in the *Nouveau Mercure*, one of the "officers" said that they took "great freedom in their pleasures" and that it was, in his opinion, difficult to resist "the temptation of such objects." While at first appearing to condemn this excessive intimacy that existed between the native women and the French settlers, he actually went on, in a kind of praise of sexual slavery, to encourage the male settlers to give expression to their desires. There was, after all, nothing to fear from these unions, the natives having found an "infallible" way to protect themselves against "the fruits of love," namely, a contraceptive plant the secret of which the author of the letter would reveal to his mysterious correspondent.

FIGURE 4.3. Engraving entitled *Le commerce que les Indiens du Mexique font avec les François au port de Missisipi* (Paris: Chez François-Gérard Jollain, ca. 1717–19). Courtesy Bibliothèque nationale de France, Département des estampes et photographies, EST QB-1 (1717).

Moreover, a "chemist" by the name of Duval had also supposedly discovered so many plants and balms that "everyone goes to him to be healed."[12] Freed from hunger, landlessness, and the fetters of sexual propriety, the settlers would also find themselves free of almost all illnesses in this earthly paradise. And they were promised even more.

The preparatory report of 1717 specified that "this great continent abounds in mines of gold, silver, copper, tin, lead, iron, and several other minerals." The topographic logic of Le Maire's reports and Delisle's first map provided the raw material for these narratives. "Yellow iron" could be found in abundance in upper Missouri, and the mines of Louisiana were located in the same mountain range as those of New Mexico. Moreover, it would not be difficult to extract the deposits given that "the King sends vast numbers of Slaves to work in the mines" and, regarding lead, "so much is currently being mined, with almost no effort."[13] The *Nouveau Mercure* also published information along the same lines. In July 1719, for example, it announced the discovery of two gold mines in Mississippi, in a place that was, of course, not specified. In April 1720, it published a report on the tests carried out in a Louisiana silver mine. The yields were reported to be "extraordinary," the metal coins made from this silver being "better than those of Peru."[14] Another engraving published by François-Gérard Jollain, circa 1717–19, clearly captured what was at stake (fig. 4.3). The scene in this engraving depicts an unspecified place that did not exist. There was no such walled city with a castle overlooking it (in the background to the right) or a convent or prison (to the left), and only very rarely were such powerful ships (in the center) seen in the mouth of the Mississippi.

As well as this fantasy city, the center of Jollain's engraving represents peaceful natives, ready to convert to the one true faith, and bringing game and various goods to the newcomers. Women are also present, depicted as being strong and in a state of relative undress. The French are represented by soldiers, gentlemen, and fishermen, some of whom are carrying tools or weapons. The whole engraving suggests both good order and civil harmony. Its title refers to "trade" with the natives "of Mexico," not those of "Louisiana." The text below the engraving emphasizes the three points already mentioned: the fertility of the soil, the docile nature and innocence of the natives, and especially the precious metals. Repeating Le Maire's report almost word for word, the text evokes the "perpetual spring" that reigned in these parts, this garden where "the trees without being grafted or cultivated naturally bear fruit of exquisite taste": "Gold and silver being so commonly found, and the savages being unaware of their value, they trade pieces of gold or silver for such European goods as knives, iron pots, wooden axes, and even for a small mirror, a little brandy, or some other such thing they find to their taste." The text thus refers to "mountains filled with Gold, Silver, Copper, Lead and Quicksilver in upper Mississippi."

Dating from December 1720, the engraving in figure 4.4 depicts one of the two concessions that Law claimed for himself in Louisiana.[15] With its cabins, boat, and other scattered dwellings, it gives an idea of what the French settlements in the mouth of the Mississippi looked like during the Regency. Contrary to the previous maps, engravings, and narratives, key to this image is its disarming simplicity. Still, the document suggests an enviable destination. First, indeed, it is the concessions of "Mr. Law" that have been represented. This simple fact and the participation of the Scotsman in several logging companies in Louisiana suggest that the minister and other important figures of the kingdom—notably, as we have seen, the principal members of the circle of Verrue—were seeking to provide an example and that they did not consider the colony to be a sterile quagmire. Second, it shows a fairly large village of solidly built houses, a large store in the background, and active settlers: some are plowing, others tanning hides or transporting goods. Order and prosperity seem to reign, and trade is possible, but this time on the condition that people actually work. With the System in decline at this time, are we to understand that the fantasy had given way to reality? All those who tend to consider the propaganda surrounding Louisiana as nothing but

FIGURE 4.4. Engraving entitled *Veüe du camp de la concession de Monseigneur Law au Nouveau Biloxy, coste de la Louisiane, designée par Jean-Baptiste-Michel Le Bouteux le dixe Décembre 1720*, by Jean-Michel Le Bouteux (1720). Courtesy Newberry Library, Chicago.

deceit and anecdotes will no doubt interpret it in this way. However, it would be a great mistake to scoff or make light of this propagandist discourse, the performativity of which is obvious. Naming and expressing all these things contributed to making them a reality. If we leave aside the widespread concubinage between the settlers and the native women, which paved the way for sex outside marriage and sexual exploitation, the case of the precious metals is paradigmatic.

As Paul Mapp points out, there was nothing fanciful about the reasoning of Le Maire, Bobé, Delisle, or Jollain: "However dubious their reasoning might seem, these authors were not foolish to think that there might be ore deposits in the unknown regions west of the Mississippi. Spain had been scraping fortunes in silver out of Mexico for two centuries, and the discoveries of massive gold deposits in Brazil in the 1680s and 1690s had demonstrated that new El Dorados might still be found. The California Gold Rush of the nineteenth century would later offer one such bonanza."[16] All kinds of useful discoveries followed these times of generalized gold rush fever, and, even though El Dorado remained a myth, the quantities of precious metals coming from the American continent over the centuries following its conquest were to change the face of the world.

In 1719, the Compagnie des Indes created the position director of mines that it assigned to the adventurer from Picardy Philip Francis Renault (d. 1750), an explorer from the family of an ironmaster in Cousolre, in the

Hainaut region, a family that had developed a significant mining and metallurgical complex in the area from the late seventeenth century on. Renault left France with two hundred settlers, among them dozens of workers and miners. His convoy made a stop at Santo Domingo, where he bought five hundred enslaved people; then it went up the Mississippi River to the Illinois Country and settled in the south of what is today the city of Saint Louis in Missouri. Renault received land grants from the Compagnie, and he founded communities on the banks of the Mississippi River that are named today "Old Mines," "Potosi," "Silver Mines," and "French Village" where people spoke French until the mid-twentieth century. Renault launched exploratory expeditions in search of mineral ores and exploited silver, iron, copper, and zinc deposits. However, these ores were found to be very disappointing, and mining operations were quickly abandoned. However, he did find around Potosi and Silver Mines a huge deposit of lead, or, to be more precise, of argentiferous galena, a mineral species consisting of lead and silver sulfide. This deposit is one of the most important of the United States, exploited even today in what is now known as the Lead Belt. In Europe in general, and in France in particular, there are no silver mines in the strict sense, only galena (lead) mines, more or less argentiferous (this is the case of the famous mines of Laurion in Greece). From the Middle Ages through the modern period, the kings of France and private entrepreneurs extracted silver, using well-mastered combustion techniques, from galena deposits, for example, in Melle (today in Deux-Sèvres), in the southern Alps, and in Ardèche, Lorraine, and Brittany (where silver extraction from galena mines reached its peak in the eighteenth century). The *Enquête du régent* of 1716–18 devoted much attention to the kingdom's lead mines and their carefully documented silver-bearing capacities. On discovering a lead deposit, the adventurers of the Compagnie des Indes thus found what they knew and, in part, what they were looking for. We know today that some galena deposits in Missouri have turned out to be silver bearing and that, at least since the nineteenth century, silver has been extracted from mines in the region (as indicated by the names "Potosi" and "Silver Mines"), as on the site of the "La Motte mine" (founded by Antoine Lamothe-Cadillac around 1714). Renault operated galena mines for years before returning to France in the 1740s, and southern Missouri experienced a real mining fever at the end of the eighteenth century (especially among French settlers from Brittany).[17] It is very likely that the sample of silver reported by the *Nouveau Mercure* in 1720 and other mineral ores sent to the Académie des sciences in the following years from Louisiana were from Renault's mines. The publicity of the System did not always lie. There may not have been "yellow iron" or cities of gold, but there were large stocks of lead and silver. From this point of view, the propaganda surrounding Louisiana formed part of the major research program in ores initiated by the *Enquête du régent* in view of the regeneration of the kingdom.

What some commentators have too easily termed pure propaganda still helped make the logic of the System work. We have seen the importance of naval convoys during the period 1719–20. It was with them that colonization truly began: hundreds of German-speaking emigrants were recruited, the construction of New Orleans began, the deportation of enslaved people accelerated, and dozens of concessions were worked.[18] Better still, exoticism as a *promise*, to use the terminology of Edward Said and Benjamin Schmidt, also worked, at least to some extent. Shannon Dawdy has proved that social mobility was possible in Louisiana during the period 1717–25: smugglers or criminals (*forçats*) became farmers, craftsmen, even dignitaries. They were able to marry European women and also to marry into native tribes, especially in the country of the Illinois. This is the case, for instance, with Mathurin Roger, former salt smuggler who arrived in 1717 as a prisoner and by 1721 was an honorable shoemaker in La Mobile. He set up a household with a wife and children. Marie Michel was also a former prisoner, "exiled for fraud" in 1719. Nine years later, she became the owner of land and a house in New Orleans. Louis Manseau, a tobacco smuggler and former prisoner, arrived in the colony on the same ship as Marie Michel. An enterprising character, he associated with a certain Louet, and they both went to the village of Natchez with enslaved people to cultivate indigo. Manseau seems to have prospered, for in 1731 he bought a house and settled in New Orleans. The so-called Chavanne arrived in Louisiana in 1719 at twenty-five years of age after having killed a man in an alcoholic brawl. He settled in a French-native village and became a farmer. During the following years, he managed to buy enslaved people and began to build up assets. He converted this wealth into symbolic capital, beginning an administrative career in the colony. Others did not seek respectability and stability. They immediately fled the scene in order to live in "semi-wild independence," whether among natives or as adventurers or pirates in the Gulf of Mexico (this is the golden age of piracy in this area). Those who had been sent to Louisiana after being issued with a *lettre de cachet* for leading dissolute lives would be able to resume those lives in another form. What Dawdy calls *rogue colonialism*[19]—this underworld of dangers and smuggling—can be seen from another perspective: it is either a utopia or a dystopia, especially for women and enslaved people, translated into deeds. Here are the promises of Lahontan, of Gueudeville, of the propagandists, that the settlers try to put into practice. What the publicity promised settlers—sexual freedom, excess, adventure—to some extent came about. Louisiana at this time was not a world without laws, but it was a place where men and women from Europe really could reinvent themselves. They changed their names, used nicknames, embellished or modified their pasts, and built a future different from what they had faced in France. It was much easier in Louisiana than in metropolitan France to acquire status and rise up the social scale during this period.[20] Again we find the idea of a purified rebirth in this other world capable of washing away sins.

The literature and the iconography associated with the liberation of desires generated various facts, gestures, and behaviors. The poor, the *taillables*, as well as gentlemen with a spirit of adventure were promised a world of leisure, wealth that was just waiting to be picked up off the ground, health, no taxes, and unbridled sexuality. All this took place within a well-known fantasy, that of a new Garden of Eden where human beings had dominion over animals and nature. Bread and wine, the elements of the biblical ritual, would be given, without effort, to those men living among innocent creatures who did not know sin. Even illness, death in childbirth, and the burden of large families would become no more than distant memories thanks to the fabulous pharmacopoeia to be found there. On the spot, the officers complained of the settlers. But who would be surprised at their behavior after what we have seen? They were just trying to realize the good life that they had been promised. Louisiana was not, or not only, an exotic hell.

Of course, during what has been described as a "heroic" period, the mortality rate was high, and the living conditions were very difficult. This is the counterpart of all adventures in search of one's desire, whether voluntary or not, from the Dionysian rites of antiquity to the punk culture of the twentieth century, including most revolutionary experiences. Utopia often comes with a heavy price to pay. As segregation, racism, and exploitation quickly set in,[21] enslaved people captured in and deported from Africa, as well as many natives, were sacrificed on the altar of the dream of liberation. They were the instruments of the Regency's fantasies as the System played an important and deleterious role in the beginning of the plantation era in the south of the continent. But, for the settlers, the System had played its marvelous role. It had aroused new hopes, new beliefs, in order to change behaviors. The propaganda did not preach patience and rewards in heaven. This time the authorities promised a better future, a *truly* enchanted land. The System clearly stated the problem faced by, not just individuals under the ancien régime, but people everywhere. In this sense, it was, strictly speaking, an eschatology, for both settlers and shareholders alike.

The Secret of the Real Chemists and the Eschatological Expectation

In a variety of ways, the letters and reports written by Law, Terrasson, Pannier d'Orgeville, and Buchet exuded an air of mystery. In the *Mémoire sur la Banque générale*, Law explained that the success of his undertaking depended on "the very secret support of a few people." The *Idée générale d'un nouveau système des finances* stated that, if the reign of Louis XIV had been so catastrophic, it was because "the secrets of credit and commerce" had not been known at that time. Finally, in the preface to his "History of the Compagnie des Indes," Buchet told his readers: "I will give you that which I hold, in other words, all that Paris sees and knows. The surplus of the System being a secret of the State."[22]

At the turn of the seventeenth and eighteenth centuries, it was still considered that politics had to be conducted on the basis of the concealment of knowledge, that the knowledge held by the king and his counselors did not have to be disclosed. In a world where the glory of the prince lay first and foremost in his conquests, secrecy was, indeed, indispensable to obfuscate and confound the enemies of the kingdom. Thus, the Oratorian priest Jean-François Senault (1604–72) said: "[T]he most important condition of a minister is secrecy." He added: "[W]hen secrecy is banished from the Council [of the king] . . . , the Prince cannot be well served." Father Dominique Bouhours (1628–1702) considered that, for princes, secrecy formed "part of their authority, & their greatness." Like God, of whom he was the representative, the prince must rule through "ways unknown to men," and it was to be an "enemy of the public good, to discover the mysteries of his counsel." Jacques-Bénigne Bossuet (1627–1704), a close friend of Bouhours, also used a theological analogy: "The counsel of kings is a mystery; their secret which concerns the salvation of the entire state has something of the religious & sacred about it." The king's plans were like those of God; the profane must never be able to understand them.[23]

Secrecy could, however, take several forms: something left unsaid, silence, or a lie. In the seventeenth and eighteenth centuries, the theoreticians of the secret of the state generally concentrated on defending the "white lie" (*mensonge officieux*), in other words, a lie that was useful, made with the purpose of being of service. While before the French Revolution certain philosophers had begun to demand a policy of truthfulness, the competition organized by the Prussian Academy of Sciences in 1780 entitled "Is It Useful to Deceive the People?" resulted in several dissertations that discussed the subject of the white lie. This was the case of the award-winning paper by Frédéric de

Castillon (1747–1814), which advocated the need for dissimulation and lying in politics but only for the benefit of the governed masses.[24] A little less than a century before, Fontenelle and Terrasson had defended the same idea.

In one of his "Dialogues between the Deceased Ancients and the Moderns," published for the first time in 1683, Fontenelle imagined a conversation between Artemisia and the Majorcan philosopher, theologian, and mystic Raymond Llull. Artemisia asked: "Is it thus useful for men to be deceived?" To which Llull replied: "Useful? Were by misfortune truth ever to reveal itself as it is, all would be lost." Terrasson applied this idea in politics by writing in his *Philosophie applicable*: "The Statesman could harm his Government were he to express the principles or the grounds on which it makes him happy." The Moderns therefore considered it necessary to govern under the seal of secrecy. But of what nature was secrecy? The politics of raison d'état generally leads to reasoning in terms of the "arcanization" (from the word *arcana*) of political action. The latter must be the business of one or more "arcanists," that is, people with secret (technical or political) expertise. So all the project makers who wanted to arouse the interest of a court until the middle of the eighteenth century were well advised to emphasize their arcane character. This political science of the secret habitually used a rhetoric, arguments, and even practices linked to magical phenomena.[25] And so Houdar de la Motte's "Ode to the Regent" extended a chemical metaphor. At the beginning of the poem, the leader of the Moderns emphasized the deplorable state of the kingdom at the death of the warring king, then expressed his gratitude to Philippe for making peace last, before going on to say:

> . . . But Peace without Abundance
> Is but one fruit of your virtue;
> Your prudence must yet
> Revive the worn-down State. . . .
> Must we await a new Llull,*
> Proud of his chemical works,
> To promise our credulous hope
> The art of controlling metals:
> To praise in his delirium
> This sovereign sand that he draws
> From a skillfully measured fire;
> To command his vain powder
> To change all, to dissolve all,
> And to bring forth gold at will?
> No, the Heavens offer us a Genius
> Whose beneficial talents

Shall realize the obsession
Of these supposed Creators.
Bolder than our hope,
In the heart of France itself
He opens a new Potosi
His more efficient System
Seems by its sublime daring
To be revealed rather than chosen.

*Famous chemist reputed for having discovered the philosopher's stone.[26]

While, at the beginning of this passage, Houdar de la Motte mocks the vain research into the transmutation of metals, he ends on a highly dubious note. He uses the past participle in claiming that the famous System was "revealed," in other words, was a revealed truth. In this sense, the System belonged to the mysteries of faith because chemistry is a gift from God.[27] The ambivalence of this poem is part of the tensions around the definition of *chemistry* that, during the Regency, ran through the Académie des sciences. On the one hand, Fontenelle, a friend of Houdar de la Motte, attempted to rebuild this science on the principles of Cartesian physics. The idea was to set aside everything that had hitherto been undertaken by numerous scholars (including Robert Boyle and Isaac Newton), in other words, attempts to transmute base metals into gold, a process known as chrysopoeia. Fontenelle did not regard the latter as a useless endeavor because, by seeking the "Philosopher's Stone," "many exceptional secrets that were not being sought have been discovered."[28] Chrysopoeia had, however, heaped so much disgrace on the science of chemistry that it was not encouraged. On the other hand, there were Homberg's students and particularly Étienne-François Geoffroy (1672–1731), an academician and professor at the Royal College. As we have seen, Homberg was fascinated with metals, and Fontenelle carefully tried to erase all traces of the chemist's work on transmutation. However, this work was extensive. "In 1684 he worked on a process to transmute mercury into silver. In 1702, when Philippe II, Duke of Orléans, by then Homberg's tutee in chemistry, purchased the enormous burning lens made by Ehrenfried Walther von Tschirnhaus, the first experiments Homberg performed with it were attempts to use the sun's light to transmute silver into gold." Homberg's laboratory was at the Palais-Royal, and we know that Philippe himself regularly participated in these experiments. At Homberg's death, Geoffroy pursued his work, and, when, on April 15, 1722, he presented the Académie with a report entitled "Hoaxes concerning the Philosopher's Stone," it was with a view not to rejecting any attempt to transmute metals but rather to denouncing incorrect chemical processes. "It is through laboratory work, the exploring of mines, and the reading of ancient authors that the real chemist shall manage to achieve knowledge of nature, and it is precisely these efforts that the 'pseudo-chemists' are so reluctant to perform, preferring to use fraudulent methods." For Geoffroy, it was a question not of marking a clean break but rather of good practices in chemistry. Indeed: "[I]n 1718, the transmutation of metals into gold remained a serious topic of study for many and one of the enterprises that most readily characterized chemistry for the general public."[29] The regent was, moreover, not the only Modern favorably disposed toward these practices. In January 1711, Dufresny entered in his journal a discussion of chemistry written in the first person. He mentioned a book that had just been published and that demonstrated the impossibility of the discovery of the philosopher's stone but hastened to add that "other books will prove the contrary by reasons that may be every bit as good." He himself claimed to be "in a supposed uncertainty, exactly where one must be in relation to an obscure science" that may allow for discovering "an infinity of secrets."[30]

Consequently, what Houdar de la Motte suggested in his ode dedicated to the Duke of Orléans was that the regent was a good chemist. The reference to the signifier *Potosi*, which Defoe had already used in his *De jure divino*, is very clear. The metaphor had become reality. Indeed, it was not transmutation itself that was at work but a secret operation, revealed and chemical, the mystery of which Bossuet spoke, that produced prosperity in a manner unknown to the public. The economic program of the System was, indeed, a chrysopoeia of a new genre that used two instruments: the search for metals and paper money.

Through his *Enquête*, the regent continued Homberg's research program. Since it was not possible to transmute base metals into gold in the laboratory of the Palais-Royal, mining exploration and knowledge of the properties of metals became a national priority. It was a matter of creating several Potosis—in the literal sense of the word—in both France and its colonies, as explained by Terrasson in May 1718 in the *Nouveau Mercure*.[31] It was also a case of importing gold and silver from the real Potosi and its avatars in Spanish America through foreign trade, and in this respect the Compagnie-Banque was the perfect instrument.

A song in twelve stanzas, untitled but dedicated to Law and his System, played on a very large number of registers, the second six-line stanza of its handwritten version making a complete reference to alchemy:

> . . . Without coal, furnace or bellows
> Did a man discover the Secret

Of the Philosopher's Stone
In a Western land
He proves that up to this point
We were but ignoramuses.[32]

It was not the traditional instruments of the chemist that were necessary to discover the "Great Work," but rather ships, settlers, enslaved people, and merchandise. By creating a trading monopoly, gold and silver from the colonies (the "Western land") would not only enter the kingdom more easily than when deleterious competition reigned among traders but would also do so in a very different way. Through the heart, the Royal Bank, precious metals were directly paid in to the state treasury, but for a very short time only. Indeed, they were immediately withdrawn to promote trade and colonization and, thus, to create a new inflow of gold and silver. Nor should we forget that the Compagnie des Indes held a monopoly on the manufacture of currency and that even in the eighteenth century the borders between metallurgy, the minting of coins, and alchemy were still uncertain.[33] For the principle to work, however, it was necessary for a second instrument to be in place, namely, paper money, metal coinage remaining the tool of the power of the state. Once again, chemistry was at the heart of the problem.

In the England of the 1640s, the "Hartlibians" were, according to Carl Wennerlind, "[a] group of scholars, natural philosophers, and social improvers gathered around the Prussian émigré Samuel Hartlib in the 1640s" who "launched an ambitious alchemical—and Baconian—informed project for the improvement of nature, society and mankind." Their basic idea was that, since wealth could potentially increase indefinitely through trade, it was necessary proportionately to increase the amount of currency ensuring the transactions. Where this did not happen, the nation risked seeing trade dry up. The way in which this was to be done was through the transmutation of metals. Knowledgeable in the latest chemical innovations, the Hartlibians launched a serious research program to achieve this end. After many failures, they started looking at a stopgap solution, an expedient that could help remedy the shortage of currency. They thus imagined another form of transmutation. One of them, William Potter, suggested the establishment of a private bank by a small number of merchants who would put into circulation paper money guaranteed by a system of collateral and insurance. This time it was no longer base metals that were transmuted into gold but the metal coins and property (both real estate and personal property) of the merchants that were transformed into currency. Gold became paper. The spirit in which the experiments of the "Great Work" were conducted led to an earnings process of a whole new but equivalent type: "While alchemical transmutation failed to eliminate the scarcity of money problem, alchemical thinking nevertheless contributed to its eventual solution by inspiring and informing the development of a generally circulating credit currency."[34]

The ideas of the Hartlibians regarding land banks, credit, and paper money preceded by at least half a century John Law's work on these issues. In the view of some historians, the former gave the latter the idea of his *Money and Trade* (1705), while others, more circumspect, think that it is impossible to state that Law was familiar with the work of the English scientists.[35] This point is, nevertheless, irrelevant with regard to the subject at hand. Indeed, the question is not whether Law actually read Potter or more generally was familiar with the work of the Hartlibians. What is important is that Houdar de la Motte's allegory and other items of the propaganda were highly accurate, the development of trade and paper money having, indeed, an intellectual origin that was chemical in nature. Once again, it is wrong to brush aside this publicity of the System. The secret in general is the trademark of the inventors and engineers of the early modern period; it is the normal language of all the projectors. Better still, the System extended the metallurgical issues of the academicians and of the *Enquête du régent*. It had chemical implications. The experiment became part of an "economy of secrets": the propagandists explain that they are arcanists in power and that, thanks to them, natural constraints disappeared and man had the power to change reality intentionally. This was undoubtedly a dangerous and provocative idea, hence the recourse to that of a "revelation," signifying that the regent and Law were God's instruments. In his poem entitled "Challenge to Monsieur Law," the artist Charles-Antoine Coypel drew an analogy with one of Christ's most well-known miracles:

> With five little loaves and three small fish
> Did God once feed a countless number:
>   Law by his admirable genius,
> Does thus feed his blessed infants;
> The five little hundred francs, unbelievable wonder!
>   Multiplied a hundred ways
> Have satisfied the most insatiable hunger. . . .[36]

The same language is used in the following verses: thanks to the shares in the Compagnie des Indes (the "five little hundred francs"), Law had accomplished "resounding miracles." He "gave birth to abundance" from "the bosom of infertility." Better yet, he was "the Joseph of France" or, in other terms, the new son of Jacob who had brought prosperity to Egypt. Law was God's instrument, as suggested in another poem mixing references to pagan antiquity and biblical exegesis:

> Minerva is in these places and Law is this Mentor, . . .
> Both great and small experience his mighty deeds,
> He is for all the French a guardian angel,
> The whole world resounds to his good deeds.[37]

Accompanied by the conservative Minerva depicted in the engraving published by Jollain (fig. 3.2), and with Christ Himself as his model, Law spread his "good deeds" with justice (to "great and small") throughout the world. He was a "guardian angel" watching over the kingdom. This "purely spiritual and intellectual creature"[38] could not be quite of this world. Nor, it goes without saying, could his works. The *Nouveau Mercure* of December 1719 published a poem about a poor lover of the Muses mourning the fact that he did not have enough money to buy shares. Lamenting his fate, he praised the incredible benefits of the "paper of the West" (the shares):

> . . . O new paper of the West,
> Child of a wise ministry,
> Come into the light, we are awaiting you,
> You our guardian angel. . . .[39]

This time it was no longer Law but, by metonymy, his paper that was considered a "guardian angel." The latter was the miraculous instrument of the creature who had created it. But this assimilation of the creator of the System to an angel could result only in a Manichaean struggle.

Guardian was defined at that period as that which "guards, protects": "[U]sed only when speaking of angels and saints. *The Guardian Angel of France*."[40] In the mythology of the French monarchy, the archangel Michael was the guardian of the kingdom. It is he who, in the book of Revelation, triumphs over the armies of Satan, the angel who carries the souls of the dead to heaven and holds the scales at the Last Judgment. It was, therefore, Law-Michael who had to lead the fight against the forces of evil. In his last letter published in May 1720, Terrasson stated: "[T]he victory of good over evil being nigh, not in the mind of the ignorant and powerless rebel, but in the views of the Prince & the Master, we shall soon see the fruits that this imaginary good [paper money and shares] is alone capable of producing."[41] Two factors were at work here: a form of Manichaeanism and an eschatological theodicy.

Much of Terrasson's *Traité de l'infini créé* is devoted to the heavenly Jerusalem. On Earth, or rather on the infinite worlds inhabited by human beings, men were one of two things, "either righteous or unrighteous." At the destruction of their planet, the bodies of the righteous would disappear, and they would become angels capable of traveling throughout the universe, while the unrighteous would be transformed into demons and tormented in hell until the end of time. Planets and humans were born every moment, Terrasson believing in the infinite nature of both the spirit and matter: "Every moment, God creates an infinity of spirits and, to give them bodies, He is forced to increase the already infinite amount of matter He has already created infinitely. The omnipotence of God therefore consists in creating an infinite work and in being able to increase it infinitely."[42] Matter was created by succession, in proportion to the number of spirits.

The homology with the System is obvious here. Law's experiment was a divine work in the sense that it formed part of the permanent re-creation of currency by the heart represented by the Compagnie-Banque. The real chemists had discovered how to operate a process of "generation" of monetary coins that was infinite, depending on the state's requirements. The heart worked like the heavenly Jerusalem in that it swallowed up the matter (metal coins) to leave only the spirit (paper money). But, as the matter was infinite, it was thus used to re-create coinage through the expenses of the Compagnie des Indes, which maintained foreign trade and mineral exploration and, consequently, the inflow of precious metals. The spirit, paper money, traveled throughout the kingdom and even across Europe like a "guardian angel," accomplishing all good deeds. But for this heavenly Jerusalem to become reality, for the heart to function correctly, an eschatological battle was at work. It was necessary to separate the "righteous" from the "unrighteous," and that is why, in the System, Terrasson continually opposed two groups, those he called the "confident," on the one side, and the "distrustful," the "rebels," or the "dissidents," on the other. The former participated enthusiastically in all the System's undertakings, while the latter spoke out against them and refused to exchange their gold and rentes for paper money or shares in the Compagnie. Regarding the latter, Law clearly stated what would happen to them: "If they keep their money, they will be punish'd by their idleness, or by their dissidence in the one and the other case, and not merit the compassion which the *Parlement* pleads for towards them."[43] The idea of divine punishment is clearly present here, Law placing himself in the position of the archangel judging the rentiers and misers who have both disobeyed the master and contributed to their own misfortune. The "confident" and those who gave their money to the System, however, were to all intents and purposes promised the same benefits as the settlers in Louisiana.

Spending, Lottery, and Theodicy

It is very unlikely that the *Fable of the Bees* (1705, 1714) of the philosopher Bernard de Mandeville (1670–1733) was known in France during the Regency. Besides, his famous economic point about "private vices, publick benefits," or the idea that the prodigal is a blessing to society as a whole, was expressed by Jean Pottier de la Hestroye as early as 1699–1700. The thought of the latter, as we have seen, has certainly played a greater role in the construction of the System than did Mandeville. But it does not matter because we are faced with a theoretical moment, on both sides of the Channel, in which several theoreticians express the same idea, that, as identified by Michael Kwass, of the "virtues of prodigality": "Spending, they reasoned, pumped money into the economy, connected countryside and town, and sustained artisanal labor."[44] We have seen why the heart of the System spent a great deal: it crucially needed the commercial and colonial enterprise to work. The same had to apply to individuals, who would thus allow wealth to trickle down to all classes in society.

In 1715, the *Nouveau Mercure* had published portions of Monsieur Roy's aforementioned dissertation on the subject of "the disadvantages of wealth," which had won the eloquence prize of the Académie française. In his paper, the author attacked luxury spending, considering that only charity could relieve the poor, not consumption by the rich. In 1719, this same institution awarded the same prize to a dissertation the arguments of which were the exact opposite of Roy's. This was Pannier d'Orgeville's "The Throne of the King Who Judges the Poor in Truth Shall Be Established Forever." The *Nouveau Mercure* eagerly published excerpts of it in August, and, on reading it, one can easily understand why. On the one hand, Pannier defended the idea that the state would die out if it oppressed "the poor," the latter being the most useful to the former. "[W]ere the State to declare war on them, if of these fruits produced by the labor of their hands it were to deprive them of what they need to sustain it [their labor], their weakness would avenge them." On the other hand, he argued that only the flow of wealth would allow that same state to be prosperous. In his view, it was, therefore, necessary for the rich to imitate the poor, in other words, to spend quickly and fully all they received. Pannier thus criticized "these large gulfs" "that avarice or suspicion contain," these treasures "from which nothing is taken, around which the dry and barren countryside suffers from famine."[45] He considered spending by the rich as a "public benefit": "These goods lost to him are riches that, so to speak, emerge anew from the bowels of the earth: it was in his hands a hidden talent that becomes useful to civil society." In short, spending had to be encouraged. Already, in December 1718, the *Nouveau Mercure* had summarized a sermon given at the Collège Louis-le-Grand by the Reverend Father Charles Porée (1675–1741) supporting this same idea. In his sermon, Porée explained that, while the "excesses" on the part of the "Prodigal Son" had brought about his own ruin, they "were in a way beneficial for society in general."[46] We can understand better why Voltaire, a former student and a great admirer of Porée, so strongly defended worldly pleasure in *Le mondain* (1736) and especially why he was so receptive to the English controversy surrounding Mandeville's *Fable of the Bees* in the mid-1720s. Porée was close to the Moderns,[47] and we have already seen how hostile the latter were to austerity and frugality and how much in favor they were of luxury spending. This idea is clearly expressed in a staggering passage of the letter that Pannier d'Orgeville published in April 1720 in support of the System:

> [To] speak dispassionately, it is important to the State that its Subjects be wealthy, but it is mostly indifferent to whom among them hold this wealth, other than the King. . . . [R]egardless of who holds this wealth, it circulates through Trade. All those who have made a quick fortune are also quick to pour out their wealth. Vanity does for some what sentiment does for others. The ridiculous pomp of an unwise expense does not make it any less useful to society, & mad profusion makes better amends than reasonable use for the injustice of fortune.[48]

This passage contains two essential ideas that had both advantages and disadvantages for the System. The first concerns the virtue of spending, the second the notion of a lottery. For the proponents of the System, if greed had to be channeled, directed by the state, the same did not hold true of prodigality. Consumption, even excessive, and the dissipation of wealth were considered to be intrinsically good. The propagandists' reasoning was subtle. None of them believed that the material prosperity of society could be the result of a desire for enrichment on the part of individuals. Their vanity, however, their taste for luxury, in short anything that drove them to spend lavishly, led to a circulation of wealth that contributed to the working of society as a whole. General prosperity occurred when the money that was previously held "captive" by "the spirit of avarice" "escapes," as alleged by the anonymous author of the *Histoire des finances*.[49] Similarly, in his *Projet d'édit*, John Law explained that the king wanted not to "accumulate" but rather to "spread" wealth. These passages clearly echoed the various reports by Pottier de la Hestroye, who, between 1698 and 1699, did not hesitate to write: "[N]o matter where the riches, or who among the subjects possess them, provided that everything be in the Kingdom, or that the State enjoy the benefit of them." He had already criticized the "hoarders" and praised the nouveaux riches who "engage in superfluous spending beyond their means, [for] it is a vice that does nothing to the State, or rather that far from losing, the State wins in this situation."[50]

From the poet and economist Antoine de Montchrestien (1575–1621) to Vauban, and not forgetting Colbert and Locke, the so-called mercantilist writers did not always condemn luxury spending, which was considered acceptable if the goods purchased were manufactured in the kingdom. They nevertheless felt it was preferable to sell such luxury goods in foreign markets to receive precious metals in return. The reason for this was simple: domestic trade was a zero-sum game. If what Peter produced was purchased by Paul, then the kingdom would be none the richer.[51] The propagandists of the System did not see things in the same way. They believed in the possibility of an organic growth of wealth within the kingdom. This was true in the case of Terrasson, who never ceased to ask his readers: "[W]hat profession has not experienced the riches resulting from the new System?" The end of his first letter described the incredible prosperity that the renewed flow of spending had supposedly generated: merchants and workers incapable of supplying the astronomical demand on the part of buyers, debtors freed of their debts, and even the lower classes "find[ing] the means to live, to earn money, to grow rich." In his last letter, he added that, in order to realize that everyone had become rich, "one has but to enter private houses indiscriminately, . . . to make one's way through the streets of Paris." This was also the case of Pannier d'Orgeville, who described, not a transfer of wealth, but rather a form of contagious prosperity: "The Common People who trade the most with the Rich are the first to feel their abundance; but gradually, & over time, everyone participates."[52]

It was necessary to encourage spending, to educate the rich in this new virtue in order to increase this prosperity. The fable entitled *L'amour et la fortune*, published in January 1720 in the *Nouveau Mercure*, used this pedagogy:

> Said Love one day to Fortune
> We each of us have our Court:
> No one has both my favors & yours at the same time,
> Some are lacking in possessions, others in the art of pleasing.
> Let us both agree this day:
> Let us have the pleasure of making a man happy,
> Let us choose a mortal of lovely appearance. . . .

It is at this point that the two deities decide to "drop" wealth in the lap of a poor but handsome young man. And to perform this miracle is yet another magical entity:

> I have few such favorites,
> Then said with a smile
> The Deity of the Royal Bank:
> With barrel after barrel shall I pour down gold upon him,
> That according to his desires shall he draw from my treasure:
> That without fearing my fickleness
> Shall he indulge the whims of his generous heart, . . .
> No sooner said than done:
> His generosity shall not be limited:
> In the evening he shall not be satisfied,
> If during the day he has not made himself
> Known through a few kindnesses.[53]

If money was hoarded, if the circulation of wealth was stopped, then the whole body would no longer be fed. Hence the famous declaration of February 18, 1720, prohibiting goldsmiths from manufacturing and selling gold and silver objects above a certain weight and the order of February 27, 1720, prohibiting paying and even holding large sums in cash.[54] Both the state and individuals were expected to spend a lot and quickly, to "indulge their every whim." In other words, the "Deity of the Royal Bank" allowed for giving expression to the hitherto repressed desires of the individual. It took the most famous fairy tales of the Western imagination, such as *Donkeyskin* and *Fortunatus*, which had experienced unprecedented popularity among a very wide readership in France between the late seventeenth century and the early eighteenth, and turned them into reality. The story of Fortunatus features a generous giant with a purse that is continually replenished, much like the donkey in Perrault's tale. Fortunatus is given the power magically to produce gold, a power conferred on him by "Lady Fortune." This good fairy adopts a parental role in this tale, providing Fortunatus with both protection and inheritance. She also teaches him how he should use his gifts, notably by being generous. It was the same in the previous fable and in the System: the Compagnie-Banque, this totalizing goddess, acted as a mother and/or father figure (depending on which glory the propaganda needed to mobilize, that of trade or that of the king), giving each of his/her disciples this wonderful power and explaining to them how it should be spent.[55]

The actor and playwright Marc-Antoine Legrand gave to the Comédie française his farce *Plutus* in February 1720, from Aristophanes's play. In the ancient version, the god of wealth, Plutus, is blind because villains as well as good people benefit from his generosity. In Legrand's play, on the contrary, he recovered his sight and began to give wealth to an honorable family of poor farmers. In accordance with the principles of the System, which has destroyed the General Farm, Plutus is now the enemy of the "usurers and partisans": "He has forced four underfarmers [of taxes] to disgorge so as to enrich a painter, & two skilled poets; a younger son of Paphos, & two wise *grisettes*." As in *L'amour et la fortune*, wealth "falls" on those who are usually forgotten—artists, young people in need—while former financiers are punished for their arrogance. Plutus faced at the beginning Poverty, personified as a beggar. What is interesting in this play is that Poverty uses a logic that is the reverse of that employed by Boisguilbert and the great majority of the political economists of the eighteenth century. She demands a mercantilist way of thinking since she does not consider self-interest a sufficient cause to make the poor work. They must be forced to work by low wages, by indigence. Rather, Plutus is openly in support of the System: everyone must be rich, even the former poor, in order to consume. In the play, one character says of the god: "[I]f he enriches folks who spend a lot of money, this is the means to see the abundance begin to return, all the arts flourish." In a satiric scene of the fable *Le savetier et le financier* by Jean de La Fontaine (1621–95), Legrand's characters explain to "Master Birennes," the craftsman, who is concerned about having been given wealth by Plutus, that the solution is simple: he just has to spend the money, on wine, on clothes! In La Fontaine's fable, the unfortunate craftsman, who cannot sleep, gave back the treasure to the financier. Legrand had to find another solution more in line with the System: expenditures. Birennes found that solution very good: "Your advice, Carion, is the best. Buy some wine, and drink until being drunk." Legrand's *Plutus* takes the connection with *L'amour et la fortune*—of which he was perhaps the author—to the point of explaining: "Love & I have never, despite our best efforts, been united in a sincere friendship. But today we agree to please you. Lovers, fear no longer that fate will oppose you, you can defy it in marriage [*hymen*] on this day, when you have both Plutus & Love on your side." The play ends with this observation on marriage, harmony, opulence, and liberality.[56]

Generosity was fashionable at the time. For example, in December 1719, the *Nouveau Mercure* published the anti-*Turcaret* theater play *L'actionnaire bigame*, which was certainly written or inspired by Dufresny.[57] The scenario of the play was identical to that of Lesage's *Turcaret*. The main character is a financier who married in the provinces but is now living in Paris and in love with a young widow whom he wants to marry. The widow in question does not, however, love him back. Rather, she has set her sights on a greedy young aristocrat and decides to use the financier to achieve her ends. Unlike the ruthless Turcaret, the shareholder—known as the "Mississippian"—is generous and tender. He agrees to a secret marriage with the young widow because she does not want to give up her illustrious name. All she is interested in is his money, which he gives her in abundance. And it is this generosity that finally solves everything. The young widow is furious when she learns that the shareholder is already married but is soon consoled on receiving a few hundred thousand livres from him. Finally, she can marry the young aristocrat, and the generous shareholder's first wife comes to Paris to live with him.

In this play, the men are heroes as Terrasson imagined them: if the Mississippian left his first wife, it was not out of malice but because she was a harpy. In all his actions, the shareholder displayed the qualities of nobility, courage and restraint, except when it came to spending, where his extravagance and generosity were legendary. The women, on the other hand, are portrayed as greedy, interested only in money. The following poem was published after *L'actionnaire bigame*, further emphasizing the moral of the play:

May you prove, o lovers, by commercial bills
The gentle power of our attraction still . . .

Send us such bills, not billets-doux,
With frivolous writings do not us woo.

Suppress your passion,
I demand submission,
And not confidence,
To paint your affection
With more eloquence;
O lovers, talk to us of Shares;
Or else prefer silence.[58]

In the May 1719 issue of the *Nouveau Mercure*, a poem explained that a woman grew rich with a shareholder but poor with an officer. A few months later, a vaudeville in verse described how the daughter of a prosecutor courted by a shareholder asked him "how much he earned each month." Hearing the answer, "she was satisfied" and agreed to marry him. Thus, while the System promised natives to the settlers, it also promised greedy Parisians to the shareholders.[59]

But the "Deity of the Royal Bank" was also the "Lady Credit" of Defoe and Addison and, therefore, the Fortuna that Pocock identified. However, in this interpretation, she was an unstable deity, prone to mood swings, making the allegory ambivalent. Fortuna was the opposite of Virtù, who symbolized the stability of the old order, the absence of any eventualities or contingencies.[60] The way in which this was manifested here was through the random nature of the distribution of wealth. The goddesses of *L'amour et la fortune* "chose" a young man, supposedly at random. Then another goddess paid him money. As in the letter by Pannier d'Orgeville, wealth was "dropped" in a person's lap, without anyone knowing very well how or why. Was it due to work, productive activity, or effort? Was there a principle of inheritance, a military or civilian position that induced wealth? Absolutely not. In French, as in English, the word *fortune* means both wealth and luck. The goddesses chose one mortal among others, a young man who had only one thing going for him: his looks. In summary, the blessed had no merit. There is probably some irony here. *Plutus* and *L'amour et la fortune* promoted the merits of expenditures, and, on this issue, there is no ambiguity. The System needed a lot of spending. On the one hand, if the shareholders hoard money, the machine of the heart, the Compagnie-Banque, cannot function properly; on the other, if domestic consumption is relatively strong, prosperity touches every class of society. But the fabulist did not fail to notice the ambiguity of the System, which is a kind of lottery. The young man has done nothing to deserve his wealth. Irony is twofold because the meaning of the fable is not fixed; it remains fleetingly open. The reader may find it shocking that the System enriches anyone, but he can also find that it is a nice snook to traditional hierarchies. Is it not wonderful if, for once, it is not always the same one who wins? This is what was suggested in Legrand's *Plutus*,[61] and this was the way some authors of the Théâtre de la foire (the collective name given to the theater productions put on at the annual fairs in Paris) would interpret it. They would have liked the fable actually to happen and the poor of the day before to be able to laugh a little and pull the rich down from their height forever.

The System viewed its operation as follows. First, it was necessary to manufacture more and more rich people (at random). Next, those rich people had to spend their money, thereby sending wealth down to the working classes and toward the heart, the Compagnie-Banque, which, finally, was itself continually investing. Ultimately, the quantity of labor increased, to the benefit of all classes of society. Of course, the phenomenon was inflationary. But it was a healthy rise in prices and wages that occurred: "When we shall have nothing more to fear but the high prices that result from consumption, then all we shall have to fear is public opulence." Wanting to refute the idea that it would be the devaluation of currency or the increase in the money supply that would cause an increase in prices, Pannier d'Orgeville believed only in a period of demand-pull inflation. In other words, prices would rise because the factories, merchants, and farmers would not be able to meet the demand for goods and services. Wages, meanwhile, would increase "proportionately," with little or no loss of purchasing power.[62]

The letters written by Pannier d'Orgeville and Terrasson as well as several poems and fables published during the winter of 1719–20 thus developed two ideas. First, there was a notion of lottery, where money would be distributed randomly, as discussed by Pannier d'Orgeville and in *L'amour et la fortune*. Moreover, the state was perfectly indifferent to who was rich or who was not given that, second, there was no need to be worthy to become rich. Or, more precisely, the old criteria of merit (birth, services rendered, public office) were disqualified. Indeed, through Terrasson, the System promised that, henceforth, "the door of wealth has been opened to everyone, & this is what constitutes the main difference between the fortunes of the former administration and those of the current."[63] In his *Mémoire pour servir à justifier la Compagnie des Indes*, Terrasson openly returned to the random nature of the experiment, in the same way as everything we have seen regarding Louisiana:

> [I]t is rare to find Treasures, to gather Diamonds or Pearls. . . . But while this is rare, it does sometimes happen. The event of the Shares in the Compagnie des Indes is & will ever remain without precedent. These profits that chance has so unequally divided, at least prove that gains and losses have not been fraudulently devised. . . . In Commerce as in Gambling, wealth does not conform to the rules of the Police; it does not distinguish between Gentleman and Commoner. This may shock you, but it is as God has ordained.[64]

Terrasson's discourse raises at least three points. The first relates to the internal consistency of the propaganda, which appears to be in doubt here. Payment for shares should be equated with a rente, a fixed and stable income, like the activity underlying it. Yet, as we have seen, Terrasson introduced the notion of gambling to explain the huge gains that some had made thanks to their shares. He sought, however, to reconcile both positions and probably saw no contradiction in his statements. Indeed, the wealth he mentioned came, not from the remuneration of the shares, but rather from the increase in their price. He explained that this increase—and the ensuing wealth of the shareholders—could be compared to a deceased person's estate, the full value of which was unknown during the person's lifetime. The same applied to the Compagnie, which was subject to increasingly great expectations as the extent of its trade became known. The stock price rose; people became wealthy. The idea was, therefore, not to question the stability of the trading nation's activities, but simply to arrive at the conclusion that they continually increased.

Moreover, the "Commerce" referred to here was not the trade undertaken by the Compagnie des Indes but rather the selling and purchasing of shares by individuals. Terrasson was very clear on this point: he condemned "greed" and "stockjobbing" but considered that one could not prevent people from "trading" shares or "other commercial paper." The increase in wealth was, therefore, not the result of a suddenly exponential dividend paid out to the shareholders. Another potential problem in the internal consistency of the System concerned the issue of laziness. We have seen how the propagandists criticized the "idle" rentiers. But was this phenomenon not produced by the shares, given that one could grow rich while sleeping? Here we find the whole ambiguous nature of these *actions rentières*. The propaganda constantly had to find a balance between a conservative discourse (the System as a return to a former order of a protonoble life) and one that was more innovative (productive and rich shareholders).

The second reflection concerns the more general question of gambling. At the start of the eighteenth century, the vice-ridden salon gambler was a recurring theme in criticism,[65] but the discourse on a more specific form of gambling—lotteries—began to change. These lotteries developed at the end of the seventeenth century in Europe under the impetus of hospitals and religious communities. The way they were structured was that the total amount of the prizes offered was less than the sum collected by the sale of the tickets. The surplus, or "precipitate," was allocated to the relief of the poor and needy. The discourse of jurists and theologians, who until then had strongly condemned lotteries, also changed at that time. In fact, two elements must be distinguished in their reactions: the question of the distribution of winnings randomly among the players and that of the precipitate generated for the institution. In 1697, Cardinal Noailles entrusted two Parisian seminaries (one of which, Saint-Magloire, was the main center of French Jansenism) with the task of setting up moral debates that were to reconcile the dogmas of the church with the jurisprudence of the kingdom. The results of this work were the subject of the 1718 *Conférences ecclésiastiques de Paris sur l'usure et la restitution*, a publication edited by a movement sympathizer.[66] This text explains that lotteries "can be allowed only for a public good": "Such were the lotteries that in recent times have been allowed in favor of parish churches, for the subsistence of the poor, or to support communities in need. The reason is, that according to the principles of Saint Augustine, & Saint Thomas, it is not allowed to use chance [*le sort*] for recreation or for one's entertainment; & it is for this reason that all the Laws condemn games of chance where the possibility of winning is abandoned to the hands of fortune."[67] Thus, the legality of the random distribution of winnings was contingent on the purpose of the lottery itself. A few years earlier, the Jesuit Father Claude-François Menestrier and the lawyer Jean Barbeyrac had started to open up a less rigorous path, explaining that, under certain conditions, all lotteries were lawful, whatever their goals. The question of the distribution of gains was no longer crucial when one considered, as Menestrier did, that "God, who is the author of all goods & who dispenses them unequally for reasons that his providence has reserved to itself, exercises his justice in these inequalities."[68] So let us return to the System. On the one hand, its propagandists openly maintained that its aim was the "public good": increasing the wealth of the kingdom, relieving the poor, lowering the tax burden, etc. Better still, works such as *Plutus* or *L'amour et la fortune* suggested that it would actually be the permanently destitute whom the experiment had enriched. Therefore, the System was a charitable operation, and some of the gains it generated could in fairness be distributed by chance, as the *Conférences* stated. On the other hand, Terrasson could argue for a providential plan that led the lotteries to do good in a way that eluded human understanding, as in Menestrier. This is the path he seems to have favored. Was the System therefore a kind of lottery? Not according to Terrasson, for whom it was a theodicy.

As a disciple of Fontenelle, Terrasson no doubt recalled Fontenelle's "In Praise of Monsieur de Leibniz," a speech he gave to the Académie des sciences in 1716, and Leibniz's "Principles of Metaphysics Founded in Reason," published in the *Nouveau Mercure* of November 1718.[69] Fontenelle praised the *Essais de théodicée* (1710) as "the greatest work by Monsieur de Leibniz." The academician summarized the subject of the book thus: God having found an infinity of possible worlds, he chose the least bad, in which there certainly existed "some evil," "allowed" but not "wanted": "This world so deserving of preference included the pain & evil deeds of men, but in a smaller number, & with the most advantageous results possible."[70] We have seen that Terrasson supported a form of eschatological theodicy in the sense that those who believed in the System would be rewarded after the victory of the archangel Law-Michael. He also supported a theodicy of hidden harmony. Men without merit were elevated above other men, the "righteous" were sometimes persecuted by the "unrighteous": "[W]e do not always comprehend God's plans: but we cannot doubt that they are just."[71] If wealth was distributed somewhat at random, there was a preestablished, hidden plan that would undoubtedly lead to widespread prosperity. Thus, even evil itself was useful: "The new System is so fortunate that the trust & the distrust that one may have with respect to it also turn to the advantage of the Kingdom. Trust leads to investing in the Commerce of the Indies, while distrust leads to clearing land & building houses." In other words, the believers bought and held shares, while the bad disciples converted their cash into land or buildings. The latter undoubtedly slowed down the establishment of the System, making it necessary continually to show them where their advantage lay. But a theodicy nevertheless led them to do good against their will. Naturally, this mediate way included the logic of spending: the more that was consumed, the more that was invested, and the more work that was created for the entire social body.[72] While the System contained a random dimension, it was not this aspect that produced prosperity. Rather, it was the generalized increase in spending and the circulation of wealth.

The third point raised by the Terrasson quote regarding "Treasures" concerns the issue of social taxonomy. In a kingdom haunted by the maintenance or, conversely, the subversion of hierarchies, within an administration that sought at all costs to maintain a good daily order, that of the market, the stalls, the open shops, and the taverns, the prospect of a wealth that more or less "fell" on anyone and with which you could do anything (spending it in any way at all) had a frightening scope. "When we promised that the System would enrich the Kingdom," affirmed Terrasson, "this promise in no way signified that it would retain the wealth for the same Individuals who possessed it."[73] This time it was no longer the theater but the state that suggested that servants could become rich. It was the authorities who insinuated a subversion of the social order.

State Carnivalesque Literature and a New System of Nature

Carnival is a time of the reversal of values, hierarchies, truths, and power. In the Middle Ages and under the ancien régime, at certain times of the year and for periods extending from a few days to several weeks, individuals were permitted to adopt ridiculous, subversive, and even sacrilegious behaviors. Free speech was tolerated by both the worldly and the spiritual powers. In his classic studies of Rabelais and Dostoyevsky, the literary theorist Mikhail Bakhtin extended this notion of carnival. In *Problems of Dostoevsky's Poetics* (1929), Bakhtin asserted that, like the carnival itself, carnivalesque literature broke with traditional forms of writing and thinking to pave the way for emancipation projects. From the mid-seventeenth century until the late nineteenth, a specific genre of writing, Menippean satire, was substituted for the subversive capacity of the real carnival. Menippean satire was "a striking combination" of "philosophical dialogue, adventure and fantasticality, slum naturalism, utopia, and so forth": "[T]he clamping principle that bound all these heterogeneous elements into the organic whole of a genre . . . was carnival, and a carnival sense of the world."[74] More generally, the main characteristic of carnivalesque literature is its capacity to replace the vertical hierarchy of official culture with horizontal contact between different cultures, which interact without precedence. It mixes the opposites the sacred and the profane, blurs identities, and reveals what was previously concealed or repressed.[75]

Between summer 1719 and summer 1720, it was the semiofficial government gazette the *Nouveau Mercure* that endorsed the three main characteristics of carnivalesque literature. The concept of the familiar, which placed different cultures and languages on the same level, was omnipresent in it. In October 1719, the newspaper published a prophecy by Nostradamus, the famous astrologer well-known to readers of the *livres bleus*, that is, inexpensive publications of various sorts—almanacs, astrological predictions, practical advice of all kinds, poetry, novels, and miscellaneous facts—sold by hawkers and comparable to English chapbooks of the period. Nostradamus had supposedly predicted the prosperity of the kingdom of France under "lavv" (Law), and his strange affirmation was published alongside foreign news, royal edicts, and the like.[76] The previous month, the actor Marc-Antoine Legrand had used Rabelaisian vocabulary ("Bouteille fait glou glou," "Ja l'on fait la nique au Pérou") to extol the merits of the System. Again, such a piece of writing did not belong to the same language register as other parts of the *Mercure* or even the poems and propaganda songs published in the same issue. Regarding carnivalesque mésalliances, the festival reached its peak in October 1719. In the section "Fugitive Facts," Buchet went beyond measure. It was impossible, he wrote, to speak of the fortunes made through the System because "this would require naming almost all Paris." He specified that the few examples that he would mention, "while somewhat improbable, are nonetheless true." He thus referred to a formerly poor man who wanted to buy a coach but did not know the technical terms and spoke in street vernacular, another who was in a hurry to find silverware for a dinner he was organizing the very same evening and bought out a silversmith's shop, and an "ex-footman" who bought the coach "belonging to his former master." (Every time it started raining, he "climb[ed] on the back through force of habit.") Everywhere, servants were leaving their positions as they were, henceforth, richer than their masters, while provincials were buying "two or three lords' domains." In November, this litany was repeated: richly dressed and bejeweled, but of course very ugly, a former laundress was given away at the opera by her speech. In a word, everything was mixed: language registers, hierarchies, and identities.[77]

Thus, the rumors from the capital, the ports of the kingdom, and Louisiana were transformed by the authorities to serve as propaganda. The government fantasy, this magical politics in prose, verse, maps, and engravings, spread among the people. The fable of the poor man suddenly become rich went on to become one of the great topoi of the post-System literature and especially of the counterpropaganda of the traditional elites, for obvious reasons. And, at the peak of the experiment, the dissemination of pro-System propaganda was working at full capacity. The *Lettres historiques*, a periodical printed in the Netherlands, simply reproduced the pages of the *Nouveau Mercure* devoted to these extraordinary stories in its issues of November and December 1719. Also in Holland, the *Gazette d'Amsterdam* considered it necessary to say about the System in February 1720 that "as many abuses have crept in among the servants, a Regulation is being drafted by which those who leave their stations without certificates shall be driven out of this City, and, for repeat offenders, sent immediately to Mississippi." With some delay, *La suite de la clef, ou Journal de Verdun*, published, in May 1720, a poem in praise of the System that recounted the story of a poor man turned millionaire "driving around with much pomp in a superb coach." This poem was immediately followed by Terrasson's first two letters. As for the *Mercure historique*, it embroidered the same topic in its issue of January 1720, writing that "he who has been poor for a long time . . . in but a few days found himself with huge property and possessions." While the *Nouveau Mercure* of October had just been published, one of the Parisian correspondents of the marquise de Balleroy, who lived in Normandy, told her on November 12, 1719, about the nouveau riche who rode on the back of his own coach, the one who bought out the silversmith's shop, etc. He even paraphrased Buchet's sentence in his letter, specifying that he was recounting "a tale that will seem somewhat improbable to you and yet is very true." One retypes government fairy tales. Chronicler Jean Buvat wrote in February 1720 how he had heard that in the homes of some lowly speculators there had been found "a prodigious amount of silverware of all kinds, exquisitely crafted and more beautiful than ever was seen in princely demesnes or in the residences of others of a rank distinguished by their nobility and their dignities."[78]

All these situations were highly improbable. But let me be clear: there is nothing to say that a few isolated cases of gain made by people of low birth did not occur. The idea, however, that the period was a carnival of poor people becoming rich, living in high style, and mixing with the nobility is obviously a fable, but it is precisely this which is interesting.[79] The state propaganda also took up the myth of the lackey-financier in an attempt to give it some consistency, a government unction. This point alone is exceptional. As the physiocrat Pierre-Samuel Dupont (1739–1817) said in 1769, the problem was not the exploitation of people's credulity that was annoying during the System of 1720; it was exploiting or "abus[ing] the government's trust, by putting its respectable seal to fables, to illusions."[80] The public authorities adopted a literary genre that, while not the enemy of authority, did at the very least serve to caricature and scoff at it. Carnivalesque literature considered life "drawn out of its *usual* rut": "[I]t is to some extent 'life turned inside out,' 'the reverse side of the world.' "[81] In other words, a state carnivalesque literature was a complete oxymoron.

Why did the Moderns go so far? This is the right question to ask. Taking on the register of fable and story was normal for them—indeed, it was what distinguished them. The problem was that this literature was here at the service of power. It took on a different meaning from the fictions they usually published. The System's propaganda promoted and endorsed new behaviors. What was unconscious, inconceivable, forbidden, became possible. But this was not entirely a configuration in which readers or spectators went to bed dreaming of that wonderful world that existed only in fables. The danger here was very great. Of course, the government carnival could be interpreted as a little hysterical surge of jubilation resulting from exceptionally new circumstances (sudden enrichment). But we must measure the seismic risk it represented. The kingdom of France was a hierarchical society made up of orders, bodies, and states. It drew its organization from the divine, which determined the sacredness of the functions and the privileges of the groups that composed society. While this essentialized vision was tested by mobile identities, social, religious, and ideological conflicts, and the rise of the central state and big business, it nonetheless remained the point of reference with which contemporaries thought about the society in which they lived.[82] How, in these circumstances, could one present in a positive way what might seem a reversal of the social (and divine) order? The Moderns had to know the price that needed to be paid for such a propaganda, one that valued the elevation, enrichment, and lavish expenditure of anyone, even people who had little: it was the outcry of the traditional holders of power, who did not fail to protest that it meant the destruction of society. But these same Moderns saw a number of advantages in this carnivalesque state propaganda. First, the enriched poor of government fables spent money. Showing off their fortunes was, indeed, what characterized them. In other words, they were virtuous rich people; they behaved as the System demanded. Then, those in power staged a debasement of the traditional ruling classes, in particular the *noblesse de robe*, a process that the government sought to bring to completion. It did so in an exaggerated manner and in the form of a symbolic killing: since officers, rentiers, certain major merchants, etc., were openly at war with the System and would in the future need to disappear to give way to the economic Leviathan, they must be metaphorically got rid of. The authorities expressed their (future) joy at the prospect of one day seeing people emerging from nowhere to replace part of the dominant elites, with the exception of the upper nobility. The nouveaux riches, indeed, were at a twofold advantage: they did not hoard, and they laid no claim to political power. The government carnival therefore announced that it was possible to live nobly, that is to say, without working, but only if the System so decided. It created its own dominant class, it distinguished its "believers." The shareholders bought land, buildings, and coaches, all without any condition of birth, lineage, function, or office—but on the condition that they did not oppose anything the state wanted. The propaganda said to all judicial officers, pensioners, etc., in no uncertain terms, that they would be well advised to consider changing their identities—becoming rich anonymous figures, disheveled spenders—rather than hanging on to prerogatives and forms of capital that would soon no longer exist.

Finally, valuing the enrichment of the dominated, of those without capital, above all meant playing the card of the debtors against that of the creditors. It was not a matter of treating the poor as fools. The propagandists of the System did not want them to believe that tomorrow they would all become wealthy. It simply wanted to get them to notice what benefits the System could offer. All the microhistorical studies indeed converge toward the same conclusion: the massive deleveraging, unprecedented and unparalleled, at least until the Revolution, of small plowmen, craftsmen, servants, and journeymen, thanks to paper money. In the towns and even in remote villages of the Pyrenees and Normandy, the North and Languedoc, these permanently oppressed people repaid their debts and the rentes they gave to religious institutions, notaries, big merchants, and nobles. The debtors did not buy coaches and dresses worthy of princesses; perhaps they may not have been able to walk away with the contents of a goldsmith's store; but they lived better. They consumed more alcoholic drinks (as in *Plutus*), they ate a little more meat, they bought new clothes and small plots of land. Walls, canopies, and "flat mats" (*paillassons plats*) were built to develop peach growing in Montreuil through the reimbursement of rentes. "You need to make the best of time" became the rallying cry of the peasants of Provence in 1719–20.[83] The magistrates of the *parlement* of Toulouse lamented in the spring of 1720 that the borrowers would henceforth be "richer than those who len[t]" since "it was necessary to relieve debtors of a huge amount of their debts." Tremendous amounts of land were reportedly purchased from the nobles in the countryside by their former creditors, so "more money came out of old houses in six months than in a whole century." For the *parlement* of Paris, "the greater part of the debts is currently discharged," and the debtors had "imposed conditions so onerous on the creditors that your majesty should no longer be concerned with anything but their relief."[84] This was certainly not the reversal of people's social conditions as found in the *Nouveau Mercure* tales, but in the villages and suburbs one could read or hear these tales of lackeys who had become rich without laughing. What might happen in Paris could now be imagined by comparing it with one's own situation, which was improving, and that is precisely what the government carnival sought to stage. The poor who benefited from the System would, perhaps, not understand quite what was going on; this needed to be vividly illustrated for their benefit.

For the propagandists, this involved an attempt to rely on strength in numbers against certain wealthy members of the *noblesse de robe* and businessmen. They sought to forge an alliance between the poor and the higher nobility (debtors) against the grumblers (the creditors) who were in-between. But they also sought to speak out for a new social stability, which was only superficially a paradox. At the start of the eighteenth century, in fact, the mercantilist conception of forced labor was combined with the religious conception of labor as redemption and as a discipline imposed on the common people, who were thought of as brutal, restless, lazy, and little inclined to intelligence. Idleness was conceivable only for honest people—the wellborn and well educated—whose bad inclinations did not need to be combated.[85] The System's propagandists offered a radically different view of things. In a bruised France, drained of blood, they did not find it worrying that the poor could now profit. Their reasoning was in line with their judgment of the Louis-Quatorzian monarchy: the latter was seen by the Moderns, not as a world of stability, but on the contrary as a vast chaos. The carnival for which they called was not something they saw as an appeal for moral relaxation and dissipation; rather, they viewed it as the subversion of a deeply incoherent, unstable, and unjust social order. The enriched poor, who spent money and made a profit, marked the advent of a finally prosperous society, one in which the spoilers and destroyers—rentiers, justice officers, the General Farm, etc.—would be crushed. The new wealthy class, devoted solely to spending and, therefore, to nourishing the social body, would generate much greater stability than did the old one, which lived solely on fiscal and agricultural plunder and, therefore, on the destruction of this same body. Consumption would to some degree replace work in buying salvation here on Earth.

The Moderns thus uttered prophecies that they hoped would be self-fulfilling. They narrated behaviors that may not actually have existed, at least not on this scale, but that they invited people to imitate, generalize, and spread. Much of the power of their fictions lay in the transformation of the media space that was taking place at the same time and, in particular, in the development of the then booming periodical press. We have seen that the so-called letters from Louisiana that appeared in the *Mercure* and certain maps from the Delisle–Le Maire–Bobé workshop were reproduced in the form of independent brochures intended for future American colonists. They were also reprinted in collections of travelogues and in other periodicals in 1720. Legrand's *Plutus* had sixteen performances, which was far from a ridiculous number and even testified to a small success; moreover, the play was immediately printed. Terrasson's letters, reproduced several times in the French-speaking press and then reprinted, were widely distributed. Above all, the *Nouveau Mercure* was undoubtedly the most widely read periodical of the time in France, and, as we have seen, its information was taken up by other newspapers and gossip writers of the time. It mainly reached an urban and literate audience, but it was cheaper than many of its competitors because of its large circulation; it benefited from royal privilege, and it was found in many public spaces (such as cabarets). It was the most widely distributed periodical in the provinces and the only one, along with the *Gazette de France*, available in rural areas thanks to hawkers. Reading it was not the only way to access it since its contents were often related at social evenings and some of the literary pieces it published were declaimed or sung on bridges, squares, and crossroads.[86] The propaganda of the System first, therefore, used different media supports, containing registers of language and heterogeneous literary genres, to address not so much individual subjects as an audience that was undefined in advance but needed to have the characteristic of simultaneously sharing the same beliefs. It was a matter of building a community of faithful followers of the System through a phenomenon of collective cohesion. Second, the Moderns hypothesized—and this does not seem completely wrong if one remembers Carlo Ginzburg's miller or the future readers of Jean-Jacques Rousseau—that individuals would be disposed to model some of their behavior on their readings.[87] Terrasson postulated that one could present good models to the public so as to shape it, to educate and form it, and this is what the System's propaganda did. This of course involved walking on the edge of a precipice that its supporters had dug themselves since then the possibility opened up that these media discourses would be transformed, falsified, turned around. When Terrasson declared in March 1720 that "the public is, so to speak, the arbiter of fortune,"[88] he knew that this collective cohesion, this imaginary community of believers, was at the same time being resisted by others, who were doing all they could to stop it coming into being.

The propaganda was not intended simply to advertise the System; it did not aim to make the System acceptable or desirable; it was not simply a confidence-generating machine. The marvelous power of fiction was at work, setting the economic Leviathan in motion, changing the expectations and, subsequently, the behaviors of individuals. Its aim was to shape the System as one does children. As Terrasson put it, the marvelous and the carnival were pedagogies. Indeed, on the one hand, they demanded adherence, belief, and wonder, suggesting that there was an impenetrable mystery behind the System. On the other, they demonstrated and explained the mechanisms at work. There is no contradiction in this. The System was so new that its workings had to be explained, otherwise no one would have understood anything about it. However, it was important not to reveal everything, the ambition of the experiment so upsetting the monarchical form of rulership that a part of the truth had to remain in the shadows. Many passages of the *Idée générale d'un nouveau système des finances*, that great revolutionary text, therefore remained in manuscript form. Specifically, these novel ideas were disseminated not through transcription and publication in rational terms but through literary and visual propaganda. It was, after all, the privilege of fiction, as Terrasson maintained, to "sacrifice the accuracy of the facts" in order to "ensure [that] instruction is better received."[89] Light was shed on the secret through metaphors, allegories, and dreams. In this way, minds were prepared for the new truths that would replace the old ones, later. Thus, some texts speak to reason and others to the imagination. But, as explained above, this division of labor in the publicity and propaganda is not part of a concerted and hierarchical plan. The intervention of the authorities is obvious when scholars, cartographers, or journalists such as Bobé, Delisle, de Fer, Terrasson, Pannier d'Orgeville, and Buchet are mobilized. One uses their geographic, philosophical, theological, and journalistic knowledge in an attempt to legitimize some reasoning in a rational way, even if their texts and maps have a tendency to leave this register for something more esoteric. These men speak of what they know and whatever is of interest for them. Terrasson and Pannier develop the metaphysical dimension of the System because they are great theologians. Le Maire, Bobé, and the cartographers publications' cover both promotional and scientific knowledge. They outline checked elements and others that would have to be verified. By means of a feedback loop, these elements will confirm or invalidate ill-founded and even imagined knowledge. The greatest poets of the Regency, the theoreticians of the fable and of the *merveilleux*, were not forced to intervene on behalf of the System. Their habitus, their taste, their agency, lead them to intervene and to contribute to an experiment driven by their powerful friends and to which they subscribe. They have invented nothing. They have translated in their language, their aesthetic, the functioning of the System. They have promoted its fabulous dimension, its wild hope.

Was it a case of imaginary beliefs? "What does 'imaginary' mean?" asked Paul Veyne in his famous study of Greek myths. "'Imaginary' . . . expresses a dogmatic judgment concerning certain beliefs of another." Thus, with their sophisticated faith the scholars of the late seventeenth century spoke scornfully of the "imaginary beliefs" of the people. But the imagination was and is a historical force. Referring to the invention of the atomic bomb, Veyne added: "[T]he Russians did absolutely not have to spy on the Americans; they only needed to know that it was possible to make such a bomb."[90] The reasoning of the Moderns was similar. The System was no more false, likely, or real than the so-called reality. They explained that one had only to believe for everything that was said, read, and seen actually to have happened. If the subjects behaved according to these new beliefs, then they would change reality. If the anticipations become self-fulfilling, the old monarchical form would be swept away. Naturally, this radical change in conditions directly called into question not only beliefs but also the place, power, and fortune of the traditional ruling classes. Here we find precisely what happens in the story *Fortunatus*: the giant's generosity provokes social conflict with the dominant, who feel dispossessed and belittled. And, indeed, this idea that the state would henceforth be indifferent to the birth and the functions of those who became rich, this carnivalesque literature of state, was intolerable to rentiers, justice officers, big merchants, religious communities, and princes of the church. They immediately understood the danger and, thereafter, defended themselves by turning against the System the weapons that its propagandists had forged.

5
Counterattacks

As the historian Roger Chartier recalls in *On the Edge of the Cliff*, we would be wrong to take literary fictions for mere "supposed reflections of historical reality." Their specificity stems from the fact that they are situated "in relation to other texts . . . the organization and form of which are intended to produce something other than a description."[1] The history of the System is entirely that of a formidable reuse of cultural materials. Those materials enter into dialogue, and their meanings evolve as usage changes. Their purposes are never limited to the intention of those who proposed them. Several stages of the fictionalization of the experiment thus played different roles. The first was at work in the letters and articles by Terrasson, Pannier d'Orgeville, Law, and Buchet. Their texts deviated from the facts to construct another world, at least in the minds of their readers. What had hitherto been commonly accepted was no longer. It was not experience or testimony that established truths but rather, from a clearly Hobbesian perspective, the state. The second stage of this fictionalization concerned the propaganda in songs, poems, plays, maps, and engravings that extended the fantasy register even further. This time it was a case of promoting such new values as the lottery, spending, unbridled love, or the carnival. More generally, these two stages constituted a fairly coherent whole describing and promoting new beliefs. The third stage was ensured by those who turned these government fictions around to make the experiment something else again.

This third stage begins with the reaction of the merchants and traders to the new monarchical form proposed by the System. Against the fact that the trading companies were merged, and against the creation of this state-managed totalizing entity, the major merchants in Saint-Malo, especially, defended their interests and doubted such a project would be possible. Even more interesting was the reaction of the trading sector to the possible consequences of a state capitalism. We will see that a document dating from the time of the experiment was concerned that such a public Leviathan (the Compagnie-Banque) would produce but few innovations, result in generalized laziness, and in the end provide no incentive for the creation of wealth. The second counterattack that we will then examine concerns the Jansenist circle. Several theologians as well as the chancellor of France, Henri-François d'Aguesseau, who was very close to the party, spoke out against both the shares in the Compagnie des Indes and the banknotes of the Royal Bank. The very notion of *actions rentières* was considered sinful by the canons of the day since it was impossible to invest money and to receive a fixed interest without giving up one's capital, in other words, without forever renouncing the sum loaned. The shares, however, could be held, but they could also be sold and bought back. Terrasson tried as best he could to answer this objection but was then confronted with a second set of criticisms concerning the notion of just price. Drawing on Thomistic scholasticism, the theologians tried to show that the price of the shares was established without cause or foundation and that it represented nothing more than deceit. They called on all good Christians to jettison their shares and to reject an "unjust and ungodly" system. Next, a profusion of humorous counterpropaganda in verse, prose, and engravings took up this theme. Finally comes the literary and iconographic criticism from traditional ruling classes (mainly cheated rentiers and humiliated magistrates). This is an inversion of the great magical and religious figures from the propaganda: Law becomes an evil wizard, Louisiana a hell on Earth, the French kingdom a large hospital. But, here again, this chapter refuses to consider this literature or these representations as a description of the fall of the System. The profound stake behind these fictions is a battle of memories. What account of the previous decades would go down in history? Would it be that of the System, which aimed to revolutionize the monarchical form by continually calling to mind the unmitigated disaster of the preceding reign? Or would it be that of its enemies, who would transform the fall of 1720 into a lasting national trauma? The dangerous register of the carnival used by the state proved a boon for the dominant classes, who had been wronged by the experiment and hastened to substantiate the government fiction in order to convey the idea that a true "topsy-turvy world" would have been created. Only the playwrights of the Théâtre de la foire sang a different song. While plainly mocking the exaggerated government propaganda, they nevertheless early on expressed a certain nostalgia regarding the opening up of possibilities that the System had represented.

Indeed, the literature mocking the System was not always anti-System. In fact, for many, Law and his experiment ultimately counted little. They delighted in its fall, but it was something else that they denounced, something that the System had simply revealed. Certain moralists in verse and prose—even Defoe, who had been so militant at another time—were actually indebted to Law for having revealed the true heart of men and their miserable, greedy, and credulous nature. In the same way that the ruling classes hastened to disseminate a counterhistory of the System, which said much about what they really feared in this matter, it was the theme of shame and redemption that started to pervade the cultural productions between 1720 and 1722. What resulted was stigmatization: the people had believed in it, and, consequently, they had been deceived and debased. The fall of 1720, in France and elsewhere, took on the role of a new signifier, that of the original sin of the eighteenth century.

"In France there will remain only idiots and idlers"

The edict of May 1719 merging the Compagnie des Indes orientales and the Compagnie de la Chine with the Compagnie d'Occident represented a major milestone on the road to the creation of a public monopoly on French trade. In its preamble, this edict extolled the return of "felicity and abundance" since the advent of the young Louis XV to the throne. It implied that the Compagnie d'Occident should be praised for the major role it had played in this restructuring but hastened to add that the same could not be said of the other trading companies of the kingdom. It sorely lamented the fact that, despite the liberalities of the late king, these companies could not have survived and would have eventually become obsolete owing to a lack of capital, ships, and competent directors.[2] In short, the rhetorical strategy of the edict was clear: it was a case of discrediting these private companies in order to justify the merger and subsequent passage of trade to state control. The directors and shareholders of said nationalized companies could not stand by and do nothing, and it is their unsuccessful attempts to oppose the merger that I will examine in what follows. However, it is less the legal battle and the opposing forces than the arguments put forward by the contemporary critics that I consider interesting with regard to the subject of this book.

Concerning the Compagnie des Indes orientales, the edict of May 1719 accused it of having "totally abandoned its Navigation" and of having "determined to cede its Privilege to Private Individuals for 10 percent of the proceeds of its sales in France." This criticism was partly founded given that the company, created in 1664 by Colbert, had indeed fallen into a state of lethargy toward the end of the seventeenth century. Strangely enough, however, the edict recalled a little further on that its privilege had been extended for ten years from April 1, 1715 (thus, theoretically, until March 31, 1725). This raises the obvious question of why Louis XIV and Minister Pontchartrain would have renewed the monopoly of a phantom company. Indeed, the edict was careful not to specify that, at that time (early 1715), it was not a few weak and dispersed "private individuals" who were setting sail for India by paying a commission to the old company of 1664. On the contrary, it was a new, extremely powerful company, known as the "Compagnie des Indes orientales de Saint-Malo." At that time, this company was, in fact, the sole monopolist of the trade with Asia, even though the former Compagnie des Indes was artificially kept active in order to repay its debts by receiving 10 percent of the profits of the Breton company.[3] The edict of 1719 blamed this commission for making French "private individuals"—the Saint-Malo company was never actually specifically named—less competitive with respect to its foreign counterparts. Moreover, the directors of the first company, that of 1664, were accused of mismanagement, the debts it had accumulated in India ensuring that the "individuals" (the Saint-Malo merchants) would not risk "sending their Ships to Surat, the principal City of the Mogul, from whence come the woolen and spun Cottons, and almost all the trade in medicinal plants and spices of the Indies & Arabia, so that our Subjects are obligated to obtain from foreigners the greater part of the merchandise of the Indies consumed in the Kingdom."[4]

While the first part of these allegations was true (the Saint-Malo merchants did not send ships to Surat), the second, however, was a shameless lie. Indeed, since 1715, France had had little need of foreigners to obtain supplies of Indian merchandise. "We form the most powerful company in the kingdom," the shareholders of the Saint-Malo company had declared at its creation. And it was, indeed, a stable company that was founded in 1715. Its capital of several million livres had been paid in full and in cash by a small number of merchants and financiers (including Antoine Crozat) who all knew each other personally. As a result, numerous ships of considerable tonnage were fitted out for Asia over the period 1715–19. In Saint-Malo, pepper, cotton, cowries, dyes, and large quantities of coffee were imported directly from Mocha and India, bypassing the merchants of Marseille, who had until this point traded in Alexandria. This trade ensured that the kingdom was supplied with goods from Asia. It was also extremely profitable, the company's rate of profit being greater than 100 percent. Where the edict referred to failures, it was actually in order to mask a brilliant success. In other words, it was not a question of saving a dying trade, of "reestablishing and increasing French commerce in the Indies," but rather of nationalizing the exceptional private profits that had long whetted the appetites of the public authorities. A legal despoilment of this nature could not happen without causing a stir. However, the French merchants did not take a united stand, those from Saint-Malo receiving only the support of the *parlement* of Paris in this matter.[5]

Indeed, the Parisian magistrates decided on Friday, June 16, 1719, to question the directors and shareholders of the companies that had been abolished as well as the trade deputies of the cities concerned. The first part of the hearings concerned only the question of the actual merger of the companies, and the directors of the former Compagnie des Indes orientales, that of 1664, declared that they humbly submitted to the terms of the edict. However, with their future hanging in the balance, they profited from the forum given them to defend their honor where the management of said company was concerned. As for the shareholders of the new Saint-Malo company holding the privilege of the trade in Asia, they were outraged by the takeover of their enterprise by Law's Compagnie. They were furious that the exploitation of Ile Bourbon (Réunion), which had barely begun, had been stripped from them. At a time when the shareholders founded great hopes on the cultivation of coffee and spices in the Mascarene Islands, the merger represented a real despoilment for them. Indeed, they asserted that it was not a "union" that "Sieur Law" was proposing but rather a buyout that left them no hope of participating in the profits of the trade in the Indian Ocean. They were mortified and hoped that the *parlement* would come to their aid and that "the justice of the King, a father to his subjects, will not suffer any one to profit at the prejudice or the expense of others." Luc Magon de la Balue (1685–1750), one of the main shareholders of the company, was also trade deputy of the city of Saint-Malo. It was he who expressed himself thus as *syndic* of the shareholders and bitterly complained of the "very great prejudice" suffered by "persons who have done naught but procure the public good." He recalled the terms of the treaty that had given the company the rights to the monopoly for ten years and noted that since that time the merchants in Saint-Malo had been responsible for bringing "more than 12 million [livres] into the kingdom."[6]

The choice of the man sent by the Breton port and his choice of words were no coincidence. Luc Magon de la Balue belonged to the first generation of inhabitants of Saint-Malo with a dual habitus, that of merchant and lawyer. After having participated in one or perhaps two long-distance trade expeditions, Magon was appointed master of the Chambre des comptes and established himself in Paris between 1708 and 1711. In 1711, he returned to Saint-Malo to marry and, after the division of his father's estate, became involved in major Atlantic and Asian trade. Belonging to the first class of Saint-Malo merchants, he was one of the twelve founders of the Compagnie des Indes de Saint-Malo of 1715.[7] When speaking before the *parlement* of Paris, Magon chose the language of the public good and placed the discussion in line with the principle of liberty and protection. In his opinion, an entity that did not derive its legitimacy from a political authority, a private company, had contributed to the public good through the pursuit of its own interests. Mirroring the rhetoric of the memoirs commissioned by Pontchartrain at the opening of the Council of Commerce (discussed above), Magon explains that his company had not only provided useful goods from the East for many years but also contributed to filling the royal treasury and to increasing the coins in circulation. His company met the needs of the state and the citizens. According to Magon, these elements were not outside the objectives of trade. They went hand in hand.[8] Magon does not consider tolls, monopolies, and privileges as shameful. He simply thinks that a combination of good laws and great commerce is able to ensure the welfare of merchants, citizens, and the state. From that perspective, there is no need for the System; one need simply revise the Colbertist policy.

During the second part of the hearings, the trade deputies of the cities of Bordeaux, Lyon, Rouen, Marseille, and Saint-Malo were invited to speak before the *parlement* on the substance of the order, in other words, on the consequences for French trade in general resulting from the merger of the companies. And, with the exception of Magon, all of them demonstrated great circumspection. Very hesitantly, they declared that they saw little problem, taking refuge behind the fact that trade deputies should not have to decide on royal dictates. Those of Lyon and Rouen, textile-manufacturing cities, expressed only their fears that the new company would bring dyed Indian fabrics into the kingdom. The deputy from Marseille considered that, with this merger, "trade is in good hands." Only Magon de la Balue dared express his opinion, albeit timidly. He appeared skeptical of Law's plan, for, while he said he wished it success, he nevertheless considered that "the Companies established in Paris have not succeeded thus far" and, especially, that, in such a large enterprise, the main obstacle "is to be found in the fear of maladministration." In other words, he was openly worried about the bureaucratization induced by the creation of this gigantic public monopoly. Questioned as to the risks that might arise from the concentration of trade in one company, he remarked that, "unless trade is absolutely free," the danger of a monopoly was, indeed, to be feared. He said no more on this subject, but his opinion was directly opposed to that of his colleagues, Magon affirming that trade in the Indian Ocean needed to be more widely expanded. Competition among trading ports and companies was very strong during the hearings. On the one hand, the trade deputies of Lyon, Rouen, and Marseille had no reason to support their colleagues from Saint-Malo, who had hurt them financially by importing cotton and coffee from Asia on a large scale. On the other hand, the directors of the old Compagnie des Indes (that of 1664) had little reason to support the new Saint-Malo company. Indeed, while the latter allowed them to reimburse the debts they had accumulated over several decades, its ultimate ambition was to become completely autonomous.

There was no one present at the hearing to defend the interests of the Compagnie de la Chine, but a report had been sent to the magistrates. This document seems to have been lost, but another, dated after the hearing and entitled simply "Compagnie de la Chine: Report," survives in a collection of the French National Archives. The authors of this report, which was fairly brief and inoffensive, brought up the question of the merger. They agreed that, while the king was "Master of His graces," it was a fact that never in the whole history of France had a monarch rescinded a "privilege accorded to one company to give it to another when said company had in no way rendered itself unworthy of His Majesty's favors." Refuting the accusations of malpractice brought against this company, they considered, on the contrary, that it had achieved brilliant results in trade and that these results had aroused "the envy of the directors of the Compagnie des Indes." They concluded by imploring the regent to return the company to its first owners. Between the lines, the authors of this text have perfectly understood that the government was trying to nationalize lucrative private activities to place those resources at its disposal. They were not fooled, just bitter.

Despite these ultimately timid criticisms of the merger ordered by Law and the regent, the magistrates took a stand in favor of the Saint-Malo merchants for the observance of the treaties and against the new Compagnie and its de facto monopoly over all foreign trade. The *parlement* of Paris and all the chambers assembled on the morning of Saturday, June 17, 1719, thus "decreed and ordered that the King be humbly begged to leave the Trade to different Companies and to allow those to which He has been pleased to grant privileges to continue to enjoy said privileges until the expiration of their term."[9] But the state countered this very brief remonstrance with a knockout blow. On the very same day, a decree of the king's Council of State disregarded the opinion of the *parlement* and considered the edict registered, "notwithstanding all opposition and any other impediment whatsoever." It must be supposed, however, that the opposition on the part of the Saint-Malo merchants did not stop there since on June 23 the regent summoned the directors of the old Compagnie des Indes and the *syndics* of the new one. While the former complied "very respectfully with the merger ordered by the conditions laid down in the Edict," the latter simply refused to attend the hearing. They were not ready to give in and submitted to the Duke of Orléans a new report, of which we have no trace. Their request to cancel the merger of the trade companies was, however, once again rejected, the matter being concluded by an order of the Council of State of July 8, 1719, that "nonsuit[ed] the Traders & Shippers of Saint-Malo."[10]

In the takeover of these commercial jewels by Law's Compagnie, should we see merely a balance of power that was unfavorable to the Saint-Malo merchants? While it is true that they were isolated both politically (by claiming their freedom of action with respect to the royal authority) and economically (by restricting their capital to a very small number of shareholders), this was not a matter of a conflict between the finance and business circles of Paris, on the one hand, and the Atlantic trade, on the other.[11] The question here was infinitely more complex than a simple balance of power between different competing circles of the capitalism of the early eighteenth century. On the one hand, the purpose of the System was precisely to nationalize large-scale trade in order to place its profits at the service of the monarchy, and, on the other, Law and his friends wanted to ensure the complete control of the state apparatus over the economic functioning of the kingdom. From this perspective, the Saint-Malo company, very profitable but with a very limited shareholder base, was the archetype of what needed to be done away with. It was natural prey, and its elimination was necessary for the establishment of this great work that was the System, this total public entity that we could today refer to as a protodirigiste experiment. Is *protodirigiste* too strong, the anachronism too exaggerated? Perhaps not, judging by a report in the French National Archives entitled *Mémoire au sujet de la Compagnïe des Indes*, which can be dated to the beginning of 1720. This unpublished manuscript is unsigned, but various elements indicate that it originated in the merchant community of Marseille.[12]

The author of this report obviously took the words of Terrasson and the royal edicts very seriously. "We see," the preamble states, "daily proof that we are in the system of making all the subjects of the King but a single and unique trader that shall be the Compagnie des Indes." This simple fact would cause the ruin of all trade in France, with money, industry, workers, and competent seamen fleeing abroad. The reason for this was simple: "[By granting] the freedom to trade everywhere and in every kind of merchandise to each of the subjects of the King, one exercises the intellect of each one of them: the one envies the other and strives to surpass his competitor. Thus is genius formed, a sword that requires polishing, that is sharpened through use." Emulation and competition are the core of this reasoning. Where "everyone stimulates his genius," "cupidity replaces intellect," causing abundance to flourish. On the contrary, from the moment the state decided to get involved in trade, catastrophe was not far off.[13]

The essential capital sin of uniting all the trade of the kingdom in a single public company was that "there will be no one who thinks up new projects." If we are to believe the authors of the *Mémoire*, managers would be interested only in executing orders at their level, without an overview of the situation, without the desire to go beyond their sphere of competence, without any willingness to challenge the status quo. Indeed: "[W]e know from the experience of all of time that the ambition of those in charge of certain works goes no further than to maintain their positions and their salaries, and at most to do good within the sphere of the commission they have received." There may be "two or three good Directors, a good Inspector, and that is all." The result? "[O]f all these employees there will be but three who will be given to reflection; the others will do no more than obey." Almost all employees and shareholders would tend to "fall asleep under the shadow of the management": "[T]hey will no longer be actively involved; they will become lazy and depraved"; "their mind will rust and produce nothing." As for those with no vested interest in the Compagnie, they "will lead an even more indolent life, and in France there will remain only idiots and idlers."[14]

Although the term *entrepreneur* was not used by the authors of the *Mémoire*, it is the figure of the entrepreneur that is invoked. The authors distinguish "traders" from "people who perform certain tasks." The former "are looking individually how to get wealthier." They are their own masters, and they want to stay ahead of their competitors. The latter are simply happy to "maintain their stipend." They have a fixed remuneration depending on a predetermined set of tasks over which they have little control. Because it will be run by such employees, the System will have lost the very essence of trade, the urge constantly to think about the best way to get rich. This is why the authors of the *Mémoire* do not believe that the firm will succeed. The Compagnie des Indes was officially called *trader*, but its work was trading in name alone. Indeed, whereas at the end of the 1720s the banker and economist Richard Cantillon characterizes entrepreneurs in terms of their ability to tame the risk by producing order, their capacity to generate coordination between different activities, the authors of the *Mémoire* have a different perspective, that of innovation. As the eighteenth century began, there was only Defoe to promote the projectors. If not the only one, he was one of the few to consider them, not as cheats and swindlers, but as useful characters only wanting to make an honest profit from their inventions and improvements.[15] The authors of the *Mémoire* go farther: they equate the trader to someone who "thinks up new projects." He is less the agent of the organization of the world and more the agent of change. He has a subversive creative streak, and it is this that is decisive for the production and circulation of wealth. The authors of the *Mémoire* immediately assimilated the System to a bureaucratic enterprise in which the complete socialization of commerce and the end of competition would kill any spirit of initiative or any thought of change. They constantly point out the limited ambition, the triumph of routine, the absence of healthy emulation. The introduction of centralized management means that the work that an entrepreneur undertakes—taking risks, destroying, creating, and rewarding according to his own lights—is simply impossible. The problem is not a human issue, nor does it concern the training of personnel: it is impossible to be a merchant if one is imprisoned in an operating environment so regularized as to render employees powerless. This discredited the System from the outset.[16]

Getting down to details, the authors of the *Mémoire* criticized the vices they believed to be inherent in all public monopolies. Indeed, a monopoly would establish prices that were too low for it to afford the commodities (and wages) it would buy from "private traders."[17] Conversely, it would resell at too high a price what merchants need, "by which means shall we witness the decline of our manufactures." Better yet, the consequences of these predetermined prices for the profitability or, more generally, the management of the Compagnie des Indes seemed to worry the authors of the *Mémoire*. On several occasions, they expressed the idea that the merchants would have no "faith" or "confidence" in a state-run monopoly. In a very blunt statement, they declared in connection with the Compagnie: "We are assured that it shall always be sustained, thereby increasing distrust." This judgment is reminiscent of the contemporary notion of "too big to fail"—moral hazard causing the directors of some firms to do whatever they want without worrying about profitability, risk, or losses since they know that, in the end, they will be saved by the public authorities. Is this not what was implicitly implied by the authors of the *Mémoire* in connection with the Compagnie des Indes, the real purpose of which was, ultimately, not to sustain the commerce of the kingdom or even to be profitable? They are not very far from the right setting: the Compagnie des Indes does not operate according to the rules of competition; it does not intend to maximize profit; it will simply achieve goals set out on behalf of and in the name of public authority. According to the merchants, this situation would result in a transfer of economic activity abroad and, finally, widespread poverty owing to the "lack of rich and industrious inhabitants."[18]

To whom was this report addressed? The Council of Commerce, the Council of Finance, the Compagnie des Indes, or the *parlement* of Paris? The report is not annotated, but the quality of the calligraphy indicates the work of a copyist. Nothing is known of his fortune in the circles revolving around the center of power. However, the mere fact that one or more merchants in Marseille had produced such an analysis and critical review of the System is in itself of great interest for the subject at hand. First, the report is evidence that, contrary to the traditional interpretation of the process of the merger of the trade companies, voices other than those of the Saint-Malo merchants spoke out to denounce the operation. Second, this document reinforces my interpretation of the experiment. Contemporaries of Law and his System accurately identified it as the totalizing enterprise that it was, of which finance was but one aspect and probably not the most crucial. Finally, and more profoundly, the *Mémoire* introduced the issue of innovation, of new projects, as being at the heart of objections. The question posed no longer referred only to the freedom of trade, the nationalization of the profits of this trade, or individual interests, which had thus far constituted the main analysis of the experiment. The authors of the *Mémoire* were concerned with the dynamics of capitalism, in other words, with the decisive role of emulation in the future creation of wealth. While the promoters of the System unceasingly vaunted the discoveries to be made, the future wealth and new trade avenues that would be available to the shareholders, their opponents in Marseille posed a fundamental question. Who would have a good reason to engage the Compagnie in these adventures? Was not the very idea of a stable and immutable dividend, that of an *action rentière*, in direct contradiction with the essence of trade, which was to continually change? Would the System, which wanted to defuse the fears surrounding the beginnings of the reign of free trade and individual interests, be able to enrich the subjects of the kingdom? Or would it cause by degrees generalized impoverishment owing to a lack of "emulation"? In other words, the great merit of the authors of the *Mémoire* is that, at the beginning of the eighteenth century and thinking beyond the System itself, they asked the fundamental question of how compatible the incessant renewal of material wealth was with the nationalization of its mode of production. Against all state utopias, they remain skeptical that it can be possible to create material prosperity through the public production and distribution of wealth. These notions of change and the risks linked to entrepreneurial activity were also questioned by other opponents of the System, but on another level, that of theology.

An "Unjust and Ungodly" System

Between the Jansenist Party, led by a few prelates, and the majority of the magistrates, on the one hand, and the regent and his circle, on the other, the first year of the Regency had nevertheless gone well. By placing Cardinal Noailles, a rebel fallen into disgrace under the late king, at the head of the Council of Conscience in 1715, and by making d'Aguesseau, "the eagle of *parlement*," one of the members of the council and then chancellor of France in 1717, the Duke of Orléans had knowingly advanced two men who were highly favorable to Jansenism. Noailles and d'Aguesseau immediately began an anti-Jesuit policy at the same time as undertaking to rehabilitate both Augustinian theology and the social pariahs of yesterday. Carried away by the events, on March 1, 1717, four bishops called for a general council to reject the papal bull *Unigenitus*, obtained by Louis XIV from Pope Clement XI for censuring the propositions contained in a book by one of the party's chiefs, Pasquier Quesnel (1634–1719). In April, Noailles joined the revolt with several dozen prelates and thousands of priests and monks. The church of France was in turmoil. The regent could not accept such a split and, deciding to put an end to the liberal phase of his regime, turned away from the Jansenists. With the recentralization of decision-making and institutional control by the Duke of Orléans, the Council of Conscience fell into disuse, Noailles finally resigning on September 16, 1718.[19] As for d'Aguesseau, who had been opposing Law's policy for months, he had been stripped of his office as keeper of the seals and exiled to his estate at Fresnes as early as January 1718. While this was not a sensational divorce between the Jansenist movement and the new state authority, it did mark the beginning of a muted hostility that would increase soon after.

The spring of 1720 saw the publication of two theological texts that were very hostile toward the System, while a third, more in-depth and better constructed, evidently circulated in manuscript form at the same time. The first (published anonymously) came from a member of Noailles's entourage, his friend Father Joseph Lambert (1654–1722). Renowned for his extreme austerity, Lambert was a Sorbonne-educated doctor of theology who had never made any mystery of his Jansenist sympathies. The author of a bestseller on how to educate the poor, reissued through the middle of the nineteenth century, Lambert advocated great detachment with respect to the things of this world, praising material poverty.[20] It is, therefore, not surprising that in 1720 he published a virulent pamphlet entitled *Décision théologique sur les actions de la Compagnie des Indes*. The second text was a letter of May 18, 1720, addressed directly to Law by one of the "ultras" of the Jansenist camp, Jean Soanen (1647–1740), the *appelant* bishop of Senez. The letter was immediately published and, as noted by the prelate's panegyrist, "found worthy of a Bishop, who is not afraid to tell the truth to the very ones that it can hurt."[21] The third text was the *Mémoire sur le commerce des actions de la Compagnie des Indes*, written by d'Aguesseau in his exile at Fresnes. While the chancellor stated in his introduction to this report that he left to the "Theologians & the Casuistes" (casuists were theologians whose studies involved resolving moral dilemmas) the task of judging whether "the trade in shares was contrary to the laws of charity, to the perfection of the Christian," it was, nevertheless, as a Catholic moralist that he was writing. His librarian, publishing his works in 1777, was not mistaken when he explained that d'Aguesseau treated his subject "from all the perspectives that concern the duties of man, *Religion, Prudence & Justice*."[22] To take religion first, the texts by d'Aguesseau and Lambert did, indeed, put forward similar arguments, using a very similar method of presentation.[23] Terrasson replied to these "Casuistes." Indeed, who better to respond to a counterattack than a man who had been brought up by the Oratorians, an order very receptive to Jansenist ideas? According to d'Alembert and Voltaire, although Terrasson was probably an atheist, he was an eminent theologian. In this respect, he was openly hostile toward Jansenism in his *Philosophie applicable*, mocking the church of Utrecht, constantly criticizing Pierre Nicole, and denouncing the fanaticism of the movement.[24] In the *Mémoire pour servir à justifier la Compagnie des Indes*, he rejected the arguments of Lambert, Soanen, and d'Aguesseau, explaining that the sovereign could not govern by following the opinions of this or that "party." Clearly reusing his Hobbesian tone against the factions, he denounced those "Doctors" who "seemingly of the law speak out against the conduct of the Prince" when they "are themselves obliged to submit to him with all simplicity & docility."[25]

What constituted the foundation of the Jansenist anti-System texts was the idea, repeated over and over again, that the System was profoundly unjust. In order to comprehend the meaning of this accusation, it is important to understand what for the French Jansenists of the seventeenth and eighteenth centuries constituted a just profit. To achieve this, we need to reconsider the *Conférences ecclésiastiques de Paris sur l'usure et la restitution*. The second volume dealt, among other things, with the shares of the trade companies. The author thus asserted: "[I]n order to discourage their subjects from making usurious loans, & to induce them to form companies [through shares], they [the princes] have always defended loans at interest, and established companies for commerce, of which they have been willing to declare themselves both the heads & the protectors." The *Conférences* added, however, that these companies were legitimate only if the shareholder participated in both the gains and the losses, a situation that was normally not the case for a person lending his money through a bank or to an individual. The whole discussion of the legitimacy of the share dividend turned on this issue of potential losses. "[T]he peril to which one exposes his money makes all these profits very just and very legitimate," declared the *Conférences*, the text driving home this view one page later: "The risk that one runs in the companies should not cause them to be banished; it is this risk that renders them legitimate." The

Jansenist theologian François Genet (1640–1703) insisted heavily on this point in his *Théologie morale* (1676–77). As Genet pointed out, for what we would today refer to as a *joint-stock company* to be permitted, "[t]he first and foremost condition is that those who give money or livestock to other persons in the company are not assured of the fate of their capital, nor of receiving any certain interest on what they give." In other words, where the certainty of recovering one's capital and/or receiving a fixed interest existed, this was a case of usury because the risks and damages were not shared with the co-contractors. From this point of view, we can immediately see how the *actions rentières* of the Compagnie des Indes came up against this stumbling block that the issue of usury represented.[26]

Lambert stepped into this breach in 1720: "It is positively against the laws of society to be assured of a definite & certain profit; since the capital that one possessed is not disposed of, & that the uncertainty of whether there will be gain or loss must hold everything in abeyance." There were, thus, two possibilities according to Lambert. The first was that the shareholders were certain of the revenues they would make, did not participate in the losses of the Compagnie, and were able to recover their capital whenever they saw fit. In this case, it was no longer trade but usury and, thus, an injustice. The second possibility was that these same shareholders would participate in the losses of the Compagnie and would not always receive a dividend. In this case, the directors had made a "promise they could not keep." They had lied, an "iniquity" that the church could not accept. In the same vein, Soanen was concerned that the disappearance of the rentes would oblige the religious communities to invest in the Compagnie: "For whether or not it involves risk, it appears that, for several reasons, this sacred asset cannot be exposed. First, because if there is no risk, the profit cannot be just; & where there is risk, then it is even less permissible for us to entrust the Heritage of our Lord Jesus Christ to chance."[27] Naturally, the merger of the Compagnie and the Royal Bank aggravated the problem. Lambert asserted that, since the shareholder dividends were partly the result of loans made by the bank "in coins or in notes at 2 percent interest for all sorts of employment," these were "usurious gains," forbidden by the laws of the church.[28]

On all these points, Terrasson appeared uncomfortable in his attempt to defend the System. His answer to the accusation of usury against capital providing a fixed revenue without having been disposed of was evasive. In a "trade company," he stated, "there is nothing to prevent certain funds from being disposed of & destined to produce a fixed revenue, & other funds . . . , subject to gains and losses." But what was the nature of the shares of the Compagnie des Indes? Terrasson did not say. He attempted only to produce an analogy between rentes, the capital of which was formerly renounced and, thus, irrecoverable, and these same shares, the first having been exchanged for the second. Unlike with rentes, the shareholder could still recover his capital by selling his shares. This same capital was, therefore, not disposed of, but Terrasson refused to enter into this debate. Concerning the dividend, he justified it by the extrinsic title of *lucrum cessans*. He argued that the merchants could have made money in another way from the money they used to buy shares. He thus equated these shares with a loan that constituted compensation for the opportunity cost incurred by the shareholders.[29]

If we return now to the theologians and the matter of the price of shares, what rules of justice made it possible to establish this price? Here again—and unlike the Jesuits—the Jansenists stuck to a strictly Thomistic dimension of the question. The *Conférences ecclésiastiques* argued that it was "violating the rules of justice to sell goods for more than they are worth." By referring to the notion of just price put forward by Thomas Aquinas, the author of this text wanted to refute the idea that price was solely the result of competition between sellers and buyers. For Thomas Aquinas, it was obvious, prices varied depending on the quantities offered and required in the marketplace. These variations were, however, subject to the principle of the conservation of the social body as a whole. In other words, it was not because a commodity was rare under certain circumstances that there was a pressing need for it, that the merchant was able to raise its price as he pleased. Scholastic logic refuted the idea that prices could be the result of an individual estimation of needs. They had to vary according to a *communis aestimatio*: first, they had to reflect the value of a good as considered by the community as a whole at a given time, and, second, they had to guarantee the social status of those who sold and bought, these different "organs" of the social body, without disrupting them. Selling to a worker or a peasant at prices that were either too high or too low would tend either to result in his death or to advance his station in life, two extremes that were not desirable within a society based on a stable hierarchy. The same thing could be said with respect to the merchant. For this, he must, as repeated in the *Conférences*, "limit himself to an honest profit, & sell only at a reasonable price."[30] Prices therefore had social, common, and identifiable causes and limits that had to be respected. But it was precisely these elements that were lacking where the shares of the Compagnie des Indes were concerned, if Lambert is to be believed: "As to the variation of the price of the Shares, the cause is as unknown as that of the ebb and flow of the tide, with this difference that the ebb and flow are bound by rules and limits, whereas the raising and lowering of the Shares are not." D'Aguesseau spoke at length on these questions, abundantly quoting the *Summa theologica* by Thomas

Aquinas. The chancellor thus considered that the price of a good or a service must be the result of a "cause" that could not be a matter of individual appreciation. There was systematically a social dimension at the root of every cause. On one side, that of the buyer, the price was, thus, the result of the "common & ordinary need of men, not of the singular necessity to which an individual may be reduced." On the other, that of the seller, this same price was the fruit "of the advantage or utility proposed by contracting": "[B]ut this can be understood only as the advantage that a reasonable man, & one making use of his reason, may find in a contract by means of a natural suitability & proportion with the end that he proposes to achieve." Indeed, the "blind & foolish desire to enrich oneself is not a cause constituting the foundation of a legitimate commitment." Prices could vary depending on the competition, but always within narrow "bounds." D'Aguesseau constantly employed *bounds* in his writings, referring directly to the notion of bad Aristotelian chrematistics and Thomistic "greed," in other words, to the idea that money could not be sought for itself in an endless quest. Money should serve only to satisfy needs, themselves limited depending on social status. According to d'Aguesseau, the accumulation of money was a pathological behavior, "an aberration of the mind," and it could result only in "injustice."[31]

Now, this is precisely what happened with the shares of the Compagnie des Indes. How can the fact that its prices rose so high and that some individuals were able to get rich so quickly be explained? Were there legitimate causes for such significant price movements? No, replied d'Aguesseau, only "shameful" causes, namely, "the ignorance or greed of the seller or the buyer." While he did not discuss the precise mechanisms that led to such highs in the price of the shares, d'Aguesseau did insist that there was no real, legitimate, or known cause—an increase in the profits of the Compagnie, notably—that could explain them. Worse, most of those who purchased the shares were not seeking a moderate gain by holding on to an asset for many years. They wanted to buy only to resell. There was, therefore, no legitimate need to be satisfied behind this trade but rather a "madness" that led to wanting to get rich "without measure," sometimes by spreading "false rumors" that disturbed both "the peace and the public tranquility."[32]

Terrasson attempted to justify the increase in the price of the shares by noting the increase in the trade of the Compagnie des Indes. At the end of his *Mémoire*, he took a particular interest in "the speculation," in other words, the incessant purchase and resale of shares. The latter, he said, were "bills of Commerce like other bills." Thus, a man who had money to spare sometimes buys a house "if he believes he is making a good deal, & then he sells it when he believes he can make a profit": "All this can be done without deceiving anyone."[33]

While d'Aguesseau was horrified by this practice, Terrasson sought to make it familiar, almost ordinary. We can, thus, see the chasm separating the two men: always to buy in order to resell was a practice of merchants, not rentiers. And, even for the merchant, the scholastic theory of just price implied that these purchases and sales be made with "measure" since enrichment could not be an end in and of itself. Still from their Thomistic point of view, the Jansenist opponents of the System denounced the so-called generalized modification of the distribution of wealth, referring to it as an "injustice." Lambert used the example of the coachman, the lackey, and the maid who had "lately been placed, as in the twinkling of an eye, above the masters whom they served & have ceased to serve." The theologian was stupefied: "Our society is no longer recognizable. The last have become the first; & many of the first have become the last. If the late King were to return to the world, he would seek his Kingdom in his Kingdom." One more time, the performativity of propaganda can be measured, here in its eschatological dimension. Lambert reiterates the message of the Gospel of Matthew ("the last shall be first" [Matt. 20:16]), but he highlights the unholy and outrageous nature of a system that pretends to fulfill the Last Judgment here below and to advance the heavenly kingdom on Earth. It is for him a frightening and sacrilegious prospect: the social order willed by God must never be called into question. By disrupting social conditions, the System had taken a stand against divine will. And for d'Aguesseau it was obvious: it was "the most virtuous families" who had been struck down. The chancellor denounced "the excess of misery in wise and virtuous houses, the excess of luxury in those of usurers, speculators, the bankrupt, our servants, and even our lackeys." Taking up almost word for word Pannier d'Orgeville's and Terrasson's arguments, he asked rhetorically: "What matter, it will be said, that property is in the hands of some rather than others, provided that the same wealth remains within the state." But he saw precisely several disadvantages to the sudden enrichment of new individuals.[34]

D'Aguesseau considered that it mattered very much indeed that wealth remained in the hands of those "to whom birth & education have taught how to make it of use to themselves and to the public, rather than being delivered, as it were, to the hazard of pillage." Responding to the argument of the generalized material prosperity that would result from luxury spending, he again treated the question from a moralist point of view. Few of the nouveaux riches would usefully and virtuously spend their fortunes "to pay their debts, or to acquire land." Each would "consume them in pleasures, in luxury, & in other equally frivolous expenses, much like those who have won vast sums at the gaming tables, & to whom, after a certain time, there remains naught but the memory." In other words, there would soon be nothing left of this so-called wealth that was not renewed, that was not invested in legitimate assets as per the fixed social statutes of an immutable monarchy.[35]

We would also be left with the fact of the System having instituted a trading nation. Far from having reestablished trade, the experiment would have further corrupted the merchants. We find here one of the main topoi of Jansenist morality against idleness.[36] While certain poems favorable to the System mocked merit and work, and while Terrasson, Pannier, and Buchet condemned the "laziness" of the rentiers, d'Aguesseau believed that the industrious people had become indolent and idle. Now, "[n]othing is more opposed to the spirit of the most holy Legislators, . . . &, if we may be so bold, to the law of God Himself, Who condemned man to earn his bread by the sweat of his brow, than to introduce a new kind of industry, which, without difficulty, without toil, without laborious application, produces more riches in a moment than the natural & ordinary ways would provide in a year, & often even in a century." Employing his usual language register of classical republicanism, the chancellor quoted examples from ancient history of peoples "weakened" by idleness, who "never recovered their former vigor, . . . & became less than women." With the nobility of sentiments and the "love of the public good" gone, "there is no one who should not fear that such a state be threatened with ruin." This "revolution of sentiments" is "often not only the omen, but the source of a revolution of events that change the face of a whole Kingdom, & that determine the fate of a Nation."[37]

While the merchants of Marseille saw in the totalizing enterprise of a public trading company the end of emulation and the beginnings of idleness and passivity, d'Aguesseau arrived at similar conclusions but in a different way and using a different vocabulary. The lottery was the mother of laziness and laziness the vanguard of ruin. Here, the opponents of the System attacked the most fragile part of the government propaganda that glorified enrichment without toil. But, for d'Aguesseau, the System was, ultimately, even worse than the destructive forces of freedom of trade and individual interests. Like freedom of trade, the System needed greed, but it united this vice with idleness and a random distribution of wealth. The revolution that followed in its wake was, ultimately, more serious than the "civil war" that he denounced in 1715 when he was still only the attorney general. This chimera that was Law's experiment did away even more definitively with the traditional values and hierarchies than did the regime of unbridled freedom. D'Aguesseau thus emphasized another problem that went beyond the System itself. What explained the establishment of prices (and, thus, revenues) in the field of finance? Was it the underlying assets, as Terrasson sometimes suggested, or the "madness" mentioned by d'Aguesseau?

Whatever the case, Lambert, Soanen, and d'Aguesseau considered that it was forbidden for Christians to buy, hold, and sell the shares of the Compagnie des Indes. They were the cause of so many injustices that no one should try to hold on to them in the expectation of hypothetical future profits because they would have done too much harm in the meantime. If, unfortunately, someone already had some of these shares, he most emphatically should not try to sell them to a private individual if he wanted to get rid of them. They should be returned to the Compagnie, along with any gains made and dividends received while he held them. Did not such conduct make Christians bad subjects of the prince who wanted the System? Lambert, Soanen, and d'Aguesseau were unanimous in placing religion above temporal powers in this affair. God, said Lambert, "is the first Master to Whom we owe obedience; religion and conscience are barriers that it is not permitted to force." Because the king had authorized something, this should not prevent "the just man" from examining its nature. Was this a case of *salus populi suprema lex esto*? Was the state in such bad shape that the System was the only remedy? D'Aguesseau did not think so, but, even if this had been the case, he did not hesitate to say that "it is not necessary for the state to be saved if its salvation can be achieved only by evident iniquity." The heroism of the magistrate, an avid reader of the authors of antiquity, extended to the gift of one's own person: "No necessity can excuse the one who betrays his duty. It is better to be an unhappy innocent than to be a happy culprit; it is better to disappear from this world than to live in it a criminal."[38]

To counter this argument, Terrasson attempted again to prove that, in delivering the debtors, the System had tried to drive sin from this world and had practiced charity without equal. It would even have resulted in the return to a form of primitive equality since, "in the natural order whereby men come into the world," they owe nothing to each other. Explicitly targeting the magistrates, he accused them of crying injustice only because they were the main bearers of rentes and because with the extinguishment of debt there were "no more trials" and, therefore, no more revenues for the officers of justice. Were they thus going to become poor while others became rich? This is what Terrasson believed, and he was very frank in this respect. Would it be better to increase the taxes of the poorest classes? It was on this kind of injustice that he invited the casuists to reflect. For, since it was necessary to relieve the state of the burden of its debt, "what could be done but to choose the System under which fewer people would suffer, & the loss would fall on those who were well-off rather than on those who had nothing": "That is what we did."[39] Terrasson opposed a morality that could retrospectively be described as consequentialist to the Jansenist authors who drew on ethical principles. In other words, the partisans and the opponents of the System did not speak the same language. Should a policy be judged by weighing up its positive and negative effects or, on the contrary, by evaluating its compliance with certain principles? In this debate, which would finally see the victory of the "deontologists," Terrasson and his friends put forward strong arguments. Had the System put the burden on the rentier class, whom it had impoverished? Undoubtedly. Terrasson admitted this fact freely. Had there been a few sudden fortunes? Perhaps. But what did it matter who became rich? The real debate was, What did society really want? To maintain the Louis XIV way of doing things and, thus, return to this policy of pressure on the working classes? The System had made another choice, one that the ruling classes would see as a world gone mad, a "topsy-turvy world."

A Topsy-Turvy World?

With the System reeling on all fronts by the summer of 1720, Law gradually losing control, inflation increasing, and a few hundred (or even thousand?) shareholders on the point of losing a lot of money owing to the fall in the price of the shares, the propaganda dried up. Other forces came into play, finding an inexhaustible wealth of material ready to be employed to discredit what had just happened. Given the heights to which Law's supporters had risen, it was child's play for the opponents of the experiment—or simply for the mockers—to reverse the roles of the figures of the government propaganda.

A first interesting theme was the reversal of the chemical motive, the importance of which was discussed in the previous chapter. As we saw, the gold of the New World and paper money were presented as two forms of great work, two transformations of metals by secret principles accomplished by the obsession of the chemists. A very famous literary work dating from 1720–21, the "Genealogy," presented itself as a counterpoint to this register. The "Genealogy" was a short poem explaining by a principle of kinship the fall of the System. The verb *engendrer* (to engender, produce; to father, beget) connected between very meaningful substantives, as in:

> And Law begat My Lord System
> And My Lord System begat the Bank
> And the Bank begat Mississippi
> And Mississippi begat the West.

This narrative principle referred directly to the gnosis of the initiates, for, as Jean Ehrard points out, "in hermetic literature the idea of Nature [is] always linked to that of generation, thus enabling the old theme of metamorphoses to be rationalized."[40] It was explained thus by the chemist Le Breton in a work published during the Regency:

> Nature tends always to produce from a certain seed an individual similar to that from which the seed has sprung; but often it is diverted and produces a different species, to the proportion that this seed has lost its first state and degenerated from its nature, by the impression of the corrupting power of external agents. Thus does wheat degenerate into ryegrass; thus are imperfect animals and monsters born.

The hope of (al)chemical literature was precisely to prevent this phenomenon of corruption by external agents. Only then would nature attain perfection, as metals matured and were transformed into gold. If this was not achieved, "the corruption of one thing is the generation of another," explained Le Breton, the process continuing until the final destruction.[41] The System fell into this second category. Many versions of the "Genealogy" have survived, but each refers in its last verse to the same idea. Here are three examples:

> The balance produced zero, which was stripped of all power to produce.
>
> Zero finally found itself powerless.
>
> Balance finally produced Zero, from which the power to produce was stripped and Babylon reduced.[42]

The "Genealogy" agreed that Law and the regent had tried the science of metamorphosis for themselves. But had they succeeded in checking the natural process of putrefaction that presides over the evolution of all seeds? Apparently not. They had not found the path to perfection, their principles having resulted in sterility. They had been chemists, but no more successful than many others; a fact that would not have been worthy of blame if the experiments conducted in the laboratory of the Palais-Royal had not contaminated Paris, the kingdom, and even foreign lands. This theme of sterility found a natural development in the reverse imagery of Louisiana. The *Great Mirror of Folly* is a compilation of texts and engravings (in Dutch and French) relating to the events of 1720. Several versions have survived, the first published in Amsterdam at the very end of the year 1720. Despite its high cost, the first edition was highly successful, and the book was reissued several times. Images contained therein are essentially a matter for mockery. The engravings—some struck particularly for the *Mirror* and some modified versions of existing plates—employ scatological and grotesque registers. The book mocks paper money, the Royal Bank, the Compagnie des Indes, and its European avatars such as the English South Sea Company.[43] These

FIGURE 5.1. Engraving entitled *Mississippi, or The World-Famous Goldland in the Fancy of the Wind Trade*, from *Het Groote Tafereel der Dwaasheid* (The great mirror of folly) (ca. 1720), pl. 55. Courtesy Yale University Library.

undertakings are regarded as hoaxes, malicious fabrications, and the *Great Mirror of Folly*, a book tainted with anti-French second thoughts, participates in some form of counterpropaganda, since many of the engravings respond to existing propaganda. So it is with the engraving *Mississippi, or The World-Famous Goldland in the Fancy of the Wind Trade* (fig. 5.1), which is the inverse representation of figure 4.3.

The cartouche at the top of the engraving announces this "New colony of the winds,"[44] and at the bottom appears the Latin motto of the Flemish poet Willem Godschalck van Focquenbroch (1640–70): "The Glory of the world is but smoke." This reference was not accidental. Indeed, Focquenbroch had been disillusioned with his colonial experience and actually died young in the Gulf of Guinea of a tropical disease while working for the Dutch East India Company. The background, mountains, river, and trees are identical to the propaganda engraving. But this time there are no cities, fortifications, or powerful ships in the mouth of the Mississippi, no civil harmony. Quarreling

Indians are portrayed in a tense scene in the center. An unpleasant alligator is present in the foreground, and the text accompanying the engraving mocks this supposed Garden of Eden that turns out to be a hostile quagmire:

> For your appearances
> So royally presented,
> Are now unmasked, their essence
> Eclipsed by the truth . . .
> For here were people planted in vain
> Where neither Gold nor Silver is to be found.

According to the Dutch engraving, the propaganda was nothing but deceit, and the "truth" beginning to break through revealed a barren country without riches and without precious metals. We have seen how much more complicated things actually were, and we have discussed the performative character of the publicity surrounding the Louisiana venture, which prompted reactions (among them reactions to mining issues). But here the engraving explicitly links the Mississippi, this "pledge to the god of the wind," to the history of the System, narrated by the vignettes numbered 1–4. Louis XIV was scarcely on his deathbed "than a Scot wind arrived" (vignette 1). He advised Orléans, and the idol Mississippi "was placed above law, virtue, and reason" (vignette 2). Money flowed in (vignette 3), but the joy was short-lived, followed very quickly by "disaster" and "poverty" (vignette 4). The last vignette, on the register of the pathetic, depicts sobbing women who seem to be reviling the one who ruined them. This feminine presence and conjugal discord are reminiscent of the theme of sexuality promoted by the government propaganda. To the colonists, as to the shareholders, a liberation of desires had been promised, and a short poem, perhaps of Jansenist inspiration, once again contradicted this promise:

> Women sell their jewelry
> To leave for the new Peru
> Girls sell their virginity
> All they can pawn they do
> When they have nothing better
> To give the speculator.

Instead of the innocent sexuality of the fickle native women and the loving and obliging *grisettes* of the rue Quincampoix, the pamphleteer literature evokes sordid prostitution. The conclusion of this theater of illusion is summed up by the general theme of "France in the Hospital," that of a poverty-stricken and desolate kingdom. Take, for example, the "Chanson sur l'agiot" ("Hymn to speculation"):

As formerly for Pharaoh,
And by his great wisdom,
The famous economist
Did relieve the Kingdom
Thus Law foreseeing the evil
Whose fate threatens us
Brought funds to the hospital
Where His project has placed us.[45]

This song contains two distinct references. The allusion to the Joseph of the Old Testament, Pharaoh's vizier, with whom Law was identified in the propaganda, is obvious, but there is also the Scotsman's visit to the Hôtel-Dieu, a hospital for the poor and needy, to make a generous donation, which the *Nouveau Mercure* had been quick to report in September 1719.[46] This theme was so widespread that it is unnecessary to list the numerous documents relating to it. What is more interesting for the subject under discussion is the relation between, on the one hand, this anti-System literature and the principle of the lottery and, on the other, the fantasized consequences that the lottery would have entailed: a topsy-turvy world in which the poor take the place of the rich. The "Méfaits de Law" ("Law's Wrongdoings") is a short work in verse in answer to the propaganda concerning the "Benefits":

Ruining the nobility, favoring the wretch,
Rapidly raising the station of the servant,
To this, these unfortunate days bear witness
Where honor and justice are no longer emergent.

A short untitled epigram is even more explicit:

Since a Jew, hailing from Scotland, a plan
To seize all our money did constitute,
Scoundrels and beggars now live in high style,
While the former rich are become destitute.[47]

The Régiment de la calotte, a literary drinking society, is symbolic of the aristocratic reaction to developments in the early years of the eighteenth century. Abhorrence of commoners, a reluctance to mix with people of other backgrounds, a dislike of egalitarian ideas, and outright racism were the hallmarks of this society.[48] Not surprisingly, Law, Fontenelle, Houdar de la Motte, and Terrasson eventually became targets of "Calottine" poetry, in which members of the society voiced their aversion to the great carnival of the wealthy poor that would have been France in 1720.[49] We find in the society's work a discourse similar to the found in Lambert, d'Aguesseau, Montesquieu, or the magistrates of the *parlement* of Paris. It is also similar to passages of the *Persian Letters* (1721) in which Montesquieu evoked this "topsy-turvy world." The following passage is particularly characteristic:

> They that were rich Men six months ago, are now fallen into Poverty; and such as had not Bread to eat, now wallow in riches. . . . This Foreigner [Law] has turn'd the state, as a Taylor turns an old Coat; what was undermost he made uppermost, and what was uppermost he puts undermost. . . . How many Footmen are now serv'd by their Fellow-Servants, and perhaps To-morrow by their Masters![50]

It is unlikely that a man as well informed as Montesquieu would have been duped by government propaganda. But he was appalled by the carnivalesque myth, the possibility of a random distribution of wealth. The fact that wealth could be dropped in just anyone's lap—and especially the fact that the state promoted such an undertaking—he found quite simply unacceptable. This attitude was not so much the reaction of a man nostalgic for the social taxonomy of Louis XIV's reign as that of a man who defended the traditional and morally acceptable means of enrichment, in other words, "commendable Labor and generous Industry."[51] If he repeated the fables about the servants, it was because they were useful in that they underlined his purpose. Montesquieu, like all the Nobles of the Robe, was revolted by the reduction in the rentes and the overthrow of the balance of power between creditors and debtors: "I have seen covetous Debtors, proud of an insolent Poverty, become the most scandalous Instruments of the Fury of the laws, and of the Rigour of the Times; pretending a Payment, instead of making one, and cutting the very Throats of their Benefactors."[52] For him, the problem lay in the reimbursement of rentes, whether in shares or in banknotes, and the inflation that reduced debts to precious little, and it was drawn directly from the remonstrances of his colleagues in the *parlement* of Paris that Montesquieu drew his material.

On April 17, 1720, the Parisian magistrates sent the young monarch a petition concerning the reductions in the rentes that were to incite those who still possessed them to exchange them for shares in the Compagnie des Indes. This process was considered by justice officers to be "a reversal of the kingdom's laws": "Trade, Navigation, and participation in the General Farm of your majesty are not appropriate and, even more, are denied to a significant share of your subjects." According to these critics, clerics are by canon law expressly forbidden to engage in trade, which would inspire in them "a spirit of greed." As for officers and magistrates, they cannot buy shares "without depreciating and degrading their nobility." At almost the same time, on the same subject, the magistrates of the *parlement* of Toulouse are even clearer concerning the ethos of the landed nobility and the forms of legitimate income. What would happen to the heads of noble families if they were forced to invest "seemingly at random in a new form of commerce [i.e., shares] about which they knew nothing and risk the capital that is necessary to their families' subsistence?" The essential characteristic of trade—its risky nature, which Terrasson and Pannier d'Orgeville had done so much to mitigate in the System—is perceived by the magistrates as anathema to their nobility and, more broadly, as an unlikely and even dangerous basis on which to ground the monarchy, unless the aim is to overthrow the constitution. These remonstrances related, with many touching examples, the ruin to which creditors and rentiers had been reduced and denounced the terrible injustice done to them: "[T]he creditors have been forced to rely on the discretion of their debtors. . . . They have seen the Heritage of their Fathers perish in a single day . . . , & reduced to want, they have the grief of seeing enormous fortunes rise before their eyes." This topsy-turvy world was clearly implicated, and the magistrates wanted to inspire pity via the usual references to the rentier dispute. Thus, they spoke of poor widows, "unfortunate servants," and "ruined families." The picture they painted was naturally apocalyptic: no more dowries, fewer marriages, less education, the bourgeois classes leaving the cities to try to live on their country estates. And, in the midst of this litany, a terrible sentence was inserted, characteristic of the magistrates' background: "The most onerous Taxations have never come near the Evils which such a Reduction entails."[53] This short passage provoked the ire of John Law himself. In a letter published in London a few weeks later, he expressed his indignation at the accusations of the magistrates:

> The gentlemen of the *parlement* say with confidence that the heaviest taxes have never approached the wrongdoings brought about by such a reduction [in the rentes]. These are the very terms of their own remonstrances. . . . This comparison will deceive no one, but shall it not cause the indignation of those who love their country?[54]

Law thus recalled the "extreme calamities" caused by the extraordinarily high taxes of the previous reign. He emphasized again and again the terrible and incredible violence against "the most unfortunate" to extract from them some additional taxes: "One cannot hear without shedding tears the account of the sufferings that the commissioners were forced to inflict in order to ensure the collection from those who were obliged to pay, at a time when the allowances were considerably diminished."[55] For Law, the observation was simple: on the one hand, the vast majority of the subjects—and the taxpayers—did not hold any rentes; on the other, almost all the magistrates and nobles who held them had revenues that came from their land.[56] He admitted that there were probably some people who had only rentes to live on but objected that they could invest in shares and that they were so few in number that it was a lesser evil than having placed the burden on this minority. This was also Terrasson's argument against the casuists and a point at the heart of the controversy surrounding the monarchical form promoted by the System.

Among the opponents, d'Aguesseau was the most lucid. He agreed that at the top and the bottom of the social ladder everything was well. Of the three classes of citizens making up the state, "the two extremes make a fortune; the workers earn more." The most numerous, those engaged in "agriculture and the arts, subsist comfortably," and the least numerous, "[t]he rich of the first order . . . , live in opulence." The problem lay with those who were "between these two extremes," those who had received a "liberal education" and for whom it was "not possible to start working." D'Aguesseau considered that this class that he pitied so much was the most useful part of the kingdom.[57] This was precisely, as we have seen, what Law, Terrasson, and their allies contested. What was being played out here, through this myth of a topsy-turvy world conveyed by this class—which represents, in reality, a large part of the dominant class and in no way a "middle" class—was actually the creation of a *screen memory* in the Freudian sense of the term. This concept refers to a very clear, very powerful memory, with very vivid images, that serves to mask one or more other repressed memories, much more unpleasant. By adopting the point of view of the state propaganda, which promoted a carnival, the critics and opponents of the System participated in the birth of a myth that suited them—better yet, that relieved them. These government fantasies were not to be mocked; they were to be propagated and substantiated. Between the last two decades of the reign of Louis XIV and the years 1720–30 a memory was, thus, created, that of the fall of the System, set up as a disaster. That this so-called disaster was incomparably less than and even ridiculous in comparison to the appalling social suffering of the vast majority of the subjects of the kingdom during the terrible years 1708–13 was not the problem. On the contrary, it was the solution. Those whom d'Aguesseau called "the most numerous" had made a little noise at the end of the preceding reign, but the echo would be weak throughout the century. The fall of the System, however, was deafening and became the founding myth of the economic ruin of the kingdom. This second memory would go on and partly mask the first, to the great benefit of those who had no interest in witnessing a fiscal, administrative, even political revolution. For the dominant classes, the stake was enormous.

As long as Law and his followers intended to leave only baubles and trinkets to the nobility, to dispense with the *parlements*, to shift the tax burden from the productive to the idle classes, to melt down the kingdom into a "body of Merchants" with a single head and a few great figures, it was necessary to present this project as a total disaster. This is the image that would be remembered later in the eighteenth century and beyond.

But another narrative emerged in 1720–21. While, like Montesquieu, they were not duped by the state propaganda, the authors of the Théâtre de la foire produced at the same time a different discourse concerning the fall of the System. In the end, they actually argued in favor of the principle of the lottery and would have liked this topsy-turvy world to become reality rather than remain a fantasy. At the time that concerns us, there were two important fairs (*foires*) mounting theater productions in the capital alongside the official theater, the Comédie française. The first was the Saint-Laurent Fair, held at the top of the rue Saint-Denis from August 9 to September 29. Outdoors and inexpensive, it brought together craftsmen, merchants, and the bourgeoisie. The other major event was the Saint-Germain Fair, held from February 3 to the eve of Palm Sunday in the district of the same name. This fair attracted a much wealthier crowd, for obvious geographic reasons, but also because it offered a number of luxury businesses, operating out of wooden stalls of fairly solid construction. Under the Regency and until the 1730s, four men were the driving force behind the theater that took place during these fairs (the Théâtre de la foire): the playwrights Alain-René Lesage (permanently at odds with the Comédie française since *Turcaret* in 1709), his two associates Louis Fuzelier and Jacques-Philippe d'Orneval (called Dorneval), and Denis Carolet, of whom we have already spoken. In the valuable *Recueil des pièces du Théâtre de la foire* published from 1721 on, almost all the plays were scripted, rewritten, rearranged, and ultimately attributed to these four men.[58]

Two examples suffice to introduce their point of view on the fall of the System. The first is that of *La foire des fées* (1721) by Le Sage, Fuzelier, and Dorneval, and the second *La lanterne magique, ou Le Mississipi du diable* (1723) by Carolet. Presented at the Saint-Laurent Fair, the first was performed by a troupe of Italian actors hired by the Duke of Orléans. In the midst of a swarm of fairies and wondrous adventures, we meet a "Mr. Millioni, speculator." The poor man is a well-known figure: a former coach driver, yesterday a millionaire, today poor once again. The authors took their mockery of the former government propaganda to extremes: "We were a bunch of nouveaux riches, who made up a world apart. We emptied shops, we seized castles; and we deprived the public of wandering beauties." The references to the tales of the *Nouveau Mercure* are crystal clear, but, as Catherine Labio points out, a form of nostalgia can also be detected in this little scene.[59] The fairies have a certain softness for all those who believed and for that world that could have been turned upside down and would not have been without interest. Carolet was more specific. In the *Avantures de la rue Quincampoix* (1719), Carolet inserted the tale of the lackey become rich who rode on the back of his own carriage:

WAITER: You see, Monsieur, habit is second nature. He has not had his equipage long, and is not yet well versed in the customs. But after all, masters on the back and servants inside is but *ver jus, jus ver*, and I find no difference betwixt them save their clothes.

INNKEEPER: You are right, but there is no question at present of commenting on the rue Quinquempoix.[60]

Here Carolet used a phrase from Furetière, "it is *jus verd* or *verd jus*, that is to say, the same thing."[61] The waiter and the innkeeper agreed that there is little "difference" between master and servant, and this short dialogue suggests that the authors of the Théâtre de la foire did not see the new random distribution of wealth promoted by the System as such a bad thing. In *La lanterne magique*, Carolet mocked the government propaganda, this "devil of Scotland" and his "bag of Illusions." But, beyond this obvious connection with the experiment, the dramatist affirmed in his preface that satire was a serious thing "since the theater is no less entitled to correct the ridiculous nature of men than the Pulpit or the Bar." And, from this point of view, he did not deliver a monologic message; far from it. In other words, while the play criticized the politics of utopia initiated by the state and the cupidity and credulity of certain subjects, it was also a fierce caricature of the honest bourgeois class and the state of the world at that time.

The character of Folly is, in fact, the moralist of the play. Folly continually ridicules the old-school merchants and traders, the haughtiness that causes them to look at "good things in the wrong light," their money, "which allows them to despise those who have none," and the false "wisdom" "that one can obtain from a tailor." Implicitly recalling Molière, Folly affirms having never met among the bourgeois "an ingenious jest, politeness, or an easy turn of conversation," just "pretentiousness and self-interest." She likens all bourgeois customs—the obsession with cleanliness, the display of precious objects that must not be touched—to ridiculous "idolatry." The simpleton of the play is the honest merchant, whom Carolet named "Mr. Prudent." All Mr. Prudent wants is to confine himself to "what the experiment permits." He intends to "exercise prudence in all things." Folly replies that this seems to her to be very imprudent indeed and that "there is nothing so constant in the world as variety and change." As for the military glory that the System hoped to overshadow, Carolet also presented it in a somber light, officers having "for all merit the right to kill only men whom they have never seen." More generally, while Fortune claims that she will enrich seamstresses, coachmen, and grooms, Folly adds: "This will form a third kind of nobility." At the end of the play, all the actors buy the products of illusion and exchange their clothes with each other, but "Mr. Prudent" keeps his shirt and hates this deceit.[62]

Lesage, Fuzelier, Dorneval, and Carolet had seen the state intervene in their usual playground. As connoisseurs, they immediately realized that this represented both a problem for the authorities—a dangerous register for the state to take on—and a boon for them, provided they profited even more from the situation. From this point of view, they were in no way duped and participated in the criticism of the government carnival. But some aspects of the latter did not displease them. They had no particular respect for the nobility. They were not unhappy to see the honest bourgeois class defended by Montesquieu and the like being supplanted and brought down by a giant lottery. Even if they did not believe in it, they found the idea of inverting the social hierarchies pleasing. What is very interesting is that at the same time, after the fall of the System, the official theater did not embrace the same perspective at all, as will be seen in the following chapter. The authors of the Comédie française took a completely different attitude, that of the need for redemption after all these sins promoted by the government. Along with the moralists and all the enemies of the System, they were ashamed of what had happened and dreamed of making the post-System period one of atonement.

Shame and the Need for Redemption

Recall that among the figures of the government propaganda was that of the archangel Law-Michael, struggling with the forces of evil, the distrustful who fought against the advent of the System. It was easy for the counterpropaganda literature to reuse this eschatological allegory that was to see "the triumph of good over evil": all it took was to return to the book of Revelation and reverse the roles. Several satiric plays thus made Law a fallen and rebellious angel, the complete opposite of the archangel Michael. This was the case, for example, in the famous "Genealogy," which always begins in the same way: "And Beelzebub begat Law." Other literary works, such as a short tale in verse dating from 1720 and entitled "The Public Ruin," described Law as "Satan's firstborn."[63] In this literature, which scoffed at the System and its consequences, the devil was depicted as using all kinds of tricks and manipulations, which obviously did not produce the fantastic effects alleged by the propaganda. But was it really Law and his System being denounced here? Undoubtedly, but not only. To comprehend fully what was at stake here, we first need to explain what was understood by the use of images of the devil in the first decades of the eighteenth century.

The figure and notion of the devil experienced a twofold shift in France between 1680 and 1720. The first shift was based on dedramatization. The devil gradually ceased to be present in an everyday life that was directly lived. The myth no longer generated persecutory behavior, at least in western Europe. The figure of the devil fell into the sphere of dreams and artwork. It started to raise smiles and even laughter. The second shift concerned the devil's incarnation, no longer in obscure sorcerers or witches in the countryside, but in ordinary human beings—and all human beings. The devil was present in the human mind and became a driving force behind societies, as in Defoe's *The Political History of the Devil* (1726), translated into French in 1729.[64] The *Nouveau Mercure* of September 1719 published a paper entitled "Why We No Longer, or Almost Never, See People Possessed by the Devil," by a "M. de Chansierges." The author explained how, by dint of exorcisms and conjurations, the church had succeeded in chasing demons out of the bodies of men, these demons having since "employed a strategy that was quite the opposite of the former": "Let us seek all that can flatter them, they said amongst themselves. It is necessary that the Demons of vanity, avarice, self-interest, envy, &c., employ all skill and cleverness to possess the hearts of these men whom we have been powerless to overcome through pain and suffering."[65] The lesson was clear: the devil was, henceforth, present in everyone, and people needed to be wary of their own nature. On this register, the *Diable d'argent* by Lesage, Dorneval, and Fuzelier, a short prologue enacted in 1720 at the Saint-Germain Fair, brings us back directly to the subject at hand. On the stage, the Devil, accompanied by his good friend Folly, holds an audience, and several people come to ask for money: a banker, a prosecutor's wife, a soldier, a dancer, a Swiss guard, a poet, and so on. The Devil and Folly are most often generous (especially with the cleverest people), and Arlequin despairs that the authors of the play "have abandoned Parnassus, & retired to the celebrated *Province* of Quinquempoix." Folly adds: "'Tis true. They are almost all become Shareholders. And while they shall be rich, adieu to works of wit."[66] Thus, all succumbed to the call of fortune, the authors of the prologue using this entertaining devil as a "revealing and enlightening" being "at the service of critical reason." Indeed, the iconographic theme of this "devil of money" had been an allegory of disorganized greed since the end of the seventeenth century.[67] Moreover, the very famous satiric engraving of the *Great Mirror of Folly* entitled *Fortune Driven by Folly* also associates the devil and folly, as in the play by Lesage and Dorneval. The description of the scene begins as follows: "FORTUNE OF THE SHARES on her Chariot driven by FOLLY. . . . [A] large crowd of people of all states & all sexes is running after Fortune to catch Shares. In the clouds, a Devil is making bottles of Soap, which mingle with the notes distributed by Fortune."[68] The meaning is clear: envy—this miniature and universal demon—has led Parisians to collect false money that will lead them to despair, the notes and shares having no more value than soap bubbles.

Two short tales in verse dating from 1720 or 1721, of which several handwritten versions have survived, describe the same idea. The first is entitled "The Banker Devil" and the other, written in the manner of Rabelais, the "Story of Prince Papirius Nicknamed Money-Plunderer, Governor of the French Fools." In the first, Lucifer wants to punish his demons, accusing them of not sufficiently tormenting the humans, who all pride themselves on being of great integrity. One of the demons speaks up, asserting that he will hasten to undeceive his master:

> To convince you, I pray, allow me to be so bold.
> He said, and then went somewhere I was not told.
> No matter, the place means naught I fear;
> Besides, it is not in all this hemisphere
> A place where the love of money drives men mad.
> Through this bait was each and every one of them had,
> By the promise of treasure did the demon find
> How to unmask the heart, how to reveal the mind.

He promises that each person will earn a thousand écus for every sol invested in "a new Peru." Carnage ensues: people are killed in the headlong dash to take part in the enterprise. Here again, all the states are mocked: men "[i]n the city, in the court," "[t]he rabble and the nobility," the men of the church, etc., all want to be involved. They sell everything they possess, no longer work, leave the other "funds" so as to be able in a mere instant to ride in "golden carriages." Driven by an insatiable thirst for gain, the humans want to invest more and more sols with the demon:

> Those who gained, to gain still ever,
> Brought to him their gold and silver.
> And with each new profit, their thirst insatiable
> From this flow, gave back to the devil
> What he had taken from his treasure.
> But when with the wherewithal his master to undeceive,

Devil and treasure disappeared without a by-your-leave.
He took all and thus he fled
The nation he had stripped and bled.[69]

The reference to Law's flight is clear. He was that facetious little demon, but he was not the most guilty party since all he wanted was to undeceive his master. He had opened the eyes of human beings.[70] He was the instrument of God who had revealed how numerous were the imbeciles and the greedy and how easy it was to build a new Babylon on the foundations of corrupt human nature. The "Story of Prince Papirius" does not say anything different and actually goes even further in this register. In this bawdy and ribald anecdote made up of false "summaries" of chapters, the regent is "Papirius" and Law "Plunder-Oats," or *pille avoine* in French, this nickname directly inspired by the takeover of the lease of the General Farm in 1719 by the Compagnie des Indes under the name of Armand Pillavoine. Thus, Papirius called to his rescue "the famous apothecary, the great charlatan Plunder-Oats." The latter distributed boxes of paper said to contain "admirable remedies": "[T]hen, when they were opened, there was often nothing at all inside." Nevertheless, being a master of illusion and propaganda, Plunder-Oats "waved such strange signs . . . and bragged . . . that he had found a country where gold and silver grew, where the walls and houses were made of fine sugar." The text speaks of Plunder-Oats as a buffoon in "his theater" and of the French as avid and consenting spectators. Papirius and Plunder-Oats "waving a piece of silver at the end of a stick that the French fools caught in the air like docile poodles, and swallowed without question," had to be seen. In the last chapter, nothing is settled, for, even though certain men, "the Ciceros," denounced the "charlatans" "and thus quoted law, paragraph, etc. and so many other good laws, they were mocked by the governor of the holy laws [i.e., the regent], who turned them upside down, and therefore nothing remained recognizable in the isle of the French fools."[71]

Since the carnivalesque literature had been temporarily appropriated by the state with astonishing audacity, criticism of the System had no choice but to produce a false Menippean, the very essence of a monologic and serious discourse, under the cover of Rabelaisian language and imagery. Indeed, we should not forget that it was the *Nouveau Mercure*, the semiofficial government gazette, that in 1719 had employed bawdy vocabulary, cock-and-bull stories, and even the prophecies of Nostradamus to praise the merits of the System. This dangerous balancing act contributed much to the taste of the people of that time for the fantastic. Those who were not duped by such an undertaking therefore had to guard against employing any carnivalesque register. On the contrary, it was necessary to denounce the topsy-turvy world proposed by the government propaganda, to renounce the true fantasy in order to keep in mind the fundamental laws, the proper role of the magistrates, and the immutable principles of the kingdom. Under the guise of an ersatz subversion, the criticism of the System lamented the complicity and the duplicity of the French. This register was the complete opposite of the tongue-in-cheek attitude toward the propaganda of the Théâtre de la foire, which portrayed the government carnival in a positive light. The author of the "Story of Prince Papirius" believed, on the contrary, that greed and illusion would emerge triumphant thanks to the subversion organized at the level of government. This would have several consequences.

"The Banker Devil," the "Story of Prince Papirius," and Folly on her chariot in *Fortune Driven by Folly* all reveal the same fear. It was not so much the System that posed a problem as the fact that it had been so easily implemented and that it actually could have endured. Law here was but the revealer of two profound tendencies inherent to the subjects of the kingdom of France: their venality and their credulity. The experiment had made them appear in their true light. They had been tempted and had not resisted enough. In "The Banker Devil," it was Law himself, in his flight, who revealed the stratagem. The spectators had understood nothing. They probably would have wanted more. As for the "Story of Prince Papirius," it does not say whether the "Ciceros" succeeded in reversing the illusion, but it seems that this was not the case. The real-life "Ciceros" had actually been frightened by what they had witnessed. In a way, it called for a reflection, not so much on the System itself, almost anecdotal, as on the corrupt nature of mankind. Montesquieu expressed this idea with the greatest clarity and force. In one of his *Persian Letters* (1721) relating to the System, he explained that the greatest evil a minister could do was not that of "harming his monarch or bankrupting the people" but rather something much more dangerous, namely, setting a "bad example." There then follows a whole tragic litany: the narrator seeing a nation "instantly perverted from the humblest to the greatest among them," "the most virtuous Men doing the unworthiest Actions; and violating on all Occasions the first Principles of Justice," "honest citizen[s] . . . never go[ing] to bed without saying: I have ruin'd one Family to-day and to-morrow I'll ruin another," and "suddenly spr[inging] up in every Heart, an insatiable Thirst after Money." Montesquieu concluded: "What will Posterity say when she must blush for her Forefathers?"[72] This notion of shame is also found in the text accompanying *Mississippi, or The World-Famous Goldland in the Fancy of the Wind Trade* (fig. 5.1 above): "The hope that with the Shares came / Is fully paid in harm and shame."

England was also incriminated. In 1719, the new directors of the South Sea Company took advantage of the French experiment to also attempt a vast plan to convert the British public debt into shares in the company. Other companies were founded (with more or less phantom activities), some of the government elites supported and promoted the project, and a speculative fever seized Exchange Alley, the London equivalent of the rue Quincampoix. It should be remembered that Daniel Defoe had actively participated in the propaganda campaign around the launch of the English company back in 1710–11, and that the scheme, which was much less extensive, had already succeeded in converting part of the public debt into shares. This time, however, Defoe considered that the new directors had gone much too far—that they had deceived the public and that the project was unfeasible. To this end, he discussed what had happened in France and in Great Britain. He decided to denounce the "chimeras" and "new Oceans" that the Compagnie des Indes in France and the South Sea Company in England had sold to the public. In *The Anatomy of Exchange-Alley* (1719), he expressed concern over the "false News" and the "Terrors, Frights, Hopes, Expectations," aroused by "Imagination." He even denounced an "Original System of Cheat and Delusion." This was all the more serious because, as he saw it, the "Treason" came from the highest spheres. The main promoters of this plan were the "Whigs, Members of Parliament, and Friends to the Government." In *The Chimera* (1720) and *The Case of Mr. Law, Truly Stated* (1721), he lamented the minister of finance's promotion of the great rival kingdom of "Imaginary Stock" and projects that were "impracticable and imaginary, as the Missisippi."[73]

Defoe had not been so wary back in 1710–11. Even though he himself had not gone so far, his team's pamphlets depicted the South American continent as a land filled with gold and other minerals, in short an inexhaustible source of wealth that would forever transform the trade of England. The appeal to the imagination and the use of powerful signifiers (*Peru*, *Potosi*, etc.) were already very much present within a vast enterprise of propaganda initiated and financed by the British government. Defoe no doubt believed at the time that Harley was engaged in a credible project of limited scope that had nothing whatsoever to do with speculation. Nevertheless, the tools forged in 1710 to promote the first version of the South Sea Company were reused by the Moderns of the *Nouveau Mercure*, by the team of cartographers of the Le Maire–Bobé network, and by all the propagandists of Law's System. Passed through the French filter, this rhetoric crossed the Channel once again between 1719 and 1720 to place itself at the service of the South Sea Company. In this affair, Defoe denounced a monster that to him was no stranger. As he began to take a step back, he devoted an important part of *The Case of Mr. Law, Truly Stated* to a sort of mea culpa: "The Baits were laid so superficially, and the Hook appeared so open, that had we not been blinded by a voracious Avarice, it had been impossible to have brought a whole Nation to be plundered as they were, even running into the Pit with their Eyes open."[74]

The world of illusions on which the great project of the South Sea Company of 1719–20 had been built would not have succeeded without the active consent of the subjects of the kingdom of England. Defoe believed that there had been little need to "lay Traps and Plots" for everyone to throw themselves into this collective delirium. He described a people impatient to be duped and wanted to show "how mad we were then": "[W]e were a Temptation to our selves, our own Avarice led us on." He seemed to be sincerely affected by these events, almost wounded. What is symptomatic is that in 1719 he had spoken in very harsh terms of the speculators and the figure of the other, whereas, in *The Case of Mr. Law*, when he spoke of himself and the rest of the British public, he consistently used the personal pronoun *we*. Guilt was, thus, universally shared after the event. Defoe applied it to himself, and he no doubt did, indeed, have a few reasons to be ashamed. "Lady Credit," that so fragile divinity, had gone away, this time perhaps for good. For the time being, Defoe stated: "[T]he whole World cannot restore Credit in England to what it has been." The country would require the assistance, over a long period of time, of probity and integrity.[75]

It was not so much the actual or supposed ruin that would provoke the great European trauma of the year 1720 as it was guilt and shame. The people were ashamed of having been shown in such a miserable light when they had thought themselves so respectable, ashamed of having seen the state praise the merits of the carnival that it was supposed to contain or prevent, ashamed of having sometimes believed that the fantasy could become reality while at the same time mocking the beliefs of the common people. The ruling classes of the magistracy and the intellectual sphere were ashamed of human nature in general and of their own in particular.

In his famous chapter of the *Philosophical Essays concerning Human Understanding* entitled "Of Miracles," the Scottish philosopher David Hume (1711–76) stated that one must constantly defy all "supernatural and miraculous relations" precisely because of the "strong propensity of mankind to the extraordinary and the marvelous." He continually referred to the proclivity of mankind to believe the incredible, the natural inclination to fall into all the traps of impostures and illusions.[76] The contemporary critics of the events of 1720 did not have the capacity to stand back and reflect on themselves and on mankind: they were astounded by what they had witnessed. They too quickly subscribed to the idea that the fantasy register was henceforth an instrument of critical reasoning. The intellectual elites of the time of the Regency thought that the majority of their contemporaries could not see anything in the publicity around the System other than shameless propaganda. Yet that is not what happened. Some wanted to believe; others did, indeed, believe. They threw themselves into the illusion all the more easily because they ardently desired it. What worried the traditional elites was that in fact the system of nature proposed and imposed by the authorities seemed much more attractive, more beautiful, more appealing than anything they had seen so far. Of all the plays that had been enacted by the powers in office over several decades, the latter seemed the best to some bad subjects. This scary observation could generate only a strong reaction, which involved nothing less than making Law's experiment the original sin of the eighteenth century. Individuals and society had to be encouraged to produce a return on themselves. The System and its avatars had to be transformed into a work of moral edification, an enterprise of collective redemption, a vaccine against all revolutionary enterprises. It was at the cost of creating the great national and even international myth of the sin of 1720 that resilience could begin. If Fortuna, the goddess of gambling, the lottery, and luck, was defeated, it was necessary to return to Pocock's Virtù, her antithesis. Since both the advent of private initiative and the Hobbesian form of public management of interests were feared, what remained on the market of ideas? The return to humility, uprightness, and the repudiation of wealth, at least for a time.

6

The Hour of Reckoning

At the very end of 1720, John Law left France, never to return. The dismantling of the System was under way, as was the great intellectual and cultural reconfiguration of the whole experiment, which was transformed into a French and European myth. In his *Mythologies*, the philosopher and semiologist Roland Barthes observes: "[M]ythology can only have an historical foundation, for myth is a type of speech chosen by history: it cannot possibly evolve from the 'nature' of things." However, the task of myth is precisely to bring a concept, an event, or an object into history by naturalizing it: "[M]yth is constituted by the loss of the historical quality of things: in it, things lose the memory that they once were made. . . . Myth does not deny things, . . . it purifies them, it makes them innocent, it gives them a natural and eternal justification, it gives them a clarity which is not that of an explanation but that of a statement of fact."[1] Here I touch on an essential point of what became obvious after the experiment: *1720* became a fact of nature, a clear, obvious, and popular sign, that of the fall of Law and his paper money, a sign characterized by words such as *finance*, *bankruptcy*, *despotism*, and *jubilee*, a sign that anyone could use according to his needs, either for evil (in the overwhelming majority of cases) or for good (on rare occasions).

This myth was manufactured and used throughout the eighteenth century. What were the intentions of the playwrights, poets, philosophers, economists, and politicians, in different registers and genres, who drew on it? Were they seeking to extinguish or rekindle the subversive dimension of the experiment, to defend or overthrow the social organization, to fabricate or destroy certain memories, to think like moralists or like economists? Aided and abetted by the discourses of the propagandists about the System, Enlightenment writers played with the myth until the French Revolution reopened the controversy—whereupon the concrete effects of the experiment and its underlying logic, for a time sublimated and defused in myth, resurfaced en bloc during the great storm of modernity.

If 1720 was a sin, then its forgiveness needed to be encouraged. This is how the official theater proposed a form of redemption: since the solution of the economic Leviathan had failed, since there could be no general enrichment, since greed had produced so many catastrophes, there needed to be a return to an individual morality of simplicity. By reactivating the figure of the noble savage, many playwrights of the 1720s transformed the character of Arlequin into a moralist of his time: he turned contempt for wealth into a virtue; he praised the kind heart, the honest soul, naïveté. It was not that social organization was good—it was bad, but the carnival did not produce anything good either. The point was to retire, to cultivate your garden, to work with the sole aim of living a decent life. Rather than liberating desires, it was necessary to limit them. Some new utopias from those years—those based on the ideas of François Fénelon—proposed the same ideal of simplicity while seeing the stability of hierarchies, power, wealth, and absolute respect for the law as the counterpoints of the System.

As early as 1720, the *conte merveilleux* (tale of marvels) was used by both opponents and supporters of the experiment. This literary genre, the fruit of propaganda, was given a twist by the experiment's opponents so as to express the theme of charlatanism: Law was presented as a fairground juggler, and the System's expectations were projected into a fantastic elsewhere. The idea was to shame those who had believed in it and reassure the skeptics. How foolish people must have been to believe these cock-and-bull stories! But it was all over, and the society that lay in front of everyone's eyes could be contrasted with the illusions of propaganda. The problem was that this rhetoric could itself be reversed: the supporters of the System in the years 1720–30 used the tale to point out that this same society was utterly miserable compared to the society that might be devised. By returning to the field of the marvelous, they sought to renew the spectacle, to reopen possibilities, to replay the exotic, to release new desires. The imagination as a historical force was returning to center stage. The aesthetic of the 1730s turned the System into a tale that was also a guide on how to live one's life.

The following decades were marked by the ebb of this aesthetic genre and by the advent of political economy. The important point now was how this new monarchical form, this nation as a "body of Merchants," this potentially authoritarian total state, was viewed by Enlightenment economists and philosophers. From the 1730s until the debates over the liquidation of the Compagnie des Indes at the end of the 1760s, most theorists denounced the public management of the French economy. For the Physiocrats, the capital vice of the System was that it had refused to trust competition, individual interest, and the market principle. By violating property rights and free trade, Law's experiment had been unable to ensure the creation of wealth. For others, by destroying the rentiers, those natural supporters of the monarchy, and by making the Compagnie all-powerful, the System had raised an entity that would bring down the king and establish a "republic of merchants." The general relief among debtors and the so-called carnival of the poor who had become rich was seen by many as a jubilee, in other words, as an egalitarian redistribution of wealth. Montesquieu, for his part, spoke of *despotism* in the sense of social leveling. By turning the fall of the System into a trauma of memory, he emphasized, at the very heart of the Enlightenment, this screen memory that masked something else—not a despotism, but the tyranny of the previous reign. Some contemporary historians, dependent on the myth of the trauma of 1720, believed that the System relied on force and authority to maintain itself. We will see that this was a paper authority and that it was the System's weakness—its inability to enforce its mandates—that precipitated its downfall.

Finally, under the French Revolution, debates crystallized around the assignats. Hitherto, it had been thought that Law's experiment was used as a foil by both supporters and opponents of this new currency. The former did not want the assignats to be equated with Law's paper and argued that they were much more solidly grounded (by the land and the general will). The latter either drew an analogy between the fall of the System and the Revolution or decided that the comparison tended to favor Law as his stocks and his paper had a more secure basis than did the assignats. But, as we shall see, this was a much deeper debate, one that gave a new lease on life to the play that the System had constituted. Just as rentiers were more important than any other subjects for the monarchy, owners and creditors were more citizens of the Revolution than were debtors and employees for the adversaries of assignats. Likewise, the adversaries of assignats thought that there were natural laws of economics that no human will could force. The "exaggerated" republicans and all the radicals felt, on the contrary, that it was the despotic steering wheel of the System that must be set in motion again: it was necessary to redistribute wealth by canceling debts, plundering the property of rentiers to put them to work, and violating property rights if necessary. The Convention would even seek to demonetize gold and silver for individuals and make the revolutionary heart the sole holder of cash, in a logic close to that of the System. This project would ultimately fail owing to its radicalism and also because it was too close to the myth of 1720.

The Return of Virtue

With *La querelle des théâtres* (1718), *Les funérailles de la foire* (1718), and *Le rappel de la foire à la vie* (1721), the Lesage team staged the hostility to which the *opéra-comique* was subjected on the part of official theaters. The latter, the Comédie française and the Comédie-italienne, were not to be outdone and responded sharply to these criticisms in several short plays that mocked the so-called mediocrity of the Théâtre de la foire. The stakes in the dispute were many but can be reduced to a problem of competition between institutions: the subsidized theater complained about competition from the Théâtre de la foire and sought to assert its monopoly over entertainment in the capital.[2] Above all, this economic rivalry was coupled with different relationships to recent events. After the fall of the System, some authors of the Théâtre de la foire did not, as we have seen, hesitate to return explicitly to the experiment by expressing a certain nostalgia for an era that was not lacking in interest and piquancy. After 1721, the official theater expressed quite different feelings. The plays that were performed there were much more cautious. They rarely directly describe events, and, when they did so, it was only allusively. After all, the official theater was now the defender of simplicity and poverty. Contempt for wealth—but also for society and its laws—became the leitmotif of a return to a primitive and "savage" virtue. Other cultural productions struck the same note, using Law's experiment as a counterpoint to new utopias.

On September 12, 1721, the Italian actors of His Royal Highness the Duke of Orléans performed at the Hôtel de Bourgogne a play entitled *Le fleuve d'oubly*. The plot is very flimsy. Trivelin is in the underworld, standing on the banks of the River Lethe; he explains that Pluto has authorized all mortals who wish to come and drink from its waters, which induce complete forgetfulness. Trivelin does not doubt that it will be very crowded, "for there are many malcontents up there." So a marquis, "recently created such, who has found the secret of earning a million in less than six months," would like to forget that he was once a "petty clerk."[3] The play waxes ironic about all the ways to ease the consciences of both losers and winners under the System. After all, for a year or two now, everyone has had something to forget—starting with the author, Marc-Antoine Legrand, who no doubt wished to forget his role as a propagandist in the years 1718–20. However, faced with the myriad moral and psychological solutions proposed by the Comédie-italienne during the post-System era, we are forced to conclude that forgetting was not the most satisfactory solution. Legrand's play was relatively successful, but had little impact, either at the time or at any time since. Things were quite different for two plays also performed by the troupe of Italians in the pay of the regent: *Arlequin sauvage*, which premiered on June 17, 1721, and *Timon le misanthrope*, which premiered on January 2, 1722. These two texts by Louis-François Delisle de la Drevetière (1682–1756), who had become a playwright after studying the law, achieved significant success.[4]

In *Arlequin sauvage*, Arlequin is an American "savage" who arrives in Marseille with Lélio and is amazed by European customs. In *Timon le misanthrope*, by contrast, Timon, a wealthy Athenian, has isolated himself from the world. He agrees to return to it after the gods have transformed his donkey into a human being, Arlequin, who is here again a kind of incredibly naive savage. The main focus of the two plays revolves around enrichment and the function of money in human societies. The Arlequin of *Arlequin sauvage* does not understand why Europeans need "laws" and "justice" to rule. He does not know what money is. He takes the goods offered to him without paying, and his behavior gives rise to several comic scenes. When Lélio explains to him what money is, Arlequin replies: "So tell me quickly where people give out this money so that I can stock up on it." He is told that "it isn't given out." He then asks: "[W]ell, where can I get some?" And Lélio replies: "You can't get any either." Thus ends the wealth that fell on anyone and everyone in the days of the System's grand lottery. Everything is back to normal, and Lélio sums it up with disarming Boisguilbert-style simplicity: the rich have all the money, and, "if the poor are to have some, they have to work for the rich." So does one have to be rich to be happy? asks Arlequin. Certainly not, says Lélio, because the rich are insatiable: their desires know no bounds; they thirst for new things, for money, for luxury. Arlequin concludes: "But if this is so, the rich are poorer than the poor themselves since they lack more things." The American savage, who says he has seen more impertinence in a day in Europe than in a thousand years in his forests, exclaims:

> I think you are foolish people who think you are wise, ignorant people who think you are clever, poor people who think you are rich, & slaves who think you are free. . . . You devote much effort to seeking for countless unnecessary things. . . . You are slaves to all your possessions, which you prefer to your freedom & to your brothers.[5]

The moral of *Timon le misanthrope* is the same. When he was rich, Timon thought that he too was "a slave to a thousand unnecessary things," and he does not miss his former state. However, he returns to Athens accompanied by Arlequin with a treasure that Mercury, disguised as a woman (another Lady Credit), has given him. However, he categorically refuses to use it. Arlequin steals it from him, but Timon does not hold it against him: "I could have him punished, but the treasures he has laden himself with will be enough for his punishment." Indeed, Arlequin, now rich, suffers nothing but setbacks and complains bitterly about men who make up "with riches for all their faults of heart and mind." He is horrified by the love that is for sale and the prejudices that favor fine clothes and decides that "there would be fewer fools, if everyone remembered their origin." At the end of the play come "Truths," who sing for the edification of the spectators: "I despise the advantages / Of clothes and attendants."[6] Fortunately, Mercury decides to take back the wealth entrusted to Timon, who will be able to get married, have Arlequin working for him, and at last be happy. Thus, the liberation from desires promised by the System is, in fact, just another bondage. The nouveaux riches pursue goals that always elude them. They are chained to the illusion of happiness that comes from spending money. Money replaces moral qualities in the social game, but such a play casts doubt on whether this is a stable way of regulating human societies.

Three years later, on July 9, 1725, the same Italian comedians performed, at the Hôtel de Bourgogne, a play entitled *L'embarras des richesses*. Once again, this was a huge success for an author who would experience such success rarely in his career. Léonor-Jean-Christine Soulas d'Allainval, known as Dallainval (1700?–53), belonged to the class of men of letters who lived in poverty. After a life of wandering, he died in complete destitution at the Hôtel-Dieu in Paris in the middle of the century.[7] Did he despise wealth, like his characters? His obscure existence does not allow us to draw any conclusions, but his play certainly does have several connections with those of Delisle. The plot is inspired by a fable by La Fontaine that we have already discussed, *Le savetier et le financier*. The scene is located in Athens, where Arlequin again embodies the naive savage (here he is a gardener) who reveals human truths. He lives next to the palace of a financier, Midas. Arlequin sings every morning while on his way to work, which annoys Monsieur and Madame Midas, outraged by his carefree life and good humor. They ask him why he is not unhappy about being poor, and that makes him laugh. Arlequin does not understand the point of being rich since he cannot eat for two. To avenge themselves for this happy simplicity, the couple appeal to Plutus, who manages to convince Arlequin to accept a treasure. From then on, nothing goes right for him. He neglects his mistress, becomes irascible, tortured, and insatiable, and "no longer recognizes himself." He absolutely wants to return the treasure to Plutus and complains to Midas about wealth: "What devilish blessings they are that make the world miserable!" Finally, poor and happy once more, he will no longer hear of "becoming a great lord" because, he says, "it's not the fashion." The vaudeville that ends the performance is very clear about the moral of the play:

Riches, vain honors
Are chains that hinder life,
Happy the one who, far from these grandeurs,
Spends his days enviably;
He knows only pleasures,
His meadow is all that he desires.[8]

Unlike Legrand's *Plutus*, *L'embarras des richesses* returns to the original meaning of La Fontaine's fable: in order to be happy, we must not keep treasure (in the sense of spending it) but return it as quickly as possible. It was again at the Comédie-italienne in 1725 that Marivaux mounted a production of his *L'île des esclaves*, which in many ways belonged to this set of moral plays. The plot is once again set in Greece, on an island where former enslaved people have established a republic that has set itself the task of amending the great and their way of life. So all those who have been the masters until now become enslaved for three years, and vice versa. Cléanthis and Arlequin, formerly enslaved, are given their freedom and provide some moral lessons to their former masters. Cléanthis, for example, admonishes them thus:

> How awful it is to have as one's sole merit gold, silver and dignities! It was hardly worth being so boastful! Where would you be today if this was our only merit for you? Come on, wouldn't you be in a fix? The point is to forgive you, and in order to be kind enough to do this, what, if you please, does one need to be? Rich? No. Noble? No. A great lord? Not at all. You were all of that; were you any the better for it? So what does it take? Ah, here we have it. One must have a kind heart, virtue and reason; this is what is needed, this is what is estimable, this is what distinguishes a person—what makes one man more than another.

Should the masters be punished? Should the lords be thrashed or even killed? Certainly not, for they are just poor unfortunate people who had nothing but their wealth and their titles. Their former servants have showed them that they themselves were worth a hundred times more than their masters and then forgave them. All return to Athens in their former roles in life, and the play ends with vows of harmony and union. The periodicals that Marivaux published in the 1720s, such as the *Spectateur français* and *L'indigent philosophe*, echo the same themes. In them, the author castigates the rich and "all the jumble of worries and superfluous needs with which they are tormented, which are born from their inflamed corruption, which spoil their hearts, which lead their minds astray, and plunge them, for mere trifles, into an abyss of deceit and villainy against each other." Marivaux contrasts these individuals with the figure of the plowman and his "innocent desires," "his cheerfulness," who "resumes his work with pleasure, and finally dies as serenely as he has lived."[9]

This distrust of both greatness and money was still center stage five years later at the Comédie-italienne, for example, in a play by the poet and playwright Louis de Boissy (1694–1758) entitled *Le triomphe de l'intérêt* (1730). Performed with great success, the play takes place "in a Financial Palace" where Mercury, who represents honor and former military glory, challenges Interest, personified as a deity. At the end of the play, Mercury is abandoned by his troops, who are lured by the immense riches of Interest. The conclusion is that greed reigns, but once again it is Arlequin who provides the meaning of the story. Interest is portrayed throughout the play as a heinous character, but honor and glory are no better. Arlequin wants none of them: "They are both dubious. Interest is Norman & Honor is Gascon." Of Interest, Arlequin says: "[He] takes away sleep, provides troublesome care: I have no desire to learn how to be miserable. . . . As for honor & for virtue, all things considered, I will take of them just what I need so as not to be hanged."[10]

Commentators who have examined these plays in the twentieth and twenty-first centuries have sometimes noted, without offering any explanation, the development of the character of Arlequin from the 1720s on.[11] Initially the clodhopping *zanni*, a heavy drinker whose back is always being belabored with blows, Arlequin later becomes the great moralist of the period, a "universal censor,"[12] in the guise of a newly minted noble savage. The System—that original sin of the new century—naturally had a great deal to do with this. The myth of the noble savage was used as a heuristic device before Delisle de la Drevetière, and his Arlequin is none other than the savage of Lahontan-Gueudeville. The latter figure was, as we have seen, a reaction against individual interest and greed erected as virtues. The fantasized life of American Indians served as a counterpoint to the social organization of Europeans, which was deemed to be inegalitarian and oppressive. Updating the figure of the savage as a critical tool after the System thus involved seeing the System as an inadequate response to such injustices. By seeking to enrich everyone and promote superfluous spending, the experiment actually fell into the same paradigm as that of the world of Louis XIV. The great Leviathan certainly wished to do the right thing: he sought to make people prosperous and happy, he tried to improve the lot of the poor, but he failed because there is no economic solution to the problems of human societies. Only morality is capable of regulating them satisfactorily.

The reversal of conditions, the desire of commoners to imitate the nobility, and the blunders that ensue are comedic devices widely used in the theater from the seventeenth century on. What is interesting in the plays just discussed is precisely that the humble heroes no longer want to escape from their condition. They do everything to remain poor and simple or to become so again. They no longer want to replace their masters and ape their behavior. Seeking to be a "great lord" has been a "fad," in other words, a passing craze. A man à la mode is, for dictionaries and writers of the time, a character whose star shines brightly but fades quickly. He owed his rise to a whim, usually that of the prince. The same goes for things: a small group of initiates creates a fleeting fashion that will be a flash in the pan. The moralists of the late seventeenth century and the early eighteenth saw this as a factor in the destabilization of the social order. Fashion does not make a good man. Quite the contrary. It ruins him, corrupts him, makes him ridiculous. Fashion gives authority to something or someone simply through the allure of novelty.[13] Fashion and the fashionable man demean true greatness, and, from this point of view, there is something both absurd and outrageous about having wanted to turn great lords and their practices into a fashion. In a stable monarchy, to be great is a fact, an immutable reality that cannot be subject to fashions. It should be added that greatness involves responsibilities and inconveniences that not everyone can take on. It is, thus, a contradiction in terms: the great lords, decreed to be such arbitrarily by the System, were in fashion (à la mode) only because their greatness was fictitious and their behavior inappropriate. Post-System theater reminds us of this simple but essential truth: greatness and wealth are undesirable if one is not meant for them; they will cause only worry to those who cannot use them. All fashions claim victims, especially those who do not have the means to be fashionable, which is always the case of those who start out with little but think they can succeed. Thus, power promotes the praise of poverty, simplicity, even naïveté. One may well doubt the performativity of this type of discourse. However, some people did start singing from this particular hymn sheet. The diarist Mathieu Marais tells us that *Timon* is creating "a real stir," and he praises the author for "sowing the seeds of a very strong moral, derived from pure reason." Regarding the same play, the journalist from the *Mercure* does not hide his enthusiasm for a new genre of play "unlike anything we have seen before": "Everything is simple, naive, & the Metamorphosis is used with so much art, that it brings out the bare truth from the bosom of nature, & the comedy from nature & truth." *L'île des esclaves* was a great success, if we are to believe another review in the *Mercure*, which praised the play and found it "very touching." Regarding *Arlequin sauvage*, the marquis d'Argenson went even further: "You can criticize this piece as much as you like for being too philosophical; this is the same, as they say, as complaining that the bride is too beautiful. In it, our whole way of life is corrected, while ordinary plays cover only a few vices in particular. Long live the natural law!"[14]

Shame, that poison of the soul, brought about a post-System guilt that generated its natural antidote, the incitement to virtue. In this sense, the trauma produced by the experiment was useful because it settled the questions posed by the crisis of conscience in the society of Louis XIV. The System sought to defuse both the disturbing effects of free trade, by state regulation of the economy, and the absolutist raison d'état, by uniting the king and his subjects in a new body, that of the trading nation. In doing so, it was necessary to open the way to riches for everyone and anyone, resulting in a form of liberation from hitherto repressed desires. Since this attempt had fizzled out, since it seemed futile to try and put an end to inequalities and unfair conditions, any idea of economic or political regulation of social relations had to be abandoned in favor of a return to moral regulation. This is very clear in the work of Delisle, Dallainval, and Marivaux, for whom it was no longer a question of producing a permanent carnival or even an ephemeral one (in the sense that the servants imitate the masters for a time). Rather, it was a morality that would put an end to the desire for generalized enrichment and the subversion of the social order. It was less about freeing desires—for money, titles, dignity, autonomy, sex—than it was about extinguishing them. The moralists of the 1720s opposed the hedonism of the System with a happy austerity, a form of ataraxia. This could be read as a clever way of defusing any dispute but also as the promotion of an individual morality that invited everyone to a form of withdrawal, asking them to step aside from society. Instead of fine clothes and a retinue, feigned praise, fictitious glory, and inconsequential love affairs, the Arlequin of the post-System period constantly promoted the memory of his origins, the feelings of the heart, the nobility of the soul, virtuous poverty, priceless love. Men were invited to reflect on themselves.[15] They were encouraged to transform themselves—their needs and wills—rather than changing the way society was organized. What was the use, deep down, of endeavoring to change an order that was admittedly unjust but the overthrow of which would produce even more disastrous consequences? In a secular version of Christian moralism, it was about being content with what you had and seeking happiness in yourself. What do you really aspire to as an individual? What are your real desires? Are they those that the System's propaganda has put forward or, on the contrary, the simpler ones that suit your condition? Besides the authorities' desire to extinguish the subversive fire, how can we not see here a return to the subject or even to the construction of the subject after the great, all-encompassing whole, similar to the state utopias, that the System had sought to be? While Terrasson, Pannier d'Orgeville, and Law openly proposed the reunification of individual wills into one, and while they promoted a Hobbesian entity of subjugation, involving the birth of a great economic

Leviathan, the end of the experiment led to a swing of the pendulum that fostered individualism. This praise of singularity instead of imitation and the spirit of the system, which Marivaux embodied in his journals of the 1720s,[16] was, among other things, a by-product of the System.

Alongside these anthropological reflections, some authors, either implicitly or explicitly, drew a contrast with Law's experiment with republican utopias—more or less following the lead of Fénelon. Take, for example, *Les femmes militaires* (1735) by Louis Rustaing de Saint-Jory (d. 1752), a man of letters who worked for the Comédie-italienne and was in touch with Marivaux. This work employs prosopopoeia, the narrator giving voice to a Dutch navigator who claims to have discovered a fabulous island. The opening lines of the play serve as a perfect counterpoint to the well-ordered and well-regulated society that will be described a few pages later: "The year 1720, so famous for incredible revolutions, was more fateful for me than for anyone. The loss of a lawsuit cost me half my property, a reimbursement robbed me of all the rest." In other words, a debtor has discharged his debt to the narrator in depreciated paper money. The narrator then decides to embark for England. He invests his last funds in a long-term trading company and, thus, meets a famous navigator. Then begins the description of an island colonized in the Middle Ages by a French fleet stranded on its coast. We discover a strange political organization with various deliberative assemblies made up of "virtuous gentlemen" and at their head a duke or a duchess elected by the grandees. As in the theater, even though there are inequalities in income and conditions, these people "have hardly any money": "[B]ut in return, they have none of the vices produced by the thirst for wealth." The islanders are unacquainted with refinement; their politeness is that of "the depths of their feelings."[17] The society is a sort of mythical golden age of the French nobility, agrarian, virtuous, and simple, with the sole exception of the great role played by women, who are more or less the equals of their husbands. Stability and laws are the hallmarks of this utopia; its political, economic, and legal structures have not budged an iota since the arrival of the Frankish knights several centuries earlier. It is precisely this ideal of stability that lies at the heart of Armand de Madaillan de Lassay's utopia, *Relation du royaume des féliciens* (1727). Lassay was close to Law and the Compagnie des Indes, but, more importantly, in the 1720s he was a member of the Club de l'Entresol founded by the historian and librarian Pierre-Joseph Alary (1689–1770). The club had around fifteen members and met in the Place Vendôme in Paris to discuss international and political issues. Fénelon's work exerted a strong influence on the men involved. They loathed the tyranny of the reign of Louis XIV and its incessant conflicts, sought the material prosperity of the regime's subjects, but wished for the maintenance of a strong social hierarchy and the strict control of the lower orders.[18] Lassay's *Relation* is imbued with all these themes.

The *Relation* begins by telling the story of the narrator, who leaves France in a hurry, probably for financial reasons, and ends up in Holland, where he embarks on a ship of the Dutch East India Company. After being shipwrecked off what is now Cape Town, he discovers an island where people speak "a very beautiful Latin." No wonder since it was founded by Romans who arrived there around two thousand years ago, then mingled with the locals and established a new civilization. Lassay warns the reader—there is an evident contrast with *Arlequin sauvage*, and the reader is also put in mind of *Télémaque*—that he will speak of a kingdom "where one is ruled by Laws rather than by men." In this way, we discover an extremely prosperous, civilized society with very strict laws. It is a republic made up of several assemblies, with a government very close to that of England but much more stable since none of its institutions or laws have changed for twenty centuries and the reigning family is the same as it was at the beginning. It is neither "ambition [nor] greed" that moves the inhabitants of this island but virtue alone. From an economic point of view, trade is supposed to be free in the sense that there are no exclusive privileges or corporations, and customs duties are low. Luxury is not forbidden since people feel that it allows the circulation of money; however, the prices of goods are fixed by the government and do not depend, in any case, "on the will of those who sell them." There are also public granaries that regulate the price of grain, laws requiring parishes to support the poor and the old and taxes them enable them to do so, and a division of land that observes the strictest equality when it comes to the lords.[19]

Lassay's utopian society is based on traditional republican ideas, elements of the System that would have worked (the logic of spending, the control of the economy), and a handful of institutions copied from England. If there are certain differences between the projections of Saint-Jory and Lassay, they converge in their defense of stability. Basically, this point is as essential as the criticisms they both level against greed. Virtue, for them, is not that of the noble savage who denounces inequality, wealth, and hypocrisy; it is that of an absolute respect for laws and institutions. In this sense, these utopias are, indeed, hollow critiques of the System, which had frequently violated them. Was this for better or for worse? While the theater and the post-1720 utopias did not openly answer this question and preferred to shift the terms of the debate, the expectations and the results of the experiment returned at the same time to the heart of another literary genre, one that was less direct, more suggestive, and very fashionable: the *conte merveilleux*.

The Time of Stories

State propaganda and the revolutionary expectations that it brought with it fixed the grammar of the debate—that is, the grammar of the marvelous. The years following the fall of the System were, thus, dependent on this register. It was the tale—often the Oriental tale—that was the main vector of the clashes between adversaries and supporters of the System in the following decades. Between 1721 and 1748, an important intertextual network—that is, a network of relations, direct or indirect—between these texts was created, culminating in the *Histoire du Système des finances* by Marmont du Hautchamp, published in 1739. Circles close to power regularly resorted to the mode of enchantment, from Louisiana to alchemy, and including the "Deity of the Royal Bank" and the diamonds of Terrasson. If we adopt the classic categories put forward by the theoretician of literature Gérard Genette,[20] there were several "travesties" and "charges" of this discourse, that is to say, the first satires that used the marvelous register of power, transforming or imitating it to mock it. This was the case with the allegories of the devil of money (*diable d'argent*) and also with the "Story of Prince Papirius" as well as many engravings in the *Great Mirror of Folly*. We will also note that the chansonniers of the time produced several variations on the theme of Cinderella;[21] it was, thus, quite natural that two important authors of the period, Montesquieu and Antoine-François Prévost d'Exiles, known as Abbé Prévost, should have used the satiric marvelous tale to talk about the experiment.

Montesquieu included in his *Persian Letters* (1721) the short fable the "Fragment of an Ancient Mythologist," and in the same vein he wrote his "Lettres de Xénocrate à Phérès," published posthumously in 1892. Taking up the metaphor of Addison, also present in the *Great Mirror of Folly*, in the "Fragment" Montesquieu turns Law into a son of Aeolus and a nymph from Caledonia who distributes the wind, which he has enclosed in wineskins, and grabs the gold of the poor kingdom of Bétique (France) before disappearing for good. In the "Lettres de Xénocrate," the Scotsman does not appear directly, unlike the regent, named Alcamène, who reigns in Sicyon (Paris):

> The gods, angry with Sicyon, sent a dream to Alcamène one night; he believed he was the master of all the treasures in the universe; this dream was the cause of the people's poverty.
>
> However, Themis took off her blindfold and saw that temples to Plutus were being erected on all sides in Sicyon: "Mortals," she cried, "beware of the god whom you serve"; but she herself was driven from her temple, fell silent and no longer gave her oracles. In one night all the altars of Plutus were

overturned, his priests fled, and all those who had followed his worship were delivered up to the four Titans.[22]

The satire is serious in appearance. How could it not be when Plutus had so often been used in whimsical plays that were favorable to the System? Montesquieu therefore contrasts him with the goddess of justice, who is first abused and then resumes her rights after the fall of the deity of wealth and abundance. She ultimately triumphs over what was inspired by a dream. Prévost, meanwhile, treats the experiment in several ways in his *Aventures de Pomponius, chevalier romain* (1724), which he describes in the epistle less as a novel "than the History of our time under borrowed names." The hero of this extraordinary adventure travels to the moon, where the Greek philosophers have founded colonies and all the books written and to be written on the history of mankind can be found. We learn in various ways what is happening around the year 1715 "in Gaul." Prévost first reports a catalog of fake book titles, mocking the nouveaux riches of Mississippi. He then relates "The Story of the Prince of Relosan," an anagram of Orléans, in a whimsical and licentious manner. He ends finally with the "Summary of the chapters, contained in the chronicle of Chevalier Sotermelec," in the playful Rabelaisian and *merveilleux* styles. In this little Oriental tale, the Duke of Orléans is Sotermelec and Louis XIV Den Sadik. After having wrested from the "round caps" (justice officers) the power of the "testamentary tables" of the late king, Sotermelec gives the "office of great calculator" to a "certain Caledonian charlatan and defector," whereupon the grandees "became merchants of paper." They invented "a great crucible to melt gold & silver," and "the debtors paid their debts with bran, & gave smoke instead of gold." Sotermelec undertakes a traffic "bailed out to a company" of "walnut shells, eel skins, matches &c."[23] This text is a pastiche of "Papirius" that echoes several elements of Montesquieu's "Fragment of an Ancient Mythologist" (Caledonia, the "smoke").

Thus, "Sotermelec" and the "Fragment" are framed in an identical register, that of charlatanism. Law becomes a fairground juggler, and the French are naive spectators drawn into the "empire of the imagination."[24] The conjurer has made people take wind and smoke for money; he has tried to make them believe that metals are worth nothing, that paper is everything, and even that a trading company that did not exist could bring in millions. By travestying the marvelous nature of propaganda, these satiric tales attempt to provoke the embarrassment of all those who have or might have paid it serious attention. They mock the unrealistic expectations that the System has fostered by placing them in a fanciful elsewhere that defuses them and makes them ridiculous. Post-System shame is staged by Prévost and Montesquieu.

But, if they insist on gullibility (more than greed), it is in order to reassure their readers. For who could ever have given credence to such dreams? Who could have got so passionate about this lamentable spectacle? A few gullible people. These anti-System tales are there to reassure the mistrustful and the nonbelievers whom Terrasson had castigated not long ago. They seem to say to everyone, You were scared, but it's all over. If this was all indeed a fanciful mystification, which can easily be transposed into cock-and-bull stories, then anyone who laughs or smiles when reading them is immediately relieved. He closes the book, and returns to real life. What does he see? That the dream or the nightmare is gone, that the story is behind him, that a familiar world is now before his eyes: the world of rentes, intermediary bodies, land ownership. He may have endured pain, the stigma may still be visible, but he has simply been the victim of a fleeting swindle that will not return. The tale instills the idea that things are back to normal for good. The problem is that this process can be reversed. More precisely, it is this same familiar world that may look pale and even be judged disastrous, nightmarish, delusional, compared to the tale. This is precisely one of the factors that explains the arrival on the market shortly after Montesquieu and Prévost of the ideas of those defenders of the System who seek to fight back on the same ground.

From a chronological point of view, first on the scene was Jean-François Melon, a former collaborator of Law, a Modern from the circle of Verrue, and his Oriental novel *Mahmoud le Gasnévide* (1729). The book describes an empire in its heyday under the leadership of a wise and conquering monarch who is said to have lived on the borders of India and Afghanistan around the year 1000 CE. To compose his work, Melon drew many historical details from the *Bibliothèque orientale* (1697) of Barthélemy d'Herbelot de Molainville (1625–95) and Antoine Galland.[25] As in the *Persian Letters* and the *One Thousand and One Nights*, it is a process of embedding that is at work, with several stories inserted in what is neither an allegory of the Regency,[26] nor a book of historical scholarship, but an Oriental tale. In his states, Mahmoud has entrusted the wise minister Amrou with the management of finances and trade. Gold and silver are the main means of trade. However, to compensate for their insufficiency, Amrou sometimes uses "*Algors*, on the Tributes from the Province of *Kovarems*," in other words "rescriptions or assignements," as indicated in a footnote inserted by Melon. These papers are identical to the bills of financial obligation payable by the treasurers of the General Farm, bills that serve as advances for the expenditure of the state on its future revenues. Melon praises this means of payment, which, however, remains limited and was used before and after the System. However, he goes further by inserting a story told to Mahmoud by the queen of another kingdom, that of

Redoc. Faced with the scarcity of shells for currency, Saugar, one of Redoc's ministers, found a happy expedient, the introduction of "red leather squares" of different sizes, which not only facilitated trade but was also the condition of unparalleled prosperity: "This Kal, which the Senate always ensures is in sufficient quantity for the needs of the state, makes our lands better cultivated, our provinces more populous, & multiplies our manufactories. . . . Abundance reigns everywhere."[27] Unlike the "Algors," leather has completely replaced shells (the previous currency). (The amount of "Kal" in circulation is regulated at the discretion of the public authorities, who can create or destroy them at will.) Mahmoud is filled with admiration as he listens to this tale, and Melon takes up this process by making the reader another Mahmoud five years later in his *Essai politique sur le commerce* (1734).

In the *Essai*, with its perfectly rational style, heralding the political economy treatises of the second half of the century, Melon introduces a fable-like allegory just once. It takes place in chapter 17, relating to public credit. After having castigated rentes and spoken favorably of the banks of Amsterdam and Venice, the author turns to the "Bank of France," whose history he transposes to the island of Formosa. We learn that the Brahmin Elnai (Law) has given his daughter Panima (the bank) in marriage to Prince Aurenko (the regent). As in the allegories of Defoe and Addison and in the image of the "Deity of the Royal Bank" of the *Nouveau Mercure*, Panima is not only beautiful: she is also "educated in all the secret sciences":

> Once Panima was established, she wrote some magical words, & immediately a mighty citadel arose, & the earth produced all kinds of fruit. She did not limit her benefits there. She had had a daughter named Linda from her marriage: she taught her some of her secrets: Linda cast new spells & the riches of the Universe arrived in abundance.[28]

So Panima, the bank, and Linda, the Compagnie des Indes, combine to produce miracles until they completely replace an "old magic" inscribed on "animal skins" (rentes), by a new magic (stocks and paper money). A fight breaks out. The goddesses could have won but Panima, "intoxicated with her successes," indulged in fantasies and a "dangerous imprudence" which have made her "odious to the whole Nation." Aurenko decides separate from her, while imagining that he might recall her one day. However, death takes him from his people before he can do anything at all.[29] Thus ends the Formosan tale and the regrets of Melon, who was the intermediary between Law and the regent, working for a possible return to favor of the former. The same is not true of the second edition of the work published in 1736. Following the tale, Melon switches back to the style prevailing in the essay: "Let us speak without allegory, & at last reveal simple things by means of a faithful tale."[30] The author does not substitute rational explanation for allegory, which he does not modify. He juxtaposes the two by adding about ten pages in which he relates the story of the System, this time using real names (except Law's) and exact dates. So it was not in order to avoid any kind of censorship that Melon repeatedly used the Oriental tale. There was something else at stake. But, before we explain the sources of this literary process, we must consider the culmination of this intertextual complex: the work of Marmont du Hautchamp.

There is a chapter in Melon's Mahmoud called "The Circassian Woman" that tells the story of an adorable Georgian enslaved whom the ruler wants to free. There is little doubt that it is from this outline that du Hautchamp composed his novel *Rethima, ou La belle Géorgienne*, published in 1736. In the preface, the author announces: "It will be the same in this book as in many others: everyone will recognize some familiar event in it."[31] The work is made up of different short stories that intertwine and fit into one another using the *One Thousand and One Nights* nesting process. Many have little to do with each other, and all are highly improbable. So it is with the adventures of Lydamon and Vandusbon, stockjobbers who have at some undisclosed date made their fortunes in a paper business and to whom all kinds of incredible things happen. These adventures of sultanas, corsairs, and barbarians say nothing specific about the System; however, we find them in a work by the same Marmont du Hautchamp published in six volumes in 1739 and entitled *Histoire du Système des finances sous la minorité de Louis XV*.

The *Histoire* is anything but a reasoned chronicle of events. The narrator intends to "present some clearer & more specific ideas than those that many people have hitherto formed" in the face of "the frivolous tales that evil & uneducated spirits have spread" about the regent, Law, and the System.[32] Yet the *Histoire* is actually a great, fable-like allegory of the experiment. Let us be clearer. It is possible and even probable that certain elements related by Marmont du Hautchamp, a professional speculator imprisoned for some time at the end of 1719,[33] are true in the sense that they refer to a certain historical reality. The *Histoire* is, however, a gigantic mélange of official documents, unverifiable but often sensational stories, satiric pamphlets, and pure and simple tales, invented or copied from elsewhere. First, and contrary to his profession of faith, in the preface the narrator gives a hearing to all the rumors of the time: the alleged incest of the Duke of Orléans with his daughter, the alleged attempts to poison the young Louis XV, and the so-called debauchery of Abbé Dubois.[34] Then, Marmont du Hautchamp takes up the elements of government propaganda and in almost the same terms. Like Buchet in the *Mercure*, he announces that he has to report "a detail of events so prodigious that they seem incredible." This is a reference to the so-called carnival; the *Histoire du Système des finances* is filled with poor people who have become rich and millionaire lackeys encountering their old masters in comical scenes. Louisiana's fabulous riches are also mentioned, although Marmont doubts that they alone would have helped support stock prices even if they had been employed properly. Like Terrasson, the author constructs a Manichaean combat by fabricating the myth of what he himself calls the *anti-System*, in other words, a conspiracy of financiers led by the Pâris brothers, who had tried to bring down Law and his projects. Finally, and above all, Marmont du Hautchamp employed theatrical tropes in his presentation of the event. As at the Théâtre de la foire or the Comédie-italienne, "Fortune" becomes a "Goddess" who comes to take people "as by the hand." The nouveaux riches "will thus be brought forth as actors who wanted to play a role on the Mississippi stage that would perpetuate their memory."[35] The entire lexical field of representation is mobilized to tell stories of Gascons deceived by female adventurers, of mysterious escapes to evade justice, of roasted hazel grouse sold for 200 livres, of former marquises deported to the islands who have become buccaneers and whose story continues on the rue Quincampoix, where they disguise themselves in ecclesiastical clothes. There are courtesans, weddings à la Dufresny, etc. Many of these little stories are in dialogue to bring them to life. And Marmont du Hautchamp sets out his thoughts on all this literature: "If sometimes I venture to go into the detail of some adventure, or to wax merry over some portrait, it is only to draw the reader out of a certain drowsiness that an often uninteresting series of stops & operations could cause him."[36]

As if that were not enough, Marmont du Hautchamp also inserts dozens of pages of *Rhétima*, his Oriental novel, in which several characters apparently meant to represent real speculators appear. Then it is the turn of Prévost's *Pomponius*, from which he copies long passages, in particular the history of Sotermelec. This theatricalization is also expressed through images. After having greatly enriched himself by means of the System, Henry-Jacques Nompar de Caumont, Duke of La Force (1675–1726), apparently tried to convert his shares in the Compagnie des Indes, not into gold and silver, but into apothecary products, which he allegedly stocked in huge quantities in the hope of reselling them later. This picturesque episode gave rise to poems, songs, and some famous engravings. Marmont du Hautchamp published one of them in his *Histoire*.[37] I offer another version (fig. 6.1). The character whose "Force" (Strength) we must admire manages to carry this large quantity of products all by himself. And the caption explains that this is a caricature of the duke condemned for "monopolizing goods" by the *parlement* of Paris in July 1721.

FIGURE 6.1. Engraving entitled *Admiré La Force, ou Un homme dont les jambes sont formées par deux colonnes porte sur un crochet des tonneaux, des boites et des pots de toute sorte* (1721). Courtesy Bibliothèque nationale de France, Département Arsenal, EST-204(44).

The crucial question posed by all this literature is why writers used the tale. Why did authors favorable to the experiment, such as Melon and Marmont du Hautchamp, resort to this literary genre? If some commentators are to be believed, this form of writing opened up the realm of possibilities, dispelling certain prejudices that surrounded economic innovation in general and paper money in particular. By narrativizing his introduction, Melon was giving meaning to something devoid of it.[38] As a result, Law's collaborator was inviting readers to reinterpret what was believed to be a "bankruptcy" in a different way so as ultimately to "generate confidence."[39]

We can first generalize about the question of the opening up of possibilities by going back to the process used by Montesquieu and Prévost in their tales, but in the opposite direction: by contrasting the fable with real life, these authors invite the reader to question what is desirable. What was better—what was in the tale or what people could see in reality? Unlike opponents of the System, Melon and Marmont were implicitly inviting the reader to wonder whether he would not be happy if what he had read really happened, if the marvelous should actually come into being. By posing the problem in this way, they restored to the System one of its original meanings: liberation from desires. Far from having been a silent mechanism, the introduction of the paper and more generally Law's experiment were buried under explanatory discourses, in very varied forms. Terrasson, Pannier d'Orgeville, and the Moderns told different stories to account for the phenomenon and the expectations of the System. As has been noted, they laid down the terms of the debate, which the enemies of the experiment and then its supporters simply recapitulated over the ensuing decades. In the case that concerns us here, Marmont du Hautchamp and Melon were perfectly aware that the window opened by the System had closed abruptly but that nothing prevented people from thinking about it again, from desiring again, from reembarking on the adventure. It is, therefore, not surprising to find strong intertextual links between the propaganda of 1717–20 and the stories in the period 1720–40. In this sense, the storyteller's process did much more than merely generate confidence: it was the reformulation of a great hope that the System bore within it. This is because the System itself was a *conte merveilleux*. It was so not only because it was presented, at the time, as such but also, and more deeply, because its aim was to blur the line between fiction and reality.

It is clear that the rococo was the normal mode of writing in the period 1717–40. But more important for our purpose is the fact that one of the fundamental characteristics of this literary genre was "to breach the fence that separates art from life, an operation encouraged by the theatricalization of the latter."[40] In discussions of the System while it was still in place, the barrier between real life and art was blurred. Not only the defense of the lottery, the logic of spending, and the liberation of sexual fantasies but also the way the slate was wiped clean of traditional institutions and the resetting to zero after the cancellation of debts and the start of a new monarchical form all strongly contributed to a theatrical effect. What had until then been confined to fiction had entered real life, shaking it, and turning it upside down. What was once represented onstage (the lackey-financier) had been consecrated by the government. The System had become a true adventure in which the French were the heroes. What happened seemed so astonishing that one could quite legitimately wonder whether it was a dream. It was power itself that had reshuffled the cards, and in this respect the experiment was, indeed, a tale of wonder since people wished it to be one. Theater entered life in the form of new beliefs that were to change behavior and fundamentally disrupt social organization, as on a life-size stage. The System—its architecture, its expectations, the way it was presented—can, thus, be considered a work of rococo art. If this revolutionary hope were to be rekindled a few decades later, then pleasure, hedonism, surprise, and the quest for novelty would need to be deployed, with a shift into eroticism, presentism, and the avoidance of death, as happened in the work of Melon and Marmont du Hautchamp. The rococo tale replayed the hopes, fears, and struggles that the System had aroused. If the latter had transformed life into a theatrical scene, the work of the partisans of the experiment would turn the tale into a guide to life.

The 1740s marked the last gasp of this mode of writing. Two authors in particular resumed the fight between the enemies and the supporters of the System. The first was François-Vincent Toussaint (1715–72), a lawyer, encyclopedist, and man of letters who in 1745 published *Mémoires secrets pour servir à l'histoire de Perse*. The second was Claude-Prosper Jolyot de Crébillon (1707–77), a chansonnier and writer of novels and licentious tales, better known under the name Crébillon fils. In 1746, he published *Les amours de Zeokinizul, roi des Kofirans, ouvrage traduit de l'Arabe du voyageur Krinelbol*, a coded history of the Regency transposed into an African kingdom.[41] In the first tale, the regent, under the guise of Ali-Homajou, finds an "extreme disorder" in the finances, as the treasury has been exhausted by the long wars of Cha-Abas (Louis XIV): "The Countryside was deserted, the land uncultivated, commerce languished, confidence & credit were lost; in short, the Kingdom was undergoing the most violent crisis." It was then that a "Japanese" man (Law) arrived, "a man with a systematic spirit." He decided to "replace the gold and silver Rupees, in which Persia abounded, with small bitter almonds." And the author concludes that, "in less than eighteen moons, the fortunes of individuals were shattered, & the kingdom ruined."[42] Crébillon believes, on the contrary, that the Kam of Anserol (the regent) managed to reestablish the finances that Zokitarezoul (Louis XIV) had exhausted: "It is true that the way he did it ruined several families; but apart from the fact that their number was small, & that their greed led to their being lost to desperate ills, less such violent remedies were needed."[43] We find in these two accounts the contrast between the catastrophist interpretation of the event, as a carnival leading to ruin, and the interpretation that, on the contrary, makes it a salutary enterprise, the negative effects of which affected only a few individuals. It was precisely on this assessment of the System that the next generation of storytellers focused.

The Despotic Interpretation of the System

With the emergence of the science of commerce in the 1740s and 1750s and then the advent of political economy in the 1760s and 1770s, it was now time to judge the System both from a theoretical point of view and in terms of the macroeconomic balance sheet. The result of an unprecedented conceptual effort focusing on the principles of the wealth of nations, made possible by chronological distance from the event and a cultural shift away from rococo, these analyses inaugurated the long tradition of economic and financial reinterpretation of the experiment. It was time to take stock, and Enlightenment economic theorists took the opportunity to debate the new monarchical form, the totalizing state capitalism of a potentially despotic nature.

Taking over in some ways from the Marseilles merchants, the "Project to Improve the Statutes of the Compagnie des Indes," published in 1733 by Abbé de Saint-Pierre, vigorously opposed the mode of management of the Compagnie that had been chosen in 1719. In particular, Saint-Pierre stresses the commercial inexperience of the directors appointed by the king: they resided in Paris, not in the ports, and would always have "the same salaries and the same consideration" whether the Compagnie was a success or failure. Returning to the question of change, he denies that innovation is possible: those who have the misfortune to propose new projects must be regarded as "job spoilers" by their peers. Thus, only a management entrusted to self-interested traders, guided by their "particular interests," would "increase earnings."[44] This familiar rhetoric resonated in the following decades with those who sought to put an end to the Compagnie des Indes. This was the case of the intendant of commerce Jacques-Claude-Marie Vincent de Gournay (1712–59), who in 1755 denounced "the negligence & the lack of interest that the managers take in running a business that is not really the business of anyone in particular." He points to the mismanagement of uncontrolled spending and argues for the retrocession of trade to "individuals" and to "competition."[45] This rhetoric culminates in the debates preceding the abolition of the Compagnie's privilege and its gradual liquidation from 1769 on.

The Physiocrats and their associates took action, and it was Abbé André Morellet (1727–1819) who launched the first assault, in his *Mémoire sur la situation actuelle de la Compagnie des Indes* (1769). We know how Terrasson and Pannier d'Orgeville praised the notion of *actions rentières* to the skies. For these zealots of the System, such shares were the tool that the most discerning legislators had lacked. If one believes Morellet, conversely, they are the capital vice. The confusion between fiscal activities, on the one hand, and commercial activities, on the other, entailed using the profits of the former to conceal the losses of the latter. In Morellet's view, the Compagnie des Indes never had any real desire to develop its business. It would have been "much more inclined to be a rentier than a merchant body." Always "the rentier spirit prevailed." And, if we are to believe the physiocrat Dupont, what did it lead to? To ruin. In Dupont's mind, when you have no competitors, when you use the public's money and not your own, when nothing invites you to make a profit, then the Compagnie "always goes, no matter how much it loses, to extremes."[46] Here we touch a central point of the market principle: veridiction through profits and prices. In Physiocratic theory, the completely free competition of sellers and buyers indicates the "right price" for goods. It helps direct capital from the less profitable sectors to the more profitable ones: "Because when a business is not profitable for free entrepreneurs, they leave it as soon as they realize this." But, if capital is not getting to where it should be as prices and profits are distorted by exclusive privileges and state management, then wealth creation is no longer assured. For Dupont, this is precisely what happened in the time of the System, "the most remarkable and most singular epoch in the general history of the dangers of ignorance, & of the faults & inconsistencies of the human mind abandoned to itself, without any insight into the Laws of reproduction & distribution of wealth."[47] By forcing individual interests to come together as a single body, by desecrating property through forced exchange of rentes and confiscatory edicts, the System disregarded the laws of the natural order—the inviolability of private property and the unlimited freedom of trade.

Against this rhetoric, in 1769 the supporters of the Compagnie des Indes appealed to the spirit of 1719. The banker, economist, and future minister of Louis XVI Jacques Necker (1732–1804) repeated that the Compagnie had to "unite the various interests in their movement," and an anonymous author noted that it represented "the Body of the Nation." The Count of Lauraguais, heir to the shares in the Compagnie des Indes held by the marquis de Lassay, pointed out that it was "the competition of the nations of Europe for the trade of India, [that] has infinitely reduced the profits from this trade." He then asks Morellet how he can conclude "that trade between individuals will not increase the effect of competition between nations, & perhaps bring it to the point of making this trade impossible." Further on, he considers the freedom of trade that would result from the disappearance of the Compagnie to be deleterious because, as he explains (using a vocabulary close to Pannier d'Orgeville's), "[the] interest of each individual will prevail over their common interest."[48] It is this kind of discourse that is madness from a Physiocratic point of view since it is precisely from competition and the clash of particular interests, so decried by the propagandists of the System, then by their heirs of 1769–70, that prosperity can emerge. The very idea of merging particular interests in a public enterprise was a capital vice for the Physiocrats, one that by itself explained the failure of Law's experiment. In the penultimate chapter of *Du commerce de la Compagnie des Indes* (a work that was anti-System and anti–Compagnie des Indes), Dupont ends with the idea that the rule of good conduct of a state is precisely to do the reverse of what happened in 1719–20. The public power must "want only what the nature of things prescribes, & what it would do on its own": "[I]t is to order *nothing* but peace, & the preservation of property rights; it is to forbid *nothing* but theft & violence."[49]

The proto-Systems of Pottier de La Hestroye and La Jonchère and the one contained in the memoir attributed to Boulainvilliers, followed by the System itself, have been interpreted as responses to the first anxieties raised by this disturbing utopia in which, if the state does not do nothing, prosperity will come about spontaneously. But is the reverse not just as threatening? In other words, does the economic Leviathan bear within it the seeds of an alarming dystopia? In his *Réflexions politiques sur les finances et le commerce* (1738), as in his *Histoire du Systême de John Law*, the Scotsman's former collaborator Nicolas Du Tot takes up fairly faithfully the factors deployed by propaganda to support the System. Following Terrasson, Du Tot interprets it as a Manichaean struggle. The System is an edifice of indescribable "beauty," against which a "powerful cabal" was formed, marking the victory of ill-intentioned people who very soon conceived the "intention to destroy it."[50] In short, the theodicy had gone wrong. For Du Tot agrees that the System was to produce painful ailments, particularly for the rentiers. Their sacrifice was the price to pay for general relief, which he vigorously defended. The liberation of the borrowers—which "freed all groups from oppression" and "awakened industry and restored value to all real estate"—could not be balanced against the despoilment of a small number of wealthy people. And Du Tot concluded, in a concise formula worthy of Terrasson, that a "particular evil must never halt the progress of a general good."[51]

Rentes are the enemy. They prevent productive investment in agriculture and commerce. They contribute, via tax transfers, to the "pillaging" of the working classes. They maintain "laziness & idleness." To destroy them is to reverse the priorities. It is to relieve and encourage the plowmen, workers, and merchants, the most numerous among those "who support the state, the nobility and other citizens."[52] In particular, it is maritime trade that attracts Du Tot's close attention.[53] He was intoxicated by the advent of the Compagnie des Indes and wished the government would do more to favor merchants whom he judged to be at least as useful as the nobility, if not more so. So it was goodbye to the rentiers and, thus, to the dominant "middle" classes dear to Aguesseau; the tax system was overturned, the bodies of middlemen scorned, the small and middle nobility humiliated, the working classes exalted. This extreme endangerment of the kingdom's economic and social organization had been denounced in 1720 as an unbearable carnival, a sin for which penance had to be done. So it comes as no surprise to see the financier Joseph Pâris-Duverney commissioning a talented man to respond to Du Tot, the playwright François-Michel Chrestien-Deschamps. Published in 1740, the *Examen du livre intitulé Réflexions politiques sur le commerce* paid special attention to the upheavals of the monarchical form that the System was to bring about.

Chrestien-Deschamps is not completely at ease with the mountain of debt that structures the capitalistic form of old France. He agrees—at length—that ways must be found to provide relief to borrowers. However, we must not fall into the extreme solutions promoted by the System: "If the debtor were to be favored entirely, the creditor would be deprived of the reward & the legitimate fruit of his labors, or of those of his fathers; libertinism, laziness, even fraud would be favored . . . ; we would ruin the credit that is the soul of commerce."[54] Besides his traditional economic analysis—the rente is the legitimate fruit of past labor; without credit, no more trade—it is interesting that Chrestien-Deschamps overturns the arguments of the opponents of usury. It is not rentes that encourages idleness but the possibility of never having to pay the interest on and/or the principal of a loan. If debtors think the slate will be periodically wiped clean, what is the point of working? You just need to borrow in order to live, to keep the creditors waiting, and eventually everything will work out. Living nobly, in the sense of the ancien régime—in other words without working—requires that you can enjoy the largesse of a prince, that you can live off your land or other real estate, or, finally, that you can buy rentes. For the dominant "middle" classes, rentes are, as has been said, a means and an end, an ideal of life that goes far beyond economic considerations. For the monarchy of the seventeenth and eighteenth centuries, they are a sort of vassal-like homage for modern times, a point on which Chrestien-Deschamps believes he must insist:

> Politicians have always regarded rentes from the king as an asset that most closely binds peoples to their sovereign. . . . We would have wished for all the citizens, freed from their interests with H.M., to have, by having their fortune committed, an indissoluble bond with a company that already dominated all the industry of the kingdom. . . . But while this arrangement was in the interests of the company, did it fit in with those of H.M.? The reestablishment of rentes, which united the greatest number of Subjects to their Prince, was much wiser, & more suitable in a State like France, where harmony requires that the Peoples are bound to the King alone, not only out of duty, but also out of interest.[55]

We are here at the heart of the monarchical question raised by the System. Apart from the caste solidarity that binds the *noblesse d'épée* to him, the solidarity of the offices that binds him to the *noblesse de robe*, the corporations that maintain the idea of the kingdom as a living body, and a clergy keeping an ideological lid on the whole structure, the king of France is still a father to his subjects through the pact of subsistence. But as if all this were no longer enough, as if these links had partly become a fiction, Chrestien-Deschamps stages the buffer zone of rentes. In his view, this is the decisive link between the king and the wealthy part of his people, a part that can, thus, provide unwavering support for the monarchical form and its tax system. Chrestien-Deschamps reads rentes as a form of political participation and does not envision the potential conflict between the monarchy and the holders of public debt. The question of sovereignty seems to be settled by this notion of a community of interests that binds the rentiers to the monarch.[56] Now, if we substitute shares for rentes, we dissociate the pecuniary interest of the wealthy subjects from the current form of government. In other words, if the debt disappears and, with it, the fiscal and financial system, who will be the new supporters of the monarchy? It could be the landowners and the big farmers, as Physiocratic theorists and many English writers of the 1750s and 1760s would claim. However, it was not land that the System had promoted but commerce. And, for men like Chrestien-Deschamps, a shareholder company was not only a world of risks, of unpredictable profits and ventures, all of which were incompatible with a stable monarchy; it was also a world in which there was a complete upheaval of conditions, a world calling for a new form of government. What need was there of a king, of a nobility, of *parlements*, if a totalizing and benevolent entity satisfied people's interests? Therein lay the danger. The Compagnie des Indes could become a state within a state, basically requiring simply to replace the monarch: "Such a powerful body is interposed between the Prince & his subjects. . . . So was it impossible that one day the exorbitant power of the Compagnie des Indes would become suspect to the Sovereign?" Opponents of the System did not believe in the solidarity of the two glories of propaganda: sooner or later trade and the crown would clash, and one or the other would have to triumph. However, if there were only shareholders, no one would come to the aid of the monarchy, and the Compagnie would take its place. Chrestien-Deschamps fully understood this risk, that of undivided sovereignty, but in favor of the commercial enterprise. However, he struggled to find a name for this frightening prospect: "The Kingdom is not meant to be a Republic of merchants; it is based on arms, & the first principle of the art of government is never to shake the foundations of a state."[57]

This was the conclusion of Chrestien-Deschamps's argument. The nation as a "body of Merchants" was for him a dangerous folly that would destroy the set of values and beliefs that supported the monarchical edifice and replace it with a republic of merchants with "exorbitant" power. This vocabulary was connected to the abolition of privileges, to a society of equals, but it also combined a form of government deemed moderate or at least in which counterforces existed, namely, the republic, with something else that the author had trouble defining and that made his point ambiguous: a power so strong that one should fear its omnipotence. This critique of one of the System's opponents made the discussion depend on the potentially authoritarian, if not despotic, nature of the experiment.

In his letters, Terrasson uses twice over, and in a positive manner, the expression *despotic power*[58] to describe the functioning of the System, and we have seen that his conception of the monarchical state was not unrelated to the ideas of Thomas Hobbes. But what does the use of the adjective *despotic* mean here? Was this a violent authority exercised by the monarchical power to coerce the subjects of the kingdom? The active search for potential emigrants to Louisiana—vagrants, "unconfirmed" people, prostitutes—led to actual kidnappings.[59] Deportation to the colonies was part of the movement to put the poor to work that had begun in the Middle Ages, and already in the seventeenth century individuals removed from hospitals were taken to Canada without their consent. However, the Regency developed the practice on a quite different scale.[60] From this point of view, without a doubt, the government resorted to authoritarian and violent measures. The obligation to pay in bills and even the prohibition against holding gold, silver, or precious stones in one's home were still seemingly arbitrary and brutal laws. They horrified Chrestien-Deschamps, who speaks of "the abuse of the King's authority" that led "to exact searches being carried out in people's Houses": "Informers were listened to, the Servant was a threat to his Master, the brother was suspect to the brother, & the son even to the Father. Mistrust broke the family union, & put citizens on guard against each other." The tragedian was in full flow. It was like a return to the days of the civil war in Rome. In 1758, the economist and man of letters François Véron de Forbonnais (1722–1800) explained, that, as he saw it, Law "relied too much on authority & flattered himself that he could support credit by violence, until its good effects made it voluntary." As for the Physiocrat Nicolas Baudeau (1730–92), he seemed terrified: "An attempt was made to force the citizens to give up their coin money & their silverware, an odious & frightening operation, which alone would take away all confidence & bring about the ruin of the system."[61]

The problem was that the same writers tended a few lines later to qualify their remarks considerably. Did these judgments and edicts that threatened anything and everything even start to be applied? It is unlikely. However highly hostile he was to Law and his System, after his lyrical flights Chrestien-Deschamps admits that "the greatest number of subjects . . . kept their gold and their silver": "They should have been convinced that it was a crime to keep any. Criminal laws that are difficult to apply are hardly ever enforced." Forbonnais explains in turn that these same laws "were merely authentic monuments of the constriction of cash & the general confusion": "[T]hey were not obeyed." In the "Memoir on Discredit" sent by Law to the regent in June 1720, the Scotsman asked to "[re]establish authority," "to enforce the judgments," "to abolish usage of gold coins," to "[re]renew the ban on keeping more than 500 pounds without permission." It was a litany of what should be enforced, precisely because nothing was enforced and authority lay with absent subscribers. Mathieu Marais confirms this impression when he reports on July 4 the "judgment that renews the ban . . . on wearing diamonds . . . and even keeping them at home," concluding with the words "if this judgment is carried out" since the first one had obviously produced no results. The song "Les adieux du parlement" said it well: "No one wished to lend a hand / To many a misleading edict."[62]

This rhetoric of arbitrariness and violence has been reactivated recently by some historians, who believe that the government applied discretionary force on a wide range of subjects throughout 1720: intimidation against the butchers who were putting up their prices, threats against criticisms of the System, pressure on priests, etc.[63] But again, nothing was really convincing.

Law certainly caused some alarm among the butchers in October 1719 and April 1720, but did he threaten them with the galleys or just hanging, as with the grain monopolists during the grain riots?[64] Not at all. He threatened those honorable craftsmen with a new tax if they did not lower the price of meat, and we know of no decrees or edicts that enforced this threat.[65] Regarding the repression of criticism and antigovernment acts, there was nothing new or specific to the System in this. The police continued to try to arrest and punish those who sang about, chanted about, and spread rumors hostile to the government.[66] In his journal, Jean Gilbert, sieur de l'Isle, clerk and secretary of the administrative service at the *parlement* of Paris, recounts the events as they reached him in Pontoise, where the magistrates were exiled in 1720 by order of the regent. Obviously, in Paris, people did not seem to be overly concerned by government threats. In the summer, high prices provoked "a lot of discontented people who even voiced their criticisms quite loudly." Some time later, Gilbert describes the insults aimed at the Duke of Bourbon: "A large number of people were shouting loudly that they should kill all these people and not leave one behind, which greatly frightened him." These scenes were repeated even at the heart of power since "they shouted aloud in the courtyard of the Palais-Royal against the Regent and against Law, calling them B[astard] dogs, B[astard] thieves, etc."[67] Mathieu Marais also reports that, while the regent was criticized and insulted in early July 1720 by peasants on the road to Asnières, "[the] guards did not dare to say a word."[68]

Apart from the deportations to Louisiana, it is therefore highly doubtful that the government used more violence than usual during the System. On the contrary, it was at odds with itself, threatening a great deal, repressing very little. It got tangled up in its own helplessness. The situation resembled that of the circus clown threatening the strong man, a scene that provoked laughter more than terror. And it was perhaps in this way, ultimately, that monarchical power lost its luster: by the lack of credibility of force, which gradually provoked the sarcastic wait-and-see attitude of individuals in the face of a paper authority. The System thus failed not by excess but by a virtual absence of authority, force, and violence, despite a cartload of threats. In other words, the limits of the monarchy's discretionary power came to light, not because the violence and arbitrariness unleashed met with fierce resistance from "public opinion,"[69] but rather because the state never really tried to carry out the crackdown it had threatened.

Of what, in this case, is *despotism* the name if not a violence that was barely employed? The use of the term by a scholar as astute as Terrasson is not trivial, and commentators should have paid more attention to its semantic weight. We know in fact that, since the end of the seventeenth century, *despotic* had taken on the meaning of "social equalizer," as Louis XIV was presented, in pamphlets and work by aristocratic theorists, as the great leveler of the ordered society. With the System, this idea spread. It was not just a matter of ending the hierarchies inherited from the past; it was also about redistributing wealth. By settling the debts of the poor and the rich, by reducing the fortunes of the classes that d'Aguesseau called *middle* (in reality, the dominant classes), by abolishing taxes, at least in spirit, and by employing a generous lottery, economic conditions were to be reshuffled.

In 1751, the Neapolitan Abbé Ferdinando Galiani (1728–87) conceptualized this great myth as follows: "Finally, all debts, property taxes and public rentes were settled. Once such change had taken place in the state of France, we can say that 1720 was for her a jubilee year like that of the Hebrews." In 1738, Voltaire had already made a similar reference. In his "Observations sur MM. Jean Lass, Melon et Dutot," he explained that there was no other policy under the Regency than that of settling all debts: "[T]his is how it was among the Egyptians, and among several peoples of the East, after fifty or thirty years."[70] Leviticus 25 details Yahweh's teaching to Moses that every forty-nine years the Hebrew people were to undertake an egalitarian review of land tenure, with the remission of debts and the release of enslaved people.[71] If one relied only on the Old Testament, it was in 1758 still a little early to see the return of the jubilee year of 1720, but Forbonnais, no doubt with a touch of humor, stated: "[I]t is all too common to see people who do not want to free themselves from their debts, living in the chimerical hope of a similar revolution."[72] The readings of Galiani and Forbonnais were certainly dependent on that of Montesquieu's *Spirit of the Laws*:

> Mr. Law, through an equal ignorance of republican and monarchical constitutions, was one of the greatest promoters of despotism yet seen in Europe. Besides the unusually, abrupt, uncommon, and unprecedented changes he made, he wanted to suppress the intermediate ranks and abolish the political bodies: he was dissolving the monarchy with his fictional reimbursements, and seemed to want to redeem the constitution itself.[73]

When he uses the noun *despotism* to speak of the System, Montesquieu is, indeed, referring to the equalization of ranks and the modification of fortunes that he deplores. This idea brings us back to the concept of screen memory that was developed in the previous chapter. The supporters of the System wanted to compare the despotism of equality with the fiscal tyranny of the previous reign:

> If one wished to think about all the force needed to carry out the violent operations that were employed to extract money from the peoples *for nearly*

> *30 years*, operations that led to carrying out others that were even more violent, might it be at all difficult to apply this authority to the execution of a *beneficent operation*? . . . People grow bold to the point of fury when it comes to oppressing the people and the King; and this is because they are *in the habit of doing so*.[74]

For the anonymous author of *Histoire des finances pendant la Régence*, the practices of the System should be compared with those of Louis XIV. Who caused the most damage? Who used and abused force and authority? Montesquieu deliberately uses the memory of the System when he evokes despotism so as to avoid speaking of another despotism, older and more painful for the majority of French people. It was not so much force, authority, or tyranny that raised a problem for him in the System as the myth of the carnival, of which he was, moreover, one of the great publicists. It is in this respect that, in his eyes, the despotism of 1720 was far more dangerous than all the exactions, famines, ravages, destructive wars, and humiliations of the reign of the Sun King. This panicked fear of egalitarian overthrow through the System recurred a few decades later under the first Necker ministry (1776–81).

Anonymous pamphlets worried about the excessive use of credit and bills the minister might use with the quasi-public bank the Caisse d'escompte.[75] They equated the public credit of Law with that of Necker and tried to show that they were incompatible with the French monarchy: "Law was banker . . . and so he knew neither the constitution of the kingdom, nor the principles of royal authority. Credit cannot be combined with absolute power. . . . So a state bank in a republic or a mixed monarchy can be of great help; but for one hundred and fifty years we have done everything to prevent France being one of the mixed monarchies."[76] These texts do not refer to a so-called excessive use of force by Law and his supporters. On the contrary, when they mention *absolute power*, they speak of the nature of the French monarchical government, which in their eyes represents the reverse of what Law wanted to do; they liken him to a promoter of equality, republics, and moderate monarchies.[77] In fact, these pamphlets worry only about the so-called carnival of the System: the "disaster of France," the "extravagances of the rue Quincampoix," Law's desire to destroy the tax system and the offices. Believing they could see Necker doing the same, accusing him of "disregarding respect for the ranks" under the pretext of saving money, they simultaneously saw the System and public credit as akin to republican and egalitarian regimes.[78] This was the designated enemy, as it had been for Chrestien-Deschamps in 1740.

The System therefore had a despotic character for both its supporters and its adversaries because it has been thought of as a machine for destroying privileges and equalizing conditions. The criticisms that would be leveled a few decades later at the notorious "legal despot" of the Physiocrats—that hereditary sovereign subject only to the laws of the natural order—were consistent. Relying on private property, free trade, and capitalist agriculture, legal despotism was to abolish fiscal privileges, level the ordered society, and lead its subjects rationally to their prosperity. The System had envisaged things in a somewhat similar way since a force that was to hold sole power, the Compagnie des Indes, also aimed to achieve the enrichment of individuals who were powerless and equal before it, the difference—a major difference—being that the great economic Leviathan of the System was based on the violation of private property, the destruction of competition, and trade rather than land, all of which the Physiocrats would reject. What would the French Revolution, so attached to both private property and equality, do with the memory of the System? Believing the System to be definitely over by October 1720, Mathieu Marais was relieved: "The servants will be returned to their masters, the craftsman to his trade, the peasant who came to use his money to purchase bills in order to redeem rentes returns to his plow, and everyone will gradually return to his natural place."[79] To hell with "natural places" in 1789. But was this the advent of the marvelous or of a republican and egalitarian despotism filled with papers?

The French Revolution and the Question of Assignats

From the advent of the System on, the experiment was fictionalized by propagandists and counterpropagandists. From 1720, a battle of memorandums began around this original sin of the coming century, a fight that the Constituent Assembly would replay in great detail. For, if Law was omnipresent in the debates on the assignats, it was above all "like a ghost—like a projection of various fears concerning the past."[80] At first glance, both the artisans and the opponents of this fiduciary currency "assigned" in exchange for confiscated clerical property seemed to use the Scotsman and his paper as a foil. On closer inspection, however, things were not that simple. Some devotees of the assignats—the radical republicans in particular—saw the System as containing interesting elements and did not hesitate to endorse the eschatological expectations of the experiment of 1720.

The assignats voted in April 1790 were, in the minds of their promoters, a way of stabilizing the Revolution. Being conservatives, these men wanted to ward off state bankruptcy and above all sought to protect individual property rights.[81] Thus, they could not endure the rapprochement with 1720. Their mantra was simple: the assignats "are of a completely different nature from what is commonly called *paper money*." The latter, explained the economist and deputy of the Third Estate Pierre-Louis Roederer (1754–1835), was "a sign to which the sovereign attaches a value." It is a currency, added Pierre-Hubert Anson (1744–1810), another deputy of the Third Estate, that was widespread "in a kingdom by the sole authority of a monarch" and that consequently carried "a character of injustice in [its] origins." If we are to believe these legislators, this was the case with Law's paper money, which was based only on "hopes" or, as the deputy Louis-Alexandre La Rochefoucauld d'Enville (1743–92) grandiloquently put it, "on gold mines, that *might perhaps be discovered in another* world." The future mayor of Paris Jérôme Pétion de Villeneuve (1756–94) used a rhetoric that was well-known in empiricist philosophy to contrast Law's bills with assignats, namely, the opposition between the senses and the imagination:

> [T]he bills of Law were mortgaged on chimeras, on seductive prestige, or, to put it more precisely, on nothing; it was paper money put into circulation using trading stocks; whereas assignats are based on solid, immutable properties that everyone knows, and has right in front of his eyes. . . . Law's system had no basis, the assignat system has the surest basis, the only true and invariable . . . land.[82]

As meaningful fictions survive across the ages, it was again pointed out that the currency of the Revolution was an "authentic delegation, not on the Mississippi of Laws [*sic*], but on the Peru of the Church."[83] The assignats still had the advantage over the paper of the System of bringing in interest (this would no longer be the case in subsequent issues) and, above all, of being in the hands of the general will. Who could believe that this would allow them to be multiplied and lose value? Only a "despot," explains La Rochefoucauld, could use them thus. Their value would never vary since they resulted "from the solemn agreement of a large family made up of creditors and debtors, who, for the common interest, settle their debts with mortgaged contracts on real estate, until the next sale of property, which must extinguish the debt."[84]

From the podium of the Constituent Assembly, this fairy tale was far from meeting with unanimous approval, and two attitudes prevailed among the deputies who opposed the assignats. The first consisted in comparing the projects of the Revolution and those of Law by recalling, as did Dupont, now deputy for Nemours, "the illusion of the ghosts of profits that could never be realized, which its magic had initially made dazzling." This is where the long-term effects of the propaganda of the Moderns can be gauged. The beneficial effects of the Compagnie des Indes took time, and the gap between the expectations of 1719–20 and the way these effects could actually be exploited helped cast suspicion on the enterprise, which was soon deemed illusory by the counterpropaganda. Losers are always wrong, and Dupont did not have much difficulty imposing this account of Law's experiment as it was an account with which many supporters of the assignats concurred.

The second attitude consisted in comparing 1720 with 1790, but to the advantage of the System. This was the rhetorical process used by Nicolas Bergasse (1750–1832), a jurist, deputy for Lyon, and monarchist who would be forced to go into hiding under the Terror. According to him, Law's bills "were secured by a far more solid mortgage than the one presented to us for the currency assignats: the produce of the General Farm, the tobacco farms, the Indian trade, the African trade, the West Indian trade, all the Kingdom's receipts, the privilege of manufacturing cash." The famous Irish philosopher and politician Edmund Burke (1729–97) took the same side in 1790:

> A noble indignation rises in the minds of your popular leaders, on hearing the magic lanthorn in their shew of finance compared to the fraudulent exhibitions of Mr. Law. . . . They do injustice to that great, mother fraud, to compare it with their degenerate imitation. It is not true, that Law built solely on a speculation concerning the Mississippi. He added the East India trade; he added the African trade; he added the *Fermes* of all the farmed revenue of France. . . . They did not think of feeding France from its own substance.

The supporters of the assignats did not fail to rush into what they viewed as a manifest error: it was the shares of the Compagnie, they said, that were backed by the collateral, not the currency.[85] This point was debatable since the Royal Bank had been merged with the Compagnie des Indes and paper could be exchanged for shares. But let us ignore this imprecision and this technical debate and return to the rhetoric of the enemies of the revolutionary currency. Abbé Jean-Sifrein Maury (1746–1817), barely objecting to the Civil Constitution of the Clergy, who later fled from the Revolution to Koblenz, subscribed to Bergasse's idea and in September 1790 stated: "Law himself, the charlatan Law, had mortgaged his bank on all the King's income. All these mortgages, so imposing, however, have never preserved & will never preserve paper money from the depreciation which is inherent in its nature." The argument was simple: when you start to create paper money, you never stop, and it inevitably loses its value relative to gold and silver. And it is here that this tirelessly repeated argument gets to the bottom of the problem: the "forced" character of assignats. If citizens are obliged to accept them in any payment whatsoever, at face value and not real value, all creditors will be cheated because they will receive less than what they had loaned. Therefore, assignats should be seen as "an inevitable misfortune for creditors, an infamous resource for debtors," if

Bergasse is to be believed. Jean-André Périsse-Duluc (1738–1800), Bergasse's colleague from Lyon, explains: "[T]o force a paper into circulation is to attack liberty and property; it is to distort the commitments already made between individuals; it is to authorize the debtor to pay in a value different from that which he has promised to provide." This "attack on freedom, on the property of citizens and the existence of our homeland," is "a scourge that, before our eyes, is today ravaging the empires of despots."[86] Abbé Maury specifies the nature of this despotism:

> To put into circulation a paper money, the value of which is lower than its title, and to force the creditors to receive it as if it were worth the same, is to consecrate, as in Greece & Rome, the establishment of democracy by abolition—quite logical, I confess—of a part of the debt; it is to renew, to the detriment of creditors, the jubilee year of the Jewish people; finally, it is to authorize, I will not say just one bankruptcy, but millions of partial bankruptcies.[87]

In addition to echoing the jubilee of Voltaire and Galiani, Abbé Maury seems to take back from Forbonnais the idea of bad subjects who have been waiting for paper money for a long time since he castigates those "brigands" "who got into debt systematically for several years" in the hope of this bankruptcy.[88] What is fundamental for our purpose is that the adversaries of the assignats constantly return to the "despotic" screen memory of 1720. According to these representatives, to overthrow and redistribute wealth in a paper jubilee is to bring about an egalitarian democracy. So what is society, after all? That is the big question. First, for these men, society rests on creditors and owners. Antoine-François Delandine (1756–1820), deputy of Forez who would soon go underground and be arrested under the Terror, explained that it was the "creditors, thrifty owners, real supporters of the state" who would bear "alone the burden of the use of papers." The whole evil would fall on "the real families of the state, on the owners." Burke echoed these words but also those of Chrestien-Deschamps, saying that the assignats would undermine the spirit of effort. They were a "subversion of all the principles of property" and would expose the fruits of labor "to the pillaging of the negligent, the embittered, the disinherited." As the economist, member of the Constituent Assembly, and future emigrant Louis de Boislandry (1750–1834) put it: "[T]he great principle consecrated by the writers of all centuries, and adopted by the Americans, our masters in freedom, that owners alone have an immediate interest in the maintenance of a Constitution, so that it is also in property alone that power can reside."[89]

So not all citizens are equal, and this is where the System's great struggle begins again. For the opponents of paper money, the liquidation of the public debt, under the Regency as under the Revolution, will never justify the subversion of the existing order. The ethos of these men always leads them to turn their attention to those who seem to them to be essential, to form the basis of society: the owners. For—and this is the nub of their arguing—no political force can arrogate to itself the power to break the faith of contracts freely made between individuals. According to them, there is legislation—with a strong Physiocratic flavor—prior to constitutional forms, "eternal laws of morality & justice," Bergasse argues, that prevents anyone from granting himself "the extravagant power to change in a moment, & by a simple effect of our wills, the nature of all commitments": "[W]ho are you, who are we to authorize, by our decrees, among twenty-four million men, the violation of individual trust? Who gave us such terrible powers?"[90] In such an argumentative logic, there are laws of nature that it is not permissible to violate. Now this is precisely what the Revolution sought to do and what Law did in his time with his totalizing ambition. It was by "embracing the entire economic system of the state in the same way in all his operations, that Law overturned the public fortune and brought about a disastrous revolution in individual fortunes." "It is to time alone," affirmed Boislandry, "that belongs the task of increasing the monetary system of Nations, & not to their legislators." It fell to the physiocrat Dupont to generalize the point: "There are things where public authority comes to an end: these are values; it is nature that gives them; competition and usage that determine them. The value of money is based on usual proportions. In no country does it depend on the denomination, but on competition and goods."[91]

The mistake of Law and the revolutionaries was quite simply to have sought to oppose natural laws because "in political economy, as in medicine . . . the less you try to do things by yourself, the better you do them."[92] Should we conclude, however, that the French revolutionaries considered economic life in general and monetary questions in particular as subject to the forces of nature alone?[93] While it is true that many supporters of the assignats did not embrace this formidable ambition, inviting humans by force of will to build a society according to their wishes, there were, nonetheless, some who openly defended it.

There were important similarities between John Law's land bank projects, in other words, those before the Regency, and the issuance of assignats. Since these were pledged on the church's lands, they were not all that different from what the Scotsman proposed in his *Considerations on Money and Trade.*[94] The System itself had envisaged the confiscation of the property of the clergy, which brought the two periods and the two models even closer. But, even more importantly, the eschatological expectation of Law and the Moderns resurfaced under the Legislative Assembly and under the Convention. Men refuted the principle of natural laws in economics and did not hesitate to defend the idea that legislators could decide the value of currencies, organize economic life, and even, yes, overturn the fortunes of individuals if that were desirable for the social body. Sin becomes a good deed and the marvelous a useful social reality—a reality that was, for once, fully revolutionary.

In *De J. J. Rousseau considéré comme l'un des premiers auteurs de la Révolution* (1791), Louis-Sébastien Mercier (1740–1814), a famous writer and deputy of the Convention, vigorously defended assignats and the genius of John Law: "If you had resuscitated Law instead of Necker, you would have seen the great man correct his plans, immediately adopt the point of view of the revolution, and march majestically to immortality, embracing the *constitution* and regeneration of France with an imposing firmness worthy of himself and of her." Mercier had already championed the System a few years earlier in his *Tableau de Paris*: "The machine, although broken by a violent effort, bore the imprint of a new and daring genius. The moralist was not sorry at this prompt exchange of goods; for they must in turn water different families."[95] These things were seldom said so clearly, but Mercier took the plunge. The good thing about the System was this jubilee of wealth and property so fiercely denounced by the enemies of Law and the assignats.[96]

We discover quite similar discourses under the Revolution. Louis-Salve Albitte de Vallivon, of whom little or nothing is known, published (probably in 1790) a pamphlet entitled *La nécessité prouvée de l'émission du papier-monnaie en assignats, pour payer la dette générale de la nation*. Against the "antipatriotic" members of the National Assembly, he maintained that there had been no failed experiment under the Regency and that, on the contrary, "Agriculture, Manufactures & Commerce flourished during the course of these banking papers." He wanted 4 billion assignats to be issued immediately. Would they lose their value to the detriment of creditors? It did not matter. Or rather, So much the better: "Those rentiers who lived in the shade of their rentes in society, without being useful or putting anything into that society, will be forced to engage in emulation; they will have to pay out their funds in the acquisition of goods, or in the draining of marshes, or the clearing of a number of lands that have remained uncultivated for lack of means." The physician and physicist Jean-Baptiste Jumelin (1745–1807) expressed similar views. He explained that one of the good effects of assignats was that an "endless number of small rentiers who lived lazily, have been forced to engage in work, and are now producing, as they always should have done. These same characters, by increasing production, consume less than in the past; and their conduct, by enriching the country, has the further advantage of turning to the benefit of morals, and turns them into republicans, even when they do not want this." Thus, the Revolution has, in effect, impoverished the rentiers, who can buy less than they could before. They are now forced to work or to invest, and here we find the rhetoric of Terrasson and Du Tot. The end of rentes produces only benefits since it means both putting an end to idleness and usury and transferring capital to wealth-creating sectors (trade and agriculture) rather than to public expenditure (which is questionable). The useless men of the past are being replaced by productive ones. As in the fiction of the "body of Merchants," there is no contrast here between the language of commerce and that of virtue; the two must come together in perfect harmony through the extinction of debts and claims.

Wanting to reverse the discourse of the opponents of the assignats, the founder of the *Républicain français*, Maurice Gouget-Deslandres (1755–1827), took up almost all the arguments of the promoters of the System. He found the main benefit of what he called *paper money* to lie in the general relief of creditors. The assignats healed "a deep wound in the fortunes of the majority of the citizens." And Gouget castigated "[t]he owners of gold & silver cash, who keep hold of them out of mistrust." The Manichaean struggle between the trusting and the mistrustful, once staged by Terrasson, now set convinced revolutionaries against those who were wary of assignats. As had happened in the past with the exchange of rentes for the shares of the Compagnie des Indes, "rejecting or discounting" the paper money of the Revolution became "as much a national insult as an economic difficulty." However, Gouget also subscribed to a form of theodicy of hidden harmony, very close to that of the letters in the *Nouveau Mercure*. Despite their ill will, the enemies of the Revolution were constrained by a force greater than them to act to strengthen it. Those corrupt men, whom he called *capitalists*, who did not want assignats "have only two ways to make their money productive; the first is to buy real estate; the second, to become industrious; & for this it is absolutely necessary that they relinquish their capital. . . . [T]he rise in property necessarily becomes the effect of their terror, & must procure even more cash in circulation." The skeptics of 1790 should trigger an increase in land funds and a fall in the interest on money, as Terrasson had hoped the dubious of 1720 would do. The price of national goods should rise and money become less scarce—two advantages that would aid the Revolution. This was how, willingly or not, all were to contribute to the prosperity of the nation. The kinship with the System is obvious, and Gouget concludes by saying: "If the *Mississippi* could have been transported to France, . . . Law's Bills would have been excellent. Now we have the *Mississippi*."[97]

But why not take the argument to its logical conclusion and completely destroy metal money? This is what Jean-René Loyseau, a Jacobin journalist who in 1792 published *Considérations sur l'agiotage des assignats*, proposed. One is reminded of the propagandists of the *Nouveau Mercure* when Loyseau says that we must put an end to "the evils that the sign of gold and silver has been inflicting on us for too long." These metals must be deprived of the quality of money forever. In this area, the power of a freely elected national representation is boundless: "The representative sign of wealth is therefore like all other social institutions, subject to Legislation, which can destroy it, modify it, or regulate its use." Loyseau also called for four billion assignats immediately, to end all debts, public and private, and to end the rentiers, those "enemies of any idea of utility": "To be rich without work, without a means of doing any work . . . was their only ambition. . . . Men of this character, imbued with such an inveterate passion, are evidently dead as regards any kind of public good." Like Albitte, Jumelin, and Gouget, Loyseau believes that, if we get rid of rentes and debts, a previously unknown prosperity lies in wait for us: "[O]ur agriculture will be encouraged; our trade will reach the highest degree of prosperity; our industry will soar higher." In short: "No Empire in the world will present such a great resource."[98]

Loyseau's theses found a wide echo during the stormy spring and summer of 1793 among the popular clubs and societies. The "exaggerated" republicans, the defrocked priest Jacques Roux, and his extremist "Enragés" declared in their *Manifeste* of June 25, 1793: "But it's the paper; people still say that it's the cause of the high cost of food: ah! the sans-culotte hardly notices that there is so much of it in circulation. . . . Besides, the prodigious amount of paper being issued is proof of its value and the price attached to it. If the assignat has a real mortgage, if it is based on the loyalty of the French nation, the quantity of national bills thus does not deprive them of their value." For these men and women, it is the "speculators," the "monopolists," all the "merchants," "grocers," and other money handlers who, by their weakness, have raised the price of goods, certainly not the overflow of assignats. Against all those rich people who "have abused the freedom of trade to oppress the people," the sans-culotte demanded the most energetic measures, in other words, the death penalty.[99] We know the rest of the story. Under popular pressure and the weight of economic difficulties, driven by a desire to restore the circulation of goods against land-grabbers and monopolists, the deputies of the Convention, the overwhelming majority of whom were loath to envisage any attack on private property and freedom of trade, voted in August and September a series of decrees and laws that gave extended powers to the executive, to the army, and to the communal and municipal authorities in economic matters: granaries of abundance, a maximum of grain, then a general maximum of prices and wages.[100] On the monetary level, while for months petitioners had been calling for the prohibition of the sale and purchase of silver, a practice accused of maintaining the depreciation of assignats, the Convention, which had repeatedly rejected this request in the name of free trade, ended up passing it in the spring of 1793, arguing that it was difficult for the state to have to buy gold and silver to pay its supply officers.[101] However, things did not end there. In order both to try to circumvent the "exaggerated" republicans and to facilitate certain payments, the Finance Committee and the Committee of Public Safety quite seriously envisaged the total and final demonetization of gold and silver coins.

The project was presented by Pierre-Joseph Cambon (1756–1820), a member of the Convention with a background in trade and a specialist in finance. The idea was to implement Loyseau's ideas by decreeing that, from "the day of the publication of this decree, the use of gold & silver coins . . . is prohibited throughout the whole extent of the territory of the French Republic," that "the Republic recognizes no other currency than assignats." All citizens who possessed metal cash would have been required to declare it and then prohibited from doing anything with it other than paying their taxes, taking out forced loans, buying national estates, or bringing them to the Paris mint, to be exchanged for receipts, themselves exchangeable in assignats: "All the gold & silver sent to Paris will be melted there & converted into ingots." The latter were, by order of the Convention, to be used to pay "for essential items supplied by foreigners, . . . or for diplomacy." This "Draft decree to demonetize gold and silver currencies" was presented to the legislators on December 1, 1793. As Cambon explains, its explicit aim was to avoid "death sentences handed down by some administrations and representatives of the people, relative to the exchange of cash against assignats," a measure that was a "usurpation of the powers of the Legislative Body." Besides regaining control of the popular movement, it was still a question of the government facilitating the payment of war supplies and subsistence for the big cities. The mechanism of the System was not far off since, in the 1793 plan, metallic money was to be used in purchases made solely by the state, as for the activities of the Compagnie des Indes, in specific supplies in France or abroad. In particular, it seems that a preproject, whose author is not known, was to prevent citizens from keeping gold and silver in their homes. They would have been forced to take their cash to the mint in exchange for receipts. Cambon opposed such an authoritarian measure because, he said, "it would bring us too close to Law's system." According to him, people should stick to declarations that would facilitate the establishment of the tax and possible future requisitions. The fact remains that, according to his project, even if the French could keep their gold and silver at home, taxation, government purchases, and loans would mean that these metals would sooner or later flow back to the heart of the Revolution and to it alone, as in the days of the System. The fiery Georges-Jacques Danton (1759–94) was fiercely opposed to this "unseemly" and useless project since, he asserted, confiscations from the clergy and emigrants were sufficient to meet the state's expenses. He described its authors as "ultra-revolutionaries" who were, in his view, "going beyond" the powers of the Convention. He asked for a postponement and succeeded in getting the plan dropped.[102]

This parallel between 1720 and 1793 is extremely significant. After the sin that the System had constituted, the time had come for redemption in the 1720s and 1730s. Against any form of liberation of desires, against the fire of egalitarian subversion, against the political or economic regulation of social relations, it was time to return to individual morality. Greatness and riches were too dangerous to be left in just anyone's hands. Contrary to the chimeras of the System, people preached a return to simplicity and virtue, especially for the poor and all those who would like, unfortunately, to escape from their condition. Stability, withdrawal into oneself, acceptance of one's fate, these were the hallmarks of the period. The rococo tales of the years 1720–50 allowed themselves to treat of that highly incendiary material, the System, but only metaphorically. The adversaries of the experiment saw it as a vast swindle and wished to contrast the tangible world with the charlatanism of fictions. The supporters of the System, on the other hand, invited everyone to think of the terrible reality—poverty, inequality, violence—in comparison with the promises of the marvelous tale, inviting readers to continue to desire, to renew the adventure. The System had blurred the boundaries between art, theater, and life, and, in so doing, it had opened up unexplored potential that should be explored anew. In the second half of the eighteenth century, the hour of reckoning led economists and philosophers, on the one hand, to condemn the economic Leviathan as a dead end in the name of the alleged natural laws of political economy and, on the other, to promote the destruction of the rentier class and the public and despotic management of the economy in the service of the productive classes. The enemies of the experiment understood perfectly well that this destruction signaled the end of the monarchy and that an egalitarian era was to be the consequence of the System. Under the Revolution, this major point resurfaced: the time had come for the sin to return for the next century. The assignat was the new medium between the citizen and the government. It was to bind the citizen to the Revolution as the shareholder had been bound to the System. It was to revitalize the economy just as the Compagnie des Indes had brought prosperity. The monarchy had its middle guard made up of rentiers. They embodied in the eyes of revolutionaries the ethos of the ancien régime: lazy, unproductive, and useless as far as the public good was concerned. Seventy years earlier, Law and his supporters had already wanted to put an end to them and, thereby, to the monarchical form that resulted from siphoning money from the land (i.e., farmers) and the poor (i.e., peasants) to enrich the idle classes (i.e., the rentiers). Engaging in such a process, however, led to a reversal of the ancien régime taxonomy and individual fortunes as well as a modification of the dominant values (warlike and hierarchical) so as to replace them with new ones (commercial and egalitarian).

But something else was at stake, something deeper and more difficult. The extreme tensions that arose during the Terror between the supporters of respect for property—Saint-Just in particular[103] and the radicals of certain clubs and the sans-culotte movement—brought to light the problem of state intervention in the economy. The System had sought to defuse the supposedly devastating effects of free trade left to individual interest by suppressing competition and socializing part of production and trade. It was a radical solution, one that to some revolutionaries, such as Dupont, might seem merely to accentuate the monarchical practice of "exclusive privileges," and, therefore, to be rejected entirely. In 1789, the banner of liberty was to be used to bring down the royal edifice, and it was in the name of this same liberty that prices, trade, currency, etc. were to be left to the free course of so-called natural laws. We have just seen how thorny this question was. What was important about the System of 1720 was that it already expressed the immutable conflict between equality and liberty. It was the original matrix of future battles between benevolent but potentially authoritarian interventionism and an often inegalitarian liberal democracy.

CONCLUSION

Over the past three hundred years, the experiment attributed to John Law has become something of a cultural product. And, indeed, how could it be otherwise? The authorities of the day had turned it into a fairy tale after all. Leaving aside the novels of the eighteenth century, of which much has already been said, a look at the following centuries shows that the essence of the experiment remained intact. In Paul Féval's novel *Le Bossu* (1857), for example, which went on to inspire a large number of film adaptations, "good Monsieur Law" provides the regent and his friends with an abundance of money, right up to the final and inevitable catastrophe. The rue Quincampoix, with its festive atmosphere, colorful characters, public writers, and alleged hunchback—willing to rent the use of his back to close transactions—becomes a myth in its own right through this novel and its subsequent film adaptations. In Louis Aragon's *Les voyageurs de l'impériale* (1941), one of the characters writes a book about John Law, who is, of course, portrayed as "a brilliant introducer of disorder," he "who invented paper money, which, in the hierarchy of the crimes and madness of men, is a feat infinitely superior to the destruction of the library of Alexandria." The manuscript in question, mentioned by another character in the novel, "was a matter of insiders," in other words, a technical, financial, and complex work. Once the hero was dead, people came to mourn at his grave in Venice. How romantic! In *Les fortunes de la gloire: Le roman de John Law*, the novelist Cendrine de Porthal emphatically describes her journey to the city of the Doges and evokes before his tombstone "this body that housed such a great spirit, such a vast heart." It is tragedy that prevails in *Nous serons comme des dieux* by Ève de Castro: we see at the end only "denunciations," "searches," "debacle," "riots," and deaths. Marie, the poor prostitute and good friend of the regent, waiting in front of the bank in the summer of 1720, "had for ten months forgotten that reality is the mother of disillusionment, solitude and poverty": "Like many millions of French subjects, she had bet her future on Monsieur Law's System. Like many millions of French subjects, at the first rays of sun she saw her property melt away." Gosh! It was now millions of people who had their assets in shares or in paper money? Yet another result of the inflation attributed to the System, no doubt. *Un palais de papier* by the novelist Françoise Hamel places John Law at the heart of the plot. He is portrayed as being in love with a young Breton woman named Espérance ("Hope"). Platonic at first, their love ignites just when everything—the paper money, the shares, the System—collapses: "Every day, people ruined by bankruptcy commit suicide. A young man who had invested the money destined for his studies at the Sorbonne threw himself out of a window. A husband slit the throats of his wife and three children before hanging himself." We tremble in fear. But no doubt the best of all these productions is Bertrand Tavernier's *Let Joy Reign Supreme* (1975). In this film, the deportations for Louisiana are abundantly described, often in a very tongue-in-cheek manner. The stockjobbing too, with the murder committed by the Count of Horn, followed by his conviction. Dubois, the regent, and their clique are portrayed as notorious debauchers, while mention is made several times of *banknotes* and *Mississippi*. Such truly revolutionary undertakings as the despoilment of church property are discussed, something exceptional enough to merit mention. But, in the penultimate scene, the Duke of Orléans organizes a macabre masquerade with some of his cohorts disguised as poor people. One of them is dressed as "the System," which signifies *bankruptcy*, *ruin*, and *poverty*, according to the characters' dialogue.[1]

In a first approximation, we could, thus, say that the dominant classes to whom we have so often referred, had won the battle of memories. The screen memory that established 1720 as a European trauma had worked to perfection. The cultural product was that of catastrophe. This analysis is too superficial, however. In the end, it does not matter whether the myth was one of an economic and financial cataclysm or, on the contrary, one of newfound happiness and felicity. To interpret the consequences of the adventure either positively or negatively is of little importance because the problem of the myth is the myth itself. As Roland Barthes showed, the myth was a depoliticizing machine. By naturalizing the events, it attributed to them "the simplicity of essences": "[I]t establishes a blissful clarity: things seem to mean something by themselves."[2] This is precisely what happened with *1720*, *John Law*, and *the System*. For three hundred years, this date and these words have had a clear, obvious, and eternal meaning: that of a financial adventure, a historical accident provoked by this Scotsman, considered either a good genie or an evil demon, depending on one's point of view. Economists and historians have studied the System very seriously, using very sophisticated mathematical or statistical tools, and produced high-quality work in economic and financial history. Other researchers have also unveiled many important aspects of the experiment, notably from the perspective of political and cultural history. Nevertheless, all without exception have remained prisoners of the myth, that of the financial event that stemmed directly from the workings of the mind of John Law. Each strongly defends his or her position and notably the economists: by producing a serious economic and financial history, what they actually did was return the event to academic history, to the canons of the scientific. But the change of direction proposed by this book is precisely, first, to consider the financial and monetary issues as quite insignificant in this case, or at least to dismiss these notions of *bubble*, *speculation*, *crash*, and *exuberant finance*, terms that have hitherto prevented us from understanding what the System really was. Second, this change in direction led to examining the experiment from the point of view of a collective history. This book considers the event from the notion of the symbolic death of the author and suggests that a "System" of a very similar nature would probably have emerged even without this character John Law. Finally, the idea was to reject the attribution of 1720 as a historical accident and to situate the experiment within a long-term context.

The purpose of this epistemological break was to enable another history, a story of the System that began at the end of the seventeenth century and ended, not in 1720, but rather during the French Revolution. From this perspective, there is no longer any teleology and, therefore, no longer any causal regime. We could take up Roger Chartier's comments in *The Cultural Origins of the French Revolution*, a book in which it is not a question of establishing the "causes" of the Revolution. Rather, it pinpoints "certain of the conditions that made it possible because it was conceivable."[3] I sought, not the causes of the System, much less its "consequences," but rather the reasons why the people of the time considered it either desirable or abhorrent throughout a century. This break also aimed to relegate John Law to the background and, thus, give voice to a large gallery of other characters, well-known or anonymous, who had given the experiment its own twist. For history cannot be reduced to a series of edicts, judgments, laws, or even facts. All that is said, published, and imagined has historical force. The way the Moderns conceived and presented the System, the stories and maps of those involved in the Louisiana affair, and the interpretations given by the employees of the Compagnie des Indes are neither more true nor more false than what Law or the regent did or wanted to do. As we have seen, the performativity of a discourse of fantasy was often much stronger than that of stillborn edicts and judgments, never applied, never taken seriously. The enemies of the System, on the other hand, often took the propaganda very seriously indeed. From this point of view, it contributed every bit as much as the financial episodes did in the making of the System, if not more so. The experiment therefore cannot be reduced to 1720, to John Law, or to anything the myth has ever made of it since. In an attempt to do away with this myth, this book thus had to *repoliticize* the System in the full sense of the term, which meant leaving aside political history, the events themselves, and issues of a strictly financial nature. It was not a question of examining the struggles of parties, coteries, or even interests, the combat led by the magistrates or the financiers against an absolute power that did not exist. It was even less a case of looking for the meaning behind this or that incident, difficulty, or technical issue. The precedence of economic ideas and financial theory was of little importance for my analysis. The cultural aspects themselves were important only inasmuch as they were manifestations and illustrations of something much deeper. This was a big step to take because it is never really possible to get to the bottom of a myth. But, when commentators talk about it as a *revolution*, we can now better understand why they either struggle to characterize it or reduce it to a mere financial dimension.

To understand this revolution, I had to start by dismissing all the facts in order to broach the subject from the perspectives of political philosophy, social theory, theology, intellectual history, literature, the sociology of networks, and even metaphysics. In short, I had to take a step back and look behind the scenes systematically. And what this approach then revealed was a truly revolutionary human adventure. If people in Europe were going through a crisis of conscience at the end of the seventeenth century, it was certainly because more and more of them believed that the monarchical social pact founded on an organic conception of the social body was no longer working. The problem was not so much that there were rich and poor, nobles and commoners. It was that the theological and political justification of the monarchical state was no longer very well ensured. The question then became to understand the real role of society. What was the true point behind the upward transfers of wealth from the productive to the idle classes (rentes and rentiers), taxes, intermediary bodies, trading companies, and so on? Not the material prosperity of everyone or the satisfaction of their desires. The emergence of the central state henceforth prevented bloody civil wars. But something new and equally dangerous had replaced those wars: fiscal tyranny and the free rein given to greed and individual interests in particular. This is why the System and other projects before and after it sought to found societies on the pooling of the wills and properties of the individuals who constituted them. Just as with a religion or a utopia, it was a true eschatological expectation that the System bore, imagining that the public power could give everyone a single direction and, thus, organize the material happiness of individuals. It said a lot about how the authorities of the time viewed population management. Moderns like Terrasson openly believed that individuals were unaware of where their own best interests lay. Thus, not only should they not intervene in the management of public affairs; the state should actually be responsible for ensuring their happiness, without or even against their consent. This was a strong idea, one that went far beyond the traditional Hobbesian recommendations and the consequences of which in the twentieth century are well-known. Moreover, throughout the centuries, the question has always remained the same. What determines the preferences and choices of social planners? Do they rely on ethical arguments to make their decisions, or do they focus only on the consequences of those decisions? In either case, there must be an underlying moral philosophy that states what is good and strong trust in the public authority to implement it.

If I had to extend this book, it would undoubtedly have to be done in two main directions. The first would be synchronic and could be introduced by the theory that, compared with England and Holland, France was considered to be behind the times. This theory began early on, toward the end of the seventeenth century, when major traders, followed by administrators and, some fifty years later, theorists, conceptualized the idea that it was the trading nations that would, henceforth, have the advantage in the balance of power. Owing to the supposed weight of the monarchical structures and the Colbertist state apparatus, France had either not been able or not known how to get the train of commercial capitalism moving sufficiently. Thus, it was possible to explain, both at the time and afterward, why the country would go on to lose its position as the leading power in Europe and, finally, why it would belatedly experience something called the *Industrial Revolution* (for which, as the historian Kenneth Pomeranz pointed out, the trade and colonial question was vital).[4] It is very interesting to note that, while many seventeenth- and eighteenth-century thinkers shared this view that France was behind the times, not everyone considered freedom of trade to be the remedy. On the contrary, it seems that state capitalism, a public trade organization, was the solution preferred by many among them. We can, therefore, reverse this perspective of being behind the times: what could explain it was, not too much state, but rather not enough. Indeed, other countries tested experiments similar to that of the French System around the same period, also planning major public projects that mostly never saw the light of day. In place of the financial contagion that we have too often wanted to see in this phenomenon, it is the discourses that prepared and accompanied this European movement of public intervention that require analysis. What were the views of the people of the time? What were the problems that needed solving? What had formerly been repressed before finally gaining expression under the French experiment? What were the anxieties of this new world? Did a truly interventionist European model of the management of society and populations emerge at that time, a model that was not that of national interest? Instead of behind the times, could the case of France be considered from the opposite point of view as being avant-garde? Was there a theoretical moment when people in Europe believed that only a great economic Leviathan could effectively develop trade and ensure the material prosperity of nations? In other words, have scholars to date missed something in history, a utopian-state element, so to speak, that began toward the end of the seventeenth century and had concrete applications at the beginning of the eighteenth? In the history of the Enlightenment, after the Cantabrigian revisionism and the introduction of civic humanism alongside individualistic and liberal discourses, after the evolution and criticism of Cantabrigian revisionism with evidence of the frequent crossing and fusion of republican and liberal discourses, and after the reintroduction of theories of natural law and religious issues as conditions behind the revolutionary movements at the end of the century, perhaps it was still possible to rely on something else. This was a discourse and a tradition much more interventionist than Colbertism, one called the *total state*. It appeared as a timely solution to the aporias generated by national interest, that of Richelieu, Mazarin, Louis XIV, and his ministers, who all failed to make society prosper. It was seen as an antidote to the worrying emergence of greed and competition erected as virtues from the end of the seventeenth century on. This great economic Leviathan had, for the supporters of a strong power with an unequal tendency (promoter of luxury), the advantage of rejecting all protodemocratic, republican aspirations, all the discourses around *virtue*, *civism*, and *counterforces* that emerged in the second half of the Enlightenment. This power was already *postpolitical* in the sense that the whole was to take care of everyone without anyone ever having to express an opinion. To take such a tradition seriously would certainly provide an interesting rereading of the European economic Enlightenment.

The second direction that this book could take would be diachronic. I have discussed the conditions that made the socialization of wealth and economic activity conceivable from the beginning of the eighteenth century on. I have studied the strong and even frightened reactions that this idea aroused. I have seen the great Homeric struggle between creditors and debtors replayed several times. I could then consider the conditions for the possibility of a new distribution of property rights, in the service of the public authorities, within the context of the twenty-first century. When an economic sector becomes hypertrophied, it sharpens appetites but does not always give rise to a desire for nationalization. It seems that this happens in specific cases or under favorable conditions, those where a society questions what holds it together, what constitutes it. Let us take the example of the real estate question today.

At the end of 2002, the United States was experiencing a serious economic recession following the bursting of the bubble—a real one this time—of Internet values, combined with the backlash from the terrorist attacks of 9/11. The country had to finance a war in Afghanistan and was about to undertake another in Iraq. It found itself at the heart of one of the most difficult periods of its recent history since the war in Vietnam thirty years earlier. On October 15, President George W. Bush delivered a speech at the Conference on Minority Homeownership at George Washington University. He recalled that, while more than two-thirds of Americans owned their own homes, this was true for less than 50 percent of those of Hispanic origin and for just over half of African Americans. He stated that he wanted to put an end to these disparities so that millions of minority Americans could also become homeowners over the following decade. He announced a whole series of federal measures for first-time buyers, but it was actually a crusade for real estate that he decreed and detailed. This crusade would go on to mobilize all public and private actors: the Federal Reserve, commercial banks, credit insurers, local governments, etc. In the months and years that followed, interest rates dropped to historically low levels, and government agencies were all mobilized to provide down payments, guarantees, and tax cuts for low-income households that invested in real estate. The result is, sadly, only too well-known: mortgages were granted in the millions to people who could not afford to pay them back, real estate prices soared, the phenomenon gathered momentum, and the whole thing collapsed in 2008 in the famous crisis of the subprime loans. This crisis, however, was but the trigger of a much bigger problem. As a result of financial globalization and, above all, the huge development of private (and public) credit throughout the world, coupled with a real estate bubble at work in many other Western countries, the crisis spread and transformed into what is considered the greatest economic cataclysm since the 1930s.

Many have so far focused on the cyclic economic and structural causes at the root of this cataclysm. The primary causes traditionally put forward include the deregulation of the financial markets since the 1980s, the poorly constructed mathematical models of finance, and the arsonist role played by the Federal Reserve and its extremely low rates, in particular. The secondary causes (much deeper) point to the explosion of private and public debt over several decades. To support the demand for goods and housing, the recourse to massive debt had become essential since the 1990s, broadly since the increase in inequality that the sharing of added value to the detriment of employees and to the benefit of capital owners had caused. The tax competition that had been taking place at the global level for the previous thirty years had led to a decline in states' revenues, offset by the recourse to debt. It is a question not of revisiting these causes here[5] but rather of looking at their impact on a specific sector, real estate.

In fact, it would seem that the crisis of 2008 was but an epiphenomenon of a fundamental trend that began in the 1990s in the West and continues today in large parts of the developed and emerging worlds. This trend is reflected in rising housing prices, but it can be described more generally as a global frenzy for private ownership of real estate, particularly in urban and periurban areas. Of course, this phenomenon accelerated during the first decade of the twenty-first century when part of the West, including the United States, was (already) experiencing an economic crisis, to which George W. Bush clearly referred in his 2002 speech: "I mean, we can put light where there's darkness, and hope where there's despondency in this country. And part of it is working together as a nation to encourage folks to own their own home." But why homes? In the same speech, President Bush explained that increasing the number of homeowners was good for the "soul" of the United States, that "owning something is freedom": "It's part of a free society. . . . It brings pride to people, it's a part of an asset-based society." Alan Greenspan, the famous American economist and chairman of the Federal Reserve from 1987 to 2006 who is often accused of having provoked and encouraged this massive debt, is even more specific in his memoirs. He thus states: "I was aware that the loosening of mortgage credit terms for subprime borrowers increased financial risk, and that subsidized home ownership initiatives distort market outcomes. But I believed then, as now, that the benefits of broadened home ownership are worth the risk. Protection of property rights, so critical to a market economy, requires a critical mass of owners to sustain political support."[6]

In other words, the rise in real estate prices over the last thirty years can be attributed to the result of a combination of two factors. On the one hand, there is a growing demand from individuals for a home, a stable foothold, owing to the increase in the population, the concentration of jobs and services in cities, the increase in the number of divorces, growing professional insecurity, and new technologies and presentism, all of which deterritorialize (historically and geographically) human activity. On the other hand, if inequalities increase, then reducing them can become a fairly shared social demand. But just how far could this go? This is a worrying potential that leads some political leaders to welcome the increase in the number of homeowners, which will tend to prevent the overly wide dissemination of ideas or policies that favor the redistribution of property rights. These leaders and their institutions can, therefore, have the objective of moderately increasing the supply of housing while encouraging the desire for private ownership. For some may have a solution to reduce inequalities and at the same time reduce public debt, namely, socializing real estate wealth. The trend of prices of real estate assets was, for decades, constantly rising. They represent a godsend equivalent to the profits of the large trading companies of the seventeenth century, and it is here that we return to the System, the true System, not that of the myth of 1720.

At the end of 2017, a French government agency made a very serious proposal to reactivate a kind of *directe royale universelle* (part of the seigneurial domain that the suzerain reserved for himself)—a kind of monarchical high domain or, more generally, an arbitrary principle of bringing private feudalisms together in the whole that is the central state. As the official document specifies, this would "allow an excessively indebted State to decree that it becomes co-owner of all constructed residential land." The authors of this study pointed out that in France "public debt has risen from 56% to 100% of gross domestic product (GDP) since the 1990s, while the net property wealth of households has risen from 125% to 255% of GDP." If the French government were to become co-owner of all the nation's real estate, it could require resident owners to pay an annual rent, or it could recover a portion of the sale price of a property at each transaction. The report's authors concluded that, if another major economic crisis were to occur, this would be a solution to be considered. Naturally, this project did not fail to arouse cries of outrage from all France's economic experts. There was talk of "ideological delirium," and the prime minister himself reacted, stating that the public agency that produced the report should have better things to do than to submit such far-fetched proposals to the government.[7]

Perhaps the latter would be well advised to moderate their jibes and comments. Indeed, the important thing is not so much what we will do if a new financial crisis were to occur as the fact that this kind of idea is beginning to emerge, no longer just among a few small, radical groups, but in the minds of state officials within government institutions. We can be sure that other projects of this nature, more or less constructed and more or less authoritarian, will emerge over the coming years, in France and elsewhere. We should try to read them in the light of the history of the System and the events that followed the fall of the Soviet Bloc. Deregulation, economic liberalism, and the decline of the state are being discussed everywhere, and we can seriously wonder whether we are not at the dawn of a demand for renationalization, a mercantilism in the sense of the seventeenth and eighteenth centuries, even in the West. While some regimes disregard property rights, it is not impossible that democratic countries may come to question them at a time when the issue is being raised of a new upward transfer of wealth from the productive to the idle classes (rentiers),[8] which give the impression that they have a desire to secede. At a time when there is much reflection as to what still constitutes a society in Europe and North America, and in a moment that is experiencing some kind of deglobalization, the return of monopolies, and hints that maritime warfare might be on the horizon, it is not surprising that the great economic Leviathan is resurfacing as a potential solution to all the anxieties and fears of dismantlement.

Acknowledgments

The Politics of Utopia is the English-language edition of *La politique du merveilleux*, a book published in 2018 by Fayard. This edition would not have been possible without the steadfast support and wise counsel of my editor at the University of Chicago Press, Dylan Joseph Montanari. I thank him sincerely. Paul Cheney played an important role in bringing this book to fruition, and I offer him my warmest thanks. Thanks to Andrew Brown for his patience in the long process of translation. I am honored that this book is welcomed in Darrin McMahon's fine series, The Life of Ideas, and I thank the team at the University of Chicago Press, especially Fabiola Enríquez Flores, Kristen Raddatz, Joe Brown, and Christine Schwab.

Financially, this book benefited from generous contributions from the University Paris 8 Saint-Denis, the Shelby Cullom Davis Center at Princeton University, and the Florence Gould Foundation.

This book began in 2015 in Princeton University's History Department, where I was a Davis Fellow. For the wonderful welcome I received there and the incomparable intellectual stimulation, I thank, in particular, Phil Nord and David Bell. My colleagues at the Davis Center, where I made many friends, helped me shape the first chapters of this book. They also made life better. Thanks to them, and in particular to Pierre Fuller, Emma Kuby, Marie Kelleher, and Susan Carruthers.

This work has been enriched by conversations at several seminars and symposia. I had the pleasure and good fortune to be welcomed at Columbia, Chicago, Montpellier, Paris 1 Sorbonne, Princeton, Rennes 2, and Stanford, as well as at the German Historical Institute and the Bibliothèque nationale de France. Many thanks to the organizers of and participants at these events.

The French edition of this book would not have been possible without the unfailing advice and support of Antoine Lilti, whom I thank once again. I am also sincerely grateful to David Bell, Loïc Charles, Steve Kaplan, Michael

Kwass, Rachel Rajalu, John Shovlin, and Christine Théré for the time they devoted to me. All of them helped me to avoid many pitfalls and to explore many points in greater depth.

I would also like to express my gratitude to Antonella Alimento, Anne-Marie Autissier, Benjamin Bernard, Jean-Luc Chappey, Paul Cheney, Linda Colley, Anne Conchon, Eleanor Davey, Dan Edelstein, Gilbert Faccarello, Pierre Force, Sheldon Garon, Lisa Graham, Katja Guenther, Paulin Ismard, Harold James, Bill Jordan, Pauline Labey, Marie Lelardoux, Florence Magnot-Ogilvy, Federico Marcon, Matthew McDonald, Philippe Minard, Yair Mintzker, Priya Nelson, Ekaterina Pravilova, Gilles Raveaud, Nicolas Rieucau, Stéphane Rossignol, Silvia Sebastiani, Pierre Serna, Jake Soll, Philippe Steiner, Francesca Trivellato, Jennifer Tsien, and Carl Wennerlind.

Notes

Introduction

1. *Nouveau Mercure* (hereafter *NM*), March 1720, 98–120.

2. Pierre Goubert, *Louis XIV and Twenty Million Frenchmen* (1966; New York: Vintage, 1972), and "Le 'tragique' XVIIe siècle," in *Histoire économique et sociale de la France*, ed. Fernand Braudel and Ernest Labrousse, 4 vols. (1970; Paris: Presses universitaires de France, 1993), 2:329–66; Robert Mandrou, *L'Europe "absolutiste": Raison et raison d'état, 1649–1775* (Paris: Fayard, 1977), 121–31; François Lebrun, *La puissance et la guerre, 1661–1715* (Paris: Le Seuil, 1997), 189–224; Danièle Rébaudo, "Le mouvement annuel de la population française rurale de 1670 à 1740," *Population* 34, no. 3 (May 1979): 589–606; Darryl Dee, *Expansion and Crisis in Louis XIV's France: Franche-Comté and Absolute Monarchy, 1674–1715* (Rochester, NY: University of Rochester Press, 2009).

3. François R. Velde, "French Public Finance between 1683 and 1726," in *Government Debts and Financial Markets in Europe*, ed. F. P. Caselli (London: Pickering & Chatto, 2008), 135–66; Thomas Sargent and François R. Velde, "Macroeconomic Features of the French Revolution," *Journal of Political Economy* 103, no. 3 (June 1995): 474–518; Alain Guéry, "Les finances de la monarchie française sous l'ancien régime," *Annales: Économies, sociétés, civilisations* 33, no. 2 (June 1978): 235–40; Philip T. Hoffman, Gilles Postel-Vinay, and Jean-Laurent Rosenthal, *Priceless Markets: The Political Economy of Credit in Paris, 1660–1870* (Chicago: University of Chicago Press, 2000), 70–71; Emmanuel Le Roy Ladurie, "Réflexions sur la Régence (1715–1723)," *French Studies* 38, no. 3 (July 1984): 286–305, 287.

4. Concerning this Christian protest movement, see Roger Chartier, *The Cultural Origins of the French Revolution* (1990; Durham, NC: Duke University Press, 1991); Catherine Maire, *De la cause de Dieu à la cause de la nation: Le Jansénisme au XVIIIe siècle* (Paris: Gallimard, 1998); Monique Cottret, *Jansénisme et Lumières: Pour un autre XVIIIe siècle* (Paris: Albin Michel, 1998); and Dale Van Kley, *The Religious Origins of the French Revolution* (New Haven, CT: Yale University Press, 2006).

5. Le Roy Ladurie, "Réflexions sur la Régence"; Alexandre Dupilet, *La Régence absolue: Philippe d'Orléans et la polysynodie* (Seyssel: Champ Vallon, 2011); Laurent Lemarchand, *Paris ou Versailles? La monarchie absolue entre deux capitales, 1715–1723* (Paris: CTHS, 2014).

6. Jean Buvat, *Journal de la Régence*, 2 vols. (Paris: Plon, 1865), 1:116, 242; *NM*, August 1718, 185, and December 1718, 96.

7. See Antoin Murphy, *John Law: Economic Theorist and Policy-Maker* (Oxford: Clarendon, 1997), 150–53.

8. Daniel Dessert, *Argent, pouvoir et société au Grand Siècle* (Paris: Fayard, 1984), 261–63; Jean Meyer, *Le régent* (Paris: Ramsay, 1985), 176–77; Edgar Faure, *La banqueroute de Law, 17 juillet 1720* (Paris: Gallimard, 1977), 124–26; Le Roy Ladurie, "Réflexions sur la Régence," 292.

9. *John Law's "Essay on a Land Bank,"* ed. Antoin Murphy (Dublin: Aeon, 1994); John Law, *Money and Trade Consider'd: With a Proposal for Supplying the Nation with Money* (Edinburgh: The Heirs and Successors of Andrew Anderson, 1705), translated into French as *Considérations sur le commerce et sur l'argent, par Mr. Law, controlleur général des finances* (La Haye: Neaulme, 1720).

10. Faure, *La banqueroute de Law*, 47–56; Murphy, *John Law*, 163–64.

11. This narrative is based on Émile Levasseur, *Histoire de la Régence pendant la minorité de Louis XV*, 3 vols. (Paris: Guillaumin, 1854); Marcel Marion, *Histoire financière de la France depuis 1715*, 6 vols. (Paris: Rousseau, 1914–31), 1:90–112; Paul Harsin, *Crédit public et Banque d'état en France du XVIe au XVIIIe siècle* (Paris: Droz, 1933), 57–62, and "La finance et l'état jusqu'au Système de Law," in Braudel and Labrousse, eds., *Histoire économique et sociale*, 1:267–300; Herbert Lüthy, *La banque protestante en France, de la révocation de l'Édit de Nantes à la Révolution*, 2 vols. (Paris: SEVPEN, 1959), 1:275–350; Earl J. Hamilton, "The Political Economy of France at the Time of John Law," *History of Political Economy* 1, no. 1 (January 1969): 123–49; Faure, *La banqueroute de Law*; Jacques Cellard, *John Law et la Régence* (Paris: Plon, 1996); Murphy, *John Law*; and François R. Velde, "John Law's System," *American Economic Review* 97, no. 2 (May 2007): 276–79.

12. A. W. Wiston-Glynn, *John Law of Lauriston: Financier and Statesman, Founder of the Bank of France, Originator of the Mississippi Scheme* (Edinburgh: Saunders & Co., 1907); Georges Oudard, *John Law: A Fantastic Financier, 1671–1729* (London: Jonathan Cape, 1928); Joseph A. Schumpeter, *History of Economic Analysis* (New York: Oxford University Press, 1954), 294–95; Amedeo Gambino, "John Law, Banker and Economist," *Quarterly Review* 9 (1956): 100–110; Robert Minton, *John Law, the Father of Paper-Money* (New York: Associated Press, 1975); Faure, *La banqueroute de Law*; Filippo Cesarano, "Law and Galiani on Money and Monetary Systems," *History of Political Economy* 22, no. 2 (June 1990): 321–40; Larry Neal, *"I Am Not Master of Events": The Speculations of John Law and Lord Londonderry in the Mississippi and South Sea Bubbles* (New Haven, CT: Yale University Press, 2012); Antoin Murphy, "Le grand débat monétaire du dix-huitième siècle entre John Law et Richard Cantillon," in *Les pensées monétaires dans l'histoire: L'Europe, 1517–1776*, ed. Jérôme Blanc and Ludovic Desmedt (Paris: Garnier, 2014), 395–434, and *John Law*; Nicolas Buat, *John Law: La dette, ou Comment s'en débarrasser* (Paris: Les belles lettres, 2015); Bertrand Martinot, *John Law, le magicien de la dette* (Paris: Nouveau monde, 2015).

13. Nicolas Du Tot (1684–1742) and Barthélemy Marmont du Hautchamp (b. 1682?) are supporters of the conspiracy theory, that of the "anti-System." See Nicolas Du Tot, *Réflexions politiques sur les finances et le commerce*, 2 vols. (La Haye: Vaillant & Prevost, 1738), 1:242, 280, 335–40; and [Barthélemy Marmont du Hautchamp], *Histoire du Système des finances, sous la minorité de Louis XV: Pendant les années 1719 & 1720*, 6 vols. (La Haye: Pierre de Hondt, 1739), 1:110–15. François-Marie Chrestien-Deschamps, a man of letters appointed by the Pâris brothers in order to answer Du Tot, stresses the vices of the structure and refutes the conspiracy theory. See [François-Marie Chrestien-Deschamps], *Examen du livre intitulé Réflexions politiques sur les*

finances et le commerce, 2 vols. (La Haye: Vaillant & Prevost, 1740), 2:9–11. In the same vein, see François Véron de Forbonnais, "Vuë générale du Systéme de M. Law," in *Recherches et considérations sur les finances de France*, 2 vols. (Bâle: Cramer, 1758), 2:574–644. Antoin Murphy rejects the conspiracy theory. See Antoin Murphy, introduction to Nicolas Du Tot, *Histoire du Systême de John Law (1716–1720)* (Paris: INED, 2000), xi–lxxvii, xlvi, and *John Law*, 432–34. Nicolas Buat has the same point of view. Marcel Marion is more severe. He claims to see both the involvement of an "anti-System" and many contradictions in the structure of Law's System. See Marion, *Histoire financière*, 1:90–99. Without entering into the conspiracy theory, but in a cutting-edge analysis of the forces involved, Jean Cartelier follows Marion by explaining that "Law's failure" is owed to the "contradictions" of the System and "the resistance of financial and parlementary oligarchies." See Jean Cartelier, "Une expérience contrariée sous la Régence: Le Système de John Law," in Blanc and Desmedt, eds., *Les pensées monétaires dans l'histoire*, 291–327.

14. In the last two decades, the supporters of this interpretive model have debated whether what happened in 1720 should be considered a financial bubble, in line with contemporary financial crisis, and whether John Law was a forerunner of central bankers in the management of public debt. See Peter M. Garber, "Famous First Bubbles," *Journal of Economic Perspectives* 4, no. 2 (Spring 1990): 35–54; François R. Velde, "Government Equity and Money: John Law's System in 1720 France" (working paper 2003-31, Federal Reserve Bank of Chicago, 2003), and "The Case of the Undying Debt," *Financial History Review* 17, no. 2 (July 2010): 185–209; Carmen M. Reinhart and Kenneth Rogoff, *This Time Is Different: A Panoramic View of Eight Centuries of Financial Crises* (Princeton, NJ: Princeton University Press, 2010); Rik G. P. Frehen, William N. Goetzmann, and K. Geert Rouwenhorst, "New Evidence on the First Financial Bubble," *Journal of Financial Economics* 108 (September 2009): 585–607; Cartelier, "Une expérience contrariée sous la Régence"; Martinot, *John Law*; and Buat, *John Law*.

15. The cataclysmic vision of a ruined France and of a long-lasting crisis after 1720 is particularly pronounced in Émile Levasseur, *Recherches historiques sur le Système de Law* (Paris: Guillaumin, 1854), 308; Henri Leclercq, *Histoire de la Régence pendant la minorité de Louis XV*, 3 vols. (Paris: Champion, 1921–22), 2:476–78; and Marion, *Histoire financière*, 1:100–104. Even if they do not subscribe to this dark approach, Charles Kindleberger, Antoin Murphy, François Velde, and Eugene White emphasize the negative effects of the System in terms of distrust in financial innovations, banks, and paper money. The System would have led to species hoarding and prevented the rise of a public credit in France, items that would have had a negative impact on the French economy during the following decades. See Charles P. Kindleberger, *A Financial History of Western Europe* (London: Allen & Unwin, 1984), 96–98; Murphy, *John Law*, 323–34; Velde, "John Law's System," 276–79; and Eugene N. White, "The Long Shadow of John Law on French Public Finance: The Mississippi Bubble," in *The Great Mirror of Folly: Finance, Culture, and the Crash of 1720*, ed. William N. Goetzmann, Catherine Labio, K. Geert Rouwenhorst, and Timothy G. Young (New Haven, CT: Yale University Press, 2013), 99–105. While the modest Jean Buvat did not specify any misery of the people after 1720, his contemporary the lawyer Edmond-Jean Barbier, who had first cried out that France was "ruined," considered at the death of the Duke of Orléans in 1723: "[The duke] has only against him the unfortunate system of 1720, which has overturned the kingdom, that is, ruined many individual families, because, in general, the kingdom has never been so wealthy and thriving. Although I am one of the injured, credit should go to the truth." Edmond-Jean Barbier, *Chronique de la Régence et du règne de Louis XV*, 8 vols. (Paris: Charpentier, 1857–66), 1:307. Du Tot follows the same line in his *Réflexions*

politiques sur les finances et le commerce. Edgar Faure's book relaunched this interpretation of a prosperous France after 1720 through massive deleveraging, both public and private, and the rise of food prices, which allowed a growth of agricultural incomes. See Faure, *La banqueroute de Law*, 610–22. See also Emmanuel Le Roy Ladurie, preface to Lemarchand, *Paris ou Versailles?*, 7–14; Cellard, *John Law et la Régence*, 377–83, and "Réflexions sur la Régence," 286–305; and Buat, *John Law*, 249–59.

16. The epitome of these shortcomings is Lüthy, *La banque protestante en France*. Also not free of them are Jules Michelet, *La Régence* (1863), vol. 15 of *Histoire de France*, 17 vols. (Paris: Éditions des Équateurs, 2008); Faure, *La banqueroute de Law*; Cellard, *John Law et la Régence*; and Martinot, *John Law*.

17. Thomas Kaiser, "Money, Despotism, and Public Opinion in Early Eighteenth-Century France: John Law and the Debate on Royal Credit," *Journal of Modern History* 63, no. 1 (March 1991): 1–28. See also Michael Sonenscher, "The Nation's Debt and the Birth of the Modern Republic: The French Fiscal Deficit and the Politics of the Revolution of 1789; Part I," *History of Political Thought* 18, no. 1 (Spring 1997): 64–103, and *Before the Deluge: Public Debt, Inequality, and the Intellectual Origins of the French Revolution* (Princeton, NJ: Princeton University Press, 2007), 108–20.

18. Le Roy Ladurie, "Réflexions sur la Régence"; Dupilet, *La Régence absolue*; Lemarchand, *Paris ou Versailles?*; Cartelier, "Une expérience contrariée sous la Régence."

19. "Public credit" was allegedly the lever used by John Law to negotiate an alliance with England and Holland, in order to drive a rebalance of Europe to the detriment of Spain. The bank and the paper money would have led Law to take little interest in colonial and commercial considerations, the Companie des Indes being just a pretext to a debt-equity swap. See John Shovlin, "Jealousy of Credit: John Law's 'System' and the Geopolitics of Financial Revolution," *Journal of Modern History* 88, no. 2 (June 2016): 275–305. This book discusses—and rejects—this proposal, following the pioneering works devoted to the Compagnie des Indes and the incredible impetus given to it in 1719–20. See Philippe Haudrère, *La Compagnie française des Indes au XVIIIe siècle*, 2 vols. (1989; Paris: Les Indes savantes, 2005); and André Lespagnol, *Messieurs de Saint-Malo: Une élite négociante au temps de Louis XIV*, 2 vols. (Rennes: Presses universitaires de Rennes, 1990).

20. Goetzmann, Labio, Rouwenhorst, and Young, eds., *The Great Mirror of Folly*, 141–262 (pt. 3, "Text, Image, Culture"); Jean-Michel Rey, *Le temps du crédit* (Paris: Desclée de Brouwer, 2002); Olivier Ferret, "Philippe d'Orléans dans les pièces manuscrites du temps de la Régence," in *Le régent: Entre fable et histoire*, ed. Denis Reynaud and Chantal Thomas (Paris: CNRS, 2003), 63–82; Yves Citton, "Les comptes merveilleux de la finance: Confiance et fiction chez Jean-François Melon," *Féeries* 2 (2005): 125–60; Érik Leborgne, "Le régent et le Système de Law vus par Melon, Montesquieu, Prévost et Lesage," *Féeries* 3 (2006): 105–35; Magali Fourgnaud, "L'économiste (Jean-François Melon) et le conteur (Thémiseul de Saint-Hyacinthe): Analyse croisée," *Féeries* 6 (2009): 151–62; Florence Magnot-Ogilvy, ed., *Gagnons sans savoir comment: Représentations du Système de Law du XVIIIe siècle à nos jours* (Rennes: Presses universitaires de Rennes, 2017).

21. See Faure, *La banqueroute de Law*, 57–58; and Murphy, *John Law*, 8–13.

22. Roland Barthes, "La mort de l'auteur," in *Le bruissement de la langue* (Paris: Le Seuil, 1984), 61–69; Michel Foucault, "Qu'est-ce qu'un auteur?," *Bulletin de la Société française de philosophie* 63, no. 3 (July 1969): 73–104.

23. Thomas Kaiser and Michael Sonenscher have undoubtedly improved our political knowledge of the System, mainly regarding the tensions between paper money, public credit, and absolute monarchy. This book returns a number of times to their analyses. These are frequently insightful but consider the System from a canonical point of view, that of a monetary reform that failed. This starting point leads them to conclusions that I do not share, such as a System that supported free trade, that abolished state grain management, and that used arbitrary and despotic violence. See Kaiser, "Money, Despotism, and Public Opinion"; and Sonenscher, "The Nation's Debt . . . Part I," 75.

24. See, e.g., the canonical narrative of Albert O. Hirschman, *The Passions and the Interests: Political Arguments for Capitalism Before Its Triumph* (Princeton, NJ: Princeton University Press, 1977). More recently, see Jonathan Sheehan and Dror Wahrman, *Invisible Hands: Self-Organization and the Eighteenth Century* (Chicago: University of Chicago Press, 2015).

25. Frédérique Aït-Touati, *Contes de la lune: Essai sur la fiction et la science modernes* (Paris: Gallimard, 2011), 111–17; Emmanuelle Sempère, *De la merveille à l'inquiétude: Le registre du fantastique dans la fiction narrative au XVIIIe siècle* (Bordeaux: Presses universitaires de Bordeaux, 2008), 153–57.

26. In February 1720, Abbé Terrasson says to a correspondent regarding the experiment under way: "I am delighted to see that you give to it by yourself the title of system." The *Dictionnaire de l'Académie française* defines *system* as an "assumption of one or several principles, from where to draw consequences, & on which one draws an opinion, a doctrine, a dogma, &c. The system of Ptolemy, the System of Copernicus." The *Dictionnaire universel français et latin* (1704) also refers to sciences: "sistem" means "in every science, a combination of principles & conclusions." It refers to the systems of Newton, Gassendi, Leibniz, Descartes, and Ptolemy and concludes: "[E]xperiments are the materials of the system." See *Dictionnaire de l'Académie française*, 2 vols. (Paris: Coignard, 1694), 2:531; and *Dictionnaire universel français et latin*, 3 vols. (Trévoux: Ganeau, 1704), vol. 3, s.v. *sistème*. See also *NM*, February 1720, 53.

27. Aït-Touati, *Contes de la lune*, 142, 166–72.

28. This approach is consistent with that initiated by Rebecca Spang in order to understand the echo of the System during the French Revolution. See Rebecca Spang, "The Ghost of Law: Speculating on Money, Memory and Mississippi in the French Constituent Assembly," *Historical Reflections/Réflexions historiques* 31, no. 1 (Spring 2005): 3–25. The *merveilleux*—a contemporary of the Oriental Enlightenment, with which it is closely linked—is an experimental and forward-looking imaginary. It builds new worlds and contributes to individual development. It produced the System and in return was fueled by it. See Srinivas Aravamudan, *Enlightenment Orientalism: Resisting the Rise of the Novel* (Chicago: University of Chicago Press, 2011), 4–9.

29. Jürgen Habermas, *The Structural Transformation of the Public Sphere: An Inquiry into a Category of Bourgeois Society* (1962; Cambridge, MA: MIT Press, 1989); Roger Chartier and Henri-Jean Martin, eds., *Histoire de l'édition française*, vol. 2, *Le livre triomphant, 1660–1830* (1984; Paris: Fayard, 1990); Roger Chartier, *Lectures et lecteurs dans la France d'ancien régime* (Paris: Le Seuil, 1990); Robert Darnton, *Gens de lettres, gens du livre* (Paris: Odile Jacob, 1992); Daniel Roche, *The People of Paris: An Essay in Popular Culture in the 18th Century* (1981; New York: Berg, 1987); Patrick Boucheron and Nicolas Offenstadt, eds., *L'espace public au Moyen Âge: Débats autour de Jürgen Habermas* (Paris: Presses universitaires de France, 2011).

30. Paul Hazard, *The Crisis of the European Mind, 1680–1715* (1935; New York: New York Review of Books, 2013).

Chapter One

1. Reinhart Koselleck, *Critique and Crisis: Enlightenment and the Pathogenesis of Modern Society* (1959; Cambridge, MA: MIT Press, 1988), 15–52; Marcel Gauchet, "L'état au miroir de la raison d'état," in *Raison et déraison d'état: Théoriciens et théories de la raison d'état aux XVIe et XVIIe siècles*, ed. Yves-Charles Zarka (Paris: Presses universitaires de France, 1994), 193–244; Fanny Cosandey and Robert Descimon, *L'absolutisme en France: Histoire et historiographie* (Paris: Le Seuil, 2002), 93–105; Michel Foucault, *Security, Territory, Population: Lectures at the Collège de France, 1977–78* (2004; New York: Palgrave Macmillan, 2007), 326–28.

2. Mathilde Moulin, "Les rentes sur l'Hôtel de Ville de Paris sous Louis XIV," *Histoire, économie et société* 17, no. 4 (October 1998): 623–48; Katia Béguin, *Financer la guerre au XVIIe siècle: La dette publique et les rentiers de l'absolutisme* (Paris: Champ Vallon, 2012), 81–83, and "La circulation des rentes constituées dans la France du XVIIe siècle: Une approche de l'incertitude économique," *Annales: Histoire, sciences sociales* 60, no. 6 (November 2005): 1229–44; Dessert, *Argent, pouvoir et société au Grand Siècle*, 21.

3. Dessert, *Argent, pouvoir et société*, 225–57; Robert Mandrou, *Louis XIV en son temps, 1661–1715* (Paris: Presses universitaires de France, 1973), 314–15; *Bibliothèque historique de la France*, 5 vols. (Paris: Hérissant, 1775), 4:92.

4. Stoyan Tzoneff, *L'homme d'argent au théâtre français jusqu'à la Révolution française* (Gap: Jean, 1934); Françoise Bayard, *Le monde des financiers au XVIIe siècle* (Paris: Flammarion, 1988); Daniel Dessert, "Le laquais financier au Grand Siècle: Mythe ou réalité?," *XVIIe siècle* 122 (1979): 21–36, and *Argent, pouvoir et société*, 83–85.

5. Léon-Emmanuel-Simon de Laborde, *Le Palais Mazarin et les grandes habitations de ville et de campagne au XVIIIe siècle* (Paris: Franck, 1846), 397.

6. Dessert, *Argent, pouvoir et société*; Bayard, *Le monde des financiers au XVIIe siècle.*

7. Florent Carton dit Dancourt, *La foire de Bezons*, in *Les oeuvres de théâtre de M. Dancourt*, 12 vols. (Paris: Libraires associés, 1760), 4:121–204, 163, and *Les agioteurs* (1710), 152.

8. Martial Poirson, "L'invention de la *comédie d'affaires*: La mobilité sociale, entre projection et contestation," in *Art et argent en France au temps des premiers modernes*, ed. Martial Poirson (Oxford: Voltaire Foundation, 2004), 203–19, 203; Nathalie Rizzoni, introduction to Alain-René Lesage, *Turcaret précédé de Crispin rival de son maître* (Paris: Le livre de poche, 1999), 8–38, 21–23; Érik Leborgne, "Les jeux de la fortune dans *Turcaret*: Grandeur et infamie du 'financier gentilhomme,'" in Poirson, ed., *Art et argent en France*, 220–29, 222.

9. See Dancourt, *Les agioteurs*, 161; Martial Poirson, "Quand l'économie était sur les planches: Argent, morale et intérêt dans la comédie à l'âge classique," in *Les frontières littéraires de l'économie*, ed. Martial Poirson, Yves Citton, and Christian Biet (Paris: Desjonquères, 2008), 27–51, 37.

10. Alain-René Lesage, *Turcaret* (Paris: Ribou, 1709), 2.3; Leborgne, "Les jeux de la fortune dans *Turcaret*," 227; Dancourt, *Les agioteurs*, 176; Lesage, *Turcaret*, 5.9, 1.95.

11. *Les tours industrieux, subtils et gaillards de la Maltôte* (London: Chez l'auteur rue des Maltôtiers, 1708), 3–5, 24, 9–12; *Pluton maltôtier* (Cologne: À l'enclume, 1708), 298–99; Poirson, "L'invention de la *comédie d'affaires*," 214–15; Charles Dufresny, *La coquette de village, ou Le lot supposé* (La Haye: Johnson, 1716), 75.

12. Dessert, *Argent, pouvoir et société*, 22; René Taveneaux, *Jansénisme et prêt à intérêt* (Paris: Vrin, 1977); Jean-Laurent Le Semelier, *Conférences ecclésiastiques de Paris sur l'usure et la restitution*, 4 vols. (Paris: Estienne, 1718), 2:422–49, 434–35.

13. Taveneaux, *Jansénisme et prêt à intérêt*, 48–50; Arnaud Orain and Maxime Menuet, "Liberal Jansenists and Interest-Bearing Loans in Eighteenth-Century France: A Reappraisal," *European Journal of the History of Economic Thought* 24, no. 4 (Fall 2017): 708–41.

14. Jean Le Correur, *Traité de la pratique des billets entre les négociants* (1682; Mons: Migeot, 1684), 69–72, 312–15.

15. Taveneaux, *Jansénisme et prêt à intérêt*, 49–50; *Journal de Trévoux*, June 1702, 74–87; Nicolas Le Maire, *Réfutation du traité de la pratique des billets entre les négocians* (Paris: Mariette, 1702), 97–106, 46–51.

16. Louis Thomassin, *Traité du négoce et de l'usure* (Paris: Roulland, 1697), 460; Jacques-Joseph Duguet, *Dissertations théologiques et dogmatiques*, vol. 1, *Sur les exorcismes, & les autres cérémonies du batême*, vol. 2, *Sur l'eucharistie*, vol. 3, *Sur l'usure* (Paris: Estienne, 1727), 3:354–55.

17. See Jean-Claude Perrot, "Portrait des agents économiques dans l'oeuvre de Boisguilbert," in *Boisguilbert parmi nous*, ed. J. Hecht (Paris: INED, 1989), 141–56, 152.

18. Jacques-Joseph Duguet, *Institution d'un prince*, 4 vols. (1739; London: Nourse, 1750), 2:292–308, 315–16. See also Jean-Arthur de La Gibonais, *De l'usure, interest, et profit qu'on tire du prest* (Paris: Delaulne, 1710), 545–46, 50–51.

19. Pierre de Boisguilbert, *Factum de la France*, in *Pierre de Boisguilbert, ou La naissance de l'économie politique*, 2 vols. (Paris: INED, 1966), 2:879–956, 908, and *Supplément du Détail de la France*, in ibid., 2:1013–20, 1016. See also Michel Le Vassor, *Lettres d'un gentilhomme françois sur l'établissement d'une capitation générale en France* (Liège: Le Bon, 1695), 101–2.

20. Michael Kwass, "A Kingdom of Taxpayers: State Formation, Privilege, and Political Culture in Eighteenth-Century France," *Journal of Modern History* 70, no. 2 (June 1998): 295–339. See also William Beik, *Absolutism and Society in Seventeenth-Century France* (Cambridge: Cambridge University Press, 1985); James B. Collins, *Classes, Estates, and Order in Early Modern Brittany* (Cambridge: Cambridge University Press, 1994); and Mireille Touzery, *L'invention de l'impôt sur le revenu: La taille tarifée, 1715–1789* (Paris: CHEFF, 1994).

21. Dessert, *Argent, pouvoir et société*, 17–20; Kwass, "A Kingdom of Taxpayers"; Pierre Goubert, "La société traditionnelle," in Braudel and Labrousse, eds., *Histoire économique et sociale de la France*, 2:567–600, 582; Michael Kwass, *Contraband: Louis Mandrin and the Making of a Global Underground* (Cambridge, MA: Harvard University Press, 2014), 46–48, 163–81; Yves Durand, *Les fermiers généraux au XVIIIe siècle* (1971; Paris: Maisonneuve & Larose, 1996), 427–29, 72; Georges T. Matthews, *The Royal General Farm in Eighteenth-Century France* (New York: Columbia University Press, 1958), 151–52.

22. Michel Bernstein, "Sur la diffusion des oeuvres de Boisguilbert et Vauban de 1695 a 1713," in Hecht, ed., *Boisguilbert parmi nous*, 163–66; Jacqueline Hecht, "La vie de Pierre Le Pesant, seigneur de Boisguilbert," in *Pierre de Boisguilbert*, 1:121–244, 157–59.

23. Pierre de Boisguilbert, *Le détail de la France*, in *Pierre de Boisguilbert*, 2:581–662, 641, 644, *Supplément*, 2:1013–15, and *Factum de la France*, 922; Duguet, *Institution d'un prince*, 2:444–45. See also Émile Raunié, *Chansonnier historique du XVIIIe siècle*, 10 vols. (Paris: Quantin, 1879–84), 1:129–30.

24. Duguet, *Institution d'un prince*, 2:439, 480–86; *L'Alcoran de Louis XIV, ou Le testament politique du Cardinal Jules Mazarin* (Roma: Stampatore, 1695), 28–38. See also Jean Nicolas, *La rebellion française: Mouvements populaires et conscience sociale, 1661–1789* (Paris: Le Seuil, 2002), 58, 121; and Kwass, *Contraband*, 92–101.

25. Foucault, *Security, Territory, Population*, 263–64; Carl Schmitt, *Theory of the Partisan: Intermediate Commentary on the Concept of the Political* (New York: Telos, 2007), 3–32.

26. Max Weber, *Economy and Society* (1922; Berkeley and Los Angeles: University of California Press, 1978), and "The Three Types of Legitimate Rule," *Berkeley Publications in Society and Institutions* 4, no. 1 (1958): 1–11.

27. Duguet, *Institution d'un prince*, 2:435–36; Boisguilbert, *Le détail de la France*, 591–97, and *Factum de la France*, 895; Sébastien Le Prestre de Vauban, *Projet de dîme royale*, in *Les oisivetés de Monsieur de Vauban*, ed. Michèle Virol (Seyssel: Champ Vallon, 2007), 751–878, 752–53, 877; François Fénelon, *Écrits et lettres politiques* (Genève: Slatkine, 1920), 149–50.

28. Perrot, *Une histoire intellectuelle*, 151; Vauban, *Projet de dîme royale*, 763; Boisguilbert, *Le détail de la France*, 618; Pierre de Boisguilbert, *Dissertation: De la nature des richesses, de l'argent et des tributs, où l'on découvre la fausse idée qui règne dans le monde à l'égard de ces trois articles*, in *Pierre de Boisguilbert*, 2:973–1012, 977–81.

29. See Mireille Touzery, "Projet de dîme royale," in Virol, ed., *Les oisivetés de Monsieur de Vauban*, 705–42, 713–15; Emmanuel Le Roy Ladurie, *Les paysans de Languedoc*, 2 vols. (Paris: SEVPEN, 1966), 1:603, and "Réflexions sur la Régence," 287; Mandrou, *Louis XIV en son temps*, 319–21; Jean-Yves Grenier, *L'économie d'ancien régime: Un monde de l'échange et de l'incertitude* (Paris: Albin Michel, 1996), 410–11.

30. Michel Nassiet, "Projet de capitation," in Virol, ed., *Les oisivetés de Monsieur de Vauban*, 279–82; Gary B. McCollim, *Louis XIV's Assault on Privilege: Nicolas Desmaretz and the Tax on Wealth* (Rochester, NY: Rochester University Press, 2012), 140; Sébastien Le Prestre de Vauban, *Projet de capitation*, in *Les oisivetés de Monsieur de Vauban*, 286–99, 286, 297; Paul Harsin, "Une lettre inédite de Boisguilbert à Vauban," in Hecht, ed., *Boisguilbert parmi nous*, 168–69; Arthur Birembaut, "Boisguilbert, Vauban et les officiers français du Génie au XVIIIe siècle," in ibid., 1:184–85; Michèle Virol, "Projet de dîme royale: Sa genèse," in Virol, ed., *Les oisivetés de Monsieur de Vauban*, 695–704; Touzery, "Projet de dîme royale," 720; Boisguilbert, *Le détail de la France*, 632–41, and *Factum de la France*, 944–51.

31. Kwass, "A Kingdom of Taxpayers," 323. See also Michael Kwass, *Privilege and the Politics of Taxation in Eighteenth-Century France: Liberté, Égalité, Fiscalité* (Cambridge: Cambridge University Press, 2000).

32. Le Vassor, *Lettres d'un gentilhomme françois*, 3–6, 16; [Pierre Jurieu and Michel Le Vassor], *Les soupirs de la France esclave qui aspire après la liberté* (Amsterdam, 1689), 5.

33. *Dictionnaire de l'Académie française*, 2:606; Cosandey and Descimon, *L'absolutisme en France*, 242–51; Le Vassor, *Lettres d'un gentilhomme françois*, 9.

34. Denis Richet, "Autour des origines idéologiques lointaines de la Révolution française," *Annales: Économies, sociétés, civilisations* 24, no. 1 (January 1969): 1–27, 18; [Jurieu and Le Vassor], *Les soupirs de la France esclave*, 17, 11; [Michel Le Vassor], *La politique françoise démasquée* (Utrecht: Chez P.D., 1695), 2–3, 134–35.

35. *Réflexions sur le traité de la dixme royale de M. le Maréchal de Vauban*, 2 vols. (1716), 2:18–19.

36. *Réflexions sur le traité de la dixme royale*, 2:18–19, 58–59, 22–24, 18–19.

37. Boisguilbert, *Dissertation*, 979, and *Factum de la France*, 881; Vauban, *Projet de dîme royale*, 760, 762.

38. Jean-Michel Racault, *Nulle part et ses environs: Voyage aux confins de l'utopie littéraire classique (1657–1802)* (Paris: Presses universitaires de Paris-Sorbonne, 2003), 25, 40, and *L'utopie narrative en France et en Angleterre, 1675–1761* (Oxford: Voltaire Foundation, 1991), 748–49; Bronisław Baczko, Michel Porret, and François Rosset, eds., *Dictionnaire critique de l'utopie au temps des Lumières* (Chêne-Bourg: Georg, 2016), 16–20.

39. Racault, *Nulle part et ses environs*, 777–78. See also Bronisław Baczko, *Utopian Lights: The Evolution of the Idea of Social Progress* (1978; New York: Paragon, 1989).

40. Racault, *Nulle part et ses environs*, 5.

41. Denis Vairasse, *L'histoire des Sévarambes*, 4 vols. (Paris: Barbin, 1677–79), 1: n.p. (epistle), 2:250, 3:12–13, 30–31, 96, 10–26; Bernard Le Bovier de Fontenelle, *La république des philosophes, ou Histoire des Ajaoiens* (1682; Geneva, 1768), 70–94; Claude Gilbert, *Histoire de Caléjava* (1700), 120–31; Simon Tyssot de Patot, *Voyages et aventures de Jacques Massé* (Bourdeaux: L'aveugle, 1710); François Fénelon, *Les avantures de Télémaque*, 2 vols. (1699; Paris: Delaulne, 1717), 1:254–58.

42. Fénelon, *Les avantures de Télémaque*, 1:99.

43. Gabriel de Foigny, *Les avantures de Jacques Sadeur dans la découverte et le voiage de la terre australe* (Paris: Barbin, 1692); François Leguat, *Voyage et avantures de François Leguat et de ses compagnons, en deux isles désertes des Indes orientales* (Amsterdam: De Lorme, 1708), 61–64, 102–3; Racault, *L'utopie narrative*, 67–74.

44. Gabriel de Foigny, *La terre australe connue* (1676; Vannes: Verneuil, 1692), 104–54; Fénelon, *Les avantures de Télémaque*, 1:166–71; Marc-André Bernier, "Amérique," in Baczko, Porret, and Rosset, eds., *Dictionnaire critique de l'utopie*, 29–49, 36; Louis-Armand de Lahontan, *Mémoires de l'Amérique septentrionale*, 2 vols. (La Haye: L'Honoré, 1703), 2:10, 133, and *Dialogues de Monsieur le baron de Lahontan et d'un sauvage dans l'Amérique* (Amsterdam and London: Boeteman & Mortier, 1704), 18–24, 68–88.

45. Réal Ouellet, introduction to Louis-Armand de Lahontan, *Oeuvres complètes*, 2 vols. (Montréal: Presses de l'Université de Montréal, 1990), 1:11–199, 113; André Lichtenberger, *Le socialisme au XVIIIe siècle* (Paris: Alcan, 1895), 54–56; Myriam Yardeni, "Gueudeville et Louis XIV: Un précurseur du socialisme, critique des structures sociales louis-quatorziennes," *Revue d'histoire moderne et contemporaine* 19, no. 4 (October 1972): 598–620; [Nicolas Gueudeville and Louis-Armand de Lahontan], *Nouveaux voyages de M. le baron de La Hontan dans l'Amérique septentrionale*, 2 vols. (Amsterdam: L'Honoré, 1705), 2:277–78.

46. Racault, *Nulle part et ses environs*, 33–35.

47. Jean Ehrard, *L'idée de nature en France dans la première moitié du XVIIIe siècle* (1963; Paris: Albin Michel, 1994), 578; Albert Soboul, "Le critique social devant son temps," in Jean Meslier, *Oeuvres complètes*, 3 vols. (Paris: Anthropos, 1970), 1:ci–cxlvi; Marcus Rediker, *Villains of All Nations: Atlantic Pirates in the Golden Age* (Boston: Beacon, 2004); Nicolas Gueudeville, "Préface du traducteur," in *L'utopie de Thomas Morus* (Leiden: Vander, 1715), n.p.

48. Lionel Rothkrug, *Opposition to Louis XIV: The Political and Social Origins of the French Enlightenment* (Princeton, NJ: Princeton University Press, 1965); David K. Smith, "Structuring Politics in Early Eighteenth-Century France: The Political Innovations of the French Council of Commerce," *Journal of Modern History* 74, no. 3 (September 2002): 490–537, 494.

49. Charles W. Cole, *Colbert and a Century of French Mercantilism*, 2 vols. (New York: Columbia University Press, 1939), 1:335–45, 287; Jean-Yves Grenier, *Histoire de la pensée économique et politique* (Paris: Hachette, 2007), 115–20; Philippe Minard, *La fortune du colbertisme: État et industrie dans la France des Lumières* (Paris: Fayard, 1998), 15–17.

50. Minard, *La fortune du colbertisme*, 17–19; John Shovlin, *Trading with the Enemy: Britain, France, and the Eighteenth-Century Quest for a Peaceful Global Order* (New Haven, CT: Yale University Press, 2021), chap. 1; Moritz Isenmann, "From Privilege to Economic Law: Vested Interests and the Origins of Free Trade in France (1687–1701)," in *Economic Growth and the Origins of Modern Political Economy*, ed. Philipp R. Rössner (London: Routledge, 2016), 103–21, 111–12.

51. [Jurieu and Le Vassor], *Les soupirs de la France esclave*, 14; [Gatien de Courtilz de Sandras], *Nouveaux interests des princes de l'Europe* (Cologne: Marteau, 1688), 156–58.

52. Shovlin, *Trading with the Enemy*, chap. 1.

53. David K. Smith, "Le discours économique du bureau du commerce, 1700–1750," in *Le cercle de Vincent de Gournay: Savoirs économiques et pratiques administratives en France au milieu du XVIIIe siècle*, ed. Löic Charles, Frédéric Lefebvre, and Christine Théré (Paris: INED, 2011), 31–61, 31; Paul Cheney, *Revolutionary Commerce: Globalization and the French Monarchy* (Cambridge, MA: Harvard University Press, 2010), 172–73.

54. Bibliothèque nationale de France (hereafter BnF), Manuscrits Français (hereafter MS Fr.) 8038, fols. 45, 49, 88, 105, 119, 236–50, 407, 425–28, 119.

55. BnF, MS Fr. 8038, fols. 94, 111, 129, 158–59, 244, 268–70, 302–9, 316–17, 433–38. Concerning Marseilles, see ibid., fols. 497–521; and Junko T. Takeda, *Between Crown and Commerce: Marseille and the Early Modern Mediterranean* (Baltimore: Johns Hopkins University Press, 2011), 44–48.

56. BnF, MS Fr. 8038, fols. 44, 87–88, 97, 107, 124, 151–57, 224–31, 321–22, 335–36.

57. "Mémoires sur divers points d'économie politique d'histoire et de philosophie, présentés à Louis XIV par M. de Belesbat," BnF, MS Fr. 1205, fols. 8–9, 79, 86–87; Duguet, *Institution d'un prince*, 2:280–89.

58. Perrot, *Une histoire intellectuelle*, 349–50, and "Portrait des agents économiques dans l'oeuvre de Boisguilbert," 152–53.

59. Pierre Nicole, *De l'éducation d'un prince* (Paris: Savreux, 1670), 203–4.

60. Boisguilbert, *Factum de la France contre les demandeurs en delay*, in *Pierre de Boisguilbert*, 2:741–818, 748–49.

61. Boisguilbert, *Dissertation*, 991–93, 987, and *Factum de la France*, 892.

62. Boisguilbert, *Factum de la France contre les demandeurs en delay*, 787; Steven L. Kaplan, *Provisioning Paris: Merchants and Millers in the Grain and Flour Trade during the Eighteenth Century* (Ithaca, NY: Cornell University Press, 1984), 25–26.

63. "Discours qui a remporté le prix d'éloquence au jugement de l'Académie françoise en MDCCXV," in *Recueil de plusieurs pièces d'éloquence et de poésie* (Paris: Coignard, 1715), 8–9, 24, 82–83, 108.

64. Henri-François d'Aguesseau, *Oeuvres de M. le chancelier d'Aguesseau*, 13 vols. (Paris: Libraires associés, 1759–89), 1:209.

65. d'Aguesseau, *Oeuvres de M. le chancelier d'Aguesseau*, 1:210–11.

66. Christian Bruschi, "Droits de l'homme et du citoyen selon d'Aguesseau," *Histoire de la justice* 19, no. 1 (January 2009): 15–40; Nicolas Delamare, *Traité de la police*, 2 vols. (Paris: Cot, 1710), 2:915.

67. [Jean-Baptiste de Lagny], "Memoire par lequel on justifie que la police établie et les reglemens donnés pour le commerce de France depuis la paix des Pyrenées ont produit l'abondance de l'or et de l'argent dans le royaume," Archives nationales de France (hereafter AnF), MAR B/7/497, fols. 406–66, 431.

68. Isenmann, "From Privilege to Economic Law," 113.

69. Lebrun, *La puissance et la guerre*, 209; Goubert, "Le 'tragique' XVIIe siècle," 363. See also Istvan Hont, *Jealousy of Trade: International Competition and the Nation-State in Historical Perspective* (Cambridge, MA: Harvard University Press, 2010). Concerning Saint-Malo, see Lespagnol, *Messieurs de Saint-Malo*.

70. Michel Morineau, *Incroyables gazettes et fabuleux métaux: Les retours des trésors améri-*

cains d'après les gazettes hollandaises (XVIe–XVIIIe siècles) (Cambridge: Cambridge University Press, 1985), 120–217; Jeff Horn, *Economic Development in Early Modern France: The Privilege of Liberty, 1650–1820* (Cambridge: Cambridge University Press, 2015), 149; Haudrère, *La Compagnie française*, 1:35; Jan de Vries, "Connecting Europe and Asia: A Quantitative Analysis of the Cape-Route Trade, 1497–1795," in *Global Connections and Monetary History, 1470–1800*, ed. Dennis O. Flynn, Arturo Giraldez, and Richard von Glahn (Aldershot: Ashgate, 2003), 35–106.

71. Philip Stern, *The Company-State: Corporate Sovereignty and the Early Modern Foundations of the British Empire in India* (Oxford: Oxford University Press, 2011), 3–7. See also James B. Collins, *The State in Early Modern France* (Cambridge: Cambridge University Press, 1995).

72. John Law, *Oeuvres complètes* (hereafter *OC*), 3 vols. (Paris: Sirey, 1934), 2:67–259; Rothkrug, *Opposition to Louis XIV*, 435 n. 132; Faure, *La banqueroute de Law*, 57–58.

73. See Pierre-Yves Legras, "L'oeuvre économique de Jean Pottier de la Hestroye" (master's thesis, University Paris 1, 1985). I refer here to "Mémoires touchant le commerce de la France et les moiens de le restablir" (ca. 1699–1700), AnF, Fonds Mirabeau, M 785, no. 4; "Mémoires touchant le commerce de la France et les moiens de le restablir" (ca. 1711), Bibliothèque de l'Arsenal (hereafter Arsenal), MS 4561; "Restablissement du commerce" (ca. 1715), in Law, *OC*, 2:67–259.

74. "Restablissement du commerce," 2:143, 203, 149, 206–7.

75. "Restablissement du commerce," 2:89; and AnF, Fonds Mirabeau, M 785, no. 4, fol. 22; Law, *OC*, 2:186–88; and AnF, Fonds Mirabeau, M 785, no. 4, fols. 126–28.

76. AnF, Fonds Mirabeau, M 785, no. 4, fols. 2–3.

77. AnF, Fonds Mirabeau, M 785, no. 4, fols. 53–54; Arsenal, MS 4561, fols. 3–4, 236–37; Law, *OC*, 2:69–70, 117–18.

78. AnF, Fonds Mirabeau, M 785, no. 4, fols. 8, 103; Arsenal, MS 4561, fols. 417–20; Law, *OC*, 2:69–74.

79. Arsenal, MS 4561, fols. 275–76, 268, 281–84.

80. Arsenal, MS 4561, fols. 303–7, 362–72, 476–83.

81. Pierre-Daniel Huet, *Le grand trésor historique du florissant commerce des Hollandois* (Rouen: Ruault, 1712), n.p. (preface), 182.

82. See Law, *OC*, 2:137.

83. Law, *OC*, 2:138–47.

84. Harsin, *Crédit public et Banque d'état en France*, 52; Law, *OC*, 2:202–59.

85. "Mémoire pour rendre l'état puissant & invincible, & tous les sujets de ce même état heureux & riches," in *Mémoires presentés à Monseigneur le duc d'Orléans, régent de France . . . par le C. de Boulainvilliers* (La Haye and Amsterdam: Aux dépends de la Compagnie, 1727), 19–20, 33–37, 41–42, 62–70. See Jacqueline Hecht, "Trois précurseurs de la sécurité sociale au XVIIIe siècle: Henry de Boulainvilliers, Faiguet de Villeneuve, Du Beissier de Pizany d'Eden," *Population* 14, no. 1 (January 1959): 73–88; and Olivier Tholozan, *Henri de Boulainvilliers: L'anti-absolutisme aristocratique légitimé par l'histoire* (Aix-en-Provence: Presses universitaires d'Aix-Marseille, 1999), 453–54.

86. Étienne Lescuyer de La Jonchère, *Systême d'un nouveau gouvernement en France*, 4 vols. (Amsterdam: Le Bon, 1720), 4:197, 300–301, 1:61, 107–29, 2:152–77, 208–35, 3:259.

87. La Jonchère, *Systême d'un nouveau gouvernement en France*, 1:170–76.

88. La Jonchère, *Systême d'un nouveau gouvernement en France*, 1:48–49.

89. La Jonchère, *Systême d'un nouveau gouvernement en France*, 1:2–3, 50–57; Alphonse Callery, *Les réformateurs de l'ancienne France: Le précurseur de Law, La Jonchère (1718–1720)* (Bourges, 1880), 2.

Chapter Two

1. See *The Ballance of Power; or, A Comparison of the Strength of the Emperor and the French King* (London: Baldwin, 1709), 10–11; Linda Colley, *Britons: Forging the Nation, 1707–1837* (1992; New Haven, CT: Yale University Press, 2005), 79; and John Shovlin, "War and Peace: Trade, International Competition, and Political Economy," in *Mercantilism Reimagined: Political Economy in Early Modern Britain and Its Empire*, ed. Philip J. Stern and Carl Wennerlind (Oxford: Oxford University Press, 2014), 305–27, 308.

2. Cheney, *Revolutionary Commerce*, 26–28.

3. See Gilles Havard and Cécile Vidal, *Histoire de l'Amérique française* (2003; Paris: Flammarion, 2006), 120–26; Cécile Vidal, "French Louisiana in the Age of the Companies, 1712–1731," in *Constructing Early Modern Empires: Proprietary Ventures in the Atlantic World, 1500–1750*, ed. L. H. Roper and B. Van Ruymbeke (Leiden: Brill, 2007), 133–61.

4. Nelson-Martin Dawson, *L'Atelier Delisle: L'Amérique du Nord sur la table à dessin* (Sillery: Septentrion, 2000); Marcel Giraud, *Histoire de la Louisiane française*, 4 vols. (Paris: Presses universitaires de France, 1953–74), 2:11–16; David J. Sturdy, *Science and Social Status: The Members of the Académie des sciences, 1666–1750* (Woodbridge: Boydell, 1995), 372–73.

5. Giraud, *Histoire de la Louisiane française*, 2:230, 272–79; Vidal, "French Louisiana in the Age of the Companies"; Shannon L. Dawdy, *Building the Devil's Empire: French Colonial New Orleans* (Chicago: University of Chicago Press, 2008), 14, 116.

6. Antoine Crozat, "Mémoire sur la colonie de la Louisiane porté au conseil de Régence le 11 février 1716," Archives nationales d'Outre-Mer (hereafter AnOM), C13A4.

7. Giraud, *Histoire de la Louisiane française*, 2:63–64, 117–29, 1:32–33, 87, 3:29; Paul Harsin, "La création de la Compagnie d'Occident (1717): Contribution à l'histoire du Système de Law," *Revue d'histoire économique et sociale* 34, no. 1 (1956): 7–42, 8–15; Haudrère, *La Compagnie française*, 1:40; Crozat, "Mémoire sur la colonie de la Louisiane"; Vidal, "French Louisiana in the Age of the Companies," 146; Dawdy, *Building the Devil's Empire*, 146.

8. Dawson, *L'Atelier Delisle*, 111–14.

9. François Le Maire, "Mémoire sur la Louisiane, pour estre présenté avec la carte de ce païs au conseil souverain de la marine, au Fort-Louis de la Louisiane, 1er mars 1717," BnF, MS Fr. 12105, fols. 16–18.

10. Le Maire, "Mémoire sur la Louisiane," fols. 6–7; Crozat, "Mémoire sur la colonie de la Louisiane," fols. 5–7.

11. Le Maire, "Mémoire sur la Louisiane," fols. 6–7.

12. See Ralph H. Vigil, "Spanish Exploration and the Great Plains in the Age of Discovery: Myth and Reality," *Great Plains Quarterly* 10, no. 1 (Winter 1990): 3–17; and Peter O. Koch, *Imaginary of Gold: The Spanish Quest for Treasure in North America* (Jefferson, NC: McFarland, 2009).

13. Guillaume Delisle, "Conjecture sur l'existence d'une mer dans la partie occidentale du Canada et du Mississipi, 1717," in *Nouvelles cartes des découvertes de l'Amiral de Fonte* (Paris, 1753), 51–60, 56.

14. Paul Mapp, "French Geographic Conceptions of the Unexplored American West and the Louisiana Cession of 1762," in *French Colonial Louisiana and the Atlantic World*, ed. Bradley G. Bond (Baton Rouge: Louisiana State University Press, 2005), 134–74, 142; Fernando Ainsa, "Mythe, prodige et aventure de l'Eldorado: Mutations sémantiques d'une légende," *Diogène* 164 (1993): 16–31; Jean-Pierre Sanchez, *Mythes et légendes de la conquête de l'Amérique*, 2 vols. (Rennes: Presses universitaires de Rennes, 1996), 1:396.

15. Giraud, *Histoire de la Louisiane française*, 2:24, 17.

16. See Christiane Demeulenaere-Douyère and David J. Sturdy, eds., *L'enquête du régent, 1716–1718: Sciences, techniques et politique dans la France pré-industrielle* (Turnhout: Brepols, 2008).

17. Sturdy, *Science and Social Status*, 226.

18. Demeulenaere-Douyère and Sturdy, *L'enquête du régent*, 12, 34, 31.

19. See John Landers, *The Field and the Forge: Population, Production, and Power in the Pre-Industrialist West* (Oxford: Oxford University Press, 2003).

20. Demeulenaere-Douyère and Sturdy, *L'enquête du régent*, 47, 56.

21. The academician Étienne-François Geoffroy (1672–1731) wrote a letter to Bignon in 1716 in which he explained that France could outperform England "if we cared as they [the English] to do some extensive research in all the provinces and to promote its [France's] wonders [*merveilles*]." Demeulenaere-Douyère and Sturdy, *L'enquête du régent*, 81 (see also 177–80, 252–56, 259–60).

22. Crozat, "Mémoire sur la colonie de la Louisiane," fol. 9; Le Maire, "Mémoire sur la Louisiane," fols. 9–13.

23. Le Maire "Mémoire sur la Louisiane," fols. 6–9.

24. Giraud, *Histoire de la Louisiane française*, 2:74–80, 1:233.

25. *An Account of What Will Do; or, An Equivalent for Thoulon: In a Proposal for an Amicable Subscribtion for Improving Trade in the South-West Part of America, and Increasing Bullion to about Three Millions per Annum, Both for the East-India Trade, and the Revenue of the Crown, Which by Consequence Will be Produced, If This Encouraged* (London: Mary Edwards, 1707), 3.

26. "These Mines Are the Fountains of That Treasure, by Which the *French* King Is Enabled to Carry on His Arbitrary Designs," in John Le Wright, *Two Proposals Becoming England at This Juncture to Undertake: One, for Securing a Collony in the West-Indies, as Her Majesty's Propriety Now to Be Enter'd upon, or for Ever Lost: And the Other, for Advancing Merchandize, and the Crown-Revenue to at Least 40 000 l. p. An.* (1706), 4. See also *An Account of What Will Do*, 3–4.

27. Shinsuke Satsuma, *Britain and Colonial Maritime War in the Early Eighteenth Century: Silver, Seapower and the Atlantic* (Woodbridge: Boydell, 2013), 86–87.

28. Julian Hoppit, "The Myths of the South Sea Bubble," *Transactions of the Royal Historical Society* 12 (2002): 141–65, 142; Carl Wennerlind, *Casualties of Credit: The English Financial Revolution, 1620–1720* (Cambridge, MA: Harvard University Press, 2011), 200–202.

29. Wennerlind, *Casualties of Credit*, 198.

30. Wennerlind, *Casualties of Credit*, 218–30; Satsuma, *Britain and Colonial Maritime War*, 160–87; Abigail L. Swingen, *Visions of Empire: Labor, Slavery, and the Origins of the British Atlantic Empire* (New Haven, CT: Yale University Press, 2015), 187–88.

31. See Arne Bialuschewski, "*A True Account of the Design, and Advantages of the South-Sea Trade*: Profits, Propaganda, and the Peace Preliminaries of 1711," *Huntington Library Quarterly* 73, no. 2 (2010): 273–85.

32. *A True Account of the Design, and Advantages of the South-Sea Trade: With Answers to All the Objections Rais'd against It* (London: Morphew, 1711), 4–6.

33. *True Account*, 32–34.

34. *The True State of the Case between the Government and the Creditors of the Navy, &c, as It Relates to the South-Sea-Trade* (London: Baker, 1711), 12–14.

35. *An Essay on the South Sea Trade* (London: Baker, 1712), 30.

36. Maximillian E. Novak, *Daniel Defoe, Master of Fictions: His Life and Ideas* (Oxford: Oxford University Press, 2001), 401–3.

37. The shareholder is a "Usurer, who has a thousand Pounds a Year coming in by Bank, *East-India* and *South-Sea* Dividends." Daniel Defoe, *Fair Payment No Spunge; or, Some Considerations on the Unreasonableness of Refusing to Receive Back Money Lent on Publick Securities: And the Necessity of Setting the Nation Free from the Insupportable Burthen of Debt and Taxes* (London: Brotherton, Meddows & Roberts, 1717), 4–6, 17.

38. Defoe, *Fair Payment No Spunge*, 4–6, 174–76, 45–70.

39. Defoe, *The Review*, January 10, 1710.

40. Defoe, *De jure divino* (London: Hills, 1706), 12.8; Defoe, *The Review*, 14 June 1709.

41. Catherine Ingrassia, *Authorship, Commerce, and Gender in Early Eighteenth-Century England: A Culture of Paper Credit* (Cambridge: Cambridge University Press, 1998), 24–25; Laura Brown, *Fables of Modernity: Literature and Culture in the English Eighteenth Century* (Ithaca, NY: Cornell University Press, 2001), 108–31. See also John F. O'Brien, "Defoe's 'Lady Credit,' *The Fortunate Mistress*, and the Resources of Inconsistency in Early Eighteenth-Century Britain," *ELH* 63, no. 3 (Fall 1996): 603–31; and Natalie Roxburgh, *Representing Public Credit: Credible Commitment, Fiction, and the Rise of the Financial Subject* (Abingdon: Routledge, 2016), 60–73.

42. J. G. A. Pocock, *The Machiavellian Moment: Florentine Political Thought and the Atlantic Republican Tradition* (Princeton, NJ: Princeton University Press, 1975), 453.

43. Sandra Sherman, *Finance and Fictionality in the Early Eighteenth Century: Accounting for Defoe* (Cambridge: Cambridge University Press, 1996), 43. Defoe writes: "Poor Credit! Sunk and dejected, sighing and walking alone; I met her t'other Day in the Fields, I hardly knew her, she was so lean, so pale; look'd so sickly, so faint, and was so meanly dre's." Defoe, *The Review*, February 1, 1711. Elsewhere: "[I]n spight of all Mr. Defoe's Allegories of a Beautiful Coy Virgin Lady, called Credit, his Virgin prov'd a Whore, a meer Common Strumpet, will lie with any Body that has but Money to supply her insatiable Cravings; Nay, the worst sort of Whores, a mercernary Whore, for she forsakes her best Friends that have spent all their Estates upon her." Daniel Defoe, *Eleven Opinions of Mr. Harley, with Observations* (London: Baker, 1711), 41.

44. Sherman, *Finance and Fictionality*, 43.

45. Joseph Addison, *The Spectator*, March 3, 1711.

46. Sherman, *Finance and Fictionality*, 52–53; Brown, *Fables of Modernity*, 101.

47. Such as *The Considerable Advantages of a South-Sea Trade to Our English Nation: A Letter to a Member of Parliament on the Settling a Trade to the South-Sea of America* (1712), sometimes attributed to Defoe, or *A True Account of the Design, and Advantages of the South-Sea Trade* (1711). Concerning the attribution of *A Letter to a Member of Parliament* to Defoe, see Wennerlind, *Casualties of Credit*, 203.

48. *The Considerable Advantages of a South-Sea Trade*, 7; Robert Allen, *An Essay on the Nature and Methods of Carrying on a Trade to the South-Sea* (London: Mount, 1712), 23.

49. *The Considerable Advantages of a South-Sea Trade*, 4–9; *A Letter to a Member of Parliament*, 8.

50. Herman Moll, *A View of the Coasts, Countries and Islands within the Limits of the South-Sea Company* (London: Morphew, 1711), 211–12.

51. Wennerlind, *Casualties of Credit*, 205.

52. Addison, *The Spectator*, July 1, 1712.

53. In "the Polite Matters of Morality, Criticism, and other Speculations abstracted from Matter; who, though they do not directly treat of the visible parts of Nature, often draw from them their Similitudes, Metaphors, and Allegories": "By these Allusions a Truth in the Understanding is as it were reflected by the Imagination; we are able to see something like Colour and

Shape in a Notion, and to discover a Scheme of Thoughts traced out upon Matter." *The Spectator*, July 3, 1712.

54. Jean-Paul Sermain, *Le conte de fées: Du classicisme aux Lumières* (Paris: Desjonquères, 2005), 53–55.

55. Wennerlind, *Casualties of Credit*, 206.

56. Rochelle Ziskin, *Sheltering Art: Collecting and Social Identity in Early Eighteenth-Century Paris* (University Park: Penn State University Press, 2012), 105; Haudrère, *La Compagnie française*, 1:43; Antoine-Louis Lacordaire, *Notice historique sur les manufactures impériales de tapisserie des Gobelins* (Paris: de Roret, 1855), 35.

57. Philippe Haudrère, "L'origine du personnel de direction générale de la Compagnie française des Indes, 1719–1794," *Revue française d'histoire d'outre-mer* 67, no. 248 (1980): 339–71, 351, and *La Compagnie française*, 1:59, 73.

58. *Catalogue des livres de feue Madame la comtesse de Verrue, dont la vente se fera en détail en son hôtel, rue du Cherchemidy* (Paris: Martin, 1737); Françoise Bléchet, "Une 'dame de volupté' bibliophile: Les collections de la comtesse de Verrue (1670–1736)," *Cahiers Saint Simon* 35 (2007): 28–43.

59. Ziskin, *Sheltering Art*, 76. See Charles-Jean-François Hénault, *Mémoires du Président Hénault* (Genève: Slatkine, 1971), 29–30. See also Krzysztof Pomian, *Collectors and Curiosities: Paris and Venice, 1500–1800* (Oxford: Polity, 1990).

60. Irène Jamieson, *Charles-Antoine Coypel: Premier peintre de Louis XV et auteur dramatique (1694–1752)* (Paris: Hachette, 1930), 58; Ziskin, *Sheltering Art*, 6, 199, 102–4.

61. Étienne Deville, *Index du Mercure de France, 1672–1832* (Paris: Jean Schemit, 1910), 53; Roger Portalis and Henri Béraldi, *Les graveurs du dix-huitième siècle*, 3 vols. (Paris: Damascène, Morgand & Charles Fatout, 1881), 2:495–96.

62. Isabelle Tillerot, "Engraving Watteau in the Eighteenth Century: Order and Display in the Recueil Jullienne," *Getty Research Journal* 3 (2011): 33–52.

63. See Larry F. Norman, *The Shock of the Ancient: Literature and History in Early Modern France* (Chicago: University of Chicago Press, 2011); and Marc Fumaroli, *La querelle des Anciens et des Modernes* (Paris: Gallimard, 2001). See also Hippolyte Rigault, *Histoire de la querelle des Anciens et des Modernes* (Paris: Hachette, 1856); and Hubert Gillot, *La querelle des Anciens et des Modernes en France: De la défense et illustration de la langue française aux parallèles des Anciens et des Modernes* (Paris: Champion, 1914).

64. Larry F. Norman, "La querelle des Anciens et des Modernes, ou La métamorphose de la critique," *Littératures classiques* 86, no. 1 (Spring 2015): 95–114.

65. François Moureau, *Dufresny, auteur dramatique (1657–1724)* (Paris: Klincksieck, 1979), 97.

66. Paul Dupont, *Houdar de la Motte (1672–1731)* (Paris: Hachette, 1898), 22.

67. See Norman, *The Shock of the Ancient*.

68. Antoine Houdar de la Motte, *Fables nouvelles, dédiées au Roi, par M. de la Motte, de l'Académie française, avec un Discours sur la fable* (Paris: Dupuis, 1719), 29; Sabine Gruffat, "Modernité de la fable selon Houdar de la Motte: La hantise du modèle Lafontainien," in *Écrire et penser en Moderne (1687–1750)*, ed. Christelle Bahier-Porte and Claudine Poulouin (Paris: Honoré Champion, 2015), 337–53, 345; Dupont, *Houdar de la Motte*, 91.

69. François Moureau, *Le Mercure galant de Dufresny (1710–1714)* (Oxford: Voltaire Foundation, 1982), 47, 65. See also Norman, *The Shock of the Ancient*; and Elena Russo, *Styles of Enlightenment: Taste, Politics and Authorship in Eighteenth-Century France* (Baltimore: Johns Hopkins University Press, 2007).

70. Moureau, *Le Mercure galant*, 88–89.

71. Melon's first book would be taken from an "Arabian manuscript found in Meudon" (i.e., Verrue's mansion). Jean-François Melon, *Mahmoud le Gasnévide, histoire orientale, fragment traduit de l'Arabe, avec des notes* (Rotterdam: Hofhoudt, 1729), vi. "I have read, Madam, the ingenious *Apologie du luxe*; I find this little book as an excellent lesson of politics. . . . I have demonstrated in my political essay on commerce, how the taste of fine art and this use of the wealth, this soul of a great State that have been called *luxury*, are necessary to the circulation of the coins and the conservation of industry; I look at you, Madam, as one of the great examples of this truth. How many Parisian families live only thanks to the protection you give to the arts?" Jean-François Melon, "Lettre de M. de Melon, ci-devant secrétaire du régent du royaume, à Madame la comtesse de Verrue sur L'apologie du luxe," in *Oeuvres complètes de Voltaire*, 52 vols. (Paris: Garnier Frères, 1877–85), 10:89.

72. Jean Bouzinac, *Jean-François Melon, économiste* (Toulouse: Imprimerie ouvrière, 1906). Melon is mentioned in the will of the countess of Verrue. See Ziskin, *Sheltering Art*, 106. See also Emma C. Spary, *Eating the Enlightenment: Food and the Sciences in Paris, 1670–1760* (Chicago: University of Chicago Press, 2012), 129–31.

73. See Aït-Touati, *Contes de la lune*, 18, 72, 172.

74. Voltaire, "Épigramme sur l'abbé Terrasson," in *Oeuvres complètes de Voltaire*, 10:490.

75. See Sturdy, *Science and Social Status*, 221–38, 351–74.

76. Moureau, *Dufresny*, 102.

77. Ziskin, *Sheltering Art*, 105.

78. Jean Terrasson, *Dissertation critique sur l'Iliade d'Homère*, 2 vols. (Paris: Fournier & Coustelier, 1715), 1:lvj, and *Sethos, histoire ou vie tirée des monuments anecdotes de l'ancienne Egypte, traduit d'un manuscript grec*, 3 vols. (Paris: Guérin, 1731), 1:x; *Dictionnaire historique, littéraire et critique*, 6 vols. (Avignon, 1759), 4:435–36; Jean-Marie Quérard, *La France littéraire, ou Dictionnaire bibliographique*, 10 vols. (Paris: Firmin Didot, 1827–39), 9:376–77; Sturdy, *Science and Social Status*, 387–88.

79. Mikhail Bakhtin, *Problems of Dostoevsky's Poetics* (Minneapolis: University of Minnesota Press, 1984), 106–78.

80. Antonella Del Prete, preface to Jean Terrasson, *Traité de l'infini créé* (Paris: Honoré Champion, 2011), 9–128, 41.

81. Terasson, *Dissertation critique sur l'Iliade d'Homère*, lix, xlix, *La philosophie applicable à tous les objets de l'esprit* (Paris: Prault & fils, 1754), 14, 28, *Sethos*, vij–ix, and *La philosophie applicable*, 41–43, 81.

82. Norman, *The Shock of the Ancient*, 84, 202–3; Terrasson, *Sethos*, v, and *Traité de l'infini créé*, 158–59, 175–77.

83. Terrasson, *Dissertation critique sur l'Iliade d'Homère*, 232, *Sethos*, xxij, xlvlj, and *La philosophie applicable*, 70.

84. Jean Le Rond d'Alembert, "Réflexions de M. d'Alembert, de l'Académie des sciences, sur la personne et les ouvrages de M. l'abbé Terrasson," in Terrasson, *La philosophie applicable*, iii–xxvi, xij–xiij; Terrasson, *La philosophie applicable*, 132.

85. François Moureau, "Nouveau Mercure galant (1714–1716)," in *Dictionnaire des journaux*, no. 0921, n.d., https://dictionnaire-journaux.gazettes18e.fr/journal/0921-nouveau-mercure-galant; Alexandre Sokalski, "Hardouin Le Fèvre de Fontenay (1686?–après 1736?)," *Dictionnaire des journalistes*, no. 491, n.d., https://dictionnaire-journalistes.gazettes18e.fr/journaliste/491-hardouin-le-fevre-de-fontenay.

86. Françoise Bléchet, "L'abbé Bignon, bibliothécaire du roi, et les milieux savants en France au début du XVIIIe siècle," in *Buch und Sammler: Private und öffentliche Bibliotheken im 18. Jahrhundert* (Heidelberg: Carl Winter Universitatsverlag, 1979), 53–66, 55; Jack A. Clarke, "Jean-Paul Bignon 'Moderator of the Academies' and Royal Librarian," *French Historical Studies* 8, no. 2 (1973): 213–35, 227.

87. Moureau, *Dufresny*, 79; François Moureau, *La plume et le plomb: Espaces de l'imprimé et du manuscrit au siècle des Lumières* (Paris: Presses universitaires de Paris-Sorbonne, 2006), 359.

88. "Buchet and other *goujats* of the Modern party," such as Dufresny, were frequently together in the café La Fiège. See Louis de Boissy, *L'élève de Terpsicore* (Amsterdam, 1718), 24.

89. Moureau, *La plume et le plomb*, 467–68; François Moureau, *Répertoire des nouvelles à la main: Dictionnaire de la presse manuscrite clandestine, XVIe–XVIIIe siècle* (Oxford: Voltaire Foundation, 1999), 1723–24.

90. Pierre-François Buchet, *Abrégé de l'histoire du Czar Peter Alexiewitz, avec une relation de l'état présent de la Moscovie et de ce qui s'est passé de plus considérable depuis son arrivée en France jusqu'à ce jour: Dédié à Sa Majesté Czarienne* (Paris: Ribou & Dupuis, 1717). See also Michel Mervaud, "Pierre le Grand en France: Les récits de Voltaire," *Revue des études slaves* 83, nos. 2–3 (2012): 847–70; Marie-Anne Chabin, "La curiosité des savants français pour la Russie dans la première moitié du XVIIIe siècle," *Revue des études slaves* 57, no. 4 (1985): 565–76; Christophe Henry, "Le séjour de Pierre le Grand à Paris: Contribution à l'histoire de la formation du cabinet de Saint-Pétersbourg," *Publications du Groupe histoire architecture mentalités urbaine*, 2011, http://www.ghamu.org/IMG/pdf/Pierre1er-txt-def-20-04-2011.pdf.

91. Marc Escola, Érik Leborgne, and Jean-Christophe Abramovici, "Présentation," in Pierre Carlet de Marivaux, *Journaux 1* (Paris: GF-Flammarion, 2010), 7–40; Édouard Fournier, "Marivaux: Sa vie et ses oeuvres, d'après de nouveaux documents," in *Oeuvres de Marivaux: Théâtre complet* (Paris: Laplace, Sanchez, 1878), i–xli, v.

92. François Moureau, "Le Nouveau Mercure (1717–1721)," *Dictionnaire des journaux*, no. 0922, n.d., http://dictionnaire-journaux.gazettes18e.fr/journal/0922-le-nouveau-mercure.

93. *NM*, September 1719, 211, republished in Charles Rivière Dufresny, *Oeuvres de Monsieur Rivière Du Freny*, 6 vols. (Paris: Briasson, 1731), 6:239; "L'actionnaire bigame, avanture," *NM*, December 1719, 87–110; "Les dédits, ou Avanture nouvelle," in Dufresny, *Oeuvres de Monsieur Rivière Du Freny*, 6:20–32.

94. *NM*, December 1719, 110–16.

95. *Oeuvres de Monsieur Houdar de la Motte, l'un des quarante de l'Académie française*, 10 vols. (Paris: Prault, 1753), 1:519–35; "A Son Altesse Royale Monseigneur le duc d'Orléans, régent de France," in Pierre Bayle, *Dictionnaire historique et critique*, 4 vols. (Rotterdam: Michel Bohm, 1720), 1:29–30. See also Laborde, *Le Palais Mazarin*, 396. "The Abbé Buchet was one of the friends of M. de la Motte, & he invited him to write some of these Bouts-Rimés." *Lettres de Monsieur de La Motte, suivies d'un recueil de vers du mesme auteur, pour servir de supplement à ses oeuvres* (1754), 213; *NM*, January 1720, 68–71.

96. *NM*, September 1719, 208–9, October 1719, 206, November 1719, 116–17, and December 1719, 110–17.

97. *NM*, February 1718, 105–52, March 1719, 184–88, September 1718, 209, February 1719, 140, July 1719, 178, September 1719, 203, October 1719, 193, January 1720, 199, April 1720, 179, and June 1720, 174.

98. *NM*, October 1719, 199–205, and November 1719, 207–12.

99. *NM*, February 1720, 53–61, March 1720, 15–31, and May 1720, 28–69.

100. *NM*, April 1720, 88–116; Mathieu Marais, *Journal de Paris*, 2 vols. (Saint-Etienne: Publications de l'université de Saint-Etienne, 2004), 1:113.

101. He died in Saint-Domingue in 1736. See *Recherches pour servir à l'histoire de Lyon, ou Les lyonnois dignes de mémoire*, 2 vols. (Lyon: Duplain, 1757), 2:290–91; *Mercure de France dédié au roi*, April 1753, 185; Édouard de Barthélemy, *Les correspondants de la marquise de Balleroy, d'après les originaux inédits de la Bibliothèque Mazarine: Avec des notes et une introduction historique sur les maisons de Caumartin et de Balleroy*, 2 vols. (Paris: Hachette, 1883), 2:146, 163.

102. *NM*, August 1719, 180–98; [Jacques Pannier d'Orgeville], "Discours qui a remporté le prix en l'année 1719 par M. Pannier," in *Pièces d'éloquence qui ont remporté le Prix de l'Académie françoise, depuis 1671 jusqu'en 1748*, 2 vols. (Paris: Brunet, 1750), 2:265–87.

103. See Daniel Roche, "Les modèles économiques du mécénat," in *Les républicains des lettres: Gens de culture et de Lumières au XVIIIe siècle* (Paris: Fayard, 1988), 51–84; Christian Jouhaud and Hélène Merlin, "Mécènes, patrons et clients: Les médiations textuelles comme pratiques clientélaires au XVIIe siècle," *Terrain* 21 (1993): 47–62; Christian Jouhaud, *Les pouvoirs de la littérature: Histoire d'un paradoxe* (Paris: Gallimard, 2000); Antoine Lilti, *The World of the Salons: Sociability and Worldliness in Eighteenth-Century Paris* (2005; Oxford: Oxford University Press, 2015), and "Sociabilité mondaine et réseaux intellectuels: Les salons parisiens au XVIIIe siècle," in *Réseaux de l'esprit en Europe, des Lumières au XIXe siècle*, ed. Wladimir Berelowitch and Michel Porret (Genève: Droz, 2009), 89–104.

104. They all lived around the mansion of the Countess of Verrue in Paris in the rue du Cherche-Midi or in her house in Meudon. See Ziskin, *Sheltering Art*.

105. Lilti, *The World of the Salons*, 197.

106. [Marmont du Hautchamp], *Histoire du Système des finances*, 1:18.

107. François-Augustin Paradis de Moncrif, "Lettre de Monsieur de Moncrif de l'Académie françoise à Milady ***," in Terrasson, *La philosophie applicable*, xxvij–xl, xxxvij; d'Alembert, "Réflexions de M. d'Alembert," vi, xxi.

108. Jouhaud, *Les pouvoirs de la littérature*, 264–68, 336–37, 368.

Chapter Three

1. Stern, *The Company-State*, 9; Kwass, *Privilege and the Politics of Taxation*, and *Contraband*; Sonenscher, *Before the Deluge*; Cheney, *Revolutionary Commerce*.

2. Rafe Blaufarb, *The Great Demarcation: The French Revolution and the Invention of Modern Property* (Oxford: Oxford University Press, 2016), 29–30; Herbert H. Rowen, *The King's State: Proprietary Dynasticism in Early Modern France* (New Brunswick, NJ: Rutgers University Press, 1980), 80–89.

3. *Histoire des finances pendant la Régence*, in Law, *OC*, 3:282–430, 335.

4. *NM*, March 1720, 30; BnF, MS Fr. 13693, fol. 297.

5. AnF, K 884, no. 4; BnF, MS Fr. 13693, fols. 273–304. The first version and some excerpts of the second have been published. See Law, *OC*, 3:77–102.

6. BnF, MS Fr. 13693, fol. 280.

7. John Locke, *The Second Treatise of Civil Government* (New York: Prometheus, 1986), 9.123. "But since gold and silver, being little useful to the life of man in proportion to food, raiment, and carriage, has its value only from the consent of men, whereof labour yet makes, in great part, the measure, it is plain, that men have agreed to a disproportionate and unequal possession of the earth, they having, by a tacit and voluntary consent, found out, a way how a man may fairly

possess more land than he himself can use the product of, by receiving in exchange for the overplus gold and silver, which may be hoarded up without injury to any one." Ibid., 5.50.

8. See Dan Edelstein, *The Enlightenment: A Genealogy* (Chicago: University of Chicago Press, 2010), 35. See also Dan Edelstein, *The Terror of Natural Right: Republicanism, the Cult of Nature, and the French Revolution* (Chicago: University of Chicago Press, 2009); and Céline Spector, *Montesquieu: Pouvoirs, richesses et sociétés* (Paris: Presses universitaires de France, 2004), 153–55.

9. "The safety of the people, or the public welfare." Thomas Hobbes, *De cive* (Oxford: Clarendon, 1982), 13.2. "Sovereigns can do no more for the citizens' happiness than to enable them to enjoy the possessions their industry has won them, safe from foreign and civil war." Thomas Hobbes, *Leviathan* (Oxford: Clarendon, 2012), 13.6. If civilian peace is ensured, power is exercised in a minimalist way. See Franck Tinland, "La souveraineté et la modération des pouvoirs selon Th. Hobbes et J. J. Rousseau," *Revue européenne des sciences sociales* 20, no. 61 (1982): 209–37, 216. See also Roxburgh, *Representing Public Credit*, 23–25.

10. Milton L. Myers, *The Soul of Modern Economic Man: Ideas of Self-Interest, Thomas Hobbes to Adam Smith* (Chicago: University of Chicago Press, 1983), 28–34.

11. Hobbes, *De cive*, 12.7. Contrary to Hobbes, Locke considers private property to be an inalienable right. See, e.g., Raymond Polin, "Parallèle entre Thomas Hobbes et John Locke," *Revue européenne des sciences sociales* 20, no. 61 (1982): 177–90.

12. BnF, MS Fr. 13693, fol. 282.

13. Terrasson, *La philosophie applicable*, 65, 37–38; Jean-Baptiste-Claude Delisle de Sales, *De la philosophie de la nature*, 2 vols. (Amsterdam: Arkstée & Merkus, 1770), 1:49.

14. Terrasson, *La philosophie applicable*, 58–59; BnF, MS Fr. 13693, fol. 276; Terrasson, *La philosophie applicable*, 62.

15. *NM*, May 1720, 57; BnF, MS Fr. 13693, fols. 297–98.

16. *Histoire des finances pendant la Régence*, 353–54; Marie-France Renoux-Zagamé, *Origines théologiques du concept moderne de propriété* (Genève: Droz, 1987), 206–53; Giacomo Todeschini, *Les marchands et le temple: La société chrétienne et le cercle vertueux de la richesse du Moyen Âge à l'époque moderne* (2002; Paris: Albin Michel, 2017), 61–62.

17. *Gazette d'Amsterdam*, 30 January 1720.

18. BnF, MS Fr. 13693, fols. 281–82.

19. "Arrêt du Conseil d'état du roi, concernant les actions de la Compagnie des Indes: Du 3 juin 1720," BnF, MS Fr. 21779, fols. 311–12. See also Isabelle Brancourt, *Le régent, la robe et le commis greffier: Introduction à l'édition intégrale du Journal du parlement de Pontoise* (La Croix d'Épine: Association des amis de Guy Augé, 2012), 129–30.

20. *NM*, March 1720, 23–24.

21. *NM*, March 1720, 26.

22. *NM*, March 1720, 26–27.

23. *NM*, March 1720, 27; Jean-Jacques Hémardinquer, "Law, Liège et la reconstruction industrielle d'Arcis-sur-Aube en 1720," in *Acte du 95e congrès international des Sociétés savantes: Section d'histoire moderne et contemporaine*, 2 vols. (Paris: Bibliothèque nationale, 1974), 2:23–43, 41. See also "Extrait des lettres de mr de la riviere retiré a l'institut de l'oratoire de Paris au pere D. Bazile d'artois chartreux," Arsenal, MS 3724, vol. 2, fol. 33.

24. *NM*, April 1720, 96–97. See BnF, MS Fr. 13693, fol. 289.

25. Haudrère, *La Compagnie française*, 1:59–60.

26. See Faure, *La banqueroute de Law*, 191–92; and Shovlin, "Jealousy of Credit," 277–83.

27. Haudrère, *La Compagnie française*, 1:52–56. See also *NM*, September 1719, 202–3; and

Martine Acerra, *Rochefort et la construction navale française*, 4 vols. (Paris: Librairie de l'Inde, 1993), 1:210–17.

28. AnF, Col. B/42/1, "Correspondance du conseil de marine," fols. 105–6, 66–67, 74–76, 82, 125, 62, 75, 82, 94, 445, 417, 336, 394. See also Haudrère, "L'origine du personnel de direction générale," 354.

29. AnF, Col. B/42/1, "Correspondance du conseil de marine," fols. 85–86, 102.

30. AnF, Col. B/42/1, "Correspondance du conseil de marine," fols. 43–44, 57, 98, 74, 75, 88, 106, 101–2, 122–23.

31. Hémardinquer, "Law, Liège," 38–39. See also Harsin, "La création de la Compagnie d'Occident," 23.

32. John R. Harris, *Industrial Espionage and Technology Transfer* (Aldershot: Ashgate, 1998), 13–25; "Relation abrégée de l'établissement de la nouvelle fabrique d'Horlogerie à Versailles," *NM*, January 1719, 141–45; Henry Sully, *Description abrégée d'une horloge d'une nouvelle invention, pour la juste mesure du temps sur mer* (Paris: Briasson, 1726); *Mémoire signifié pour les entrepreneurs de la fonderie de Chaillot contre le sieur Law* (Paris: Mesnier, 1728); AnF, K 884, no. 36; Liliane Hilaire-Pérez, "Transferts technologiques, droit et territoire: Le cas franco-anglais au XVIIIe siècle," *Revue d'histoire moderne et contemporaine* 44, no. 4 (Fall 1997): 547–79, 550, 554.

33. Antoin Murphy, *Richard Cantillon: Entrepreneur and Economist* (Oxford: Clarendon, 1986), 93–95.

34. Noémie Wansart, "Le baron Jean-Baptiste Glucq de Saint-Port (1674–1748) et l'entourage de la comtesse de Verrue," unpublished paper (Paris: École du Louvre, 2005), 33; René Le Conte, "Les Allemands à la Louisiane au XVIIIe siècle," *Journal de la Société des Américanistes* 16 (1924): 1–17, 13; Harsin, "La création de la Compagnie d'Occident," 23.

35. Albert Lougnon, *L'île Bourbon pendant la Régence* (Nérac: Couderc, 1956), 133–38, 176–80, 198–99; Madeleine Ly-Tio-Fane, *Mauritius and the Spice Trade: The Odyssey of Pierre Poivre* (Port-Louis: Esclapon, 1958), 3.

36. *NM*, March 1720, 26, 18.

37. Haudrère, *La Compagnie française*, 1:52–59; Dawdy, *Building the Devil's Empire*, 118.

38. See David Celetti, "Le commerce au détail des fils de lin et de chanvre: Acteurs, espaces et réseaux dans la Vénétie et la Bretagne d'ancien régime," in *Retail Trade, Supply and Demand in the Formal and Informal Economy from the 13th to the 18th Centuries*, ed. Simonetta Cavaciocchi (Florence: Instituto Datini, 2015), 467–87. See also Jean-Louis Monguilan, "Une enquête sur la culture du chanvre en Provence à la fin du XVIIIe siècle," *Provence historique* 155 (1989): 35–53, 41.

39. *Arrêt du Conseil d'état qui ordonne que le commerce du chanvre dans l'intérieur du royaume sera libre: Du 27 décembre 1719* (Paris: Imprimerie royale, 1720), 2. The author of the *Histoire des finances* pointed out that this project for hemp was "une affaire capitale" and that the company "would have manufactured the hemp." *Histoire des finances pendant la Régence*, 361.

40. AnF, Col. B/42/1, "Correspondance du conseil de marine," fols. 66–67, 124–25.

41. Law, *OC*, 3:166.

42. *Mémoire sur le denier royal*, in Law, *OC*, 3:38–61, 49.

43. "[T]he establishment of public warehouses will prevent the high prices of foodstuffs even during the years that will not be good." *NM*, May 1720, 67.

44. Steven L. Kaplan, *Bread, Politics and Political Economy in the Reign of Louis XV*, 2 vols. (La Haye: Martinus Nijhoff, 1976), 1:88.

45. Steven L. Kaplan, *Raisonner sur les blés: Essais sur les Lumières économiques* (Paris: Fayard, 2017), 50–51.

46. See Jean-Marie Apostolidès, *Le roi-machine: Spectacle et politique au temps de Louis XIV* (Paris: Minuit, 1981), 156–57.

47. *NM*, April 1720, 94, 98; AnF, M 1027, "Projet de deliberation," fol. 1.

48. *NM*, April 1720, 95.

49. De Vries, "Connecting Europe and Asia," 83.

50. "Arrest du Conseil d'état, qui accorde & réünit à perpétuité à la Compagnie des Indes le privilege exclusif pour le commerce de la Côte de Guinée: 27 septembre 1720," in Jospeh Dufresne de Francheville, *Histoire générale et particulière des finances où l'on voit l'origine, l'établissement, la perception & la régie de toutes les impositions* (Paris: Debure, 1738), 516–19. See also Albert Girard, "La réorganisation de la Compagnie des Indes (1719–1723)," *Revue d'histoire moderne et contemporaine* 11, no. 1 (1908–9): 5–34, 24.

51. AnF, M 1027, "Projet de deliberation," fol. 1; David Eltis, *The Rise of African Slavery in the Americas* (Cambridge: Cambridge University Press, 2000), 182–83, 120–22; Olivier Grenouilleau, *Les traites négrières: Essai d'histoire globale* (Paris: Gallimard, 2004), 148, 210–11.

52. Ira O. Wade, "The Abbe de Saint-Pierre and Dubois," *Journal of Modern History* 2, no. 3 (1930): 430–47, 438.

53. John Shovlin, "Commerce, Not Conquest: Political Economic Thought in the French Indies Company, 1719–1769," in *New Perspectives on the History of Political Economy*, ed. Robert Fredona and Sophus A. Reinert (London: Palgrave Macmillan, 2018), 171–202, 188–89.

54. See Jean Wirth, "La fin des mentalités," *Les dossiers du Grihl: Questions de méthodologie*, no. 4 (2022), http://dossiersgrihl.revues.org/284.

55. Shovlin, "Jealousy of Credit," 284–85.

56. Smith, "Structuring Politics in Early Eighteenth-Century France," 497–98.

57. Haudrère, *La Compagnie française*, 1:59.

58. *NM*, April 1720, 100.

59. Jacques Savary and Philémon-Louis Savary, *Dictionnaire universel de commerce*, 2 vols. (Paris: Estienne, 1723), 2:1223; *Dictionnaire de l'Académie française*, 2:24; Takeda, *Between Crown and Commerce*, 59.

60. Béguin, *Financer la guerre au XVIIe siècle*, 353; Grenier, *L'économie d'ancien régime*, 103; Katia Béguin, "Du présent au passé: Les dynamiques historiques de la richesse à l'époque moderne," *Annales: Histoire, sciences sociales* 70, no. 1 (Spring 2015): 91–102.

61. *NM*, April 1720, 113, 91.

62. *NM*, April 1720, 98–99.

63. *NM*, May 1720, 42.

64. Edgar Faure wrote: "It is staggering for us to see a company decide in advance the dividend of a financial year that has not yet begun." Faure, *La banqueroute de Law*, 303.

65. As specified by Pannier d'Orgeville: "[T]he Shares have the convenience of rentes, & the benefits of industry." *NM*, April 1720, 114. Talking about the shareholders, Pannier specifies: "[T]heir safety will be better based, because it is attached to the greatness & the wealth of the King." *NM*, April 1720, 115.

66. *NM*, March 1720, 18.

67. Jacques-Bénigne Bossuet, *Politique tirée des propres paroles de l'Écriture sainte* (Paris: Cot, 1709), 1.3.5; Keith Michael Baker, "Representation," in *The French Revolution and the Creation of Modern Political Culture*, vol. 1, *The Political Culture of the Old Regime*, ed. Keith Michael Baker (Oxford: Pergamon, 1987), 469–92; Jean-Yves Guiomar, *La nation entre l'histoire et la raison* (Paris: La découverte, 1990), 32, 64–65; Sonenscher, "The Nation's Debt . . . Part I,"

67; David Bell, *The Cult of the Nation in France: Inventing Nationalism, 1680–1800* (Cambridge, MA: Harvard University Press, 2001), 57–61; "Corps," in *Dictionnaire de l'Académie française*, 1:251; William H. Sewell, "État, Corps and Ordre: Some Notes on the Social Vocabulary of the French Old Regime," in *Sozialgeschichte heute*, ed. Hans-Ulrich Wehler (Göttingen: Vandenhoeck, 1974), 49–68, 55–56.

68. *NM*, May 1719, 195–96.

69. *Edit du roi, concernant la ferme générale du tabac, donné à Paris au mois de Septembre 1718 et arrest du Conseil d'état du roi du 4 Septembre 1718*, in Augustin Chambon, *Traité général du commerce de l'Amérique*, 2 vols. (Amsterdam: Rey, 1783), 1:487–90; Haudrère, *La Compagnie française*, 1:45.

70. "[T]hrough the grace of God, by the August protection that the Great Prince, who heads France, generates so liberaly to Sciences & Scholars." *Discours de Mr. Coffin, recteur de l'Université au roy, et a Monseigneur le duc d'Orléans, en leur présentant le cierge le 1. Fev. 1719 et sur l'etablissement de l'instruction gratuite dans l'Université de Paris* (Paris: Thiboust, 1719).

71. Darius A. Spieth, "The French Context of *Het groote tafereel der dwaasheid*: John Law, Rococo Culture, and the Riches of the New World," in Goetzmann, Labio, Rouwenhorst, and Young, eds., *The Great Mirror of Folly*, 219–233, 222.

72. See Valentine Toutain-Quittelier, *Le carnaval, la fortune et la folie: La rencontre de Paris et Venise à l'aube des Lumières* (Rennes: Presses universitaires de Rennes, 2017), 164–80.

73. Valentine Toutain-Quittelier, "John Law et le décor de la Banque royale: Un ensemble ornemental unique?," in Magnot-Ogilvy, ed., *Gagnons sans savoir comment*, 41–57, and *Le carnaval, la fortune et la folie*, 193–221.

74. Louis de Sacy, *Traité de la gloire* (Paris: Huet, 1715); Thomas Kaiser, "Louis le Bien-Aimé and the Rhetoric of the Royal Body," in *From the Royal to the Republican Body: Incorporating the Political in Seventeenth- and Eighteenth-Century France*, ed. Sara E. Melzer and Kathryn Norberg (Berkeley and Los Angeles: University of California Press, 1998), 131–62, 136.

75. Jean Le Rond d'Alembert, "Éloge de Monsieur de Sacy," in *Oeuvres de d'Alembert*, 5 vols. (Paris: Belin, 1821–22), 3:61–82; Sacy, *Traité de la gloire*, 17–18.

76. See Frédéric Lefebvre, "L'honnêteté du négociant: Une querelle sociologique française au milieu du XVIIIe siècle," in Charles, Lefebvre, and Théré, ed., *Le cercle de Vincent de Gournay*, 201–38, 218–19; and Marie-France Piguet, "Noblesse 'commerçante'/nation 'commerçante': Genèse d'un adjective," in ibid., 161–78, 166.

77. Sacy, *Traité de la gloire*, 99–105.

78. Takeda, *Between Crown and Commerce*, 4.

79. BnF, MS Fr. 13693, fols. 300–301.

80. BnF, MS Fr. 13693, fol. 302.

81. *NM*, May 1720, 68; Jean Terrasson, *Mémoire pour servir à justifier la Compagnie des Indes contre la censure des casuistes qui la condamnent* (1720), 34.

82. See Christopher Storrs, ed., *The Fiscal-Military State in Eighteenth-Century Europe* (Burlington: Ashgate, 2009); and R. Bonney, ed., *Economic Systems and State Finance* (Oxford: Clarendon, 1995).

83. Defoe, *Fair Payment No Spunge*, 4–5, 9, 14.

84. Clare Haru Crowston, *Credit, Fashion, Sex: Economies of Regard in Old Regime France* (Durham, NC: Duke University Press, 2013); Antoine Lilti, "Le pouvoir du crédit au XVIIIe siècle: Histoire intellectuelle et sciences sociales," *Annales: Histoire, sciences sociales* 70, no. 4 (Fall 2015): 957–77, 959.

85. Lilti, "Le pouvoir du crédit au XVIIIe siècle," 971–75.

86. *Projet d'une nouvelle forme d'asseoir les revenus du roy* (April 1718), in Law, *OC*, 3:30–37, 30.

87. *Mémoire sur le denier royal*, 56.

88. *Dictionnaire de l'Académie française*, 2:894; *Mémoire sur le denier royal*, 58.

89. Jean-Pierre Labatut, *Les noblesses européennes de la fin du XVe siècle à la fin du XVIIIe siècle* (Paris: Presses universitaires de France, 1978).

90. Law, *OC*, 3:75.

91. Defoe, *Fair Payment No Spunge*, 75; *NM*, May 1720, 64, and February 1720, 54.

92. *NM*, March 1720, 63–64. Concerning the reality of the abolition of taxes, see Haudrère, *La Compagnie française*, 1:50–52.

93. Defoe, *Fair Payment No Spunge*, 20.

94. *Mémoire sur le denier royal*, 53.

95. *NM*, February 1720, 55–56.

96. BnF, MS Fr. 13693, fol. 299.

97. *NM*, May 1720, 39–40; Law, *OC*, 3:14, 28.

98. *NM*, May 1720, 44, 53.

99. See Buvat, *Journal de la Régence*, 2:63.

100. Law, *OC*, 3:24.

101. Rey, *Le temps du crédit*, 18–19, 135, 218; Kaiser, "Money, Despotism, and Public Opinion."

102. Lilti, "Le pouvoir du crédit au XVIIIe siècle," 976; Michelet, *Histoire de France*, 15:116.

103. Jean Wirth, "La naissance du concept de croyance (XIIe–XVIIe siècles)," *Bibliothèque d'humanisme et Renaissance* 45, no. 1 (Spring 1983): 7–58, 51–56.

104. See Giacomo Todeschini, "*Date otiosam pecuniam et recipietis fructuosam gratiam* (Ambrogio, *De Tobia*, 16, 56)," in *Credito e usura fra teologia, diritto e amministrazione: Linguaggi a confronto (sec. XII–XVI)*, ed. Diego Quaglioni, Giacomo Todeschini, and Gian Maria Varanini (Rome: École française de Rome, 2005), 57–71; Paolo Prodi, "Conclusioni," in ibid., 290–96; and Wirth, "La naissance du concept de croyance (XIIe–XVIIe siècles)," 16–18.

105. Émile Bouvier, "La croyance au merveilleux à l'époque classique," in *Mélanges d'histoire littéraire, offerts à Daniel Mornet par ses anciens collègues et ses disciples français* (Paris: Nizet, 1951), 99–108; Ehrard, *L'idée de nature en France*, 29–31; Tzvetan Todorov, *Introduction à la littérature fantastique* (Paris: Seuil, 1970).

106. Concerning Galland, see Edward Said, *Orientalism* (New York: Vintage, 1979), 63–65; and Aravamudan, *Enlightenment Orientalism*.

107. Anne Defrance, "La politique du conte aux XVIIe et XVIIIe siècles: Pour une lecture oblique," *Féeries* 3 (2006): 13–41, 14; Todorov, *Introduction à la littérature fantastique*, 166.

108. Michael Sonenscher, "The Nation's Debt and the Birth of the Modern Republic: The French Fiscal Deficit and the Politics of the Revolution of 1789; Part II," *History of Political Thought* 18, no. 2 (July 1997): 267–325.

Chapter Four

1. *NM*, January 1717, n.p. (preface); Bernard Le Bovier de Fontenelle, *Oeuvres*, 10 vols. (Paris: Veuve Brunet, 1761), 10:76.

2. "[T]his facility to believe everything & this disturbed love of the marvelous that one can see in most men, is even more important in the People, it is its first character trait." *NM*, June 1718, 85.

3. *NM*, March 1720, 21, and May 1720, 46; Simon Schaffer, "Augustan Realities: Nature's Representatives and Their Cultural Resources in the Early Eighteenth Century," in *Realism and Representation: Essays on the Problem of Realism in Relation to Science, Literature and Culture*, ed. George Levine (Madison: University of Wisconsin Press, 1993), 306–7.

4. Bobé to Delisle, May 27, 1718, and July 9, 1718, in Dawson, *L'Atelier Delisle*, 239–41.

5. Steven Shapin, *A Social History of Truth: Civility and Science in Seventeenth-Century England* (Chicago: Chicago University Press, 1994).

6. "Nouvelle relation de la Louisiane," *NM*, September 1717, 128–43; "Lettre touchant la Louisiane, autrement le Mississipi," *NM*, February 1718, 105–50; "À la Nouvelle Orléans, province de la Louisiane sur le Mississipi, le 5 Novembre 1718," *NM*, March 1719, 184–89; "Dissertation particulière sur la Louisiane ou le Mississipi," in Henri Abraham Chatelain and Nicolas Gueudeville, *Atlas historique, ou Nouvelle introduction à l'histoire, à la chronologie & à la géographie ancienne & moderne* (Amsterdam, 1719), 91–94.

7. Chatelain and Gueudeville, *Atlas historique*, ii.

8. "Relation de la Louisiane et du fleuve Mississipi, où l'on voit l'état de ce grand pays & les avantages qu'il peut produire," in *Recueil des voyages au nord*, 8 vols. (Amsterdam: Bernard, 1715–27), 5:35–196; *Ausführliche, Historische und Geographische Beschreibung des an dem grossem Flusse Mississipi in Nordamerika gelegen herrlichen Landes Louisiana, in welches die neu aufgerchtete französische grosse Indianische Compagnie Colonien zu schicken angefangen* (Leipzig, 1720). For Weigel's map, see https://digital.library.cornell.edu/catalog/ss:3293722: "Totus hic tractus est plenus Metallorum" and "Regio Metallorum."

9. *Description du Mississipi par M. le chevalier de Bonrepos, ecrite de Mississipi en France à Mademoiselle D**** (Rouen: Guérin, 1720); "Découverte du Mississipi, autrement appellée la Louisiane," in *A Full and Impartial Account of the Company of Mississipi, Otherwise Call'd the French East-India-Company, Projected and Settled by Mr. Law, in French and English* (London: Francklin, 1720), 42–79.

10. "Mémoire sur la Compagnie du Mississipi et les établissements qu'elle se propose de fonder en Louisiane" (1717), AnOM, MS C13A15, fol. 13.

11. "Mémoire sur la Compagnie du Mississipi," fol. 13; *Description du Mississipi par M. le chevalier de Bonrepos*, 8; *NM*, September 1718, 131–34, September 1717, 131–40, May 1718, 106, September 1718, 214, and March 1719, 186.

12. *NM*, September 1717, 142, and March 1719, 185; *Description du Mississipi par M. le chevalier de Bonrepos*, 15; "Mémoire sur la Compagnie du Mississipi," fol. 13; *NM*, March 1719, 186, February 1718, 126–27, 148, and March 1719, 187. "As soon as we landed, the girls we had were quickly & well married," *NM*, March 1719, 186.

13. "Mémoire sur la Compagnie du Mississipi," fol. 13; *NM*, March 1719, 184, September 1717, 130–35; "Mémoire sur la Compagnie du Mississipi," fol. 13; *NM*, September 1717, 132.

14. *NM*, February 1718, 146, September 1719, 203, January 1720, 199, June 1720, 183, July 1719, 178, February 1718, 146, and April 1720, 179. For the claim that, in Louisiana, "we walk on *Silver Mines*," see *La suite de la clef, ou Journal historique*, April 1720, 289.

15. J. Hanno Deiler, *The Settlement of the German Coast of Louisiana and the Creoles of German Descent* (Philadelphia: Americana Germanica, 1909), 10–11.

16. Paul Mapp, "French Geographic Conceptions," 140.

17. André Lequeux, "L'industrie du fer dans le Hainaut français au XVIIIe siècle," *Revue du nord* 73, no. 19 (1933): 5–28; Paul Fénelon, "Les mines françaises de plomb et de zinc," *Revue géographique des Pyrénées et du Sud-Ouest* 26, no. 4 (1955): 272–91; Bruno Ancel, "Techniques

minières et maîtrise de l'espace dans les mines d'argent médiévales: Exemples des mines de plomb argentifère des Alpes du Sud (Xe–XIVe siècles)," in *L'innovation technique au Moyen Âge*, ed. P. Beck (Caen, Paris: Errance, 1998), 108–10; Demeulenaere-Douyère and Sturdy, *L'enquête du régent*; Vincent Rich, *The International Lead Trade* (Cambridge: Woodhead, 1994); *Combined History of Randolph, Monroe and Perry Counties, Illinois: With Illustrations, Descriptive of Their Scenery and Biographical Sketches of Some of Their Prominent Men and Pioneers* (Philadelphia: McDonough, 1883), 28, 382–84; *Revue de métallurgie* 5 (1908): 353–54; Gerald L. Gold, "Lead Mining and the Survival and Demise of French in Rural Missouri," *Cahiers de géographie du Québec* 23, no. 59 (1979): 331–42; Carl Tolman, *Biennial Report of the State Geologist* (Rolla, MO: Bureau of Geology and Mines, 1933); R. D. Hagni, "Ore Microscopy of the Silver Minerals in the Epigenetic Ag-W-Sn Deposits in the Silver Mine District, Southeastern Missouri, U.S.A.," in *Syngenesis and Epigenesis in the Formation of Mineral Deposits* (Berlin: Springer, 1984), 52–61; Cheryl M. Seeger, "History of Mining in the Southeast Missouri Lead District and Description on Mine Processes, Regulatory Controls, Environmental Effects, and Mine Facilities in the Viburnum Trend Subdistrict," in *Hydrologic Investigations concerning Lead Mining Issues in Southeastern Missouri*, ed. M. Kleeschulte, US Geological Survey Investigations Report 2008-5104 (2008), https://pubs.usgs.gov/sir/2008/5140. See also Antoine-Simon Le Page du Pratz, *Histoire de la Louisiane*, 3 vols. (Paris: Bure, Delaguette, Lambert, 1758), 1:166–76, 225–42, 255–64, 281–332.

18. Deiler, *The Settlement of the German Coast of Louisiana*, 11–13; Vidal, "French Louisiana in the Age of the Companies," 151–52; Le Conte, "Les Allemands à la Louisiane au XVIIIe siècle."

19. Benjamin Schmidt, *Inventing Exoticism: Geography, Globalism, and Europe's Early Modern World* (Philadelphia: University of Pennsylvania Press, 2015), 168; Dawdy, *Building the Devil's Empire*, 165–70, 192–210.

20. Things changed a few years later. See Havard and Vidal, *Histoire de l'Amérique française*, 129–35; Cécile Vidal, "Le pays des Illinois, six villages français au coeur de l'Amérique du Nord, 1699–1765," in *De Québec à l'Amérique française: Histoire et mémoire*, ed. Thomas Wien, Cécile Vidal, and Yves Frénette (Québec: Presses de l'Université Laval, 2006), 125–38.

21. See Cécile Vidal, "De l'incorporation à l'exclusion: Les relations entre Amérindiens, Européens et Anglo-Américains dans la vallée du Mississippi de 1699 à 1830," *Tocqueville Review/Revue Tocqueville* 25, no. 2 (2004): 35–54, "Francité et situation coloniale: Nation, empire et race en Louisiane française (1699–1769)," *Annales: Histoire, sciences sociales* 63, no. 5 (2009): 1019–50, and "Public Slavery, Racial Formation, and the Struggle over Honor in French New Orleans, 1718–1769," *Anuario colombiano de historia social y de la cultura* 43, no. 2 (2016): 155–83.

22. Law, *OC*, 3:25, 95; *NM*, January 1720, 119.

23. Daniel Jütte, *The Age of Secrecy: Jews, Christians, and the Economy of Secrets, 1400–1800* (2012; New Haven, CT: Yale University Press, 2015), 19–20; Jean-François Senault, *Le monarque, ou Les devoirs du souverain* (Paris: Le Petit, 1661), 405–6; Dominique Bouhours, *Les entretiens d'Ariste et d'Eugène* (Paris: Mabre-Cramoisy, 1671), 165–67; Bossuet, *Politique tirée des propres paroles de l'Écriture sainte*, 5.2.4.

24. Arnaud Lévy, "Évaluation étymologique et sémantique du mot 'secret,'" *Nouvelle revue de psychanalyse* 14 (1976): 117–29; Werner Krauss, ed., *Est-il utile de tromper le peuple? Concours de la classe de philosophie spéculative de l'Académie des sciences et des belles-lettres de Berlin pour l'année 1780* (Berlin: Academie-Verlag, 1966).

25. Bernard Le Bovier de Fontenelle, "Dialogues des morts Anciens avec les Modernes: Dialogue II: Artémise, Raymond Lulle," in *Oeuvres de Fontenelle*, 3 vols. (Paris: Belin, 1818), 2:232–33; Terrasson, *La philosophie applicable*, 68, and *Sethos*, xxiij; Jütte, *The Age of Secrecy*, 21–22.

26. “Mais quoi, la Paix sans l’Abondance / N’est qu’un des fruits de ta vertu; / Il faut encor que ta prudence / Ranime l’Etat abatu. . . . / Attendrons-nous qu’un nouveau Lulle*, / Fiers de ses chimiques travaux, / Promette à nôtre espoir crédule / L’art de commander aux métaux: / Qu’il nous vante dans son délire / Ce sable souverain qu’il tire / D’un feu sçavament mésuré; / Qu’il ordonne à sa vaine poudre / De tout changer, de tout dissoudre, / Et d’enfanter l’or à son gré? / Non, le Ciel nous offre un Genie / De qui les talens bienfaiteurs / Vons réaliser la manie / De ces prétendus Créateurs. / Plus hardi que nôtre espérance, / Dans le sein même de la France / Il ouvre un nouveau un nouveau Potosi / Son sistême plus efficace / Semble par sa sublime audace, / Plutôt révélé que choisi. / *Celebre Chimiste qui passe pour avoir trouvé la pierre Philosophale.” *NM*, December 1719, 163–64.

27. Jütte, *The Age of Secrecy*, 11.

28. Fontenelle, “Dialogues des morts Anciens avec les Modernes,” 231.

29. See Terrasson, *NM*, May 1718, 195; Lawrence M. Principe, “Alchemy Restored,” *Isis* 102, no. 2 (June 2011): 305–12, and “A Revolution Nobody Noticed? Changes in Early Eighteenth-Century Chymistry,” in *New Narratives in Eighteenth-Century Chemistry*, ed. Lawrence M. Principe (Dordrecht: Springer, 2007), 1–22; Christine Lehman, “Alchemy Revisited by the Mid-Eighteenth Century Chemists in France: An Unpublished Manuscript by Pierre-Joseph Macquer,” *Nuncius* 28 (2013): 165–216; Bernard Joly, “À propos d’une prétendue distinction entre la chimie et l’alchimie au XVIIe siècle: Questions d’histoire et de méthode,” *Revue d’histoire des sciences* 60, no. 1 (Spring 2007): 167–83; and Ehrard, *L’idée de nature en France*, 38.

30. *Mercure galant*, January 1711, 5–20.

31. Terrasson was very pleased to give an account of a memoir read by Reaumur at the Académie des sciences of Paris dedicated to tests on precious metals from the French rivers as part of the *Enquête du régent*. See *NM*, May 1718, 194–96.

32. “Sans charbon, fourneau ni sousflet / Un homme a trouve le Secret / De la Pierre philosophale / Dans une terre Occidentale / Il fait voir que jusqu’à present / Nous n’étions que des ignorants.” BnF, MS Fr. 13655, fol. 211.

33. Jütte, *The Age of Secrecy*, 104.

34. Wennerlind, *Casualties of Credit*, 54, 79; Murphy, *John Law*, 77–78; Wennerlind, *Casualties of Credit*, 71.

35. See Wennerlind, *Casualties of Credit*, 231; Murphy, *John Law*, 78.

36. “Avec cinq petits pains & trois petits poissons / Dieu nourrit autrefois une troupe innombrable: / Law par son genie admirable / Substante ainsi ses heureux nourrissons; / Les petits cinq cent francs, prodige inconcevable! / Multipliés en cent façons / Ont assouvi la faim la plus insatiable.” *NM*, December 1719, 166–69.

37. “Minerve est en ces lieux et Law est ce Mentor, . . . / Les grands et les petits ressentent ses hauts faits, / C’est pour tous les Français un ange tutélaire, / L’univers retentit du bruit de ses bienfaits.” Raunié, *Chansonnier historique du XVIIIe siècle*, 3:159.

38. *Dictionnaire de l’Académie française*, 1:39.

39. “. . . Nouveau papier de l’Occident, / Enfant d’un sage ministere, / Venés au jour, on vous attend / Comme nôtre Ange tutelaire. . . .” *NM*, December 1719, 110.

40. *Dictionnaire de l’Académie française*, 1:39.

41. The analogy was transparent in the first poem. Law had triumphed “[over] the Dragon” as Saint Michael. See *NM*, December 1719, 166–69. See also *NM*, May 1767, 67.

42. Terrasson, *Traité de l’infini créé*, 176–80; Del Prete, “Préface,” 11.

43. Law, *OC*, 3:131.

44. The echoes of Mandeville's "private vices, publick benefits" began in France only in the 1720s. See Elena Muceni, "Mandeville and France: The Reception of the *Fable of the Bees* in France and Its Influence on the French Enlightenment," *French Studies* 69, no. 4 (Fall 2015): 449–61; Michael Kwass, "Spending and Saving in the Enlightenment," *Historical Reflections/Réflexions historiques* 31, no. 1 (2005): 49–70, 69.

45. [D'Orgeville], "Discours qui a remporté le prix en l'année 1719," 70–78.

46. *NM*, December 1718, 165.

47. Joseph La Serviére, *Un professeur d'ancien régime: Le père Charles Porée, S.J., 1676–1741* (Paris: Houdin, 1899), 375.

48. *NM*, April 1720, 102–3.

49. *Histoire des finances pendant la Régence*, 414–15. Dealing with this passage, which they attribute to Law, Jonathan Sheehan and Dror Wahrman interpreted credit and money as "self-organizing powers." See Sheehan and Wahrman, *Invisible Hands*, 120. This idea is highly debatable because, in the ideology of the System, wealth creation must first be organized by the public authorities, after which the logic of expenditure would be able to create growth. Without dealing with the organization of the System itself, and unfortunately attributing the *Histoire des finances* to Law, Thomas M. Kavanagh touched on what was at stake by asserting: "[I]t is only as money moves from hand to hand that it exercises its most important power of increasing the value of everything it touches." Thomas M. Kavanagh, *Enlightenment and the Shadow of Chance: The Novel and the Culture of Gambling in Eighteenth-Century France* (Baltimore: Johns Hopkins University Press, 1993), 87.

50. Law, *OC*, 3:64; [Jean Pottier de la Hestroye], "Restablissement du commerce" (1698–99), AnF, Fonds Mirabeau, MS 785, fols. 53–54.

51. See, e.g., Philippe Steiner, "Circuit, monnaie et balance du commerce," in *Nouvelle histoire de la pensée économique*, ed. Alain Béraud and Gilbert Faccarello, 2 vols. (Paris: La découverte, 1992–99), 1:111–21.

52. *NM*, February 1720, 59–61, May 1720, 32, and April 1720, 103.

53. "L'amour disoit à la Fortune un jour, / Nous avons chacun notre Cour: / On n'a point à la fois mes faveurs & les vôtres, / Les biens manquent aux uns, & l'art de plaire aux autre. / Accordons-nous aujourd'huy tous les deux: / Donnons-nous le plaisir de rendre un homme heureux, / Choisissons un mortel de gentelle apparence. . . . / J'ay peu de pareil favoris, / Dit alors avec un souris / La Deïté de la Banque Royale: / Je vais a pleins tonneaux chez luy verser de l'or, / Qu'au gré de ses désirs il puise en mon tresor: / Que sans craindre mon inconstance / Il se livre au penchant de son coeur genereux, . . . / Aussi tôt dit, aussi-tôt fait: / Sa générosité ne peut être bornée: / Le soir, il n'est point satisfait, / S'il ne s'est pas dans la journée / Signalé par quelque bienfait." *NM*, January 1720, 69–71.

54. *La suite de la clef, ou Journal historique*, April 1720, 292–93, 295–96.

55. See *Histoire de Fortunatus*, in *La bibliothèque bleue entièrement refondue & considérablement augmentee*, 3 vols. (Liège: Desoer, 1787), vol. 2; Robert Mandrou, *De la culture populaire aux 17e et 18e siècles* (Paris: Stock, 1964); and Catherine Velay-Vallantin, "La bourse de Fortunatus," *Communications* 39 (1984): 141–67.

56. Marc-Antoine Legrand, *Plutus, comédie, représentée en 1720*, in *Théâtre de Monsieur Le Grand*, 4 vols. (Paris: Ribou, 1731), 2:229–91, 241, 253–54, 263, 277–78, 284, 291.

57. *NM*, December 1719, 87–110.

58. "Prouvez, amans, par des effets, / Le doux pouvoir de nos atraits, . . . / Faites-nous de plus doux billets, / Non des écrits frivoles. / Suprimez votre passion, / Je veux de la soumission, / Et

non de la confiance, / Pour peindre votre affection / Avec plus d'éloquence; / Amans, parlez-nous d'Actions; / Ou gardez le silence." *NM*, December 1719, 117.

59. *NM*, December 1719, 117, May 1719, 60, and November 1719, 116–17.

60. Pocock, *The Machiavellian Moment*, 31–48.

61. Legrand, *Plutus*, 255.

62. *NM*, April 1720, 110–11. Earl J. Hamilton has shown that both prices and wages increased dramatically in 1719–20: "After falling in 1711–12, real wages made a brisk recovery in 1715. In 1716–1719 the trend was horizontal, but the upward surge of prices in January, 1720, deprived money wages of 18.6 per cent of their purchasing power. Unless greater regularity of employment and the opportunity to work overtime at the peak of the Bubble more than counteracted the adverse ratio of money wages to the cost of living, real incomes were much lower in 1720 than during the preceding quinquennium. During the crisis, in 1721, real wages advanced sharply, and the gain was maintained in the following year. But 1723–25 witnessed a marked retrogression." Earl J. Hamilton, "Prices and Wages at Paris under John Law's System," *Quarterly Journal of Economics* 51, no. 1 (1936): 42–70. Hamilton has shown that the argument for demand-pull inflation is not entirely inaccurate and that real wages were better in 1719–20 than at the end of Louis XIV's reign.

63. *NM*, April 1720, 33. The promise of the System to overturn the hierarchical organization of the realm was kept. As the anonymous author of the *Histoire des finances* wrote: "[A]nyone could participate without favor." *Histoire des finances pendant la Régence*, 313.

64. Terrasson, *Mémoire pour servir à justifier la Compagnie des Indes*, 41.

65. Élisabeth Belmas, *Jouer autrefois: Essai sur le jeu dans la France moderne (XVIe–XVIIIe siècles)* (Seyssel: Champ Vallon, 2006); Sheehan and Wahrman, *Invisible Hands*, 72.

66. Taveneaux, *Jansénisme et prêt à intérêt*, 211.

67. Le Semelier, *Conférences ecclésiastiques de Paris*, 4:98.

68. Claude-François Menestrier, *Dissertation des lotteries par le P.C.F.M. de la Compagnie de Jesus* (Lyon: Bachelu, 1700), 11–12; Jean Barbeyrac, *Traité du jeu, où l'on examine les principales questions de droit naturel et de morale qui ont du rapport à cette matière*, 2 vols. (Amsterdam: Humbert, 1709), 1:129–32. See also Marie-Laure Legay, *Les loteries royales dans l'Europe des Lumières, 1680–1815* (Villeneuve d'Ascq: Presses universitaires du Septentrion, 2014), 16–26.

69. Bernard Le Bovier de Fontenelle, "Éloge de Godefroy Guillaume Leibnitz," in *Histoire de l'Académie royale des sciences, Année 1716* (Paris: Imprimerie royale, 1718), 94–128; "Principes de métaphysiques fondez en raison, par M. Leibniz," *NM*, November 1718, 3–19.

70. Fontenelle, "Éloge de Godefroy Guillaume Leibnitz," 121.

71. Terrasson, *Mémoire pour servir à justifier la Compagnie des Indes*, 42.

72. *NM*, May 1720, 42, 64.

73. *NM*, May 1720, 32.

74. Bakhtin, *Problems of Dostoevsky's Poetics*, 134.

75. Renate Lachmann, "Bakhtin and Carnival: Culture as Counter-Culture," *Cultural Critique* 11 (1988–89): 115–52.

76. Hans-Jürgen Lüsebrink, "Des *Messagers boiteux/Hinkende Boten* à la Bibliothèque bleue: Filiations textuelles et rapports interculturels," in *La Bibliothèque bleue et la littérature de colportage*, ed. Thierry Delcourt and Élisabeth Parinet (Paris: École des Chartres, 2000), 267–77, 270–71; *NM*, October 1719, 205–6.

77. *NM*, September 1719, 211–12, October 1719, 199–206, and November 1719, 207–11.

78. *Lettres historiques*, November 1719, 581–86, and December 1719, 682–87; *Gazette d'Amsterdam*, February 9, 1720; *La suite de la clef, ou Journal de Verdun*, May 1720, 358; *Mercure historique*, January 1720, 7; Barthélemy, *Les correspondants de la marquise de Balleroy*, 2:283–84; Buvat, *Journal de la Régence*, 2:32.

79. Leborgne, "Le régent et le Système de Law," 122.

80. [Pierre-Samuel Dupont], *Du commerce et de la Compagnie des Indes, par Du Pont, des Sociétés royales d'agriculture de Soissons, d'Orléans, & de Limoges, correspondant de la Société d'emulation de Londres* (1769), 2nd ed. (Amsterdam, Paris: Delalain, Lacombe, 1769), 116.

81. The carnivalesque literature endorses "all sorts of violations of the generally accepted and customary course of events and the established norms of behavior and etiquette." Bakhtin, *Problems of Dostoevsky's Poetics*, 116, 122.

82. Fanny Cosandey, ed., *Dire et vivre l'ordre social en France sous l'ancien régime* (Paris: EHESS, 2005); Gilles Chabaud, ed., *Classement, déclassement, reclassement de l'antiquité à nos jours* (Limoges: Presses universitaires de Limoges, 2011).

83. *Histoire des finances pendant la Régence*, 399; Pierre Dardel, "L'influence du Système de Law sur la situation économique de la Haute-Normandie," *Actes du 81e Congrès national des sociétés savants* (Paris: Presses universitaires de France, 1958), 121–38; Farid Abbad, "La crise de Law à Nantes," *Annales de Bretagne et des pays de l'Ouest* 82, no. 3 (1975): 297–316; Faure, *La banqueroute de Law*, 554–57; Jean-Paul Poisson, "Introduction à une étude quantitative des effets socio-économiques du système de Law," in *Notaires et société: Travaux d'histoire et de sociologie notariales* (Paris: Economica, 1985), 309–56; Jérôme Jambu, "Le Système de Law dans les campagnes: L'exemple du pays d'Auge," *Annales de Normandie* 50, no. 2 (2000): 297–320; Pierre Force, "Two Days of Financial Panic in the French Countryside: The Mississippi Bubble in the Notarial Archives of La Bastide Clairence (October 30–31, 1720)" (paper presented at the conference "The Money Series: The Architecture, Experience and Aftermath of a Financial Disaster," April 24, 2017, Columbia University, New York); Pierre Deyon, *Amiens, capitale provinciale: Étude sur la société urbaine au XVIIIe siècle* (Paris: Mouton, 1967); Roger Schabol, *La pratique du jardinage, par M. l'abbé Roger Schabol, ouvrage rédigé après sa mort sur ses mémoires, par M. D**** (Paris and Liège: Bassompierre, 1781), 142; Le Roy Ladurie, *Les paysans de Languedoc*, 1:599–600.

84. "Remontrances du parlement de Toulouse au sujet du denier 50. 1720," Arsenal, MS 3724, vol. 2, fol. 55; "Très humbles et très respectueuses remontrances que font au roy notre très honoré seigneur les gens tenants la cour de parlement après pâques: Le 17 avril 1720," Arsenal, MS 3724, vol. 2, fol. 155.

85. Robert Castel, *From Manual Workers to Wage Laborers: Transformation of the Social Question* (1995; New Brunswick, NJ: Transaction, 2003); Mathieu Marraud, "Dérogeance et commerce: Violence des constructions sociopolitiques sous l'ancien régime," *Genèses* 95, no. 2 (2014): 2–26.

86. Jean Sgard, "La multiplication des périodiques," in Chartier and Martin, eds., *Le livre triomphant*, 198–205; Alfred Sauvy, "Le livre aux champs," in ibid., 559–78; Roger Chartier, *Lectures et lecteurs dans la France d'ancien régime*; Moureau, "Le Nouveau Mercure (1717–1721)," and *La plume et le plomb*.

87. Carlo Ginzburg, *The Cheese and the Worms: The Cosmos of a Sixteenth-Century Miller* (1976; Baltimore: Johns Hopkins University Press, 1980); Darnton, *Gens de lettres, gens du livre*, 240; Antoine Lilti, *The Invention of Celebrity, 1750–1850* (2014; Cambridge: Polity, 2017).

88. *NM*, March 1720, 30.

89. Terrasson, *La philosophie applicable*, 68, and *Sethos*, xxiij.

90. Paul Veyne, *Did the Greeks Believe in Their Myths? An Essay on the Constitutive Imagination* (1983; Chicago: University of Chicago Press, 1988), 88–92.

Chapter Five

1. Roger Chartier, *Au bord de la falaise: L'histoire entre certitudes et inquiétudes* (Paris: Albin Michel, 1997), 59. The passage quoted in the text has not been translated in Roger Chartier, *On the Edge of the Cliff: History, Language, and Practices* (Baltimore: Johns Hopkins University Press, 1997). See also Roger Chartier, "Culture as Appropriation: Popular Culture Uses in Early Modern France," in *Understanding Popular Culture: Europe from the Middle Ages to the 19th Century*, ed. Steven L. Kaplan (Berlin: Mouton, 1984), 234. See also Dominick LaCapra, *Rethinking Intellectual History: Texts, Contexts, Language* (Ithaca, NY: Cornell University Press, 1983), and *History, Politics, and the Novel* (Ithaca, NY: Cornell University Press, 1987).

2. Germain Dernis, *Recueil ou collection des titres, édits, déclarations, arrêts, règlemens, & autres piéces concernant la Compagnie des Indes orientales établie au mois d'Août 1664*, 4 vols. (Paris: Boudet, 1755), 3:220–21.

3. Lespagnol, *Messieurs de Saint-Malo*, 2:658–59.

4. Dernis, *Recueil*, 3:221.

5. Lespagnol, *Messieurs de Saint-Malo*, 2:670–706; Dernis, *Recueil*, 3:222; Haudrère, *La Compagnie française*, 1:59.

6. AnF, X1A 8436, fols. 409–19, fols. 412–14.

7. Lespagnol, *Messieurs de Saint-Malo*, 2:779.

8. See also Amalia D. Kessler, *A Revolution in Commerce: The Parisian Merchant Court and the Rise of Commercial Society in Eighteenth-Century France* (New Haven, CT: Yale University Press, 2007), 48–49.

9. AnF, M 1024, "Compagnie de la Chine, Mémoire"; AnF, X1A 8436, fol. 424.

10. Dernis, *Recueil*, 3:231–32.

11. See, e.g., Lespagnol, *Messieurs de Saint-Malo*, 2:708.

12. AnF, M 1026, *Memoire au sujet de la Compagnïe des Indes*.

13. AnF, M 1026, *Memoire au sujet de la Compagnïe des Indes*.

14. AnF, M 1026, *Memoire au sujet de la Compagnïe des Indes*.

15. AnF, M 1026, *Memoire au sujet de la Compagnïe des Indes*; Richard Cantillon, *Essai sur la nature du commerce en général* (1755; Paris: INED, 1997), 31; Hélène Vérin, *Entrepreneurs, entreprise: Histoire d'une idée* (1982; Paris: Classiques Garnier, 2011), 148–51; Christian Lamouroux, "L'entrepreneur, l'entreprise et l'ordre social: Cantillon, Montchrestien et la Chine médiévale," in *Montchrestien et Cantillon: Le commerce et l'émergence d'une pensée économique*, ed. Alain Guéry (Lyon: ENS, 2011), 177–212; Bert Hoselitz, "The Early History of Entrepreneurial Theory," *Explorations in Entrepreneurial History* 3, no. 4 (April 1951): 193–220; Fritz Redlich, "On the Origin of the Concepts of 'Entrepreneur' and 'Creative Entrepreneur,'" *Explorations in Entrepreneurial History* 1, no. 2 (1949): 1–7.

16. Ludwig von Mises concluded in 1922 that the programmed failure of socialism stemmed precisely from this lack of responsibility and competition, which led to "laziness" and the end of "innovations," "reforms," and "improvements." See Ludwig von Mises, *Socialism: An Economic and Sociological Analysis* (1922; Indianapolis: Liberty Classics, 1981), 203–12. See also Joseph A. Schumpeter, *Capitalism, Socialism and Democracy* (New York, London: Harper & Bros., 1947).

17. In a letter dated on April 28, 1720, from the Council of Marine to "Mr Law," the council mentioned a memoir by La Rochelle and Canadian merchants. They complain of "the price of the Beaver paid by the Compagnie des Indes": "[T]hey request it be doubled since the dramatic increase of goods, or that trade is freed, by paying a modest fee to the Compagnie." AnF, Col. B/42/1, fol. 56.

18. AnF, M 1026, *Memoire au sujet de la Compagnïe des Indes.*

19. Emmanuel Le Roy Ladurie, *Saint-Simon and the Court of Louis XIV* (1997; Chicago: University of Chicago Press, 2001), 299–342, and "Réflexions sur la Régence"; Dupilet, *La Régence absolue*, 291–332.

20. Joseph Lambert, *La manière de bien instruire les pauvres et en particulier les gens de la campagne* (Rouen: Le Boucher, 1716), and *Instructions courtes et familieres pour tous les dimanches et les principales fetes de l'année, en faveur des pauvres, & particulièrement des gens de la campagne* (1721), 3rd ed. (Paris: Lottin, 1723); Touzery, *L'invention de l'impôt sur le revenu*, 331.

21. Jean Soanen, *Lettre de Mgr l'évêque de Senés du 18 may 1720 à M. Law* (n.p., n.d.), and "A M. Law controlleur général des finances, au sujet de l'arrêt du conseil qui ordonnoit le remboursement des bénéficiers, des communautés religieuses & des hopitaux, pour que leur fond fût porté à la banque: 18 Mai 1720," in *Lettres de Messire Jean Soanen, evêque de Senez*, 8 vols. (Cologne: Aux dépens de la Compagnie, 1750), 1:279–83.

22. Henri-François d'Aguesseau, *Mémoire sur le commerce des actions de la Compagnie des Indes*, in *Oeuvres de M. le chancelier d'Aguesseau*, 10:169–294, 169; [Abbé André], "Avertissement," in ibid., 10:vj.

23. Was this text by d'Aguesseau published during the days of the System? This is what Paul Harsin thinks, but, to date, investigations in the French libraries have produced no evidence corroborating this hypothesis. It is probable, however, that the text was known in certain circles before the fall of the System. See Paul Harsin, "Essai de bibliographie critique," in Faure, *La banqueroute de Law*, 689–722, 697.

24. Terrasson, *Traité de l'infini créé*, 313–15, and *La philosophie applicable*, 99–107.

25. Terrasson, *Mémoire pour servir à justifier la Compagnie des Indes*, 45.

26. Le Semelier, *Conférences ecclésiastiques de Paris*, 2:45–47; François Genet, *Théologie morale, ou Solution des cas de conscience selon l'Écriture sainte, les canons et les saints pères*, 8 vols. (Paris: Pralard, 1695), 1:426–27. Elsewhere than in Genet, these rigid moral standards were also clearly expressed in the text of the *Conférences* and again in the *Traité de l'usure* by Louis Bulteau, opportunely republished at the beginning of 1720 under the false name Pierre Nicole. The author insisted in his preface on the need to render this work available again in "these unfortunate times when the purity of Christian morality on the matter of Usury . . . is opposed by a great number of Christians." [Louis Bulteau], *Traité de l'usure* (Paris: Babuty, 1720), xvi.

27. [Joseph Lambert], *Décision théologique sur les actions de la Compagnie des Indes* (n.p., n.d.); Soanen, *Lettre de Mgr l'évêque de Senés*, 280.

28. [Lambert], *Décision théologique*, 11. Profits that flow from violent conquest and from slavery are equally "injust" and "unholy," such as those caused by usury, because "[o]ne is accountable for malpractices in a society to which he belongs." [Lambert], *Décision théologique*, 7.

29. Terrasson, *Mémoire pour servir à justifier la Compagnie des Indes*, 22.

30. Le Semelier, *Conférences ecclésiastiques de Paris*, 2:230, 254.

31. [Lambert], *Décision théologique*, 6–7; d'Aguesseau, *Mémoire*, 179–89.

32. d'Aguesseau, *Mémoire*, 179–89; 261–62.

33. Terrasson, *Mémoire pour servir à justifier la Compagnie des Indes*, 45–46.

34. [Lambert], *Décision théologique*, 9–10; d'Aguesseau, *Mémoire*, 272.

35. d'Aguesseau, *Mémoire*, 272, 217–18.

36. See Arnaud Orain, "The Second Jansenism and the Rise of French Eighteenth-Century Political Economy," *History of Political Economy* 46, no. 3 (Fall 2014): 463–90.

37. [Lambert], *Décision théologique*, 11–14; d'Aguesseau, *Mémoire*, 272, 239–40.

38. [Lambert], *Décision théologique*, 15–22; d'Aguesseau, *Mémoire*, 265–67, 281–88.

39. Terrasson, *Mémoire pour servir à justifier la Compagnie des Indes*, 3–9, 21.

40. BnF, MS 13655, fol. 139; Ehrard, *L'idée de nature en France*, 46.

41. Charles Le Breton, *Les clefs de la philosophie spagyrique, qui donnent la connaissance des principes et des véritables opérations de cet art dans les mixtes des trois genres* (Paris: Jombert, 1722), 22.

42. Marais, *Journal de Paris*, 2:481; Jacques de Norvins, *Extraits des mémoires relatifs à l'histoire de France depuis l'année 1757 jusqu'à la Révolution* (Paris: Desoer & Cie, 1824), 281; BnF, MS 13655, fol. 139.

43. Goetzmann, Labio, Rouwenhorst, and Young, eds., *The Great Mirror of Folly.*

44. Goetzmann, Labio, Rouwenhorst, and Young, eds., *The Great Mirror of Folly*, 319 (pl. 55).

45. BnF, MS 13655, fols. 211, 508.

46. *NM*, September 1719, 192.

47. Raunié, *Chansonnier historique du XVIIIe siècle*, 3:160, 232. See also "Memoire pour servir a l'histoire du sisteme de Law, présenté a m. le duc d'Orléans en l'année 1719" (n.d.), Arsenal, MS 3724, vol. 2, fol. 32.

48. Antoine de Baecque, "Les éclats du rire: Le Régiment de la calotte, ou Les stratégies aristocratiques de la gaieté française (1702–1752)," *Annales: Histoire, sciences sociales* 52, no. 3 (1997): 477–511.

49. G. Plantavit de La Pause (penname), *Mémoires pour servir à l'histoire de la Calotte* (1725), new ed. (Aux états calotins: De l'imprimerie Calotine, 1752), 23–26, 39–40, 90–91; [Pierre-François Guyot Desfontaines], *Dictionnaire néologique à l'usage des beaux esprits du siècle avec l'éloge historique de Pantalon-Phoebus* (1726), 6th ed. (Amsterdam, Leipzig: Arkstée & Merkus, 1750), 321.

50. Montesquieu, *Persian Letters* (1721; London: Penguin Classics, 1973), 235–36 (letter 132).

51. Céline Spector, *Montesquieu, les "Lettres Persanes": De l'anthropologie à la politique* (Paris: Presses universitaires de France, 1997), 63.

52. Montesquieu, *Persian Letters*, 244–45 (letter 138).

53. "Très humbles et très respectueuses remontrances que font au roy notre très honoré seigneur les gens tenants la cour de parlement après pâques," vol. 2, fols. 151–59; "Remontrances du parlement de Toulouse au sujet du denier 50. 1720," fol. 57.

54. Law, *OC*, 3:130.

55. Law, *OC*, 3:130.

56. The *parlement* of Paris agreed in part with that idea. See "Discours de mr le procureur general du parlement de Paris en luy presentant l'edit du mois de mars 1720 pour la reduction des rentes au denier 50," Arsenal, MS 3724, vol. 2, fol. 42.

57. d'Aguesseau, *Mémoire*, 219–20.

58. Isabelle Martin, *Le théâtre de la foire: Des tréteaux aux boulevards* (Oxford: Voltaire Foundation, 2002), 10, 86–90.

59. Catherine Labio, "Staging Folly in the Dutch Republic, England, and France," in Goetzmann, Labio, Rouwenhorst, and Young, eds., *The Great Mirror of Folly*, 143–57, 152.

60. Denis Carolet, *Avantures de la rue Quincampoix* (1719), BnF, MS Fr. 9315, fols. 10–37, 13–14.

61. Antoine Furetière, *Dictionnaire universel*, 2 vols. (La Haye and Rotterdam: Arnout & Reinier Leers, 1690), vol. 2, s.v. *verd.*

62. Denis Carolet, *La lanterne magique, ou Le Mississipi du diable* (La Haye: Roguet, 1723), 19, n.p. (preface), 4–9, 38–39, 59–60.

63. BnF, MS Fr. 13655, fol. 139; Raunié, *Chansonnier historique du XVIIIe siècle*, 3:234.

64. Robert Muchembled, *A History of the Devil: From the Middle Ages to the Present* (2000; Cambridge: Cambridge University Press, 2003); Emmanuelle Sempère, "Le diable en héritage, de Lesage à Cazotte (1707–1776)," *Dix-huitième siècle* 42 (2010): 655–71.

65. *NM*, September 1719, 11–15.

66. [Alain-René Lesage, Jacques-Philippe Dorneval, and Louis Fuzelier], *Le diable d'argent: Prologue*, in *Le théâtre de la foire, ou L'opéra comique: Contenant les meilleures pièces qui ont été représentées aux foires de S. Germain & de S. Laurent*, 9 vols. (Paris: Ganeau, 1721–34), 4:94–123, 121–22.

67. Sempère, "Le diable en héritage," 658; Maurice de Meyer, "Le diable d'argent: Évolution du thème du XVIe au XIXe siècle," *Arts et traditions populaires* 15, nos. 3–4 (July–December 1967): 283–90, 287.

68. Goetzmann, Labio, Rouwenhorst, and Young, eds., *The Great Mirror of Folly*, 286 (pl. 21).

69. Raunié, *Chansonnier historique du XVIIIe siècle*, 3:218–20.

70. In an ironic twist, it could be said that Charles-Antoine Coypel was right in describing Law as the "Joseph of France" (discussed earlier) because the Joseph of Egypt is the one who reveals the greedy heart of humans. See Augustin Calmet, *Dictionnaire historique, critique, chronologique, géographie et litteral de la Bible*, 4 vols. (Paris: Emery, 1730), 3:491.

71. "Histoire du prince Papirius surnomme Pille Argent gouverneur des francs sots," in *Le régent: Entre fable et histoire*, ed. Denis Reynaud and Chantal Thomas (Paris: CNRS, 2003), 83–87. For variations, see Arsenal, MS 2962, fols. 93–104, and MS 3231, fols. 537–47.

72. Montesquieu, *Persian Letters*, 268–69 (letter 146).

73. Daniel Defoe, *The Anatomy of Exchange-Alley: or, A System of Stock-Jobbing* (London: Smith, 1719), 3–7, *The Chimera; or, The French Way of Paying National Debts* (London: Warner, 1720), 8–20, and *The Case of Mr. Law, Truly Stated* (London: Moore, 1721), 10.

74. Defoe, *The Case of Mr. Law*, 29–32.

75. Defoe, *The Case of Mr. Law*, 33–37. See also Hoppit, "The Myths of the South Sea Bubble," 162.

76. David Hume, *Philosophical Essays concerning Human Understanding* (London: Millar, 1748), 186.

Chapter Six

1. Roland Barthes, *Mythologies* (1957; New York: Noonday, 1972), 108, 142–43.

2. Martial Poirson, *Spectacle et économie à l'âge classique* (Paris: Garnier, 2011), 135–39.

3. Marc-Antoine Legrand, *Le fleuve d'oubly*, in *Théâtre de Monsieur Legrand*, 4 vols. (Paris: Ribou, 1731), 2:376–79.

4. Ola Forsans, introduction to *Arlequin sauvage, Timon le misanthrope, Les Caprices du coeur et de l'esprit* (Paris: Société des textes français modernes, 2000), 7–68; Mario Matucci, "De l'Arlequin sauvage à L'indigent philosophe," in *Langue, littérature du XVIIe et du XVIIIe siècle*, ed. R. Lathuillère (Paris: SEDES, 1990), 381–92.

5. Louis-François Delisle de la Drevetière, *Arlequin sauvage* (Paris: Briasson, 1721), 51–54.

6. Louis-François Delisle de la Drevetière, *Timon le misanthrope* (Paris: Hochereau, 1722), 81, 96–99.

7. Martial Poirson, "Présentation," in *L'école des bourgeois suivi de L'embarras des richesses* (Saint-Gély-du-Fesc: Espaces 34, 2006), 7–24.

8. Jean Soulas d'Allainval, *L'embarras des richesses* (Avignon, Chambeau, 1767), 52–55.

9. Pierre Carlet de Marivaux, *L'île des esclaves* (1725; Paris, GF-Flammarion, 2009), and *Journaux 1* (Paris: GF-Flammarion, 2010), 253, 261–62. See also Leborgne, Abramovici, and Escola, "Présentation," in Pierre Carlet de Marivaux, *Journaux 2* (Paris, GF-Flammarion, 2010), 7–40.

10. Louis de Boissy, *Le triomphe de l'intérêt* (La Haye, 1734), 59–62.

11. Matucci, "De l'Arlequin sauvage à L'indigent philosophe"; Kim Solga, "The Savage Ambivalence of Delisle de la Drevetière," *Eighteenth Century* 43, no. 3 (Fall 2002): 196–209.

12. Jean-François de La Harpe, *Lycée, ou Cours de littérature ancienne et moderne* (Paris: Agasse, an 9 [1803–4]), 546; Casimir Fusil, "Jean-Jacques Rousseau et Delisle de la Drevetière," *Revue d'histoire littéraire de la France* 33, no. 2 (1926): 234–37.

13. Crowston, *Credit, Fashion, Sex*, 117–37.

14. Marais, *Journal de Paris*, 2:472; *Mercure*, January 1722, 205; *Mercure de France*, April 1725, 784–87; René-Louis d'Argenson, *Notices sur les oeuvres de théâtre* (Les Délices: Institut et musée Voltaire, 1966), 657.

15. See Ehrard, *L'idée de nature en France*, 583–84.

16. Christelle Bahier-Porte, "Quelques 'réflexions sur l'esprit humain': L'héritage et la modernité selon Marivaux," *Littératures classiques* 75, no. 2 (2011): 71–88; Marc Escola, "'Une singularité d'esprit et conséquemment de style': De Montaigne à La Bruyère et de Pascal à Marivaux," *Littératures* 137 (2005): 93–107.

17. Louis Rustaing de Saint-Jory, *Les femmes militaires: Relation historique d'une isle nouvellement découverte* (1735; Amsterdam: Aux dépens de la Compagnie, 1739), 1, 13, 245, 74, 96.

18. See Nick Childs, *A Political Academy in Paris, 1724–1731: The Entresol and Its Members* (Oxford: Voltaire Foundation, 2000), 140–50.

19. Armand de Lesparre de Lassay, "Relation du royaume des feliciens," in *Recueil de différentes choses, par M. le marquis de Lassay: Quatrième partie* (Lausanne: Bousquet, 1756), 345–491.

20. Gérard Genette, *Palimpsests: Literature in the Second Degree* (1982; Lincoln: University of Nebraska Press, 1997), 24–30.

21. "Messieurs, messieurs, bonne nouvelle! / Le carrosse de Law est réduit en cannelle!" André Cochut, *Law: Son système et son époque* (Paris: Hachette, 1853), 178.

22. Montesquieu, "Lettres de Xénocrate à Phérès," in *Histoire véritable et autres fictions* (Paris: Gallimard, 2011), 163–70, 167.

23. [Jean-François Prévost d'Exiles], *Les avantures de Pomponius, chevalier romain, ou L'histoire de notre tems* (Rome: Les héritiers de Ferrante Pallavicini, 1724), 118–19, 209–14.

24. Montesquieu, *Persian Letters*, 254–57 (letter 142).

25. Marie-Louise Dufrenoy, *L'Orient romanesque en France, 1704–1789* (Montreal: Beauchemin, 1946); Barthélemy d'Herbelot and Antoine Galland, *Bibliothèque orientale, ou Dictionnaire universel contenant généralement tout ce qui regarde la connaissance des peuples de l'Orient* (Paris: Compagnie des Libraires, 1697).

26. Eugène Daire, *Collection des principaux économistes* (1843; Osnabück: Otto Zeller, 1966), 702.

27. Jean-François Melon, *Mahmoud le Gasnévide*, 68, 120.

28. Jean-François Melon, *Essai politique sur le commerce* (1734), 256–59.

29. Melon, *Essai politique sur le commerce*, 256–59.

30. Murphy, introduction to Du Tot, *Histoire du Systême de John Law*, xviii; Melon, *Essai politique sur le commerce: Nouvelle édition augmentée de sept chapitres* (1736), 307–8.

31. [Barthélemy Marmont du Hautchamp], *Rethima, ou La belle Géorgienne: Histoire véritable*, 6 vols. (Paris: Musier, Chardon, Dupuis, 1736), 1:iij–jv, iiij.

32. [Marmont du Hautchamp], *Histoire du Système des finances*, 1:iv. See also Barthélemy Marmont du Hautchamp, *Histoire générale et particulière du visa fait en France pour la réduction & l'extinction de tous les papiers royaux & des actions de la Compagnie des Indes, que le Systeme des finances avoit enfantez*, 4 vols. (La Haye: Scheurler, 1743).

33. Murphy, *John Law*, 283–84.

34. [Marmont du Hautchamp], *Histoire du Système des finances*, 1:xiij, 2:10–15.

35. [Marmont du Hautchamp], *Histoire du Système des finances*, 2:52, 107–8, 3:27, 1:xlv, 183, 98–99, 110–13, 3:12–22, 2:18, 1:xlviij, 175.

36. [Marmont du Hautchamp], *Histoire du Système des finances*, 1:165–74, 188–200, 2:34–43, 51, 65–75, 193–200, 4:160–86, 2:47.

37. [Marmont du Hautchamp], *Histoire du Système des finances*, 2:225–46, 4:96–152, 102. See Louis Sergent, "Le procès des épiciers contre le duc de La Force," *Bulletin de la Société d'histoire de la pharmacie* 14, no. 49 (1926): 211–14.

38. Citton, "Les comptes merveilleux de la finance," 125–60. See also Fourgnaud, "L'économiste (Jean-François Melon) et le conteur (Thémiseul de Saint-Hyacinthe)"; and Leborgne, "Le régent et le Système de Law."

39. Citton, "Les comptes merveilleux de la finance," 159.

40. Jean Weisgerber, *Les masques fragiles: Esthétique et forme de la littérature rococo* (Lausanne: L'Âge d'homme, 1991), 214.

41. [François-Vincent Toussaint], *Mémoires secrets pour servir à l'histoire de Perse* (Amsterdam: Aux dépens de la Compagnie, 1745); [Claude-Prosper de Crébillon], *Les amours de Zeokinizul, roi des Kofirans, ouvrage traduit de l'Arabe du voyageur Krinelbol* (Amsterdam: Michel, 1748).

42. [Toussaint], *Mémoires secrets*, 6, 16–17.

43. [Crébillon], *Les amours de Zeokinizul*, 21–22.

44. Charles-Irénée Castel de Saint-Pierre, "Projet pour perfectionner les statuts de la Compagnie des Indes," in *Ouvrajes de politique*, 14 vols. (Rotterdam and Paris: Beman & Briasson, 1733), 5:255–316, 265, 267–74.

45. Jacques Vincent de Gournay, "Observations sur le rapport fait à M. le Contrôleur-Général, par M. de S*** le 26 Juin 1755, sur l'état de la Compagnie des Indes, par feu M. de Gournay, intendant du commerce," in A. Morellet, *Mémoire sur la situation actuelle de la Compagnie des Indes* (1769), 2nd ed. (Paris: Desaint, 1769), xi–xxiij.

46. Morellet, *Mémoire sur la situation actuelle de la Compagnie des Indes*, 29–30; Dupont, *Du commerce de la Compagnie des Indes*, 174, 245–46.

47. Dupont, *Du commerce de la Compagnie des Indes*, 245, 103.

48. [Jacques Necker], *Réponse au mémoire de M. l'abbé Morellet, sur la Compagnie des Indes* (Paris: Imprimerie royale, 1769), 6–7; *Éclaircissements sur le mémoire de M. l'abbé Morellet* (1769), 14; Louis-Léon-Félicité de Brancas de Lauraguais, *Mémoire sur la Compagnie des Indes, précédé d'un discours sur le commerce en général* (Paris: Lacombe, 1769), xiv, 75–77. See also Louis-Léon-Félicité de Brancas de Lauraguais, *Mémoire sur la Compagnie des Indes, dans lequel on établit les droits & les intérêts des actionnaires: En réponse aux compilations de M. l'abbé Morrelet* (1770).

49. Dupont, *Du commerce de la Compagnie des Indes*, 261–62.

50. Du Tot, *Réflexions politiques sur les finances et le commerce*, 1:335–37, 242, 277.

51. Du Tot, *Histoire du Systême de John Law*, 134–35.

52. Du Tot, *Histoire du Systême de John Law*, 111–12, and *Réflexions politiques sur les finances et le commerce*, 271–72, 300–303.

53. Murphy, introduction to Du Tot, *Histoire du Systême de John Law*, xxxii.

54. [Chrestien-Deschamps], *Examen*, 1:33.

55. [Chrestien-Deschamps], *Examen*, 2:50–51.

56. See Sonenscher, "The Nation's Debt . . . Part I," 81–89, and *Before the Deluge*, 261.

57. [Chrestien-Deschamps], *Examen*, 1:278, 2:440.

58. *NM*, March 1720, 29, and May 1720, 68.

59. Faure, *La banqueroute de Law*, 417–27; Jennifer Tsien, "Quoniam le rôtisseur et les prisonniers du Mississippi," in Magnot-Ogilvy, ed., *Gagnons sans savoir comment*, 207–20; Giraud, *Histoire de la Louisiane française*, 3:252–83. See also Jean-François Prévost d'Exiles, *Histoire du chevalier Des Grieux et de Manon Lescaut* (1731; Paris: GF-Flammarion, 2006).

60. Yves Landry, *Orphelines en France, pionnières au Canada: Les filles du roy au XVIIe siècle* (Ottawa: Léméac, 1992).

61. [Chrestien-Deschamps], *Examen*, 2:132, 1:338; Forbonnais, *Recherches*, 2:616; Nicolas Baudeau, *Idées d'un citoyen sur l'administration des finances au roi* (Amsterdam, 1763), 143.

62. [Chrestien-Deschamps], *Examen*, 1:398; Forbonnais, *Recherches*, 2:628; Law, *OC*, 3:166; Marais, *Journal de Paris*, 1:315–16, 373.

63. Kaiser, "Money, Despotism, and Public Opinion," 2, 28, 17.

64. See Kaplan, *Bread, Politics and Political Economy*.

65. Buvat, *Journal de la Régence*, 1:447.

66. Arlette Farge, *Subversive Words: Public Opinion in Eighteenth-Century France* (1992; University Park: Penn State University Press, 1995); Lisa J. Graham, *If the King Only Knew: Seditious Speech in the Reign of Louis XV* (Charlottesville: University Press of Virginia, 2000); Robert Darnton, *Poetry and the Police: Communication Networks in Eighteenth-Century Paris* (Cambridge, MA: Harvard University Press, 2010); Buvat, *Journal de la Régence*, 2:49.

67. Brancourt, *Le régent, la robe et le commis greffier*, 221–38.

68. Marais, *Journal de Paris*, 2:356.

69. This is Thomas Kaiser's argument. See Kaiser, "Money, Despotism, and Public Opinion."

70. Ferdinando Galiani, *De la monnaie/Della moneta* (1751; Paris: Economica, 2005), 505; Voltaire, "Observations sur MM. Jean Lass, Melon et Dutot; sur le commerce, le luxe, les monnaies, et les impôts," in *Oeuvres de Voltaire*, 72 vols. (Paris: Lefèvre, Werdet, Lequien, 1829–34), 37:527–44, 537.

71. See Olivier Artus, "Lévitique 25: Année sabbatique et jubilé dans le contexte des traditions bibliques et des cultures du Proche-Orient ancien," *Transversalités* 129, no. 1 (2014): 7–27.

72. Forbonnais, *Recherches*, 2:641.

73. Montesquieu, *On the Spirit of the Laws* (1748; Cambridge: Cambridge University Press, 1989), 2.4. See also Charles Duclos, *Mémoires secrets sur les règnes de Louis XIV et de Louis XV* (Paris, 1759), 563.

74. *Histoire des finances pendant la Régence*, 307–8.

75. "Lettre de M. Turgot à M. Necker," in *Collection complette* [*sic*] *de tous les ouvrages pour et contre M. Necker* (Utrecht, 1782), 1–28; "Sur l'administration de M. Necker, par un citoyen françois," in ibid., 29–71. "Lettre de M. Turgot" is, of course, not a letter from Turgot.

76. "Sur l'administration de M. Necker, par un citoyen françois," 43.

77. Kaiser misinterpreted the situation. See Kaiser, "Money, Despotism, and Public Opinion," 23–24. What the authors of the pamphlet fears is the discretionary increase of paper money, not the so-called despotic authority ascribed to John Law.

78. "The French constitution is entirely opposed to that of a Republic. . . . Resources useful in Geneva would be too dangerous for us." "Sur l'administration de M. Necker, par un citoyen françois," 31.

79. Marais, *Journal de Paris*, 1:473.

80. Spang, "The Ghost of Law," 16.

81. Antoin Murphy, "John Law and the Assignats," in *La pensée économique pendant la Révolution française*, ed. Gilbert Faccarello and Philippe Steiner (Grenoble: Presses universitaires de Grenoble, 1990), 431–48; Rebecca Spang, *Stuff and Money in the Time of the French Revolution* (Cambridge, MA: Harvard University Press, 2015), 58–59, 79–89.

82. *Archives parlementaires de 1787 à 1860: Imprimées par ordre du Sénat et de la Chambre des députés, fondé par MM. Mavidal et E. Laurent* (hereafter *AP*), 102 vols. (Paris: Dupont, 1862–2023), 13:55 (April 15, 1790), 13:63 (April 16, 1790), 12:606 (April 9, 1790), 13:55 (April 15, 1790), 13:82 (April 16, 1790).

83. Joseph-Antoine-Joachim Cerutti, *Idées simples et précises sur le papier monnoie, les assignats forcés et les biens ecclésiastiques* (Paris: Desenne, 1790), 24.

84. *AP*, 13:56 (April 15, 1790), 12:605–6 (April 9, 1790).

85. *AP*, 10:140 (November 20, 1789); Nicolas Bergasse, *Lettre de M. Bergasse, député de la sénéchaussée de Lyon, à ses commettans* (1790), 5; Edmund Burke, *Reflections on the Revolution in France* (1790; Dublin: Porter, 1791), 346–47; Cerutti, *Idées simples et précises*, 107.

86. Jean-Sifrein Maury, *Opinion de l'abbé Maury, député de Picardie, sur les assignats-monnoie* (Paris: Imprimerie nationale, 1790), 37; Nicolas Bergasse, *Protestation de M. Bergasse, député de la sénéchaussée de Lyon contre les assignats-monnoie* (1790), 29; *AP*, 12:622–24 (April 9, 1790).

87. Maury, *Opinion de l'abbé Maury*, 38.

88. Maury, *Opinion de l'abbé Maury*, 58. Bergasse's cousin, Georges Bergasse de Laziroules, deputy of Lyon, agreed, see *Opinion de M. George* [*sic*] *Bergasse-Laziroule sur le projet de rembourser la dette exigible, par une émission d'assignats-monnoie* (Paris: Imprimerie nationale, 1790).

89. Antoine-François Delandine, *Faut-il des assignats-monnaie ou des quittances de finances pour la liquidation de la dette publique?* (Paris: Imprimerie nationale, 1790), 14; Burke, *Reflections*, 312; Louis de Boislandry, *Considération sur le discrédit des assignats* (Paris: Imprimerie nationale, 1792), 18.

90. Bergasse, *Protestation de M. Bergasse*, 29–30, 37–39.

91. Bergasse, *Réponse de M. Bergasse au Mémoire de M. de Montesquiou sur les assignats* (Paris: Lallemand, 1791), 64; Louis de Boislandry, *Opinion de M. Boislandry, député du département de Seine et Oise, sur la liquidation de la dette publique et les assignats-monnoie* (Paris: Imprimerie nationale, 1790), 21; *AP*, 13:54 (April 15, 1790); Pierre-Samuel Dupont, *Opinion de M. Dupont, député de Nemours, sur le projet de créer pour dix-neuf cent millions d'assignats-monnoie, sans intérêt* (Paris: Baudouin, 1790), 50.

92. Dupont, *Opinion de M. Dupont*, 50.

93. Spang, *Stuff and Money*, 82.

94. Murphy, "John Law and the Assignats," 431–33.

95. Louis-Sébastien Mercier, *De J. J. Rousseau considéré comme l'un des premiers auteurs de*

la Révolution, 2 vols. (Paris: Buisson, 1791), 1:580–81, and *Tableau de Paris* (1781–88; Paris: Mercure de France, 1994), 1:392.

96. Concerning Mercier's complex economic thinking, see Marcel Dorigny, "Louis-Sébastien Mercier, lecteur et propagateur de l'économie politique," *Dix-huitième siècle* 26 (1994): 163–75.

97. Louis-Salve Albitte de Vallivon, *La nécessité prouvée de l'émission du papier-monnaie en assignats, pour payer la dette générale de la nation* (1790), 6; Jean-Baptiste Jumelin, *Lettre écrite au bonhomme Richard, concernant les assignats* (Paris: Courrier de la librairie), 2; Spang, *Stuff and Money*, 161; Maurice Gouget-Deslandres, *Discours sur les finances, le crédit des assignats, la circulation de l'argent, & la baisse de l'intérêt de l'argent* (Paris: Imprimerie nationale, 1790), 20–21, 32–40.

98. Jean-René Loyseau, *Considérations sur l'agiotage des assignats* (Paris: Belin, 1792), i–ij, 11–12, 39, 16, 216, 184, 154–55.

99. Bastien, *Projet pour prouver qu'il n'y a pas trop d'assignats en circulation, même qu'il n'y en a pas assez* (n.d.); Albert Mathiez, *La vie chère et le mouvement social sous la Terreur* (Paris: Payot, 1927), 112–44.

100. Richard Cobb, *The People's Armies: The Armées révolutionnaires, Instruments of the Terror in the Departments, April 1793 to Floreal Year II* (1961–63; New Haven, CT: Yale University Press, 1987); François Hincker, "Y eut-il une pensée économique de la Montagne?," in Faccarello and Steiner, eds., *La pensée économique pendant la Révolution française*, 211–24; Dominique Margairaz and Philippe Minard, "Marché des subsistances et économie morale: Ce que 'taxer' veut dire," *Annales historiques de la Révolution française* 352 (2008): 70–78; Spang, *Stuff and Money*, 161–68.

101. Spang, *Stuff and Money*, chaps. 4 and 5.

102. *AP*, 80:492–95 (December 1, 1793).

103. Concerning Saint-Just and property rights, see Louis-Antoine de Saint-Just, *Esprit de la Révolution et de la Constitution de France* (Paris: Beuvin, 1791), 35, 58.

Conclusion

1. Paul Féval, *Le Bossu: Le roman de Lagardère* (1857; Paris: Omnibus, 2001); Louis Aragon, *Les voyageurs de l'impériale* (Paris: Gallimard, 1961), 98, 584; Cendrine de Porthal, *Les fortunes de la gloire: Le roman de John Law* (Paris: Acropole, 1982), 668; Ève de Castro, *Nous serons comme des dieux* (Paris: Albin Michel, 1996), 295–309; Françoise Hamel, *Un palais de papier* (Paris: Fayard, 2017), 344; Bertrand Tavernier, *Que la fête commence . . .* (Les productions de la Guéville and Universal Pictures, 1975), 114 min.

2. Barthes, *Mythologies*, 143–45.

3. Chartier, *The Cultural Origins of the French Revolution*, 2.

4. Kenneth Pomeranz, *The Great Divergence: China, Europe and the Making of the Modern World* (Princeton, NJ: Princeton University Press, 2000).

5. Most of these elements are discussed in Thomas Piketty, *Capital in the Twenty-First Century* (2013; Cambridge, MA: Harvard University Press, 2014).

6. George W. Bush, "President Hosts Conference on Minority Homeownership," October 12, 2002, The White House, Washington, DC, https://georgewbush-whitehouse.archives.gov/news/releases/2002/10/20021015-7.html; Alan Greenspan, *The Age of Turbulence: Adventures in a New World* (2007; New York: Penguin, 2008), 233.

7. Fabrice Lenglart, Vincent Aussilloux, Marie Cases, and Christophe Gouardo, "Comment assurer la résorption des dettes publiques en zone euro?," France Stratégie, Analytic Note no. 62, 2017, https://www.strategie.gouv.fr/publications/resorber-dettes-publiques-zone-euro. For outraged reactions, see, e.g., Jean-Yves Archer, "Le délire idéologique de France Stratégie," *Les échos*, October 13, 2017; and Anne de Guigné, "Taxe sur la propriété: La colère de Matignon après la polémique," *Le Figaro*, October 12, 2017.

8. Among other things, Piketty's *Capital in the Twenty-First Century* has the immense merit of bringing back to the center of the debate the problems posed by the presence of a high proportion of rentiers in a given society and in terms that are not completely different from those of the System. With the proposal for a capital tax to reduce public debt, Piketty does not, however, propose a partial *socialization* of heritage in the strict sense of the term.

Index of Names